Banking and Finance

Finance of International Trade

Banking and Finance Series

Finance of International Trade

by

Leonard Waxman

Senior Lecturer in Banking and Business Studies
City of London Polytechnic

Graham & Trotman

First published in 1985 by

Graham & Trotman Limited
Sterling House
66 Wilton Road
London SW1V 1DE

Graham & Trotman Inc.
13 Park Avenue
Gaithersburg
MD 20877, USA

© Leonard Waxman, 1985

ISBN 0 86010 561 X (softcover)
0 86010 578 4 (hardback)

This publication is protected by International Copyright Law. All
rights reserved. No part of this publication may be reproduced, stored
in a retrieval system, or transmitted in any form or by any means,
electronic, mechanical, photocopying, recording or otherwise, without
the prior permission of the copyright holder.

British Library Cataloguing in Publication Data

Waxman, Leonard
    Finance of international trade.—(Banking
and finance series)
    1. Commerce   2. Finance
    I. Title   II. Series
    382   HF1008

    ISBN 0-86010-578-4
    ISBN 0-86010-561-X Pbk

Typeset in Great Britain by Acorn Bookwork, Salisbury, Wiltshire
Printed and bound in Great Britain

Contents

Series Foreword

The *Banking and Finance Series* has been written for students who are preparing for the Associateship of the Institute of Bankers. The structure of the series follows the syllabus closely. Although the emphasis is on the Institute of Bankers' examinations the series is also relevant to students for the kinds of other professional examinations such as the different Accountancy Bodies, Chartered Secretaries, Diploma in Public Administration, undergraduate business courses, BTEC, BEC, HND, DMS, Stock Exchange courses, Association of Corporate Treasurers, Institute of Freight Forwarders, Institute of Export.

July 1985

Brian Kettell
Series Editor

Chapter 1

Introduction – International Trade as a Special Subject

Trade – any kind of trade – consists of the exchange of one form of wealth for another, where wealth is defined as a consumption or capital good, or service of some kind, or a financial instrument (a piece of paper purporting to have value now, or in the future). All of these things can represent wealth if someone is prepared to part with money for them.

The fact that the medium of money is used to facilitate the exchange does not detract from the underlying principle that in effect, something is being exchanged for something else. Of course this phenomenon is most clearly expressed in the case of barter trade where it is a condition of the transaction that item A is to be purchased only if item B is used to pay for it. A recent example of barter trade (which can take many forms) is of the Indonesian authorities offering to buy fertilizer from foreign companies only if those same companies agreed to purchase Indonesian non-oil and gas products to the equivalent value.[1] The obvious advantage to Indonesia is that, for *these* values anyway, there will be no balance of trade problem. See Appendix 2 to this chapter for a description of counter-trade.

Most trade, including international trade, is however conducted via a monetary payment and the advantages are not difficult to list. Prime amongst them is that no one is forced to purchase items they would rather not purchase, but instead can accumulate a money balance either to use on alternative products *now or in the future*, or simply to amass a money balance.

International trade however, has both apparent and real differences from domestic trade, in degree and in kind, and the following sections attempt to point them out.

---

[1]*Financial Times* Report, 10 August 1982.

1. Language

One of the additional costs borne by exporters and importers arises from the need to communicate in a foreign language. Although English is widely used in international transactions, for English speaking traders there is always the problem of their overseas partners misunderstanding or misinterpreting a clause in their contract. This calls for carefully worded agreements and usually (for at least one of the traders) the services of a translator. Now, language differences are not restricted to international transactions. Some countries like India have many languages and in such cases too, linguistic problems can arise. In the Soviet Union there are several languages; for example, Georgian is quite different from Russian. To the extent that language differences express themselves as added costs to the seller (and thus to the buyer) the advantages of buying imports become less attractive. However, this is a relatively minor problem as evidenced by the very large rise in world trade over the past few decades.

2. Customs, Laws and Regulations

Each country has its own special laws, customs and habits that are reflected in the types of products that their consumers buy. Obvious cases include right-hand drive cars in the United Kingdom (UK), rice consumption in south-east Asia, and a very special typewriter to accommodate the large number of letters in the Chinese alphabet.

Whether these social and legal differences arise from economic or non-economic causes is beside the point. The fact is that they give rise both to deterrents and encouragements for world trade. They act as deterrents when it is costly for companies to so alter their output to meet the special requirements of an overseas market whose size does not merit such alterations. Indeed, this concept has now been eagerly raised to national policy level in many countries under the guise of technical specifications necessary for the welfare of the community. Examples include car exhaust systems, safety specifications, and drug specifications to mention just three. Such trade restrictions have become so important that the world agreement designed to limit trade restrictions, the General Agreement on Tariffs and Trade (the GATT) has had to include within its terms of reference the so-called "non-tariff barriers to trade" – meaning restrictions imposed on imports other than the use of an import duty, as well as the more obvious tariff barriers.[2] It has had to consider it again in Geneva in November 1982 when a group of Commonwealth trade experts led by Sir Alec Cairncross delivered a forty-seven point list of recommendations to it indicating how such "non-tariff" measures can be brought under greater multilateral control.[3] A list of non-tariff barriers together with further analysis can be found in Appendix 1 at the end of this chapter. Clearly, all kinds of pretexts can be invoked to

[2]Tokyo Round of Negotiations 1979.
[3]*Financial Times* Report, 12 August 1982.

justify the limitation of certain imports. Whether or not they are designed for the stated purpose, or simply to limit competition is no easy question to answer. However, to the extent that they are (increasingly) used illustrates the deterrent aspect of special national requirements.

On the other hand such differences in customs habits and laws can have the opposite effect. The Japanese predilection for Scotch whisky is one case in point, although Japanese "Scotch" is now available! The apparent preference in some African countries for imported manufactured baby foods is another example.

3. Geography

An often used word in international trade is the term "shipped" in relation to the despatch of goods from one country to another. Even when the goods are going by air, train or road the term is sometimes applied. The reason is not hard to see, especially for an island nation like the UK whose trade was with distant countries throughout the world. Yet, as we shall see, the patterns of trade are changing and not all of it by any means necessarily involves transhipment over long distances. In any case long distances are not only found in world trade. Shipments from one side of the United States (US) (or the Soviet Union) to the other also involve large distances indeed.

However, for many countries, international trade does involve much longer distances than domestic trade, and to the extent that this raises the costs of the goods, trade will be restricted or even eliminated. For example, the cost of air-freighting soft fruits and flowers may be such as to severely limit the marketability of these products in overseas countries, except perhaps at special times of the year.

Many ingenious devices have been developed over the years to limit this deterrent factor to world trade. Large ocean-going tankers tend to reduce the cost of shipment of grain, coal, crude oil, minerals etc. The use of refrigerated vessels allowed trade in meat and dairy produce to expand. More recently the use of satellites to transmit television images from one continent to another has allowed trade in "information" to develop.

4. Money

It is however, when we turn to the use of money that we see the most marked differentiation between domestic and international trade. Within the boundaries of one country there is usually just one legal tender, defined as such by the national authorities to be the one money unit that can be proffered and must be accepted in exchange for goods or services rendered. As a result in normal circumstances there is little risk in maintaining balances of cash to meet future transactions except of course that cash balances attract no interest income and may be subject to inflation. However, there have been times when due to abnormal circumstances such as the aftermath of war, people turn to whatever commodity can best perform the function of money. For example after the Second World War cigarettes became for a time the best means of "paying" for transactions.

Again, there are cases where, within the boundaries of one nation state more than one legal tender exists. Such a case is Panama where apart from the local unit – the Balboa – the US dollar is also acceptable legal tender and circulates freely with the Balboa. Here conditions become more like that of a single country than of two separate nations. For example, given that the value of the Balboa has been fixed at one Balboa equals one US dollar since 1904, it follows that balance of payments problems cannot be adjusted by the use of a currency depreciation. Nor can interest rates differ, otherwise everyone will want to hold balances in the higher interest rate currency.

However, such special cases apart, there are separate national monies which do give rise to problems not encountered in domestic trading. When traders enter into negotiations for an international contract they have to decide whether payment is to be designated in the currency of the exporting country, of the importing country, of some third country or perhaps in an artificial unit of money such as a Special Drawing Right (SDR) (see Chapter 12).

The fact is that there is no such thing as international legal tender simply because there is no international institution with the responsibility to issue money in the way that national authorities have such responsibility. On what basis then, do traders decide which money to use?

To begin with most importers prefer to *pay* in their own money and most exporters prefer to be paid in *their* own money. The reasons are obvious; there is no need to sell one money for another; no problem of fluctuating exchange rates apply; traders can calculate their costs and receipts just as if the trade were domestic. Clearly, however, both parties cannot reap these benefits at the same time. Useful work has been done to quantify the proportion of UK trade invoiced in sterling and foreign currency. It was found that in 1975 24% of UK exports and 40.1% of UK imports were invoiced in foreign currency.[4] The Department of Trade publishes periodic data in their magazine *British Business* which shows that 25% of UK exports were invoiced in foreign exchange as at November 1978,[5] and 59% of UK imports were invoiced in foreign exchange as at October 1979.[6]

It appears therefore that UK traders are increasingly turning to the use of foreign currency, especially in payment for imports and we shall discuss the reasons and implications for this in later chapters (see Chapters 9 and 10).

The point to bear in mind at this stage is that international trade is significantly different from domestic trade because – apart from anything

[4]Carse, S., Williamson, J. and Wood, G. E. 1980. *The Financial Procedures of British Foreign Trade.* Cambridge University Press.
[5]*British Business*. Department of Trade. 10 October 1981.
[6]*Ibid*. 13 February 1981.

else — of the problems associated with the choice of currencies for invoicing purposes. From the traders' point of view these problems are:

(a) Changes in exchange rates;
(b) Bank charges;
(c) Problems of exchanging some currencies;
(d) The limited usefulness of some currencies.

None of these problems (which we shall look at in detail later) apply to domestic trade. Of course, if UK exporters insisted on invoicing all their exports in sterling these problems would not arise *for them*. However, they *would* arise for the overseas buyer. Likewise, if UK importers insisted on paying in sterling they would shift the burden of the problems onto the shoulders of the overseas seller. The point then is clear; no matter what currency is used someone, somewhere, must face such problems. They can be insured against, or shared by both parties, but the problems remain to be met by somebody.

Another aspect of money as a differentiating factor lies in the macro-economic area of the balance of payments. Up to now we have only discussed the micro-economic problems faced by traders but governments too face problems associated with trade. Within the boundaries of one country balance of payments problems are confined to regions who "import" more goods and services from other regions than they "export" to those regions. But such imbalances are financed by the commercial banks whose business it is to accept deposits and make loans. To the extent that they are willing to extend credit to certain areas of the country the internal balance of payments problem is financed. In other words the internal balance of payments deficit of a region is financed by a flow of capital to that region. Should that region (or company or person for that matter) not be able to meet its debts then the banks can take the steps of either writing off the loan or liquidating the security used to support it. Either way, there is no foreign currency problem to surmount.

However, in international business, balance of payments deficits are deficits of an entire sovereign nation (albeit, made up of many of its citizens). There is no certainty of capital financing, other than forced capital imports due to the inability to meet payments when due. Further, such deficits can play havoc with the exchange rate for the domestic currency with repercussions for rates of interest and other aspects of government economic and financial policies. Once again, money differences make world trade quite different from domestic trade. See Chapter 12 for a fuller discussion of the balance of payments.

5. Factor Differentiation and Immobility

One final and important reason for treating world trade as a separate subject goes to the very heart of the theory that tries to explain and justify it, namely, the theory of comparative cost advantage. We shall be dealing with this theory in Chapter 3 but it is necessary to state at this stage that one of the major reasons why international trade takes place is because of the differences in national resource availability. This not only applies to differences in climate, land and minerals, but equally to labour and the availability of capital. Furthermore the ratio of these resources are likely to be different between nations and this also accounts for cost and price variations which lead to countries trading with each other. Now, within the boundaries of one country we can also find such differences. Natural resources like coal and oil are found in specific areas of (say) the UK. However, within the UK it is possible for both capital and labour to move to those areas offering the highest rewards and this tends to equalize the returns to these factors of production. Between countries, however, mobility is less likely for a variety of reasons and because of this relative immobility of resources, differences in costs and prices emerge. It is to take advantage of such differences that traders participate in international commerce. The mobility of goods and services substitutes for the movement of people and money.

So there we have it. World trade has the aforementioned peculiarities of language, customs, laws and regulations, geography, money, and factor immobility. None of these peculiarities are found *only* in world trade, but they are more *marked* in world trade. They are reflected as additional risks (and therefore additional costs) to traders who have to allow for such expenses as translation services, special documents, use of bank facilities and freight forwarders, etc., etc. These added risks can be off-loaded onto specialist risk-takers such as insurers, but this may serve to further raise cost levels.

However, there is one important aspect of world trade that is identical with domestic trade. Countries import goods and services because they may be cheaper or better than domestic equivalents, or both. This serves to raise the efficiency of production where the imports are of capital goods, and to raise living standards where the imports are of consumer goods. Exports, on the other hand provide these same advantages *but to the other country*! Exports, therefore are best considered as a means to pay for desired imports. In other words we need to export in order to import. Put this way we can see that this principle is also at the bottom of domestic trade. Producers make and sell products not so much for their own sake, but principally to acquire money to enable workers, managers, shareholders and governments to acquire those things they wish to buy.

Appendix 1[1]

Non-tariff Barriers

Such barriers to trade can take many forms but in 1977 the British Overseas Trade Board, together with the Central Office of Information, listed a number of possible non-tariff barriers to trade faced by UK exporters. The following is based on that list:

(1) *Customs procedures.* This includes time taken to clear goods in transit; warehousing regulations; basis of value (some countries levy import duty on the "official" price determined by the authorities of the importing country, which is usually higher than the actual price in order to increase the strength of the tariff). The purpose of this is to offset what the authorities believe to be an overseas discriminatory practice. An example of this was the so-called American Selling Price system for imports of benzenoid chemicals. Instead of levying tariff duty on the value of the imports based on its unit price, duty was levied on the basis of prices existing for the same product within the US itself. As US prices were higher than the import prices the total value of the duty was enhanced. One justification used by the US for this practice was that European tariffs were based on the CIF (Cost, Insurance and Freight) import rates while in the US tariffs are based on the FOB (Free on Board) values. As a result US tariffs were somewhat lower than they would have been if based on CIF values.[2] Such valuation differences were removed by the Kennedy Round of GATT Negotiations in 1967,[3] although the Tokyo Round of GATT Negotiations in 1979 still felt it necessary to lay down codes of conduct, amongst other things, in relation to "fictitious" import valuations.

---

[1]See also *Impact* No. 38 1982 published by the US International Communication Agency Washington, for article by Thibaut de Saint Phalle who gives a comprehensive account of non-tariff barriers.
[2]See Chap. 5.
[3]See MacBean and Snowden. 1981. *International Institutions in Trade and Finance.* George Allen and Unwin, Chap. 4.

(2) *Quantitative restrictions*. There are many examples of quotas through-out the world which, of course, deliberately restrict imports to a specific level. Examples include US quotas on Japanese colour television sets and on shoes from Taiwan and South Korea; Italian quotas on Japanese cars, and the UK–Japanese "voluntary" agreement to limit the penetration of the UK market by Japanese cars. Quotas are clear barriers to trade and have no pretence to be anything else and as such, countries tend to use them as a last resort measure.

(3) *Standards*. These have become a very important factor in world trade. Ostensibly designed for a variety of innocuous purposes such as safety or health, they can also result in imports being more severely hit than domestic products. Examples include car engines that run on low-lead petrol, safety of boilers and electrical equipment and prohibitions on the sale of certain drugs and medicines.

Now, of course, these standards apply to both imports and to domesti-cally produced goods but they can become non-tariff barriers where:

(a) domestic producers are already complying with these standards before legislation is imposed and most imports are not;

(b) domestic companies adjust to standards to be required in the future when it would be costly for overseas companies to do so for just one export market.

A further example of an alleged non-tariff barrier concerns the so-called "Anglo-French turkey war" in which the UK refused to accept European Commission proposals that UK health regulations on imports of poultry be relaxed. British import regulations effectively banned imports of EEC poultry in 1981 when there was a spectacular growth in French sales of turkeys to Britain, by imposing a requirement that only coun-tries using a slaughter policy to control fowl pest were permitted to sell to the UK market. As most EEC countries followed a vaccination policy this was seen by the French in particular as an attempt to keep them out of the lucrative UK Christmas trade.[4]

Of course, the French have been accused of following non-tariff barrier policies of their own. The French government imposed a tax on video machines of about £40 per annum with the resulting funds being diverted to the television channels who complain of competition from video recordings. However, one major effect will be on sales of video machines most of which are imported from Japan. To overcome this problem in 1982 the French authorities required all imports of video machines to enter France in a remote customs post with the clear pur-pose of making such imports less convenient and also causing a severe backlog of processing by customs.

[4]See *Financial Times*, 17 and 23 September 1982.

Other non-tariff barriers to trade not specified in the British Overseas Trade Board pamphlet include:

(4) *Export subsidies*

(5) *Government procurement policies*

(6) *Domestic taxes rebatable on exports* e.g. *VAT*. In this case where a country relies heavily for its domestic taxation revenues on such indirect methods as value added taxes, goods going for export will be exempt. However, goods which are produced in countries relying heavily on direct taxation measures, e.g. income and profit taxes, are not exempted from them when exported. As countries in the European Economic Community have moved toward the former type of taxation their exports to markets like the US have enjoyed increasing exemptions. This is in contrast to US exports to Europe which do not enjoy such privileges to the same extent. These differences have been the subject of much argument between these countries.

There are, of course, many other examples that could be cited to illustrate an alleged non-tariff barrier. The topic is an extremely complex one because it is by no means easy to discover whether any particular policy affecting imports and exports was designed for the purpose as stated with only incidental significance for external trade, or whether the policy was designed with such significance in the forefront of the authority's thinking.

Appendix 2

Counter-Trade

Counter-trade may take a variety of forms but it is basically a barter or quasi-barter arrangement to link imports with exports; either between private firms and/or government bodies.

The seller is obliged to accept on a *partial* or *total* settlement, for his exports of goods (and sometimes, services), goods (imports) from the buyer.

There are 4 Types

(1) *Barter*. This is Goods for goods. It involves a limited number of products and is a once and for all operation. Barter is comparatively rare because of the problem of matching the needs of both parties.

(2) *Compensation arrangement*. The exporter is prepared to take full or partial payment *in kind* but in fact acts as an *agent* for a *third* party who is the actual buyer of the imports. Again, not common, because of the difficulty in finding a suitable third party.

(3) *Buy-back arrangement*. Most common. The exporter (who normally supplies plant, equipment or technology) agrees to accept in payment (part or full) goods to be produced by the plant, etc. A special aspect of this arrangement is that the *buy-back* values can exceed that of the original exports, with, of course, a longer contract period.

(4) *Counter-purchase*. Common but complicated! The exporter agrees to purchase from the buyer an agreed value of goods selected from a list – that *excludes* things produced by the exporters themselves!

A trading company is used here (as in buy-back) to market the goods purchased. They tend *not* to use them themselves.

Important for East–West trade and between developed and developing countries.

Factors Leading to Growth of Counter-Trade

(1) Eastern bloc traders can more easily plan their export sales (otherwise, because of fluctuations in foreign demand, such exports would be volatile);

(2) Achieve a bilateral balance of trade;

(3) Relieve shortages of hard currency;

(4) Need for overseas technology;

(5) Overcapacity;

(6) Penetration of difficult markets;

(7) Exporters in the West may find it the only way to sell to some markets.

Counter-trade involves additional risks to traders and therefore to bank finance, because such trade *does* incur a need to value goods in monetary terms.

As a result banks need to establish special accounts for their counter-trade customers. Two such accounts are Evidence and Escrow accounts.

Evidence Accounts

Because it is the practice that exporters will be required to make counter-purchases of up to 80% of the value of their own exports over an agreed period of time – usually one year – this type of account can be used to record the values of the relevant shipments by crediting the exporter's purchase of the counter-trade goods and debiting him for his own exports. Only the final difference between the credits and the debits will call for a payment of hard currency by the counter-purchase party. The account therefore provides the "evidence" of the state of the financial relationships between the parties and also gives the exporter some time to make his counter-purchases within the specified time period enabling him to "shop around" for the best possible goods.

Escrow Accounts

In this case an exporter who makes a counter-purchase *prior* to shipping his own goods and who is uncertain as to whether the other party will honour its obligations to take *his* goods at a later date will use such an account. It operates by recording the exporter's payments for his purchases as a credit to the other party. Payments are *blocked* until the exports are actually shipped and accepted in which case the account will be debited. As a result, no hard currency is released until both parties fulfil their obligations.

Apart from operating such special accounts, banks can also assist in the following ways:

Banks can help their customers in their counter-trading activities by:

(a) giving advice on the "premium" an exporter customer should build into his export prices to offset the extra costs involved

(b) making finance available to an overseas buyer of UK exports to allow him to make payments *before* the receipt from the sale of their reciprocal exports (see Chapter 10 on ECGD)

(c) providing bank bonds to cover penalties payable by the exporter if he fails to purchase the reciprocal goods (see Chapter 10 on Bonds)

(d) matching UK exporters with UK importers in a "Link" purchase. I.e. finding a buyer for the reciprocal goods

(e) putting customers in touch with specialist intermediary companies at home or abroad who trade in reciprocal goods by buying them at a discount and then on-selling them.

For a fuller outline and examples of counter-trade see article by Norman S. Fieleke reproduced in *Economic Impact* No. 47, 1984, published by United States Information Agency, Washington.

Chapter 2

Trade Data Analysis

Any student of world trade and its finance must become familiar with at least the broad outlines of trade and trade changes. This chapter sets out to examine the more important data and to try to indicate the major changes in recent years.

Now statistics are by their nature difficult things to deal with, and when applied to huge aggregations like "world exports" take on an even more daunting air. There are many problems associated with the interpretation of such data but provided that caution is taken and allowances made where necessary, some broad conclusions may be made. However, it is important to draw attention to some of the problems of data interpretation.

DEFINITIONS

It is essential to bear in mind that terms that may seem to have an obvious meaning may, in fact, mean something rather different. For example, the term "world" need not necessarily mean every country in the world. One of the more important sources of such information comes from tables of data published by the International Monetary Fund (IMF) in Washington, USA. Although their membership is now of 146[1] countries it does not include most nations of eastern Europe including the Soviet Union (although Yugoslavia has been a member for some years, Romania joined in 1972, Hungary in 1982 and China in 1981). The IMF of course can only publish data supplied to it by its members and therefore references by it to "world exports", etc., are taken to mean the aggregation of exports of its members only, although some attempts are also made to quantify other, non IMF trade.

[1]July 1984.

Another area of aggregation that can be somewhat misleading concerns the term "developing countries". The IMF uses the term to mean all of their members who are not advanced industrialized countries. However, this depends on where the line is drawn, and there are examples where a member of the Less Developed Countries (LDCs) have the same or higher per capita Gross Domestic Product (GDP) than members of the industrial countries. One example is Singapore where GDP per capita is about the same as Italy's (see Table I).[2]

A further definitional problem arises from the use of different methods for evaluating trade. In Chapter 5 we deal with the more widely used trade terms but here we need only refer to the terms "Free on Board" (FOB) and "Cost, Insurance and Freight" (CIF); the former is commonly used to value exports while the latter is used to evaluate imports. This is usually to enable the authorities to impose import duties on the highest possible import value base represented by the CIF value! For our purposes however, it is evident that "world exports" will usually be a smaller figure than "world imports" as a direct result of the usage of these bases of value. To further complicate matters, some countries do use the FOB base to evaluate imports (e.g. Canada).

CURRENCY VALUES

A much more significant problem surrounds the use of national currencies to determine trade values. A dramatic example is the case of the Argentine peso. If we were to measure Argentine exports in terms of the peso we would obtain increases in Argentine exports from 1972 to 1981 of some 232,143%. Now of course, Argentine trade expanded by nothing like this phenomenal increase which is largely due to the fall in the value of the peso resulting from domestic inflation. (See Tables C, F and G in Appendix 3.)

The US dollar is the most widely used currency for valuing international trade. In the past this posed no major problem as the currency kept its value in terms of goods and services within the US economy and it was thus a useful measure of real changes in US trade. It was also an acceptable measure of other countries' trade provided exchange rates were flexible enough to adjust for internal purchasing power movements.

In Table 2.1 we see a hypothetical illustration of the use of the US dollar to evaluate UK export value increases. If in Year 1 UK exports are valued at £50,000 m and at an exchange rate of $2 per £1 the US dollar value of UK exports is therefore $100,000 m. By Year 2 UK exports have risen in value to £70,000 m but it is assumed that much of this rise has been due to price increases with real export values measured in terms of volume changes having a value of £55,000 m. In other words, of the £20,000 m

[2]The main tables and graphs A to L appear as an appendix to this chapter.

Table 2.1
UK Exports. "Real Value" Adjustment by Measuring in US Dollars

Currency of measurement	Year 1	Year 2			
		Nominal value	% rise	Real value	% rise
Sterling	£50,000 m	£70,000 m	40%	£55,000 m (after allowing for inflation)	10%
US dollars	£50,000 m @ $2 per £1 = $100,000 m			£70,000 @ $1.57 per £1 = $109,900 m	9.9%

nominal increase, £15,000 m was due to a rise in unit prices and just £5,000 m due to an expansion in the real (volume) export of goods. Using the US dollar at current exchange rates we get a much better measure of real value than using sterling.

We must be careful here to differentiate between relative and across the board price changes. For example, in the normal course of events there will be price changes due to changing supply and demand circumstances. Thus some products will show price rises and some price falls, and these changes must be allowed to reflect themselves in the value of a country's trade as they are part of the cut and thrust of commerce. However, where the *general* level of prices are rising reflecting an underlying inflation they must be eliminated from the figures to give a more realistic interpretation of events (see the example of the Argentine).

Prior to 1972 the world was on a fixed exchange rate regime. That meant in practice, that apart from rare but substantial changes brought about by devaluation, the dollar rate for sterling was fixed between narrow limits. Inflation in the UK however, was greater than in the US and thus when UK trade was converted into dollar values it tended to *over-value* the real size of such trade (e.g. in Table 2.1 it was as if we used $2 = £1 for the conversion in Year 2. This would give $140,000 m).

US INFLATION

Since 1972 currencies have fluctuated wildly against each other with the US dollar first falling in value against other major currencies and in 1982 rising sharply against them. This was associated with much increased inflation rates in the US relative to such countries as Germany (see Table G). The effects of such fluctuations can be illustrated by reference to hypothetical data for (say) German trade in Table 2.2.

In this hypothetical example we assume there has been no inflation in Germany between Years 1 and 2 but the DMs purchased by one US dollar fall from DM3 to DM2.5. The increase in German exports is 32% when measured by the actual exchange rate of DM2.5 in Year 2 but this is due largely to the

Table 2.2
German Exports. US Dollar Measurement gives Inferior Reading

Currency of measurement	Year 1	Year 2			
		Nominal value	% rise	Real value	% rise
D marks	DM400 b	DM440 b	10%	DM440 b. No inflation assumed	10%
US dollars	DM400 b @ DM3 per $1 = $133.33 b			DM440 b @ DM2.5 per $1 = $176.0 b	32%

dollar's depreciation. When the "old" exchange rate of DM3 is used the real change is revealed (+10%). Thus under such circumstances the *dollar value* of a country's trade will be *over-valued*. It is with this effect in mind that we must approach all data expressed in US dollars since 1972. One way to estimate the real changes net of general price rises is to compare total values with unit prices. This can be done by reference to Table A (amongst others) and Table E. For example, we note that US exports (in Table A) rose from $49.8 b in 1972 to $1233.7 b in 1981 – an increase of some 369% by value. From Table E however, we see that US export prices (in dollars) rose from index number 60 in 1972 to index number 162 in 1981 – an increase of some 170% in unit prices. Thus, a substantial proportion of the nominal increase in US exports arose from increases in US dollar prices. Nevertheless, there was *some* rise in export volume.

TRADE VOLUMES

The best way, of course, to measure real (volume) changes is to measure volume instead of value. This is easier said than done because of the difficulty in aggregating (say) changing units of nuclear power stations and thimbles! Product types are continually changing (e.g. word processors) and it is difficult to relate falls in the volume of (say) non-electric typewriters with increases in (say) personal computers! Indeed, it is one of the prime functions of money itself to deal with this problem by aggregating *money values*! It is clear from this therefore, that inflation causes a deterioration in the functions of money.

Nevertheless, attempts are made to calculate real changes and UK figures are given in Tables K and L. For example, in Table L UK export volume is shown to have increased from index number 86 in 1972 to index number 110 in 1976 – a rise of some 28% in volume. Yet in Table A for the same period UK export values are shown to have increased by some 89%! Clearly then, the export values (in US dollars) are misleading as much of the rise is due to price and currency changes. This is confirmed by reference to UK export price movements shown in Table E.

One way to calculate approximate real changes from value and price data is to use constant prices. For example, if we look at export values and price changes for the Netherlands we see the following:

Table 2.3
Netherlands Exports. Unit Value Adjustment

1972	1981	Nominal change	Real change
Dutch guilders 69.40 b	Dutch guilders 204.36 b	+194.5%	
Average export unit price 70[1]	Average export unit price 116[1] = +65.7% over 1972		
DG69.40 b raised by 65.7% = DG115.00 b	DG204.36 b		+77.7%

[1]Based on Dutch guilders.

In Table 2.3 past export values are "inflated" by percentages equal to price changes. The result is to show that real Netherlands exports rose by a more modest 77.7% over the whole period than the nominal values suggest.

(Readers should attempt this exercise themselves by reversing the process and finding 1981 values in terms of 1972 prices.)

OTHER PROBLEMS

Some other items to note in any trade data evaluation are as follows:

Roundings to nearest billion units. Where a billion is one thousand million. Inevitably, totals are unlikely to equal the sum of their parts.

DATA UP-GRADING

Readers should not be dismayed to find that data relating to a particular item is different in different sources and even different in separate publications of the same source! The reason is simply one of changing the information in the light of new data. The rule is a simple one: the most accurate data is the most recent data for past periods.

Bearing these complications in mind, let us now look at some of the presented data and try to arrive at some general observations.

Tables A and B

Here we have in column (a) exports (FOB) and imports (CIF) for the major trading nations and some important groupings measured in billions of US dollars. In addition column (b) shows national percentages of world trade; (c)

Table 2.4
World Exports. Unit Value Adjustment

1972	1981	Nominal change	Real change
$376.1 b	$1832.3 b	+387.2%	
Average export unit price 54[1]	Average export unit price 178[1] = +229.6%		
$376.1 b raised by 229.6% = $1239.6 b	$1832.3 b		+47.8%

[1]Based on US dollars.

shows exports and imports per capita all measured in US dollars; and (d) shows exports and imports as a percentage of national gross domestic product but all measured in domestic currency.

Analysis

World exports are shown to have grown in value from $376.1 b in 1972 to $1832.3 b in 1981 a percentage increase of 387.2%. (Note that the term "world" excludes some eastern European trade.) However, from Table E we see that unit export prices rose from 54 in 1972 to 178 in 1981, an increase of 229.6%. If we up-grade the 1972 export value by this percentage and compare the result with the 1981 value the real increase in world exports is seen to be not 387.2% but a more modest 47.8%. This is shown in Table 2.4.

Even this figure of 47.8% over the nine-year period is somewhat misleading as it is measured in US dollars which fell against other major currencies. One way to eliminate this problem is to convert the US dollar values into Special Drawing Right (SDR) units (see Chapter 12) by reference to Table F. This is done in Table 2.5.

By converting export values in 1981 prices in US dollars to SDRs we can see that a more realistic change in "world" exports has been some 36.1% over the nine-year period or an annual average increase of 4%.

According to figures published in IMF Survey for August 20 1982 world trade for 1981 fell by 1.5% over 1980 when measured in US dollars. How-

Table 2.5
World Exports. Adjustment by SDR Value

1972	1981	Dollar adjustment	SDR adjustment
$1239.6 b[1]	$1832.3 b	+47.8%	
@ SDR 0.9210 per $1 = SDR 1141.7 b	@ SDR 0.8480 per $1 = SDR 1553.8 b		+36.1%

[1]As calculated in Table 2.4.

ever, when measured in SDRs the 1981 figure was up 9% over 1980. Once again the importance of using a reliable measure cannot be over-emphasized. After world-wide inflation is allowed for there was in fact no increase in world trade at all in 1981. In 1980 the real increase was only 1.5%. See IMF Survey September 20 1982 and the GATT Report 1981 (General Agreement on Tariffs and Trade).

Readers should now attempt to apply this reasoning to other data in Tables A and B.

Graphs A and B

Graph A – Exports

(a) Bearing in mind the above let us now turn to Graphs A and B which are not so adjusted. In spite of this (as readers may determine for themselves) Graph A(a) represents roughly the correct hierarchy of major exporting nations. It is interesting to note that in spite of poor UK economic performance the country is part of the top six exporting nations in the world. (More on the UK later.)

(b) *Exports as a Percentage of World Exports.* These same top six exporting countries were responsible for no less than 46.6% of total world exports in 1981 compared to 51.1% in 1972. The reasons for this are due to the rise in value of oil exports from OPEC countries and the increase in exports of some of the more advanced developing nations.

(c) *Exports Per Capita.* A notable feature of this graph is the relegation of the US to the seventh place in the exports per capita league. The US has historically been much less dependent on world trade than other countries because of the size of the US economy which is much more self-sufficient than (say) the UK or Germany. However, it is interesting to see that a country like Japan is only sixth in this hierarchy.

(d) *Exports on a Percentage of Gross Domestic Product.* Here we are relating exports as a percentage of gross domestic product both measured in domestic currency. This gives us some indication of the importance of world trade to each nation. Surprisingly the UK is the second most important country (after Germany) in this category reflecting perhaps the fact that UK exports have risen (or declined less) while UK GDP has been stagnant (or declined). Nevertheless, it still indicates that the UK exports no less than some 28% of its GDP compared to Japan with a figure of some 15% (1981).

Graph B – Imports

The data here is very much that of graph A with the exception of (d) which shows that since 1976 the UK's position has slipped from first place to fourth place no doubt due to reduced imports of oil and also reduced consumer demand for goods due to the domestic recession. Another possible factor may be the fall in some imported commodity prices (real); see Table H.

One further note of caution needs to be stressed at this point. When comparing nations' exports per capita or in relation to their GDP it must be remembered that some countries perform the function of an entrepôt centre; that is to say that goods are imported for re-export. Examples include the Netherlands and Singapore who are major importers of crude petrolem which is refined and re-exported. Clearly such trade is not of the same order as imports for domestic consumption or of exports which have a significant domestic added value. Thus such countries are excluded from graphs A and B.

Tables C and D – Exports and Imports of Other Nations

In these tables we look at what might be called "Division II" trading nations. These consist of other relatively industrialized countries who participate in trade much more than the less advanced LDCs. This is a selective list and is not intended by any means to be definitive. Readers may like to consult the sources to see which other countries could easily be included in "Division II".

USSR and Eastern European Nations. Note that the so-called Soviet bloc countries do not report to the International Monetary Fund (IMF) who provide the most comprehensive array of trade data (although some exceptions have already been noted). Instead, the IMF report such trade from the point of view of those trading partners who are themselves IMF members. For example USSR exports to the Federal Republic of Germany (referred to throughout as "Germany") are reported by the latter country as imports from the USSR. In this way the IMF builds up an indirect assessment of USSR trade which by definition excludes their trade with other members of their group (known officially as members of the Council for Mutual Economic Assistance (CMEA)).

COMPARATIVE ANALYSIS TO SHOW PROBLEMS OF UNADJUSTED DATA

Let us take a low export per GDP country like Brazil and compare it with a high export per GDP country like Malaysia (Table 2.6). This analysis shows how misleading unadjusted figures can be. On the face of it Brazilian exports seem to have expanded much less than Malaysian exports (see column (b) of Table C). Yet when allowance is made for the price rise effect it can be seen that the Brazilian real performance is much better than that of Malaysia.

Graph C

Some inkling of this can be noted from Graph C(d) which measures exports as a percentage of Gross Domestic Product. Although the Malaysian ratio is much greater, the *trend* since 1976 is in favour of Brazil.

Table 2.6
Comparison of Brazilian and Malaysian Exports

1972	1981	$ price adjustment	SDR adjustment
BRAZIL exports $4.0 b Average export unit price 58[1]	$19.7 b Average export unit price 141[1] = +143%		
$4.0 b raised by 143% = $9.72 b	$19.7 b	+102.7%	
$9.72 b @ SDR 0.9210 per $1 = SDR 8.95 b	$19.7 b @ SDR 0.8480 per $1 = SDR 16.71 b		+86.7%
MALAYSIA exports $1.7 b Average export unit price 50[1]	$11.2 b Average export unit price 198[1] = +296%		
$1.7 b raised by 296% = $6.73 b	$11.2 b	+66.4%	
$6.73 b @ SDR 0.9210 per $1 = SDR 6.198 b	$11.2 b @ SDR 0.8480 per $1 = SDR 9.49 b		+53.1%

[1] Based on US dollars.

Table E/Graph E – Terms of Trade

A clear trend in trade prices is reflected in Table E and pictured dramatically in Graph E. OPEC terms of trade have improved from 35 in 1972 to 204 in 1981 while industrial nations moved from 113 to 89. In effect this means that oil exporting countries have been able to raise their export prices *much more* than the rise in their import prices.

The terms of trade is a concept which measures the *ratio* of export and import prices. The formula is:

$$\frac{\text{The Export Unit Price Index (EUPI)}}{\text{The Import Unit Price Index (IUPI)}} \times 100 = \text{Terms of Trade}$$

Thus, if the EUPI = 110 and the IUPI = 98, then we have $\frac{110}{98} \times 100 = 112.2$ Terms of trade. This is an *improvement*. However, it *only* measures changes in unit prices and says nothing about volume changes. It does not always follow that an improvement in the terms of trade – indicated by a rising index number – necessarily implies an improved trading position. The latter depends on whether *volume* of trade is adversely affected. Thus, if OPEC can raise its export prices *without* a significant fall in demand for oil, then total export values will rise. Here, improved *terms* of trade is analogous with improved *balance* of trade. However, if UK export prices of manufactured goods rise and this is offset by volume decreases, then improved terms of trade is *not* analogous with the balance of trade. Nevertheless, if, for example, prices of imported commodities into the UK fall while UK export prices rise (both in dollar terms) it follows that the UK may need to export less volume to finance the reduced cost of imports. This is especially true where the demand for imported commodities is relatively inelastic (see Chapter 3).

Table 2.7
**US and German Consumer Prices
Compared with the Dollar/Mark
Exchange Rate**

Consumer prices	1972	1981
USA	77.7	169.0 = 117.5% rise
Germany	82.5	129.2 = 56.6% rise
US $s per DM1	0.3136	0.4425 = 41.1% rise

Tables F/G, Graphs F/G – Exchange Rates and Consumer Prices

It is interesting to compare changes in exchange rates (Table F and Graph F) to change in internal consumer prices (Table G and Graph G).

An important set of such prices relates to the US and Germany who, we have already noted from Table A, are the two largest trading nations in the world.

In Table 2.7 we see that US domestic prices rose much more quickly than in Germany but that the dollar fell against the Deutsch mark (the latter deduced from figures in Table F). Thus the fall in the exchange rate for the dollar goes a large way to offset the decline in price competitiveness of US goods and services.

This kind of result tends to lend support to the theory known as Purchasing Power Parity, that in the long run, exchange rates will be adjusted to compensate for changes in international competitiveness brought about by movements in domestic price levels.

Another example is of the Argentine peso which fell from 8.2 per $1 in 1972 to 15163.1 per $1 in 1981. But domestic prices in the Argentine rose from 17.8 in 1972 to 44017.4 in 1981; a chilling example of the relationship between internal prices and external rates of exchange.

Table H/Graph H – Commodities Prices

The outstanding feature here is the runaway price increase for crude petroleum relative to other commodity price changes. While most prices have doubled or trebled over the whole period, petroleum prices have increased by a factor of 17. This is indicated dramatically in Graph H and, of course, underlines OPEC's improved terms of trade. Other commodities to have done relatively well are aluminium, cocoa, palm oil, rice, rubber and tin. While beef, coffee, copper, cotton, maize, soyabeans, sugar, tea, tobacco and wheat did less well.

Now, these broad price changes hide very important shorter-term price movements. An indication of the giddy "switch-back" price movements for some commodities can be found by reference to the IMF International Financial Statistics Supplement on Prices (1981). There it can be seen that aluminium prices rose by 18.1% in the fourth quarter of 1980 but fell by 22.9% in the third quarter of 1981. Similar fluctuations are evident for many other primary products.

Table J/Graph J – Export Patterns

Here we are concerned with the trends in the pattern of export *markets*. Some items stand out; they are:

(1) *Industrial countries* export a large part of their goods to other industrial countries although the proportion has fallen somewhat due to an understandable increase in sales to OPEC markets. The proportion going to LDCs has also risen no doubt in part due to a drive to sell capital goods on highly concessionary export credit terms (see Chapter 10).

(2) *US exports* show that a stable proportion of sales go to Canada and Japan combined and that OPEC and LDC markets have become much more important than in 1972. The EEC has remained a relatively stagnant market for US exports as has the US market for EEC exports. Thus US exports to just two countries exceed in importance US exports to the whole of the EEC!

(3) *UK exports* show how strikingly the EEC market has grown, with an even more marked percentage rise for sales to OPEC. Those two areas take over half of all UK exports. Note that the LDC market has increased by a much smaller extent than for the US or the EEC indicating perhaps the degree of lack of competitiveness in capital goods exports.

(4) *Japanese exports* indicate that over one-third of their market lies in the "Pacific" basin. This figure is in fact greater when other markets in that area are included (not shown in table). Note that in spite of agitation in the US concerning imports from Japan, the US as a market is somewhat smaller in 1981 than it was in 1972; this is also true of the UK as a market for Japanese imports. Note also that the LDCs as a market has increased very little. A reflection perhaps of the major role of consumer durables in the make-up of Japanese exports.

The EEC as a whole continues to be a major importer of Japanese goods, and when compared with Japan as a market for EEC exports, indicates just how "unbalanced" this trade is.

(5) *OPEC exports* are much less significant for the EEC market than in 1972, no doubt due in part to the self-sufficiency of the UK and Norway and also to the recession in the Industrialized world. However, the US as a market has increased significantly due, of course, to the fact that the US is a major oil importing nation, allied to much higher unit prices for oil – a factor that has affected all importers. Another point to make in this respect is the fact that the EEC – despite its decline as an OPEC market – is still much larger as a market than the US.

(6) *LDCs exports* are noteworthy for the fact that a very large part are sold to the Industrialized world, although there has been something of a falling off in recent years. This is clearly due to the increased importance of both OPEC and the LDCs themselves as markets. Note that while the US as a market takes about one-fifth of all LDC's exports, the LDCs take close on one-third of all US exports. A significant proportion of this imbalance results from the demand for agricultural products available from US suppliers.

(7) *Soviet bloc exports* (or at least that part that goes to non-CMEA[3] members) goes largely to the Industrialized countries, especially Germany. As it is estimated that about half of *all* Soviet bloc exports go to non-CMEA countries,[4] this represents a very large slice of such shipments. About half of all USSR exports to the West are oil and two-thirds of Eastern Europe's exports to the West are clothing[5]). The LDCs as a market has doubled in relative size over the period for these exports. This can perhaps be explained by increased commercial ties with countries of the Indian sub-continent and also by increases in prices for oil supplied by the Soviet bloc.

(8) *EEC exports* are largely going to EEC nations – a fairly constant proportion over the period, with the US market becoming somewhat less important. The US is a much less important market for EEC exports than the EEC is for US exports.

Tables K and L

Finally, turning specifically to UK trade we note that mineral fuels and lubricants have become a much larger share of total UK exports and that semi and finished manufactured imports now account for a large share of total UK imports.

If we look at the volume indices in Table L we see that the volume of UK exports (less oil) grew from 84 in 1972 to 121 in 1981, an increase of 44%. By contrast, the increase in import volume over the same period has been 45.5%. This deterioration in the *volume* of trade has been confined to the latter period of 1976 to 1981 and was accentuated in the first half of 1982.[6] One explanation for this trend is that UK companies were re-stocking primary commodities and semi-finished goods after a period of sharp destocking during the depths of the 1980–81 recession. Another explanation is that the UK market is increasingly being penetrated by imports of finished manufacturers. Only time will reveal the true position.

What is undeniable is that unit prices for UK exports (less oil) measured in £s have increased somewhat more sharply than unit prices for UK imports

[3]Council for Mutual Economic Assistance.
[4]*World Bank Atlas.*
[5]*Barclays Bank Review* August 1980.
[6]See FT, 23 September 1982.

(less oil). Part of this is likely to be the reduction in relative prices of primary commodities.

UK service exports show a healthier trend. Not only has the *volume* of UK exports increased faster than the *volume* of UK service imports but unit prices for UK export of services has also risen more quickly than for UK service imports.

SUMMARY

So what have we found? Let's draw some broad conclusions to our remarks:

(1) World trade has been expanding about 4% per annum in real terms.

(2) The Industrialized nations were responsible for two-thirds of all world trade and that the six top exporting countries performed nearly half of all world exports.

(3) The differences in the dependence on international trade varies widely. For example the United States exports amounted to just 9.6% of its 1981 GDP while the German ratio was 31.8% for the same year. However, it is evident that the US ratio is on an upward trend – an important matter for the largest trading nation in the world.

(4) The UK remains one one of the top six exporting countries with higher exports to GDP than Japan.

(5) Some countries exports are of the entrepôt variety and should therefore not be reviewed in the same light as "indigenous" exports.

(6) There have been sharp movements in the Terms of Trade for groups like OPEC and the Industrialized nations. Individual country's Terms of Trade tend to be offset by exchange rate movements.

(7) Commodity prices are subject to wide fluctuations and are linked to demand by the major trading nations.

(8) There are evident patterns of trade to be observed; namely:

    (a) inter-Industrial nations;
    (b) inter-Pacific basin;
    (c) inter-EEC;
    (d) inter-Soviet bloc.

    Thus there are four large circular trade flows in the world.

(9) UK imports are increasingly of the manufactured goods type.

(10) UK service exports are showing a much sharper rising trend than exports of goods.

Appendix 3

Trade Statistics

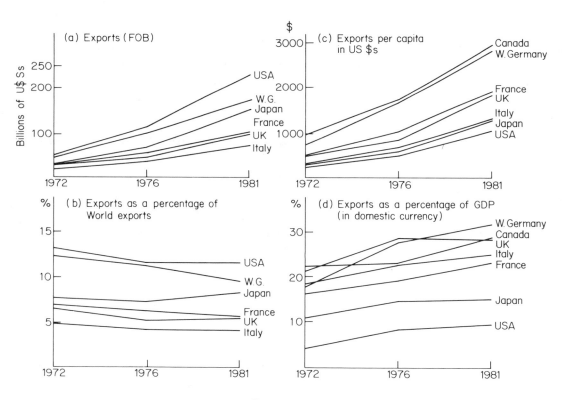

Graph A

Table A
Exports (FOB) US$ billions

Exports from	1972 (a) EX	(b) %	(c) EX PC $s	(d) EX % GDP DC	1976 (a) EX	(b) %	(c) EX PC $s	(d) EX % GDP DC	1981 (a) EX	(b) %	(c) EX PC $s	(d) EX % GDP DC
World[1]	376.1	100.0	—	—	917.2	100.0	—	—	1832.3	100.0	—	—
Industrial nations	276.7	73.6	—	—	632.9	69.0	—	—	1218.6	66.5	—	—
US	49.8	13.2	238	4.3	115.4	12.6	529	8.3	233.7	12.7	1017	9.6
Germany	46.7	12.4	757	18.0	101.9	11.1	1656	27.8	176.1	9.6	2855	31.8
Japan	29.1	7.7	272	11.2	67.3	7.3	597	14.4	151.5	8.3	1299	15.2[2]
France	26.5	7.0	513	16.2	57.2	6.2	1081	19.1	106.4	5.8	1972	23.2[3]
UK	24.7	6.6	443	21.6	46.7	5.1	835	28.4	102.7	5.6	1840	28.1[2]
Italy	18.5	4.9	340	18.4	37.3	4.1	664	22.9	75.3	4.1	1316	24.7
Netherlands	16.8	4.5	1260	47.3	40.1	4.4	2912	53.5	68.7	3.7	4824	58.9
Canada	21.2	5.6	971	22.1	40.6	4.4	1764	22.6	72.6	4.0	2999	28.2
Belgium[4]	16.1	4.3	1658	43.6	32.8	3.6	3340	47.6	55.6	3.0	5639	59.7[2]
LDCs[5]	45.5	12.1	—	—	143.5	15.6	—	—	321.5	17.5	—	—
OPEC[6]	25.0	6.6	—	—	132.7	14.5	—	—	269.7	14.7	—	—
EEC[7]	155.4	41.3	—	—	331.0	36.0	—	—	612.9	33.4	—	—
Intra EEC	80.6	21.4	—	—	171.7	18.7	—	—	306.4	16.7	—	—

Data derived from International Monetary Fund's *Direction of Trade Statistics 1982*, and International Monetary Fund's *International Financial Statistics*, August 1982.

(a) column shows: FOB exports in US billions of dollars
(b) column shows: Percentage of world FOB exports
(c) column shows: FOB exports per capita in US dollars
(d) column shows: FOB exports as a percentage of Gross Domestic Product both measured in domestic currency.

[1] World excludes Soviet bloc countries except Romania and Hungary and includes Peoples Republic of China.
[2] Based on 1980 data.
[3] Based on third quarter 1981 annualised.
[4] Includes Luxembourg.
[5] All non-oil less developed countries.
[6] Algeria, Indonesia, Iran, Iraq, Kuwait, Libya, Nigeria, Oman, Qatar, Saudi Arabia, United Arab Emirates, Venezuela.
[7] Belgium/Luxembourg, Denmark, France, Germany, Greece, Ireland, Italy, Netherlands, UK.

Table B
Imports (CIF) US$ billions

Imports to	1972				1976				1981			
	(a) IMP	(b) %	(c) IMP PC $s	(d) IMP % GDP DC	(a) IMP	(b) %	(c) IMP PC $s	(d) IMP % GDP DC	(a) IMP	(b) %	(c) IMP PC $s	(d) IMP % GDP DC
World[1]	388.0	100.0	—	—	931.8	100.0	—	—	1917.8	100.0	—	—
Industrial nations	281.9	72.7	—	—	680.4	73.0	—	—	1294.4	67.5	—	—
USA	58.9	15.2	282	5.1	132.5	14.2	608	8.7	273.4	14.3	1190	10.6
Germany	40.4	10.4	655	20.0	88.1	9.5	1432	25.2	163.9	8.5	2658	31.0
France	27.0	7.0	522	15.3	64.4	6.9	1217	20.3	121.0	6.3	2242	24.7[3]
Japan	23.9	6.2	223	8.9	64.9	7.0	841	13.7	142.9	7.5	1225	16.1[2]
UK	28.2	7.3	505	21.8	56.6	6.1	1013	29.6	99.5	5.2	1782	25.7[2]
Italy	19.3	5.0	355	18.8	43.4	4.7	773	25.4	91.1	4.8	1593	28.2
Netherlands	17.5	4.5	1313	44.4	40.5	4.3	2941	49.9	67.3	3.5	4726	55.0
Belgium[4]	15.5	4.0	1596	40.4	35.4	3.8	3605	48.2	62.1	3.2	6298	63.4[2]
Canada	20.0	5.2	916	21.3	40.4	4.3	1755	23.2	69.8	3.6	2883	27.1
LDCs[5]	56.8	14.6	—	—	180.4	19.4	—	—	442.1	23.1	—	—
OPEC[6]	14.1	3.6	—	—	63.5	6.8	—	—	160.2	8.4	—	—
EEC[7]	155.4	40.1	—	—	351.2	37.7	—	—	641.5	33.4	—	—
Intra-EEC	80.6	20.8	—	—	170.6	18.3	—	—	300.6	15.7	—	—

Sources and notes as for Table A.

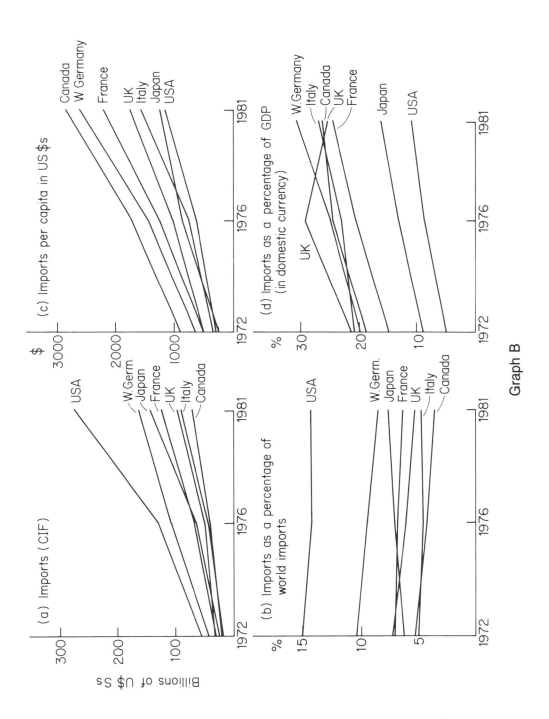

Graph B

Table C
Exports (FOB) US$ billion

Exports from	1972				1976				1981			
	(a) EX	(b) %	(c) EX PC $s	(d) EX % GDP DC	(a) EX	(b) %	(c) EX PC $s	(d) EX % GDP DC	(a) EX	(b) %	(c) EX PC $s	(d) EX % GDP DC
USSR[1,2]	5.1	1.34	20	N/A	14.4	1.57	57	2.8	35.7	1.95	135[7]	8.9[7]
Brazil	4.0	1.06	40	6.9	10.1	1.10	93	6.8	19.7	1.07	160	8.7
Spain	3.8	1.01	110	14.1	8.7	0.95	242	14.0	20.3	1.11	553[5]	15.6[5]
Hong Kong	3.5	0.93	858	N/A	8.5	0.93	1932	79.8	21.8	1.19	4449	135.2[7]
Taiwan[3]	2.9	0.77	190	42.7	8.2	0.89	502	51.9	16.1[7]	1.07[7]	753[6]	58.5[6]
China[3]	2.8	0.74	4	N/A	6.0	0.65	7	N/A	19.9	1.09	2	N/A
India	2.4	0.64	4	4.5	5.0	0.54	8	7.6	7.8	0.43	12	7.0[7]
Nigeria	2.2	0.58	38	19.8	10.8	1.18	159	30.8	18.7	1.02	138[6]	25.7[6]
Singapore[4]	2.2	0.58	1023	70.8	6.6	0.72	2882	111.6	21.0	1.15	8040[5]	184.7[5]
Poland[1,2]	2.0	0.53	60	N/A	4.7	0.51	138	N/A	5.8	0.32	165	N/A
Argentina	1.9	0.51	78	9.0	3.9	0.43	151	8.9	7.9	0.43	299	11.9[6]
Mexico	1.7	0.45	31	9.3	3.5	0.38	56	8.5	21.2	1.16	295	12.6[5]
Malaysia	1.7	0.45	155	36.0	5.3	0.58	431	51.6	11.2	0.61	777	51.6
South Korea	1.6	0.43	48	21.0	7.7	0.84	215	32.6	20.2	1.10	522	39.2
Greece	0.9	0.24	101	11.7	2.6	0.28	283	16.8	4.3	0.23	448	19.6

[1] Did not report data to IMF; does not include intra-Soviet trade.
[2] Data derived from partner countries and is on a CIF basis.
[3] China replaced Taiwan as reporting member on 17 April 1980.
[4] See text.
[5] Based on 1980 data.
[6] Based on 1978 data.
[7] Based on 1979 data.
Sources and column heading notes as for Table A, except data for USSR from UN Statistical Yearbook and CMEA Statistical Yearbook.

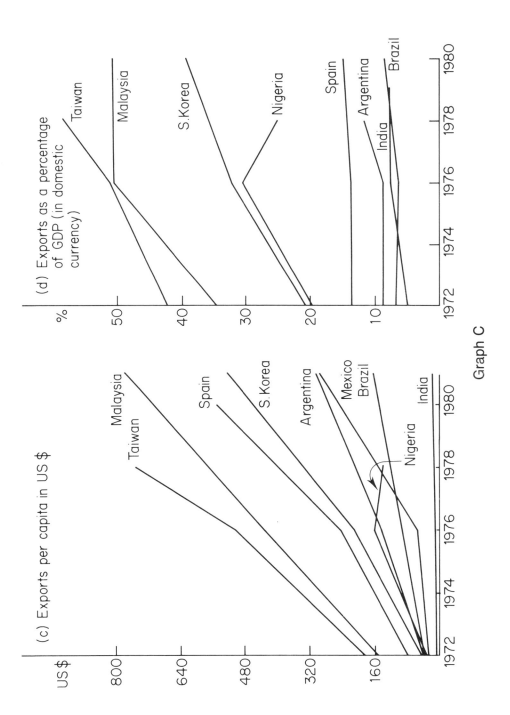

Graph C

Table D
Imports (CIF) US$ billion

Imports into	1972				1976				1981			
	(a)	(b)	(c)	(d)	(a)	(b)	(c)	(d)	(a)	(b)	(c)	(d)
	IM	%	IMP PC $s	IMP % GDP DC	IM	%	IMP PC $s	IMP % GDP DC	IM	%	IMP PC $s	IMP % GDP DC
Spain	6.8	1.76	197	14.5	17.5	1.88	680	18.1	32.2	1.68	911	18.3[5]
USSR[1,2]	6.3	1.62	25	N/A	20.2	2.17	79	5.3	36.0	1.88	136[7]	8.0[7]
Brazil	4.8	1.24	48	8.5	13.8	1.48	126	9.1	23.0	1.20	187	9.1
Hong Kong	3.9	1.01	956	N/A	8.9	0.95	2023	92.0	24.8	1.29	5061	153.8[7]
Singapore[4]	3.4	0.88	1581	108.8	9.1	0.98	3974	153.7	27.6	1.44	9958[5]	228.8[5]
Mexico	2.7	0.70	50	11.1	6.0	0.64	96	9.9	29.1	1.52	405	13.5[5]
Taiwan	2.5	0.64	164	36.3	7.6	0.82	465	49.0	14.8[7]	0.96[7]	656[6]	51.5[6]
South Korea	2.5	0.64	75	26.2	8.8	0.94	245	34.4	25.1	1.31	648	43.6
Greece	2.3	0.59	259	20.0	6.0	0.64	654	25.8	8.6	0.45	896	27.5
India	2.2	0.57	4	4.8	5.1	0.55	8	7.0	15.2	0.79	25	8.4[7]
Poland[1,2]	2.2	0.57	67	N/A	7.1	0.76	209	N/A	6.4	0.33	182	N/A
China[3]	2.1	0.54	3	N/A	5.2	0.56	5	N/A	19.4	1.01	20	N/A
Argentina	1.9	0.49	78	8.4	3.0	0.32	117	6.8	10.0	0.52	379	7.6[6]
Malaysia	1.6	0.41	145	37.4	3.8	0.41	309	41.9	11.6	0.60	804	59.2
Nigeria	1.5	0.39	26	16.7	8.2	0.88	121	27.8	18.8	0.98	177[6]	33.4[6]

All notes and sources as for Table C.

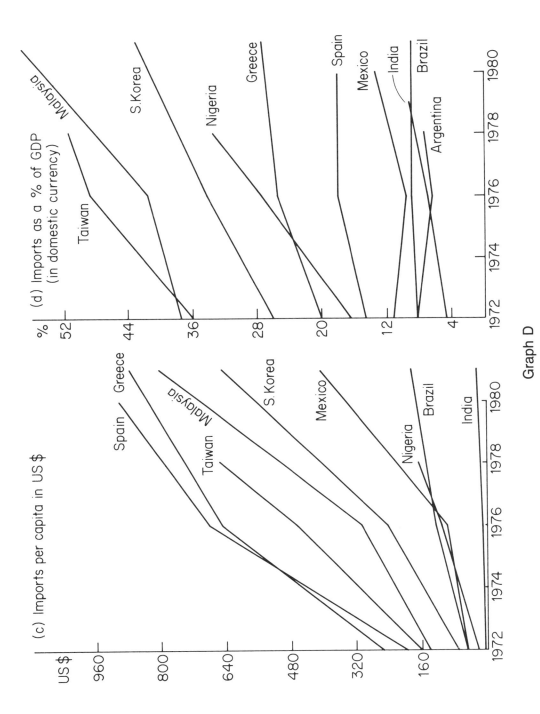

(d) Imports as a % of GDP (in domestic currency)

(c) Imports per capita in US $

Graph D

Table E
Export and Import Unit Prices and Terms of Trade (Based on US Dollars)
1975 = 100

	Export Unit Prices			Import Unit Prices			Terms of Trade		
	1972	1976	1981	1972	1976	1981	1972	1976	1981
World	54	102	178	53	101	175	102	101	102
Ind. nations	60	101	155	53	101	174	113	100	89
USA	60	103	162	52	103	190	115	100	85
Canada	61	106	152	67	103	160	91	103	95
Japan	65	99	159	44	103	202	148	96	79
Belgium	59	100	144	58	102	160	102	98	90
France	58	98	137	55	99	152	105	99	90
Germany	59	102	136	55	103	159	107	99	86
Italy	60	94	155	48	98	182	125	96	85
Netherlands	55	101	155	52	101	161	106	100	96
UK	64	97	182[1]	53	99	191[1]	121	98	95[1]
Nigeria	23	109	324	60[3]	101[3]	155[3]	38	108	209
Greece	57	96	148[1]	52	96	159[1]	110	100	93[1]
Spain	63	99	156[1]	47	103	188[1]	134	96	83[1]
Brazil	58	115	141	46	103	195	126	112	72
Taiwan	65	102	142[2]	55	100	155[2]	118	102[2]	92
India	65	99	134[2]	42	97	129[2]	155	102	104[2]
S. Korea	67	112	174	47	98	164	143	114	106
Malaysia	50	117	198	49	96	164	102	122	121
Singapore	50	102	162[1]	51	101	163[1]	98	101	99[1]
Argentina[4]	133	106	251[1]	60[3]	101[3]	160[1,3]	222	105	157[1]
OPEC	21	106	316	60[3]	101[3]	155[3]	35	105	204
LDCs	56	106	169[1]	51	100	172[1]	110	106	98[1]

Note: Terms of Trade defined as the Export Unit Price Index as a percentage of the Import Unit Price
Index i.e. $\dfrac{\text{EUPI}}{\text{IUPI}} \times 100 = \text{ToT}$.

[1] 1980.
[2] 1979.
[3] Industrial nations export unit price index.
[4] Export prices based on Argentine meat export prices only.
Sources: IMF International Financial Statistics (various) and IMF IFS Yearbook 1981.

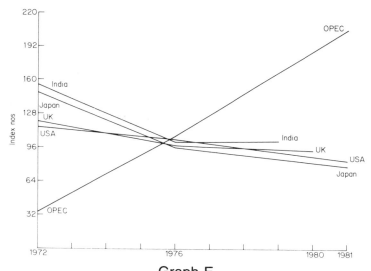

Graph E
Terms of Trade. 1975 = 100. Based on US dollars.

Table F
Exchange Rates per US dollar (Annual Average)

	1972	1976	1981	*June* 1982
SDRs	0.9210	0.8661	0.8480	0.9073
German Deutschmarks	3.1886	2.5180	2.2600	2.4298
Japanese Yen	303.17	296.55	220.54	251.04
French francs	5.0443	4.7796	5.4346	6.5791
UK pounds	0.3997	0.5536	0.4931	0.5692
Italian lire	583.22	832.28	1136.77	1356.02
Dutch guilders	3.2095	2.6439	2.4952	2.6860
Canadian dollars	0.9899	0.9860	1.1989	1.2753
Belgian francs	44.015	38.605	37.131	46.212
Greek drachmas	30.00	36.518	55.408	62.830[2]
Irish pounds	0.3997	0.5536	0.6185	0.7047
Spanish pesetas	64.271	66.903	92.314	109.153
Argentine pesos	8.2	140.0	4402.7	15163.1
Brazil Cruzerios	5.934	10.673	93.125	168.335
Mexican pesos	12.500	15.426	24.515	47.619
Taiwan dollars	40.050	30.000	36.048[1]	N/A
Indian rupees	7.594	8.960	8.659	9.276[2]
S. Korean Won	392.90	484.0	681.03	738.39
Malaysian ringgets	2.8196	2.5416	2.3041	2.3404
Singapore dollars	2.8092	2.4708	2.1127	2.1370
Nigerian naira	0.6579	0.6266	0.6140	0.6755[3]
China yuan	N/A	1.9414	1.7050	1.8970

Rates are average for years shown.
[1] 1979.
[2] May 1982.
[3] April 1982.

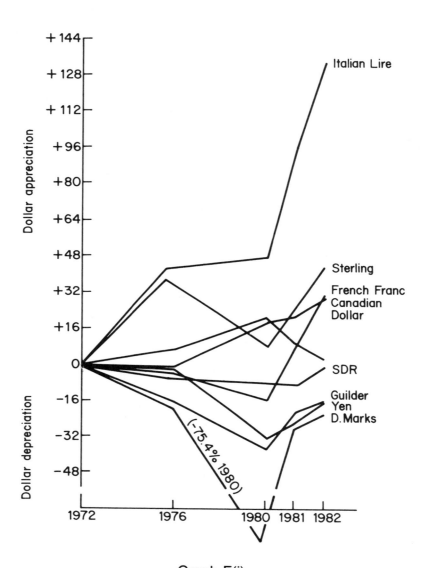

Graph F(i)
Currency rates per US dollar. Percentage changes since 1972. Annual averages.

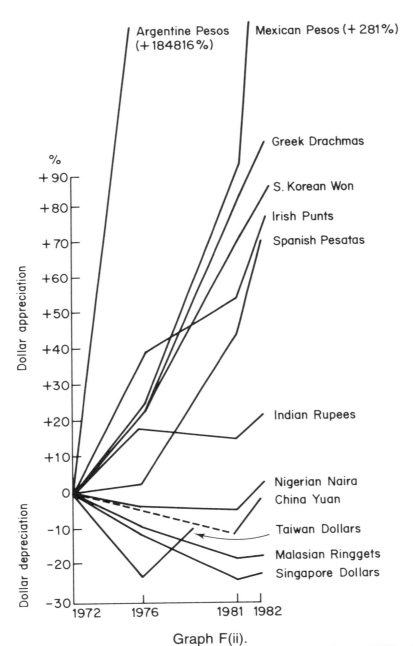

Graph F(ii).
Currency rates per US dollar. Percentage changes since 1972. Annual averages.

Table G
Consumer Prices (Index Numbers)
(*Based on domestic currency*) 1975 = 100

	1972	1976	1981
World	69.5	110.9	197.0
Ind. nations	73.8	108.3	169.1
USA	77.7	105.8	169.0
Canada	75.7	107.5	171.0
Japan	64.3	109.3	143.9
Belgium	73.6	109.2	146.4
France	73.3	109.6	183.8
Germany	82.5	104.3	129.2
Italy	64.8	116.8	251.1
Netherlands	76.5	108.8	142.8
UK	63.6	116.5	218.9
Nigeria	62.9	124.3	260.8
Greece	60.1	113.3	264.6
Spain	66.4	115.1	262.8
Brazil	53.9	142.0	1623.9
Taiwan	59.6	102.5	127.4[1]
India	62.9	92.2	137.3
S. Korea	62.2	115.3	272.9
Malaysia	73.8	102.6	136.7
Singapore	63.0	98.0	129.5
Argentina	17.8	543.2	44017.4
OPEC	65.5	116.2	206.3
LDCs	52.2	121.7	387.4
China	N/A	100.3	116.6

Sources: IMF *International Financial Statistics* August 1982
and IMF *Yearbook* 1981.
[1]1978.

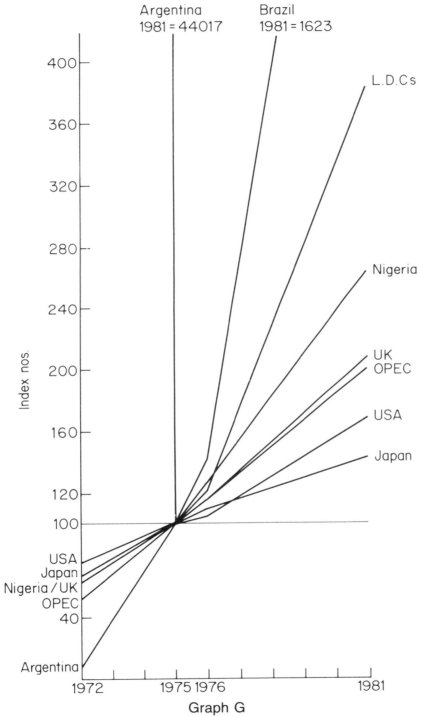

Graph G
Consumer prices. Index numbers 1975 = 100. Domestic currency.

Table H
Commodity Prices – Index Numbers (End Period)
Based on US dollars 1975 = 100

Commodity	Producer	1972	1976	1981 (3rd qtr)
Aluminium	Canada	65.7	116.4	181.9
Beef	Argentina ⎱ USA ⎰	101.8	97.6	163.2
Cocoa	Brazil	57.3	223.3	161.0
Coffee	Brazil	67.4	233.6	140.0
Copper	Canada	87.2	109.8	138.7
Cotton	Mexico ⎱ USA ⎰	63.0	150.7	148.0
Maize	USA	55.1	91.6	117.7
Palm oil	Malaysia	56.6	117.3	154.1
Petroleum	Saudi Arabia	17.4	100.0	296.8
Rice	USA	52.9	79.3	157.5
Rubber	Malaysia	65.6	141.5	202.5[1]
Soyabeans	USA	78.1	133.2	157.4
Sugar	Brazil	58.5	57.6	120.7
Tea	India	81.1	132.9	137.2
Tin	Malaysia	59.7	130.1	208.3
Tobacco	USA	77.1	101.9	137.4
Wheat	Argentina ⎱ USA ⎰	61.9	71.9	117.0

[1]2nd quarter 1981
Data calculated from prices in IMF *International Financial Statistics*
Supplement No. 2 1981.

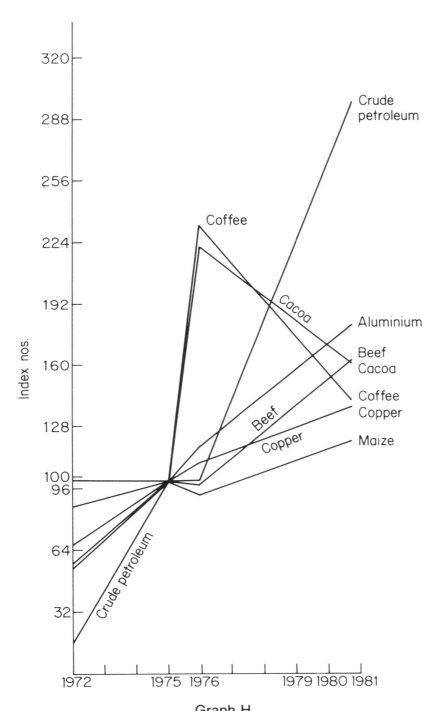

Graph H
Commodity prices. Index numbers 1975 = 100. Measured in US dollars.

Table I
Population (m) and Gross Domestic Product per Capita Measured in US dollars

	1972		1976		1981	
	Population	*GDP PC*	*Population*	*GDP PC*	*Population*	*GDP PC*
USA	208.23	5643	218.04	7785	229.81	12102
Germany	61.67	4201	61.51	7249	61.67	11142
Japan	107.19	2840	112.77	4959	116.78[1]	8873[1]
France	51.70	3762	52.89	6638	53.71[1]	12143[1]
UK	55.79	2843	55.89	4029	55.95	7997[1]
Italy	54.41	2367	56.17	3351	57.20	5062
Netherlands	13.33	3430	13.77	6597	14.24	9798
Canada	21.83	4941	23.02	8563	24.21	11724
Belgium	9.71	3671	9.82	6927	9.86[1]	12079[1]
Argentina	24.39	1230	25.72	2230	26.39[2]	2443[2]
Brazil	97.85	626	109.18	1442	123.03[1]	2021
Taiwan	15.23	504	16.34	1056	16.85[2]	1432[2]
Greece	8.89	1416	9.17	2464	9.60[1]	4181[1]
India	563.53	112	613.27	147	663.60[1]	241[1]
Ireland	3.02	1845	3.23	2549	3.40[1]	5252[1]
South Korea	33.51	307	35.85	770	38.72	1698
Malaysia	11.00	458	12.30	898	14.42	1680
Mexico	54.27	755	62.33	1426	71.91[1]	2426[1]
Singapore	2.15	1350	2.29	2576	2.41[1]	4348[1]
Spain	34.49	1548	35.97	3006	37.43[1]	5640[1]
Nigeria	59.85	196	67.76	599	72.22[2]	627[2]
USSR	247.5	N/A	254.4	2010	264.1[3]	2582[3]

[1] 1980.
[2] 1978.
[3] 1979.

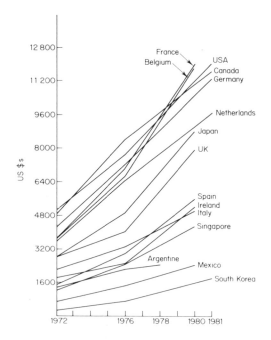

Graph I
Gross domestic product per capita. Measured in US dollars.

Table J
Patterns of Exports (FOB) Measured in US Dollars

	1972	1976	1981
Exports from			
Industrial Countries	$276.7 b	$632.9 b	$1218.6 b
	%	%	%
to: Industrial countries	68.6	67.5	65.1
OPEC	4.0	8.4	9.5
LDCs	14.0	18.0	20.3
EEC	39.1	38.6	36.9
Soviet bloc	3.4	3.9	2.9
Exports from USA	$49.8 b	$115.4 b	$233.7 b
	%	%	%
to: Canada	24.9	20.9	16.9
Japan	10.0	8.8	9.3
Germany	5.6	5.0	4.4
Netherlands	3.8	4.0	3.7
UK	5.3	4.2	5.3
OPEC	5.3	10.5	8.9
LDCs	24.0	26.1	31.8
Soviet bloc	1.6	2.8	1.6
EEC	23.9	22.6	22.4
Exports from UK	$24.7 b	$46.7 b	$102.7 b
	%	%	%
to: USA	12.3	9.5	12.1
France	5.2	6.6	6.5
Germany	6.0	7.0	10.8
OPEC	5.8	11.3	11.4
LDCs	16.0	19.7	18.0
Soviet bloc	2.9	2.3	1.8
EEC	29.7	35.8	40.0
Exports from Japan	$29.1 b	$67.3 b	$151.5 b
	%	%	%
to: USA	31.3	23.7	25.7
Australia	2.5	3.4	3.1
Germany	3.2	3.3	3.9
UK	3.4	2.1	3.1
OPEC	6.4	13.7	15.1
LDCs	28.5	29.8	31.1
Soviet bloc	5.0	4.4	2.8
EEC	11.5	11.9	12.4
China	2.1	2.0	3.5
Exports from OPEC	$24.9 b	$132.7 b	$269.7 b
	%	%	%
to: USA	10.5	15.7	17.6
Japan	15.6	16.2	18.4
France	9.2	8.6	7.3
LDCs	16.7	21.5	23.2
Soviet bloc	0.9	0.8	1.0
EEC	44.5	34.2	29.0
Exports from LDCs	$45.4 b	$143.4 b	$321.6 b
	%	%	%
to: Industrial countries	64.9	61.3	56.6
OPEC	3.0	5.6	7.1
LDCs	19.8	21.6	23.8
Soviet bloc	5.4	7.9	6.6
EEC	27.3	26.7	21.5
USSR	2.5	4.4	4.3
USA	24.3	19.2	19.8
Japan	9.4	8.6	9.1
Germany	6.2	6.9	5.4
UK	6.7	5.4	3.7

Table J
Patterns of Exports (FOB) Measured in US Dollars
(continued)

	1972	1976	1981
Exports from Soviet Bloc[1]	$13.2 b	$26.5 b	$50.8 b
	%	%	%
to: Industrial countries	55.5	60.9	60.9
Germany	9.8	10.9	11.2
OPEC	4.5	4.2	5.1
LDCs	17.3	34.9	34.0
EEC	35.1	37.6	38.2
Exports from EEC	$155.4 b	$331.0 b	$612.9 b
	%	%	%
to: USA	8.2	5.5	6.7
UK	5.3	5.6	6.4
OPEC	3.7	7.9	9.6
LDCs	10.0	14.7	15.6
Soviet bloc	3.4	3.7	2.6
EEC	51.9	52.2	50.3
Japan	1.1	0.9	1.1

[1]Excluding intra-Soviet bloc trade.

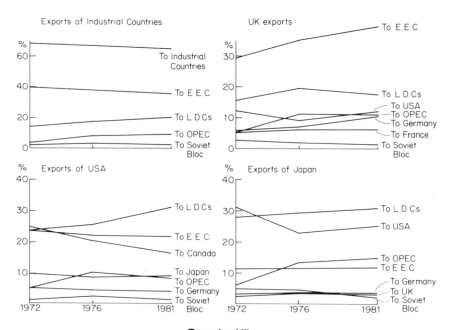

Graph J(i)
Patterns of exports (FOB) measured in US dollars.

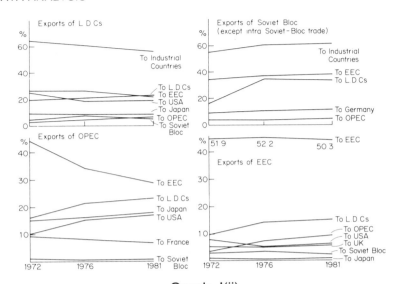

Graph J(ii)
Patterns of exports (FOB) measured in US dollars (continued)

Table K
UK Trade – Analysis by Commodity
Percentages Measured in Sterling

Exports	1972	1976	1980
EXPORTS	%	%	%
Food, beverages and tobacco	6.76	6.56	6.84
Basic materials	3.36	3.20	3.10
Mineral fuels and lubricants	2.56	5.02	13.54
Semi-manufactures	32.40	31.74	29.86
Finished manufactures	51.92	50.24	43.74
Other	3.00	3.24	2.92
Totals	100.00	100.00	100.00
IMPORTS			
Semi and finished manufactures	57.07	54.03	63.59

UK Services – Unit Value and Volume Indices   1975 = 100

	1972	1976	1980
SERVICE EXPORTS			
Unit values	64	123	189
Volumes	86	106	106
SERVICE IMPORTS			
Unit values	60	125	164
Volumes	95	99	113

Terms of Trade in Services   1975 = 100

	106.7	98.4	115.2

Source: CSO *UK Balance of Payments* 1982.

Table L
UK Trade
Unit Value and Volume Indices
(Measured in Sterling) 1975 = 100

	1972	1976	1980
EXPORTS (FOB)			
Unit Values			
All goods	57	120	193
Less oil	58	119	190
Volumes			
All goods	86	110	128
Less oil	84	109	121
IMPORTS (CIF)			
Unit values			
All goods	47	122	186
Less oil	53	120	170
Volumes			
All goods	95	106	119
Less oil	90	107	131

Source: CSO *UK Balance of Payments* 1982.

Chapter 3

The Benefits from Trade

We must now turn to the matter of why countries participate in international commerce. What benefits – if any – flow from it; what determines which products are sold abroad and which are purchased from abroad; what determines the size of the flows and the prices paid for them?

Now, these are all questions that go to the very heart of the long-running debate concerning the benefits of trade to a particular nation, and as this debate has reached a new peak of intensity at a time of high levels of unemployment in many parts of the world, it is an entirely pertinent matter to deal with in the context of international trade and finance. Indeed, many of the facilities we shall go on to discuss were created to assist and expand trade between countries.

One thing can be said very clearly at the outset; international trade is not just the exchange of goods which otherwise could not be produced domestically. Of course there are examples of goods being imported due to lack of available domestic supply – the various mineral and agricultural products come immediately to mind. Yet, it is not as simple as that. For example, as we have seen, many countries are large importers of crude petroleum. Certainly these nations produce little or no petroleum output domestically but this is not to say that they do not possess alternatives to imported petroleum. Many such alternatives can be cited, some of them likely to be available in quantity only in the future. But some unlikely ones are being utilized already – such as the use of sugar alcohol mixed with conventional fuel for driving vehicles in Brazil.

Again, if we turn to metals, there are nearly always *some* products which can be substituted for an imported product. In the case of agricultural products it is clear that certain items are produced much more effectively abroad than at home. But in all these cases the deciding factor tends not to be the domestic inability to produce but rather the *costs* of producing the same or an alternative product to the imported product. To use an oft quoted illustration, bananas *could* be grown in the UK! But at what cost?

Further, if we note one of the conclusions to the previous chapter concerning the flow of trade *between* the Industrialized nations, it is evident that much trade nowadays is *not* concerned with the exchange of food and raw materials for finished goods but rather the exchange of manufactures *for* manufactures!

Why then should a country with an ability to produce a certain product, buy it from a foreign supplier? Or indeed, to put it the other way round, why should a foreign consumer buy imported products when they could be produced in his own country?

The answer must include *cost* and assuming that the price of goods truly reflect underlying costs for materials and labour, etc., then the price of goods is a major determinant in its trade. What factors, however, determine costs? Why should a product produced in one part of the world have a different price from a similar product produced elsewhere? A number of factors are held to be responsible including monopoly or monopsony prices of private companies or state-owned industries; deliberate price manipulations designed to improve export competitiveness or barriers to imports which tends to raise prices in the importing country. Now all of these are indeed factors that cannot be ignored; yet more fundamental still is the fact that countries *do* have an indigenous ability to produce certain things more cheaply than elsewhere. These factors concern the economic and social make-up of a particular society, the quantity and quality of all the resources available to it and how those resources are organized.

Now when we refer to "economic resources" we are talking about the physical environment that provides the type of soil, mineral contents, climate, etc.; but also two other important groups of resources, namely, the level of capital available and the quality and quantity of the workforce including management and entrepreneurship.

Capital can be defined in this context as the supply of productive machinery, plant and equipment and the availability of finance to fund further capital acquisitions. The level of capital depends on the degree of output not going to consumption plus credits from a wide variety of sources.

The quantity and quality of labour depends, of course, on the size of the population and also on such social matters as school-leaving age, hours worked per week, etc. The quality of labour is another way of talking about "labour capital". That is, skilled or educated people who have had finance invested in them to improve the quality of their output.

Clearly, all these variants are likely to be different in different countries. An obvious example is that of Canada, where because of a huge supply of suitable arable land and the proper climate, plus the improvements wrought by investment in farm machinery and management, wheat and other farm produce is supplied far in excess of the amounts required for domestic needs.

Other examples include Argentine beef, OPEC oil, and South African gold. In terms of manufactures we can cite Japanese cars, US computers, and UK aircraft.

It may seem reasonable to agree that there are *some* countries which obviously do have the ability to produce *some* products more cheaply than elsewhere, but can we extend this argument to encompass *all* countries? Well indeed we can, because it is just that proposition that is contained in the hypothesis posed by the theory of comparative cost advantage. This theory was first advanced by a British economist, David Ricardo, in the early part of the nineteenth century when he made the observation that it did not matter whether a particular country had an *absolute* cost advantage in a certain product over other countries, what mattered was whether they had a *relative* or *comparative* advantage. This was a vital point at issue at the time (as indeed it still is) for it countered the arguments in favour of restricting imports which held that if some countries were more efficient (perhaps because of low wage levels) then nothing could be sold to that country in return for their exports.

It is necessary therefore, for us to distinguish clearly between these two concepts. Readers are strongly advised to follow the logic of the argument carefully if a full understanding is to be obtained. We can begin by laying out some of the implied assumptions needed to consider the theory at its basic level. These are:

(a) Competitive International Trade Conditions

We assume that consumers do not face artificial restrictions on their choices of goods or services and that there are no special incentives or subsidies granted by the authorities to maintain production costs below market levels.

(b) Free Movement of Domestic Resources

Domestic supplies of capital and labour are free to move to those regions prepared to offer the optimum returns. This requires efficient capital and labour markets unrestricted by regulations, amalgamation and monopoly for the purpose of limiting such movements.

(c) Rates of Exchange at Market Levels

Currency rates are assumed to settle at levels which accurately reflect domestic costs and prices of tradeable goods. Thus, at given rates of exchange tradeable goods (and services) will tend to have similar costs and prices as a result of *international trade*. (See purchasing power parity theory in Chapter 9).

(d) Changing Marginal Costs of Production

We must make allowances for the fact that production costs are not static but change with output quantities. Thus, over a small range of production unit costs (i.e. costs per each unit of output may not change very much. But at much larger outputs such unit costs may rise (or fall)). We assume at first that costs are static but later relax this assumption.

(e) The Impact of Demand Preferences

We assume at first that demand plays no function in determining costs and prices but later relax this assumption.

Let us put the case at its most simple yet retain the basic principle intact by imagining two countries which for reasons outlined above each produce two products at different costs. At this stage we need to select an appropriate cost measure in order to make international comparisons. One method is to consider the volume of resources needed in each country to produce a given output but because resources vary in quality and kind this would be difficult. Another method is to compare final prices by reference to the existing exchange rate. The difficulty here is simply that the exchange rate may be affected by many factors apart from prices of traded goods and services (see Chapter 9).

CASE 1

The method adopted here is the most common way out of these problems. It is simply to assume that our two countries (let's call them A and B) can produce two goods (called X and Y) and that these two goods are much the same in both countries. The cost measurement is then deduced from the ratios of output of one good in terms of the other. Thus, if country A can with a certain bundle of resources produce (say) 24 units of good X but only 6 units of good Y and country B can produce 16 units of good X but 32 units of good Y, the price/cost differential between A and B is found by reference to the ratio differentials. Table 3.1 sets this out.

Nation A can clearly produce more X than nation B and the latter can produce more Y than nation A. These figures give us the *absolute* cost advantages of these two countries. Let's assume (for the moment) that these outputs are so produced that half the resources go into good X and half into good Y. The actual pre-trade outputs is thus 12X and 3Y in A and 8X and 16Y in B. (Constant marginal costs are assumed.) Now let both countries specialize only in the good in which it possesses an absolute advantage, namely good X for A and good Y for B. In column 6 we show this specialization.

Now we need to get these countries to trade with each other. Let us assume (for the moment) that nation A is prepared to sell (export) 8 units of X which nation B is prepared to buy (import). What will the exchange ratio (the volume terms of trade) be? Well, we can find this out as follows:

If nation A exports 8 of X she will want more than 2 of Y.
If nation B imports 8 of X she will want to give less than 16 of Y.

Table 3.1

1	2	3	4	5	6	7	8	9
			Possible/Actual Pre-trade outputs		*Output with trade*	*Trade*	*Post-trade consumption*	*Gains from trade*
Case	*Country*	*Goods*						
1	A	X	24	12	24	−8	16	+4
			or	and	and	and	and	and
		Y	6	3	0	+8	8	+5
1	B	X	16	8	0	+8	8	nil
			or	and	and	and	and	and
		Y	32	16	32	−8	24	+8
2	A	X	12	6	12	−4	8	+2
			or	and	and	and	and	and
		Y	6	3	0	+5	5	+2
2	B	X	16	8	0	+4	4	−4
			or	and	and	and	and	and
		Y	32	16	32	−5	27	+11
3	A	X	8	4	8	−4		
			or	and	and	and		
		Y	16	8	0	>8?		
3	B	X	16	8	0	+4		
			or	and	and	and		
		Y	32	16	32	<8?		

The above results follow from the *domestic* ratios in column 4. For example, country A can get 2 of Y *by her own efforts* when she reduces output of X by 8. If she is going to gain from trade with B she needs to receive (import) *more than 2 of Y* to gain. Likewise, country B can produce 8 of X by reducing output of Y by 16. For her to gain from trade she needs to give up (export) *less than 16Y*.

Clearly then, any price between the range of 8X for 3Y to 8X for 15Y is possible. Let us assume (for the moment) that they split the difference and trade at 8X for 8Y. Column 7 shows this trade, where A exports 8Y and imports 8Y while B imports 8X and exports 8Y.

Column 8 shows the final result after trade has taken place. A produced 24X less 8 for export equals 16 left for domestic consumption. B produced 32Y less 8 for export equals 24 for domestic consumption.

Naturally, while exports reduce consumption at home, imports increase consumption at home.

The gains each country makes from this trade are shown in column 9. The result is found by comparing column 5 (pre-trade output and consumption) with column 8 (post-trade consumption).

Country A consumed 12 of X before trade but 16X after trade.
Also she consumed 3 of Y before trade but 8 of Y after trade.

Country B consumed 8 of X before trade, and still 8 of X after trade. Also she consumed 16 of Y before trade but 24 of Y after trade.

Both nations have made substantial gains from trade arising from their cost ratio differentials and the subsequent specialization and trade.

However this argument is very limited for two reasons:
(a) because it assumes the same bundle of resources in both countries, and
(b) because it deals only with *absolute* cost differentials.

CASE 2

So, let us now turn to Case 2. Here, nation B's output is as in Case 1 but A's output is reduced to 12X and 6Y. It is not now relevant to speak of "bundles of resources". All that has to be considered is the *ratio* of X to Y in both countries irrespective of what goes into them. For example, country B is able to produce more of X *and* Y than is A at *any* level of resource input.

Can these nations still trade as before? Well, the answer is "perhaps". Let us see. Suppose as before, they both produce one half of their possible outputs (remember that resources are limited and we are anyway concerned with ratios rather than total outputs). Thus column 5 now shows 6X and 3Y for A and 8X and 16Y for B. What trade will follow?

Well, if A specializes in X and B in Y (as before):

A will export (say) 4X but will want more than 2Y and
B will import (say) 4X but will want to give less than 8Y.

Suppose we agree on 4X for 5Y. This is shown in column 7. The results are shown in column 8 and the "gains" in column 9.

Have they both gained from trade? Well, country A certainly has; she now consumes 2 more X and 2 more Y than before. Country B however, has 4 fewer X to consume but 11 more Y. Is she also better off? That depends on whether her consumers want more Y. If they do, the cost of getting 11 more Y by trade is 4 of X. Had nation B reduced output of good X by 4 units in an attempt to produce more Y units instead, she would only have produced *8 more Y units*. Therefore, it is cheaper to buy the Y units from nation A, *even though nation A has no absolute cost advantage whatsoever*.

What A *does* possess however, is a *comparative* cost advantage in good X (or to put it more exactly, A has the *least* comparative cost *disadvantage* in good X). It is therefore quite possible for both nations to gain from trade, even where one of them has a clear cost advantage in *all* outputs!

CASE 3

To emphasize this important conclusion let us now turn to Case 3 where B's possible output is double that of A's in *both* products.

B has an absolute but no *comparative* cost advantage in anything. Does this matter? Well, let's try to get them to trade. Let A specialize in X and B in Y. (You can try it the other way around if you like.) At what rates will they both be prepared to exchange goods?

Let A export 4 of X, she will want something more than 8Y.
Let B import 4 of X, she will want to give less than 8Y.

Stalemate! They cannot agree on terms simply because they do not possess a *comparative* cost advantage. Now the reason for the lack of such advantage lies in the *identical* ratios for both goods; i.e. B can produce *twice* the volume of X and *twice* the volume of Y than A can.

It is noteworthy that in Case 2, the *least* efficient country (A) made the clearest gains while in Case 3 neither country can make any gains at all! The answer surely rests on the fact that a comparative cost advantage existed in Case 2 and is absent in Case 3 even though nation B is more productive than A in *both* cases.

The likelihood of one nation being able to produce two goods exactly more efficiently than another country is small. It becomes almost impossible when we realize that the number of goods and services run into hundreds or thousands. In other words, Case 3 is not a representative position for any two nations and we can therefore largely ignore it. It follows that given an exchange rate that roughly reflects domestic purchasing power, there is bound to be some output which can command an overseas market. Another way to put it is to say that international trade is the rule rather than the exception even for nations that are relatively inefficient in all things! (Case 2).

We need now to expand on this theory in order to permit the relaxation of certain assumptions and to give a more precise answer concerning traded quantities and prices.

Some of these assumptions are:

(1) *Constant marginal opportunity costs:* i.e. we have been assuming that countries can move from one good to another while incurring the same costs at each stage of transfer. This is unlikely as increasing marginal costs will be incurred resulting from dis-economies of scale and use of less appropriate resources. For example, industry X cannot go on increasing output ad infinitum at constant costs per unit of X because there are problems involved in the size of individual firms as they grow larger, and because as resources are drawn away from other products, their ability to adapt to good X will gradually fall as less and less appropriate resources are drawn away.

(2) *Another assumption is that demand for X and Y is indeterminate* and plays little or no role in determining cost advantage. This is not so. For example, if the population of Saudi Arabia were to expand a great deal, domestic demand for oil and by-products would rise sharply. Other

things being equal, this would tend to further raise oil prices and make oil exports less competitive than (say) North Sea oil output or alternative fuels.

(3) We also assume, by implication, that *costs and prices are set competitively* and that there are no restrictions to trade.

(4) Finally, we have taken no account of the costs associated with the *movement of goods between nations*.

Let us start by re-presenting Table 3.1 in diagram form. This is shown in Diagrams 3.1, 3.2 and 3.3, each representing Cases 1, 2 and 3 in Table 3.1.

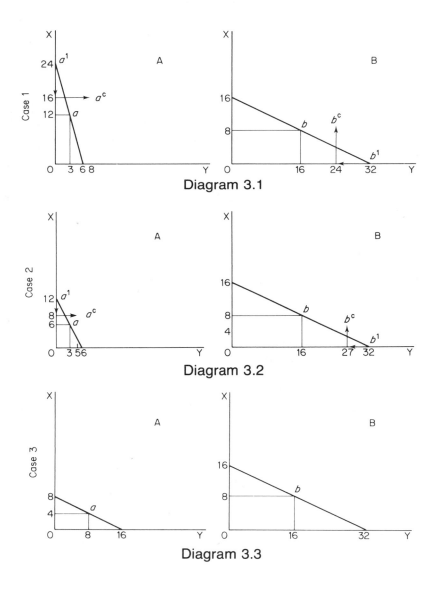

Diagram 3.1

Diagram 3.2

Diagram 3.3

Diagram 3.1

We measure units of good X on the horizontal axis and good Y on the vertical. Point *a* is the mid-way point of actual output for A and *b* for B (both these points represent column 5 in Table 3.1). Both nations can move along their straight-line "production frontier" by the process of producing more of one good at the cost of giving up output of the other good.

If A now produces only good X at *a'* and B only Y at *b'* (column 6 in Table 3.1) as in Case 1, and then trade 8X for 8Y (column 7 in Table 3.1) their final consumption is plotted at points a^c and b^c (column 8 in Table 3.1).

Now both these points of post-trade consumption lie outside the "production frontiers". That is to say that given the total resources of these countries their ability to produce X and Y is limited by their respective production frontiers. It is therefore visually evident that consumption *after* trade is superior to any combination of consumption *before* trade.

Diagram 3.2

This diagram represents Case 2 in Table 3.1. Once again final post-trade consumption is an improvement on pre-trade consumption (compare points *a* and *b* with points a^c and b^c respectively).

Note that A's "production frontier" is inferior to B's yet both nations manage to make trade gains.

Diagram 3.3

In this case (Case 3) no amount of specialization will yield trade gains. Readers may like to try for themselves! The point is now visually obvious. Both nations' "production frontiers" are parallel. We concluded before that Case 3 was one of absolute advantage for nation B but a comparative advantage for no-one. The geometry highlights this conclusion, namely, that absolute advantage is represented by a "production frontier" further away from the origin, and comparative advantage by a difference in the *slope* of the "production frontier".

We are now in a position to remove one of the basic assumptions concerning constant marginal opportunity costs. Such costs are represented geometrically by *straight-lined* "production frontiers"; i.e production can be altered along the line but always at *constant* costs in terms of production foregone.

Diagram 3.4

In Diagram 3.4 we see a more realistic production frontier. It is concave to the origin indicating that output changes always incur *increasing* costs rather than *constant* costs.

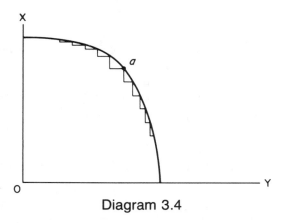

Diagram 3.4

For example, suppose one starts from point *a* and moves along the line towards more X output. It is evident that for each unit of Y foregone, less and less X becomes available. Alternatively, if we start at *a* again and move towards greater Y production, each unit of X foregone yields less and less Y output. In other words industries cannot go on indefinitely producing greater and greater amounts without suffering higher and higher unit costs of production. It may be possible that in the short-term economies of scale may be available, in which case this can be represented by a *convex* production frontier. Readers should attempt to draw such frontiers and derive trade patterns from it.

Diagram 3.5

Let us now consider our two countries A and B again but in the light of increasing marginal opportunity costs. Diagram 3.5 does this. Absolute cost advantage is described by the distance from the origin to the ends of the production frontier but now how do we find comparative cost advantage?

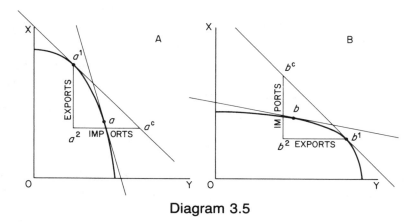

Diagram 3.5

The answer lies in geometry, namely, that the slope of the production frontier is infinitely variable over its length and that therefore, the costs of production at any one point is described by a line tangent to that point.

Points a and b are assumed to be points of preferred consumption given the limitations of possible output described by the two production frontiers. The straight lines drawn tangent to these points describe marginal costs at these points. Notice that the slope of the line through a is steeper than the one through b.

Refer back to Diagram 3.2 where we noted that nation A's slope was steeper than B's and that A's comparative cost advantage was in good X.

It is the same here. At point of output a, nation A has a comparative cost advantage in good X over nation B at their output at point b. It is clear however, that if these pre-trade output (and consumption) points were plotted elsewhere, it is quite conceivable that both tangents could be parallel and that there would be *no* comparative advantage whatsoever, in spite of there being an obvious *absolute* advantage.

From this we deduce the proposition that comparative cost advantage can be as influenced by domestic demand which determines domestic output, as by resource availability and use.

However, let us remain with points a and b as shown in Diagram 3.4 and proceed toward specialization and trade. Let nation A specialize in X and B in Y. As they both do so, however, the movements entail a change in the slopes of the two tangents. For example, if A moves from a to a' the slope is less steep and if B moves from b to b' the slope becomes steeper. Ultimately, if this process continues, a point is reached where there will be parallelism; at that stage comparative cost advantage ceases!

This takes us to the conclusion that domestic specialization does *not* proceed to the ultimate point at the *ends* of the output curve, but rather goes only to those points on the curve where no further specialization would provide gains. This, of course, is verifiable from observable facts in the real world where 100% specialization is virtually unknown.

TRADE WITH INCREASING MARGINAL COSTS

Let A proceed to the point a' output and then to export $a' - a^2$ of X and import $a^2 - a^c$ of Y. This gives final post-trade consumption at a^c.

Also, let B proceed to point b' output and export from there $b^2 - b'$ of Y for $b^2 - b^c$ of X imports. Final consumption is a b^c.

Note the following:

(1) Both nations have agreed to trade at the price represented by the slopes of their parallel tangencies to their specialization outputs (a' and b').

(2) Both nations have agreed to trade a mutually acceptable quantity of each product.

(3) Both nations reach levels of consumption (at a^c and b^c) that are impossible to obtain without trade as they lie outside production possibility levels (given current circumstances).

(4) Note also, however, that while both sets of consumers have increased consumption of one good (more Y for A and more X for B) they have forfeited units of the other good. The point, nevertheless is this; they have traded units of the good they are least anxious to possess in certain quantities for units of the good they are most anxious to possess in certain quantities.

For example, UK consumers are only too happy to exchange surplus quantities of (say) farm machinery for relatively scarce (at the price) saloon cars.

CONSUMER DEMAND – INDIFFERENCE ANALYSIS

But to round off the analysis we must approach this whole business of demand in more depth in order to show how it has an impact on trade. To do this we need to turn to the Indifference curve.

Diagram 3.6

Diagram 3.6 shows a number of lines that represent price situations for domestic consumers. The steeper the slope the lower are prices faced by the consumer for good X. Normally, consumers will tend to demand more as price falls and vice versa. Thus, it is logical to state that at price 1–1, consumers will demand a small quantity of Y relative to X – say at i.

At price 2–2 rather more Y is demanded, say at ii. At price 3–3 even more Y is wanted – say at iii. And at price 4–4, say, demand is at iv.

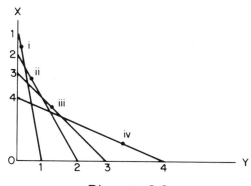

Diagram 3.6

Now we are only showing four possible situations but given that prices can change by infinitely small proportions it follows that there will be an infinite number of consumption points between i and iv and this allows us to join them all together to form a consumer indifference curve. This is shown in Diagram 3.7.

Diagram 3.7

This curve indicates that consumers will tend to react to price increases by reducing demand in favour of goods and services whose prices are falling. It is called an "Indifference" curve because consumers react to price changes by adjusting their consumption by an amount to just offset the price impact. Hence, they are indifferent between any two points on the curve. For example, if public transport fares were to fall substantially, then many car users would consider it a good bargain to leave their cars at home and go to work by public transport. They would have substituted cheap public transport for expensive private transport and moved along their indifference curve. They have swapped the *benefits* of private transport for the *cheapness* of public transport.

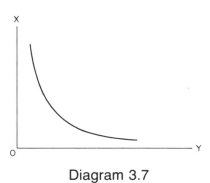

Diagram 3.7

CHANGING INCOME LEVELS

Now this proposition assumes a given, static, level of income, but the idea can be extended to any income level. For example, if incomes rise, consumers will now make their choices all over again. Some may prefer to go on spending in the same manner as before. Others may wish to buy fewer of some things but more of others.

Diagram 3.8

Diagram 3.8 represents these income and consumption changes.

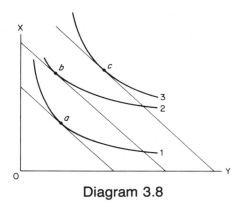

Diagram 3.8

Indifference curves 1, 2 and 3 represent different levels of income, and at prices indicated by the slopes of the price lines consumption moves from a on curve 1, to b on curve 2 to c on curve 3.

As consumer income rises, but at stable prices, peoples' preferences change to more of X on curve 2 but then to more of Y on curve 3. An example of this might be that as incomes rise people decide to spend more money on butter (good X) but at even higher levels of income they decide to switch back to margarine (good Y) perhaps because of the availability of more information about these products.

INDIFFERENCE CURVES AND WORLD TRADE

Diagram 3.9

We can now apply this reasoning in Diagram 3.9.

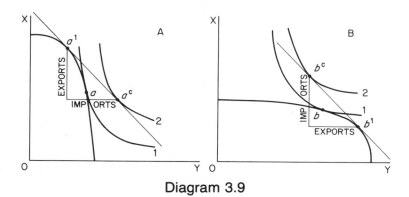

Diagram 3.9

In Diagram 3.9 we show again both countries starting from points a and b and moving to a' and b' from which A exports X and imports Y to reach point a^c and B exports Y and imports X to reach b^c.

Now we can see more clearly the effect of this trade on consumption which has moved from a to a^c in A and from b to b^c in B.

The point is that both sets of consumers have climbed the Indifference Curve "map" by moving from curve 1 to curve 2. In effect, they have increased their real income simply by a process of specialized production and the exchange of goods.

Here then, is the kernel of the case in favour of world trade. It can provide for increases in income levels primarily by allowing nations to specialize in certain outputs which are cost effective, and providing people with the choice of the things they would prefer to buy rather than being restricted to domestic output only.

Naturally circumstances can change and an interesting example of this can be found in the tomato-growing industry of the UK. As a result of climatic conditions it takes a great deal more fuel (for heating) to grow a tomato crop under greenhouse conditions in the UK than (say) in the Canary Islands. As a result, the UK has not had a comparative advantage in this product and much of the total UK consumption (but not all) has come in imports.

However, one enterprising grower in East Anglia has had the bright idea of buying a German built *straw* burner to replace his oil-fired burner. He pays £18 per ton of straw against the equivalent in oil of £150. Further, he has found that the waste product contains a high silica content which he can sell to tile manufacturers. The final result may be that his total fuel bill is *zero*.

Now if this can be repeated by other growers it could be that the comparative cost advantage enjoyed by overseas supplies could at least be reduced. Note however, that it was the efficiency of the *imported* burner that did the trick. But note also, that *increasing* costs may soon appear. For example, with increasing demand for straw – preferably rape or wheat rather than barley – the price will rise. Also, the supply of waste-products will tend to *reduce* the price offered by the tile makers.

Another example of comparative cost advantage concerns the purchase of US wheat by the USSR. A study reported by the *Financial Times*[1] indicates that the domestic costs in the USSR of producing one tonne of wheat is 3.3 tonnes of domestically produced oil.

By purchasing US wheat instead, the cost to the USSR is equivalent to only 0.625 tonnes of oil. The report suggests that for fear of over-dependence on foreign food supplies the USSR deliberately follows a policy of producing wheat which does not possess a comparative cost advantage and that, were less home wheat produced, significant resources could be diverted to more efficient sectors of their economy.

[1]*The Wharton Econometrics Report* 16 September 1982 referred to in the *Financial Times* 17 September 1982.

To conclude, we have removed two of our original assumptions, namely constant opportunity costs and no demand analysis. The others need not be dwelt upon here except to say that monopolies, by either reducing prices below market levels (dumping) or raising them above market levels, distort the international price mechanism and thus the flows of trade. Suffice it to say that trade restrictions can – and do – interfere with the processes described above, and insofar as trade *raises* income levels, restrictions may *reduce* them.

That is not to say that there are no legitimate arguments for regulating trade – there are. Readers who are interested are recommended to further reading on this topic found at the end of the chapter.

Finally, the costs of moving goods between nations is obviously an impediment and has to be taken into account in determining whether goods are to be sold abroad or not. For example, fresh, soft fruits may be air-freighted from warm climates to temperate climates at seasonal times of the year, yet it would be absurd to do this when these products are abundant in temperate climates. Trade is most certainly affected by the cost of transportation, and also by insurance and other associated costs.

Further Reading to Chapter 3

Meier, Gerald M. 1980. *International Economics; the Theory of Policy*. OUP, Oxford, Chaps. 1, 2, 3 and 4.

Havrylyshyn, O. and Wolf, M. 1982. Promoting Trade Among Developing Countries: an assessment. *Finance and Development*, March 1982, IMF, Washington.

Chapter 4

Reducing Trade Risks – The Intermediaries

International trade – like all trade – involves the incurring of risks. Whatever the actual nature of these risks – and we shall be discussing them in detail in the following chapters – they all entail the bearing of additional costs. Delay or non-receipt of payment are obvious examples; others include transit delays, damage and loss. Traders have the choice of either bearing these risks themselves, in which case their net profits may be higher, or alternatively, offloading them onto someone else but at a fee or cost. The purpose of this chapter is to consider the functions of trade intermediaries in order to show their usefulness to traders in terms of risk/cost reduction.

THE FREIGHT FORWARDER

Perhaps the best place to start is by an appreciation of the function of the Freight Forwarder. There are some 1,000 freight forwarders in the UK and 90% of UK traders utilize their services in one form or another.[1]

An obvious function of the freight forwarder is to arrange for the physical distribution of goods by air, road, rail or sea. Because of his knowledge built up over time he can obtain the best possible transportation at the lowest cost to the shipper (exporter/importer). Another important function is to operate "groupage" or "consolidation" services.

Groupage

Freight forwarders are able to fill individual containers or road freight or rail-ferry transporters as well as sea-going vessels and thus receive more

[1] *A Brief Introduction to Freight Forwarding.* Institute of Freight Forwarders Ltd., Richmond, Surrey.

favourable charges than would apply to small quantities that many traders would need to transport at any one time.

Consolidation

Likewise, when goods are sent by air, the freight forwarder can fill the airlines unit loading devices which are specially designed to fill an airplane's hold. A special low rate per kilo is thus charged. Forwarders offering consolidation services and who use House Air Waybills may be subject to increased liabilities. See section on Air Waybills.

In addition the freight forwarder – whose offices may be situated at sea and air ports – can often provide storage facilities to allow for the onward transmission of sufficient quantities to fill a container. He can also offer his own domestic vehicle fleet to move goods from the exporter's warehouse to the air or sea port or rail-siding.

Other services that may be offered include:

   advice on best routeing;
   documentation required;
   overseas regulations;
   relevant packaging consistent with costs.

In connection with this last mentioned service, many freight forwarders have their own packaging companies in order to assure the safe arrival of the goods. They will also prepare a Freight Forwarder's Bill of Lading for ocean shipment or Air Waybill for air freight (see Chapter 5). Even if more than one mode of transport is used, the forwarder submits only one invoice to the shipper.

Insurance

He can advise on and arrange for the most suitable type of insurance including the best value to insure for and the most relevant hazards to cover. He can also deal with claims in the event of loss.

Imports

Finally, the freight forwarder can assist importers also, by getting goods cleared through customs, and onward delivery to the importer. He can also advise on the correct description of the goods for the purpose of minimizing the import duty payable (if any).

An example of a freight forwarder is Moonbridge Shippers Limited of London. Although sited in the South-East of the country they attract export business from all over the UK by the use of regional agents. They are able to offer both container groupage and general cargo services; warehouse, documentation and assistance with Customs and Excise formalities for both export and import cargoes. They raise the necessary documents based on information supplied by their principals (exporters) even including a bank collection order (see Chapter 6). Many of their documents are of the "aligned" type (see Chapter 5).

Services Not Provided

While freight forwarders provide many services, it might be useful at this stage to outline some facilities they do *not* provide:

(a) No cover for the credit risk; i.e. the possibility that payment may be delayed or non-existent.

(b) No financial facility; i.e. the provision of funds to the exporter or importer on shipment or arrival of goods.

(c) No foreign exchange cover; i.e. the prevention of loss arising from exchange rate fluctuations.

(d) No provision of possible buyers abroad or suppliers at home.

(e) No sales promotion and advertising advice.

(f) No selling function abroad.

INTERMEDIARIES

New traders may be prepared to face these problems themselves or they may be prepared to use the services of a range of intermediaries to reduce or eliminate them. We shall now look at a number of these intermediaries and consider the ways in which their facilities might be attractive to both exporters and importers in certain circumstances. In doing so, we shall ignore for the moment the banks, insurance companies, etc., which will be dealt with in detail later on. At this stage we are primarily concerned with those intermediaries who – one way or another – are prepared to assist the exporter or importer with some or all of the services (a) to (f) mentioned above with the *prime* service being that of *selling* on behalf of the exporter or *buying* on behalf of the importer.

The best way to start is by emphasizing the specialist nature of international business. Much information needs to be acquired and analysed if it is going to be a profitable part of the business of the trading or manufacturing company. Many such firms have quite enough problems dealing with the functions of production and domestic selling to be able to cope properly with the problems of selling overseas, even if the services of a freight forwarder are being utilized. So what more natural than for specialist intermediaries to be established for this purpose! Naturally, some companies are able to deal adequately without the services of an intermediary and we shall be referring

Diagram 4.1
A Schematic Outline of Trade Intermediaries

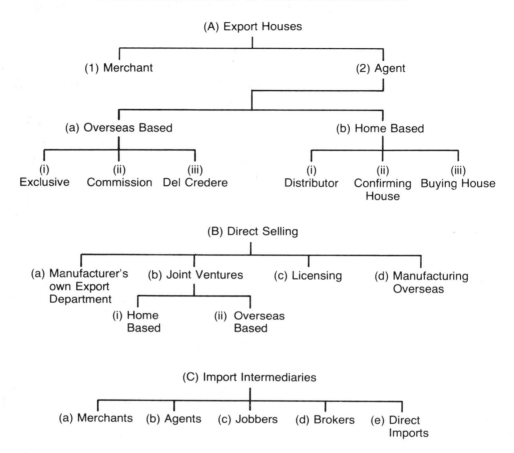

to them later in this chapter; but for the moment we need to consider and compare the intermediaries themselves.

(A) EXPORT HOUSES

We begin by looking at the functions of Export Houses. These are specialist intermediaries of varying sizes and providing a variety of services. According to the British Export Houses Association (BEHA) there are about 800 or so operating in the UK. They may be giant divisions of giant banks, old-established trading companies or one-man operations run from one-room offices. Some 225 are members of the BEHA and their services are listed in its directory.

The term "Export House" is a generic one covering a variety of specialist institutions. They include the following:

The Export Merchant
The Export Agent/Distributor
The Confirming House/Buying House

(1) The Export Merchant

These institutions derive their existence from the old Merchant Adventurers who established themselves in the overseas colonies with the purpose of supplying the demand of local residents for the manufactured goods obtainable in Great Britain. These are the oldest form of Export House but can vary enormously in size and tend to specialize in both products and markets.

The special characteristic of the Export Merchant is that he buys and sells on his own behalf. In effect, when a supplier sells to a Merchant, it is the equivalent of selling to the domestic market as the Merchant takes on the entire responsibility for on-selling in an overseas market.

Export Merchants usually provide the following services:

(a) Buys from the supplier and has the responsibility to on-sell. Goods cannot be returned to the supplier if there is no overseas market for them.

(b) The credit risk is eliminated as cash is paid on delivery to the Merchant.

(c) Most, if not all, of the mechanics of export are dealt with by the Merchant. He will provide documentation, shipping and insurance services.

(d) Sometimes Merchants have a more favourable entry into foreign markets because of their specialist knowledge and contacts. For example, sales to Eastern Europe can be enhanced as a result of Merchants' imports from this area, perhaps as part of a barter arrangement.

In other words, the whole burden of trading, including the important selling function, is shouldered by the Merchant, leaving the producer to concentrate on the functions of production.

Export Merchants thus seek to profit by charging a higher price abroad than they pay at home. They thus operate as domestic wholesalers operating in foreign markets through their own salesforce, agents and stockists.

From the points just made, it is evident that Merchants provide most advantages to the small exporter or one whose output is likely to be variable and who is unable or unwilling to shoulder the tasks associated with direct overseas selling. On the other hand some large companies who operate overseas directly in some major markets may find the Merchant a useful distribution channel in unchartered markets.

Disadvantages of the Merchant

(1) By selling to a Merchant, the producer loses control over his overseas market. For example, the Merchant may tend to lose interest in a certain product especially if its profitability is relatively low.

(2) The brand image of the product may be that of the Merchant instead of the producer's, especially where several companies are supplying the Merchant with the same product. Thus, overseas goodwill is not acquired by the manufacturer.

(3) Overseas pricing will be in the control of the Merchant who may set prices to suit his own profitability rather than that of the manufacturer. For example, a low price for a time may allow for market penetration after which prices can be raised; but the Merchant may be looking for short-term returns.

The Export Merchant — A Summary

The Merchant offers most benefits to the new exporter who has not been able to build up sufficient expertise or to the exporter whose output for overseas markets is small or variable. The Merchant may be willing to offer the producer his feed-back from the markets to enable him to adjust his product if he wishes to do so. The provision of payment on delivery to the Merchant entirely eliminates the risk of not getting paid and the need to obtain short-term finance to fund trade credit. The Merchant will be able to cut administration costs so as to keep prices competitive and, of course, all the administrative burdens are shouldered by him.

The cost of these benefits is largely a loss of control over marketing and pricing, but a new company may well find it desirable to "test" the overseas possibilities this way rather than to incur the costs and responsibilities of direct exportation.

(2) Agents

(a) Overseas Based

The Export Agent/Distributor
Like the Merchant, the Export Agent can vary in size and market-scope. His prime function is to *represent* the exporter in an overseas market. He does not buy goods for his own account but acts as an intermediary seller usually by way of a commission on the value of the sales he makes.

There are various types of Agents; for example:

(i) *The Exclusive Agent* (or Sole Agent)
Here, the appointed Agent is the only representative of the manufacturer in an overseas market. Sometimes this type is called a Sole Distributor. Often this Agent will be responsible for maintaining stock levels to meet demand fluctuations and also be prepared to offer spare parts and an after-sales service. The price charged by such an Agent would be agreed beforehand between them and would allow for the costs described above.

(ii) *The Commission Agent*
Here, the Agent usually acts as a selling intermediary, passing orders back to the producer on a commission basis. Where the Agent is selling more than

one principal's product there could well be conflict between the Agent and any one supplier. For example, the Agent will tend to push the product most easy to sell or the one that commands the best commission.

In either case, the appointed Agent will tend to be a national of the overseas market, familiar with the legal and social constraints of that market. He will be supplied with the necessary sales literature and can be expected to attend overseas exhibitions for the purpose of product promotion. The Agent, therefore, is best seen as an *employee* of the exporter, albeit one with more powers than home-based employees.

(iii) *The Del Credere Agent*
It may be possible for a principal (exporter) to arrange for his Agent to bear the credit risk by offering him a premium on his commission in return for which the Agent (a del credere Agent) promises to pay the principal whether or not the overseas buyer keeps his promise of making payment to the Agent. It thus becomes the task of the del credere Agent to ensure the collection of bad debts (if he can). In practice the provision of this facility is tantamount to ensuring that sales will only be made, and trade credit granted to, first-class buyers. While this certainly ensures prompt payment it can also lead to a more limited market for the principal's product than might be possible via an Agent who is prepared to accept sales to a buyer with an uncertain credit record. In effect, sales via a del credere Agent are credit-risk free, but unadventurous. Of course, any type of agent can offer a del credere facility.

(b) Home-Based

In addition to selling abroad via an Agent resident in the overseas market or markets, there is the possibility of arranging for sales and ancillary functions to be performed by Agents with Head Offices in the UK through their own representatives overseas.

(i) *The Export Distributor/Manager*
There are a number of Agents based in the UK who are prepared to offer a full agency service to domestic producers wishing to exploit overseas markets. One such company is A. Hurst, a subsidiary of Arbuthnot Latham, the merchant bank. They provide a comprehensive service including selling, shipping and collecting payment. They are also able to offer more attractive credit terms to the overseas buyer than the exporter may be able to provide. In effect, such an institution takes on all the responsibilities associated with overseas sales other than the central one of ownership of the goods. It is probably the nearest thing to the exporter's own export department without the expense of running such a department himself. Selling is performed by locally appointed Agents or Distributors responsible to the Export Distributor who in turn is responsible to the exporter.

The Export Manager resembles the Export Distributor except that facilities are usually not so comprehensive. For example, he may not be able to offer a financial service. Export Managers are not so closely tied to the exporter on a long-term contractual basis and are prepared to offer their functions on an *ad hoc* basis if necessary.

What then are the special benefits and drawbacks offered by an Agency facility?

Benefits

(1) A range of ancillary services depending on the type and size of the Agent.

(2) A selling ability enhanced by local knowledge of laws and social customs.

(3) Where sales are on a commission basis, some selling costs are incurred only when sales are made.

(4) The agent may be selling complimentary products that could boost an exporter's sales.

(5) The del credere Agent ensures a limited exposure to the credit risk.

Disadvantages

(1) An Agent not specializing in the exporter's lines may not give his full attention to sales, especially where competing items offer both a better commission rate and easier selling characteristics.

(2) Lack of contact between the exporter and an overseas-based Agent due to geographical separation and language problems may give rise to a conflict of interest. For example delays in export supplies would penalize the Agent by reducing his commission potential while leaving the exporter free to supply the home market from time to time which may provide a more attractive, but temporary outlet.

(3) A Sole Agency abroad responsible for stock management to maximize sales whilst minimizing stock costs may be less than adequately efficient, leading either to lost sales or high stock levels.

(4) A del credere Agent may lose potential sales by his unwillingness to accept possible credit-worthy buyers.

(5) The Export Distributor/Manager may be able to exercise an ability to influence control over pricing, quantity and specification which may not be in the best interests of the manufacturer.

The Confirming House/Buying House

We next turn to those intermediaries whose prime function is not so much to represent the exporter and to find overseas markets but to represent an overseas buyer seeking supplies in the UK.

(ii) *The Confirming House*

These institutions had their origins as UK Merchant Houses supplying goods to the colonies who eventually started to use them as Buying Houses for goods that were required. Later, the colonies sought credit terms for the goods they were ordering via the intermediary and this laid the foundation for the modern Confirming House as a representative of the overseas *buyer* and also as a supplier of credit to him.

There are many kinds of Confirming Houses, ranging from those who supply only a financial service, to those who also supply shipping and documentation facilities through to the complete range of services including that of finding the best source of supply to meet the needs of the overseas customer/ client. These days, the emphasis tends to be on their financial facilities.

Method of Operation

An overseas buyer seeking supplies either from the UK or *elsewhere* can contact a Confirming House such as W. Jones & Co. (London) and ask them to find a particular supply on the best possible terms. The Confirming House then arranges with a manufacturer to provide the required goods on terms agreed between them. The Confirming House places the order and may be prepared to *confirm* it. In effect, confirmation of an order is a promise by the House to make payment to the manufacturer/supplier on shipment of the goods. In addition, the House will usually allow the overseas buyer the usual short-term credit terms of up to 120 days.

Although the House represents the overseas buyer and is paid a commission by him for his services, it is not unknown for UK exporters to advise their prospective overseas customers to refer to a nominated Confirming House in order for them to obtain credit terms not offered by the exporter himself. This relationship between an exporter and a Confirming House can develop to the point where the latter relies on the former as a useful and constant supplier to match requests coming from clients abroad.

In this way, Confirming Houses can gain considerable experience about the export supply potential in the UK in specialized product areas as well as knowledge of the requirements of specialized overseas markets.

The advantages and disadvantages of the use of Confirming Houses by UK exporters are as follows:

Advantages

(1) Both the credit risk (of not getting paid) and the foreign exchange risk (of fluctuating currency values) are borne by the House.

(2) Associated with the credit risk is the granting of credit itself. Even when a supplier is assured of being paid (perhaps by a bank) there is still the cost of meeting the finance. Confirming Houses offer to pay the supplier on shipment and bear the *cost* of the credit themselves.

(3) As with the Export Merchant, selling via a Confirming House is the equivalent of selling to a domestic buyer, thus eliminating the need to maintain an Export Department to handle shipment, packaging and insurance or to use the services of a Freight Forwarder. Further, these costs are borne by the buyer.

(4) Where Confirming Houses are prepared to place orders on behalf of the overseas clients, the manufacturer is relieved of the function of *finding* customers. In addition, Confirming House fees are paid by the overseas buyer.

Now all these points suggest that this type of intermediary can provide considerable benefits to exporters, perhaps superior to those provided by an Export Merchant; but like the Merchant there are some pitfalls.

Disadvantages

(1) Use of such an intermediary cannot be relied upon as a constant and substantial method of exportation as the House has the ability to switch sources of supply as it thinks fit.

(2) If the House has a supply agreement with a manufacturer, then the problem of control similar to that of a Merchant is possible, with constraints on delivery, specification and price.

(3) Irrespective of whether this type of intermediary is used as a constant export medium or not or whether it supplies just a financial facility or much more, the mere fact of its use will require the supplier to trim his prices, bearing in mind that he will face no credit risk at all.

(4) Because the Confirming House represents the overseas buyer with predetermined requirements, it is less likely that a supplier of an innovative product will interest a House seeking to meet demands for established products.

Summary

From the points above we can draw the conclusions that the best use of Confirming Houses will be made by those suppliers who:

(a) cannot provide adequate credit themselves;

(b) are unwilling to accept the foreign exchange risk;

(c) do not have the resources or time to operate an Export Department;

(d) find that they have spare output from time to time and can therefore use this medium of export on an *intermittent* basis.

(iii) *Buying Houses*

From our understanding both of Export Merchants and Confirming Houses, it is apparent that these institutions have their roots in those parts of the world that are now referred to as the Commonwealth. However, we have seen from the chapter on world trade data that a major portion of world trade is performed by industrial nations who do most of their business with *each other*. It is not surprising therefore to find that the proportion of UK exports handled by all Export Houses has fallen considerably since the 1950s from about 35% then to about 20% now.[2]

As a result of this trend in trade, new channels have developed to permit UK exporters to market their products in the US, Europe and Japan.[3] One such channel is the Buying House or Indent House. This institution acts on behalf of its overseas principals – who may be department stores – by seeking attractive consumer products that would sell well in such stores. Other examples are of overseas governments opening Buying Houses in the UK. When the overseas principal gives specific instructions to the House to purchase a particular product, the House is referred to as an Indent House as its main function is to indent (requisition) by placing orders with UK suppliers. Countries with Buying Houses in London include the US, Germany and Japan. In addition overseas stores send regular buyers here to obtain supplies.

A Buying House therefore closely resembles a Confirming House except that its main emphasis is on the procurement of supplies while Confirming Houses have tended to become essentially financial institutions. Another major difference is that the former represent only one potential buyer while the latter can represent any number of buyers.

The advantages and disadvantages of using the facilities of a Buying House are similar to those of Confirming Houses. For example some of the US stores' Buying offices in London are prepared to make all the necessary arrangements for documentation and shipping on behalf of the exporter and moreover, are normally able to make payment on shipment. In addition some of the bigger ones will give advice on labelling or marking products and also on consumer preference for patterns and the use of things like dyes that may be subject to US regulations.

As with Confirming Houses, the exporter has to offer an attractive price and be able to meet his contract without trouble. In addition, if a large part of his output is going via this type of intermediary he may find that decisions on quality, volume, price, etc., are determined by the House and not by him.

One additional disadvantage may be that – unlike sales via a Confirming House – the Buying House may not be utilized for intermittent sales but requires a continuous flow of supplies.

---

[2]See Walsh, L. S. 1981. *International Marketing*, M & E Handbooks; and Tookey, D. 1975. *Export Marketing Decisions*. Trade Research Publications.
[3]Although the various forms of Agencies have also developed in these markets.

(B) DIRECT SELLING

Having considered some of the ways that trade might be assisted by an intermediary we now have to turn our attention to the gains and drawbacks of self-exportation. In fact, when this term is used in its widest sense it can take several forms.

(a) Manufacturers' Own Export Department

One obvious possibility is for the producer to handle most of the work by establishing a special department for this purpose. Its functions would vary depending on whether the services of a Freight Forwarder are used.

Larger firms might find it economic to handle all services themselves. Of course, such a system requires that the exporter also becomes responsible for selling his output in selected overseas markets and this requires a whole host of abilities, not least an understanding of the characteristics of the markets abroad. This problem can be dealt with by sending experts out to the markets to represent the company. This is a common method in selling to Eastern Europe where agents are not available.

Another method is to establish an overseas-based marketing/sales subsidiary to handle the products. By employing local people, the company can reduce the risks of market ignorance.

Advantages

These are as follows:

(1) Very suitable for sales of consumer goods sold by direct mail to overseas customers or to overseas retail stores. The overseas buyer, in effect, makes himself responsible for the usefulness of the product, thus relieving the producer of the tasks of marketing. Also, many types of capital goods can be sold directly by using a company representative abroad, especially to overseas governments, local authorities and other semi-governmental bodies. These buyers welcome the intervention of a company man who can answer their questions and with whom they can negotiate price and terms.

(2) The exporter is in full control of all the variables such as quality, type, price, delivery, etc. He can then determine what part of his total output is to go abroad and in so doing maximize his returns on his total investment. Moreover, as price is within his control, he can attempt to fix it at a level to maximize profitability or, if he wishes, to sell at below average cost for a time in order to become established in the market.

(3) The exporter can benefit from the marketing of his products under his

own brand image by building up a loyalty to that image to further assist in market penetration.

(4) Sales of engineering products requiring technical advice and after-sales service can best be done this way to ensure customer satisfaction.

Disadvantages

(1) Clearly there are going to be considerable costs involved in the setting up of an Export Department at home with control of travelling representatives or alternatively setting up an overseas sales subsidiary. The producer will have to acquire the necessary techniques connected with the mechanics of exportation as well as marketing abilities.

(2) In particular he will have to find export credit facilities to finance his trade or, if he has sufficient working capital, to provide such credit himself. The following chapters deal in detail with just such facilities which are available in many forms.

(3) Once established in an overseas market, the exporter will have to ensure that supplies are adequate and that changes in market circumstances are quickly understood and translated in altered specifications. Adequate stock levels must be maintained especially in the overseas market.

(4) Provisions for technical advice, after-sales service and spare parts must be made. Overseas personnel must be capable of dealing with such problems.

Summary

All in all, such self-exportation means that to the problems of production must now be added the problems of sales and marketing to a foreign market. However, there are circumstances where this could be the best method of exporting, namely:

(a) where the company has a substantial output with available capital for further investment or where such capital could be raised at acceptable cost;

(b) where the product is either of a fairly simple consumer type requiring little or no technical operating problems (e.g. table-ware), in which case mail-order or sales direct to overseas department stores would be best; or, in the case of engineering goods requiring an after-sales service, self-exportation might provide a superior performance than if left to the operation of an intermediary like a Merchant or even an Agent;

(c) where the producer is keen to become established with his own brand image and seeks a continuous and expanding market;

(d) where the producer can acquire competent personnel both at home and abroad.

(b) Joint Ventures

Where an individual manufacturer cannot see his way to self-exportation; it may be possible to engage in joint ventures with other organizations in order to pool resources and cut costs. This can be done both at home or abroad.

(i) At Home

Piggy-Back Schemes
Under this arrangement an established exporting firm offers its distribution facilities to another company new to exporting. In this way the established company can more easily utilize its own export department more fully by ensuring that the throughput of orders is kept to an economic level and also by ensuring that the assisted company's product is a complementary one (i.e. one that is likely to help sales of its own product). In this way its own sales can be enhanced. Piggy-back schemes were given much publicity in the UK in the 1960s but have had a somewhat mixed result probably because of the likely divergence of needs between the two firms. An example of such a piggy-back scheme is of the Singer Sewing Machine Co., helping thread producers to sell abroad.

Export Consortium
Here, two or more firms get together to supply complementary goods against one particular order. For example, where large construction projects are being considered overseas, it is possible for a number of UK firms to operate on a joint venture to supply a package of industrial products like cranes and lifting equipment, presses and pumps.

(ii) Abroad

It is possible for joint ventures to be established between home-based and overseas-based companies.

(c) Licensing

Under this heading there are a wide range of possible agreements but in essence it comes down to the sale of expertise by the licensor (the UK company) to the licensee (the overseas company).

The "expertise" can take several forms, e.g. a patent covering a product or a process; use of a brand name; or simply expert knowledge of marketing. Whatever it may be, the overseas company can benefit, in exchange for a fee, by producing the licensor's product itself.

Advantages to the Licensor

(1) It enables income to be accrued from sales in a foreign market which may be closed to direct exportation because of tariffs or quotas.

(2) It may keep production and distribution costs down especially if resources are relatively cheap overseas and transportation is reduced.

(3) The need to maintain an expensive home-based export department to cope with all the problems of exporting is largely eliminated.

Disadvantages to the Licensor

(1) A major problem is quality control. This is important to the licensor because where the "expertise" takes the form of a brand name, it is his reputation which is at stake.

(2) When the licensee period expires it may be possible for the licensee to continue using his acquired knowledge and thus become a competitor to the licensor.

Finally, we need to consider the ultimate possibility, namely that of rejecting all of the foregoing possibilities of using intermediaries, self-exporting as joint ventures and embarking on a production and selling operation in an overseas market for selling both to it and to third markets.

(d) Manufacturing Overseas

Where a potential exporter is unwilling, or unable, to offer a licensing agreement or to participate in a joint venture of another kind, or indeed, to use the services of an intermediary, then the possibility of making an investment overseas so as to produce and market from there, must be considered. This would be favourable in the following circumstances:

  (i) where import restrictions limit the quantity that can be supplied from home;

 (ii) where the raw materials and/or the market is to be found overseas;

(iii) where production costs can be lower than at home (e.g. labour and land).

The advantages and disadvantages are similar to those of licensing, except that perhaps quality control may be more easy to maintain but on the negative side the capital cost may be very large and (like licensing) there may be restrictions on the repatriation of earnings to the home country.

Final Summary

(a) *Manufacture abroad?* Depends on capital availability, size of overseas markets; possible sequestration or nationalization of assets; locality of raw materials and cost of overseas resources.

(b) *Joint ventures?* Depends on complementarity of products or acceptable overseas licensees.

(c) *Use of intermediaries?* Depends on knowledge of the mechanics of exporting; ability to provide trade credit; volume of output; need for a continuous or variable level of overseas sales.

Taken together, the scope is large and, of course, there are many variations on all the themes touched on. Readers should be aware that in the case of Export Houses, a variety of services may be available even from a single institution. For example, many Merchants are also prepared to offer Agency facilities.

(C) IMPORT ORGANISATIONS

To conclude, let us consider the channels available to firms wishing to obtain supplies *from* overseas.

In fact, we have already referred to some in passing. For example, Confirming and Buying Houses represent overseas importers and by switching the country of origin, we can consider them from the point of view of the importing nation.

Again, other intermediaries may be prepared to offer an import as well as an export facility. For example, where an Export Merchant has contact with a possible overseas supplier, he may be prepared to offer him assistance to market his product in the UK. However, there are also specialist importers we need to consider.

(a) Import Merchants

This type of importer is important in the commodities trade. He tends to specialize in certain staple products like tea or tin and is prepared to carry stocks in the UK. Like the Export Merchant he operates on his own account and thus carries all the risks of international trade. In some cases he may own overseas estates from which supplies are obtained.

(b) Import Agents

These tend to operate in the fruit and vegetable and dairy produce lines, normally buying goods on an "on consignment" basis. That is, giving orders to overseas sellers but not against firm orders in the UK. Instead, the goods will be sold here subject to demand. Both prices and volume are thus indeterminate, making it a more risky proposition for the overseas supplier although a del credere facility may be available.

(c) The Import Jobber

His function is to purchase large quantities of goods from abroad (like meat and grain) and re-sell in the UK in smaller volumes. He thus provides a wholesaling function. Like the Merchant he works on his own behalf.

(d) The Import Broker

Unlike the other intermediaries, the broker is solely concerned with putting buyers and sellers in touch with each other and usually does not provide any other services.

(e) Direct Import by Principals

Finally, many UK firms, some quite small, have established their own purchasing departments to secure overseas supplies.

Chapter 5

International Trade Documentation

All economic transactions involve the entering into of contractual obligations, not only by those parties engaged in selling and buying goods but also by any intermediary assisting in these operations.

For example there are Contracts of:

SALE	– an agreement to sell goods on certain terms;
CARRIAGE	– an agreement to arrange for movement of goods;
INSURANCE	– an agreement to cover loss or damage in transit;
AGENCY	– an agreement to represent one of the principals.

In addition there are the contracts between banks and their trading customers to provide financial, currency and other facilities.

Inevitably, in any contractual arrangement there will be the need for documentation, and this chapter is devoted to the description and understanding of the more important documents used in the international movement of goods. The one exception to this concerns financial documents like Bills of Exchange and Documentary Credits, etc., which will be dealt with in separate chapters devoted to the *financing* of trade.

FUNCTIONS OF DOCUMENTS

Before we look at individual documents it would be useful if we can list the *functions* they serve. These functions can be said to be:

(1) To provide conditions (or terms);
(2) To provide information;
(3) To provide a receipt;

(4) To request a service;
(5) To transfer title.

Let us first look at some brief illustrations of these functions.

(1) CONDITIONS OR TERMS

Whenever a contract is entered into the parties concerned will need to know the conditions on which they are engaging, in obligations or services given or received.

Many documents provide a list of terms under which the supplier of a facility or service attempts to limit liability to their customers. Examples include an *Insurance Policy* and a *Bill of Lading*. The *Contract of Sale* is itself an agreed list of details stating the precise functions of the parties and the terms on which they agree to participate. One important example is the reference to the country whose commercial laws will determine the outcome of any dispute.

It is on the basis of the agreed terms and conditions specified in the documentation that all parties to an agreement know what to expect if things go right, and what limitations exist when things go wrong.

(2) INFORMATION

An obvious function of any document is to provide pertinent information to interested parties. For example, the goods need to be described and prices need to be quoted. The places taking up and setting down the goods need to be made clear, etc. A *Certificate of Insurance* is an example of a document of information, providing as it does, a confirmation that insurance has been entered into, while the actual details of terms and conditions can be found on the *Insurance Policy*. Another example is a *Short Form Bill of Lading* which incorporates a clause referring the parties to the fact that the carrier (shipping line) is prepared to operate only on the basis of the conditions and terms specified in their Standard Conditions. This can be obtained from the carrier on request. A *Long Form Bill of Lading* incorporates these conditions on its reverse side.

Other examples of information include:

PRO-FORMA INVOICE	– giving prospective buyers details of the goods;
WEIGHT NOTE	– giving details of the weight of the goods;
PACKING LIST	– indicating the packing arrangements (i.e. details of each case or packet);
INSPECTION CERTIFICATE	– to certify the grade, quality or condition of the goods.

(3) RECEIPT

Every time goods in transit change hands some kind of document must be issued to the party handing over the goods to evidence the transfer. Examples include, *Air Waybill*; *Parcel Post Receipt*; *Road Waybill*; *Rail Consignment Note*; *Forwarder's Receipt*; *Bill of Lading*; *Warehouse Receipt*; *Sea Waybill*. In all of these documents at least one of the functions is to provide a receipt for goods entrusted to a carrier for onward transit. This is not just to provide the holder with details of the goods, but to serve as *evidence* of the *passing* of goods between parties.

(4) REQUESTING A SERVICE

In this case the document is acting as a request for a service to be provided. Examples include a *Standard Shipping Note* required by some ports and other receiving authorities to receive goods for onward transit; *Export Consignment Note* requests inland carriers like British Rail and National Carriers Ltd. to accept goods for delivery to a specified port; *Delivery Order* asks a warehouse to release goods to a named party.

(5) TRANSFERRING TITLE

We have already seen that a Bill of Lading acts as a receipt, a source of information and a specification of terms and conditions. However, its most important function is to allow the *passing of title* to the goods.

At this point it is necessary to distinguish between *Possession* and *Property*.

Possession. The possession of the goods reside in whoever has physical and legal control over them. For example, delivering the goods to a ship or a warehouse entails the passing of Possession, albeit, transitory.

Property. The property in the goods resides with the lawful owner, no matter who actually has possession. Where a *document of title* (i.e. a Bill of Lading) is used, then property passes when the *parties intend it to* pass. This is usually when the buyer makes payment or promises to pay (i.e. accepts a time Bill of Exchange).

However the transfer of property occurs only when an endorsed Bill is passed to the buyer. In effect, *property* is held by the buyer even though *possession* is held by the shipping company.

As a result, the shipping company is bound to release the goods to the presenter of the Bill of Lading without any requirement on the part of the presenter as to proof of identity. The only exception to this would be if the shipping line had reason to believe that the presenter had no legal right to the document.

Indeed, even if the carrier fully accepted the legitimacy of the claimant to the goods but the claimant was unable to deliver the Bill of Lading, the goods will not be released unless a bank provides an *Indemnity* releasing the carrier from consequential liability.

It is important to distinguish between a *receipt* and a *document of title*. For example, if a trader receives a receipt for goods delivered to a warehouse for safe keeping, and later decides to sell those goods by transferring the receipt to the buyer, the warehouse is under no obligation to release the goods to the buyer simply because he presents the receipt!

The receipt is not, of itself, a document of title, and the warehouse must release goods only on the authorization of the party it believes has the property in the goods, namely the original trader. In addition, it will require proof of identity from any claimant to the goods. However, see *Warehouse Warrants* (page 209).

A Bill of Lading in its document of title function is, in itself, a *document of authorization of transfer of property*. This makes it a most important document; one that we shall refer to again in this and other chapters.

PASSING OF RISK

In discussing the passing of possession and property it is pertinent also to consider the passing of *risk*. When goods are in transit by air, sea, road or rail, they are open to loss or damage. As goods will normally be covered by insurance, it is important to ascertain the party liable to suffer the loss in order to ensure which party can legitimately receive indemnification from the insurers. It is an important insurance principle that the claimant must have an *insurable interest*; i.e he must be the party to have incurred the loss.

It is clear therefore, that the parties to trade need to be aware at what point in the transit stage the risk passes. Theoretically, risk passes with property, for whoever has legitimate title to the goods also has an insurable interest in them. However, in practice the passing of risk also depends on the terms specified in the Contract of Sale.

Contracts of Sale

Now, Contracts of Sale can be of two broad categories:

(i) a full document listing all the agreed terms on which the seller sells and the buyer buys. We can call this a "long-hand" contract. However, due to the complexity and time consuming nature of such contracts they will tend to be used only for complex and high value trading.

(ii) a brief document listing the major items without detailed reference to a number of points such as the responsibilities of both parties in connection with passing of risk, of insurance, of freight, etc. Such a document can be called a "short-hand" contract, but in order to overcome the obvious problem of identifying responsibilities a number of internation-ally accepted "codes" called *Incoterms* are used.

Incoterms

There are currently fourteen Incoterms each specifying a particular set of conditions of contract any one of which can be used in the Contract of Sale to determine responsibility. The vast majority of international business is car-ried out by use of Incoterms, and as a consequence much time and effort is saved and both parties are aware of their rights and duties.

The International Chamber of Commerce (ICC) publishes these conditions which can be called *Trade* or *Shipping* terms. If need be, the parties to the trade can widen the definitions by agreement. For example, "CIF Incoterms WPA" means as set out by the ICC for CIF (Cost, Insurance and Freight) but qualified by WPA (With Particular Average) meaning that the seller has to arrange for insurance to cover special marine risks (see page 98).

Basically, these Trade terms (shown on page 88) are listed in order of a progressive increase in the responsibility of the seller (exporter).

Ex-works (EXW). The seller has to make the goods available usually at his own premises and inform the buyer of their availability. It is the buyer's responsibility to arrange for collections and pay all costs associated with onward transportation, etc.

Free to Carrier (FRC). The seller has to deliver the goods to a named point in his country. This could be a freight station or depot. The seller also has to provide an export licence. The buyer is responsible for onward carriage.

Free on Rail (Truck) (FOR–FOT). The seller has to deliver the goods to a wagon or truck and pay for loading. The buyer pays for freight and insur-ance and is also responsible for an export licence.

Free on Board (Airport) (FOA). The seller has to deliver the goods to an air carrier and also pay for air freightage, unless otherwise agreed. Whoever arranges for freightage receives the Air Waybill as a receipt for the goods. The goods are delivered to the party mentioned in the Air Waybill. The seller also has to provide an export licence.

Free Alongside Ship (FAS). The seller must deliver the goods alongside a vessel named by the buyer, at a port named by the buyer and within the stipulated period. He must also notify the buyer of such delivery and also obtain a clean document of proof of delivery such as a dock or warehouse receipt. The buyer bears all costs from that point.

Free on Board (FOB). The seller has to deliver the goods on board a vessel named by the buyer and also obtain an export licence. Delivery is effected when the goods pass over the ship's rails.

Cost and Freight (C and F). The seller has to deliver the goods on board a vessel and pay for freight but not insurance. He must also obtain an export licence and provide the buyer with a clean negotiable Bill of Lading.

Cost, Insurance and Freight (CIF). As for C and F but in addition the seller must arrange for marine insurance for a value equal to the CIF value plus 10%.

With both C and F and CIF, *Property* passes with the delivery of the Bill of Lading to the buyer.

Freight or Carriage Paid to . . . (DCP). Like a C and F contract except that good delivery is made to a first carrier. This could be a road haulier, a railway, an airline, a shipping company, a multimodal transport operator or a freight forwarder. The seller pays for freight to the agreed place of destination.

The buyer is responsible for all costs from the delivery to the first carrier, except for onward freightage. This type of contract relieves the seller from the obligation to make good delivery over a ship's rails. The buyer is therefore responsible for loss or damage from the first carrier onwards.

Freight or Carriage and Insurance Paid to . . . (CIP). This is similar to the DCP contract except that it calls for the seller to effect insurance to a value of the contract price plus 10% and to cover all the forms of transport relevant to the contract. The seller must also obtain the export licence.

Ex Ship (EXS). The seller is responsible for ensuring good delivery at the unloading port so that the goods can be conveniently off-loaded in a manner appropriate to the nature of the goods. This contract is therefore more onerous to the seller than the CIF contract. Import licences are the responsibility of the buyer.

Ex Quay (EXQ). As for EXS but in addition the seller is responsible for off-loading on the wharf of quay at the agreed port and also to provide an import licence.

Delivered at Frontier (DAF). The seller must deliver the goods at a named place at the frontier in the importer's country and supply the buyer with the necessary documents like warehouse warrants, etc. The seller also has to pay Customs charges, taxes and duties, etc., and be responsible for exchange control regulations at the frontier. The buyer takes delivery at the frontier and pays import duties and onward freightage. The buyer is also responsible for the import licence.

Delivery Duty Paid (DPP). As for a DAF contract, but in addition the seller must make good delivery at a named point of destination in the buyer's country. The seller is responsible for VAT (Value Added Tax) and the import licence.

Which of these Incoterms will be used depends on a number of factors. For example, where the exporter faces strong competition he may be pre-

pared to offer as many facilities as he can in order to simplify the arrangements for the buyer. Thus, he might offer "Delivered Duty Paid" (DDP)
terms. Naturally these extra costs would have to be reflected in his quoted
price.

Another determining factor is the rates at which facilities can be obtained.
Where the exporter has a large turnover he may be able to command lower
rates than could an overseas importer whose trade is small and infrequent.

Again, traders tend to be more familiar with the services in their own
countries and may tend therefore to offer only these. Any term up to and
including "Freight or Carriage and Insurance Paid to..." (CIP) would be
appropriate here. Alternatively an overseas buyer may wish to take delivery
in the country of export perhaps for the purpose of on-selling the goods to a
buyer in that same country. In this case he will require an "Ex Works"
(EXW) or "Free To Carrier" (FRC) contract.

Finally, governments may regulate the terms on which trade takes place
perhaps for the purpose of encouraging the use of domestic services. Thus,
imports may tend to arrive on a "Free on Board" (FOB) or "Free to Carrier"
(FRC) basis while exports may go out on a "Cost, Insurance and Freight"
(CIF) or "Freight or Carriage and Insurance Paid to . . ." (CIP) basis.

One important aspect of Incoterms consequent on the ICC changes made in
1980 is the new emphasis on the critical point of making good delivery.
Under the long-standing FOB and CIF contracts delivery is effected at the
point where the goods pass over the ship's rails.

However, the tendency to use integrated (door-to-door) and multimodal
(more than one form of transport) services, brought on by the advent of the
container, has meant that delivery over the ship's rails is no longer the
significant point of handing over the goods. And, as we shall see, if a major
function of the transport document is to evidence good delivery, it should be
issued at a point where the carrier has the best opportunity to conduct a
check. This is especially so where the carrier has agreed to be responsible for
"through liability" of the goods even where he may arrange for part of the
transportation to be effected by other parties. In such cases, the Incoterms
FRC, DCP and CIP may be more pertinent and the ICC expect them to
gradually replace FOB, C and F and CIF (See Combined Transport Bills of
Lading on page 93.)

Table 5.1

Trade Term	ICC Symbol	Seller's Duties	Buyer's Duties	Passing of Risk	Passing of Possession	Passing of Property
EX WORKS	EXW	Make goods available at exporter's premises	Bear all charges from exporter's premises	At point of disposal of goods to buyer	When goods taken by buyer	As intended (usually on payment)
FREE TO CARRIER	FRC	Deliver goods to named carrier in exporter's country	Bear all charges from delivery to named carrier	At point of disposal of goods to carrier	At point of disposal	As above
FREE ON RAIL OR TRUCK	FOR-FOT	Deliver goods to railway	Bear all charges from delivery to railway	At point of taking in charge by railway	Taking in charge by railway	As above
FREE ON BOARD (AIRPORT)	FOA	Deliver goods to air carrier	Bear charges from delivery to airport except (sometimes) freight	At point of taking in charge by airport	Taking in charge by airport	As above
FREE ALONGSIDE SHIP	FAS	Deliver goods alongside named vessel	Bear all charges from delivery alongside vessel	At point of delivery alongside vessel	Delivery along-side vessel	As above
FREE ON BOARD	FOB	Deliver goods on board a named vessel	Bear all charges from point of passing over rail	At point of passing over ship's rail	Over ship's rail	As above
COST AND FREIGHT	C and F	Deliver on board a vessel and pay freight charges	Bear all charges from port of destination[1]	At point of passing over ship's rail at port of shipment	Over ship's rails	On buyer's receipt of bill of lading

COST INSURANCE AND FREIGHT	CIF	As for C and F but including marine insurance	Bear all charges from port of destination	As for C and F	As for C and F	As for C and F
FREIGHT OR CARRIAGE PAID TO . . .	DCP	Deliver to first carrier (usually a cargo terminal)[2]	Bear all charges from first carrier except for freight	At point of delivery to first carrier	Delivery to first carrier	As intended, or as for C and F
FREIGHT OR CARRIAGE AND INSURANCE PAID TO . . .	CIP	Deliver to first carrier and pay insurance and freight	Bear all charges except freight and insurance	As for DCP	As for DCP	As for DCP
EX SHIP	EXS	Make goods available at port of destination	Bear all charges from port of availability	At point of availability	At point of availability	On buyer's receipt of bill of lading
EX QUAY	EXQ	Make goods available on wharf or quay[3]	Bear all charges from point of availability	At point of availability	At point of availability	As intended
DELIVERED AT FRONTIER	DAF	Make goods available at frontier	Bear all charges from point of availability	At point of availability	At point of availability	As intended
DELIVERED DUTY PAID	DDP	As for DAF but also import licences and to named place	Bear all charges from named place	At point of named place	At point of named place	As intended

[1] Also Marine Insurance.
[2] Also pay onward freightage.
[3] Also pay import duties.

DOCUMENTS

It is now time to turn to an examination of the documents themselves. At this point reference should be made to an organization called SITPRO – Simplification of International Trade Procedures Board – funded by the Department of Trade but operating as an independent entity. It was established in June 1970 and its prime aim has been to rationalize and standardize trade document formats.

It is an independent, non-profit making organization whose task it is to cut down on the costs and complexities of international trade procedures. It supplies a range of export documentation systems, computer software, publications, and audio visuals, details of which can be obtained from SITPRO.[1]

Its members include freight forwarders, bankers and insurers and it has evolved a system called the "Aligned" system which consists of a Master Document which includes a very comprehensive range of possible information about trade flows. By the use of a masking overlay only the relevant portions of information on the Master Document are reproduced on the actual documents. The common Short-Form Bill of Lading, the Non-negotiable Sea Waybill, the Air Waybill, Export Cargo Shipping Instructions, Standard Shipping Note, Dangerous Goods Note and Export Consignment Note, have all been developed by SITPRO as part of a standard system of export documentation.

SITPRO believes that by the use of the "Aligned" system, documentation costs can be reduced by 50% and and once the Master Document has been checked for errors, all other documents must be correct. The majority of the documents reproduced in this book are in the SITPRO "Aligned" format.

BILLS OF LADING

A Bill of Lading (see Appendix 4) is one of the documents of transport and has three major functions:

(a) *It evidences receipt of goods shipped by sea.* Usually issued as a signed set of two or three originals by the carrier, known as negotiable copies, any one of which can give title to the goods! The number of copies in a set is shown in each copy. Non-negotiable copies can be made available for information purposes only. These are not signed. The Bills are issued by the carrier as a receipt for goods entrusted to him for onward transportation.

(b) *The Bills will either carry the full terms and conditions of carriage* on the reverse side, in which case the document is said to be a full or *long-form Bill*; or alternatively it could be a *short-form Bill* which carries only a *reference* to the carrier's standard conditions on the front and does not include them in detail on the back. If necessary the shipper (exporter) can request a copy of these standard conditions from the carrier. Such short-form Bills have been

[1]SITPRO, Almack House, 26–28 King Street, London, SW1Y 6QU. Telephone: 01-214 3999; Telex: 919130.

recognized by the ICC since 1974 and can be accepted under Documentary Letters of Credit unless specifically prohibited. (See Chapter 7.)

In 1979 the General Council of British Shipping (GCBS) and SITPRO introduced the *Common Short-Form Bill of Lading* (see Appendix 4). Unlike the Liner Bill it does not carry an individual shipping line logo (name, mark or sign). The exporter or the freight forwarder inserts the name of the carrier to be used and like the ordinary short-form Bill does not carry the standard conditions on the back. Instead, like the short-form Bill it carries a brief incorporation clause on the front.

The common short-form Bill is a "received for carriage" document which can be converted into a "shipped" or "loaded on board" document by the appropriate notation of the carrier when the goods are received by him. The benefits of this type of Bill of Lading are that the exporter or his agent can stock one type of Bill and not several; it is in the "Aligned" form and so can be integrated with the other "Aligned" documents, and it has the "fine print" on the back eliminated so making it a simpler document.

A common short-form Bill cannot be used for Combined Transport; i.e. where the goods are being moved by at least two different modes of transport because different conditions apply and additional information has to be shown. *Combined Transport Bills* are normally computer prepared by the carrier from information supplied by the shippers.

(c) *Bills of Lading are documents of title*. The first original copy presented to the carrier is sufficient to ensure release of the goods to the presenter (see Appendix 4). Original Bills are notated "Negotiable". All others are "Non-negotiable".

Transferring Title

An exporter can if he wishes make out a Bill of Lading in favour of his buyer. By doing so he ensures that no intermediary party (e.g. a bank) can have title to the goods. The drawback of this method is that, as is customary, banks wish to retain title for themselves when granting finance, and will only hand over the Bill of Lading to the buyer either on receipt of his payment or his acceptance of a time *Bill of Exchange* (see Chapter 6). Another disadvantage of this method is that buyers cannot on-sell the goods while they are on the high seas as no other party can have title to them without his own endorsement. This will not be possible before he has the Bills in his possession, therefore Bills made out to "order" and blank endorsed are more common.

To summarize the functions of a Bill of Lading we can say that it:

(a) is a receipt for goods entrusted to a carrier;

(b) it contains details (or reference to details) of the conditions of carriage;

(c) it is a document of title permitting the transfer of property by a process of transferring the negotiable endorsed document.

In addition to the notations already discussed, and apart of course, from reference to the goods themselves, and the places of taking them up, and setting them down, certain other important notations should be considered:

(a) A Claused Bill of Lading

When a carrier receives goods which, on the evidence of the state of packing, casing, barrels, etc. appears to be defective, they must so notate the Bill by clausing it to that effect. A Bill claused in this way is referred to as a "dirty" or "foul" Bill. The absence of such notation leaves the Bill "clean" or unclaused. This protects both the carrier from liability and the buyer from accepting the goods where a Letter of Credit is used and which prohibits such a clause. (See Chapter 7.)

(b) Payment of Freight

A Bill can be notated "Freight Paid" or "Freight Forward" depending on whether the exporter or the buyer has agreed to meet this charge; that is, depending on the trade term (Incoterm) agreed upon. For example, an FOB contract will call for a Bill of Lading to be notated "Freight Forward", meaning that the carrier will only release the goods on payment of freight at destination.

A C and F or a CIF contract on the other hand will call for a "Freight Prepaid" Bill as also will DCP and CIP contracts . (Refer to Table 5.1 for details of these contracts.)

(c) An "On-board" or "Received for Shipment" Bill

In order for the buyer to be assured that the goods are on their way, a Bill can be notated "on-board" by the carrier. This can be printed on the document or inserted by hand by the shipper. Such a notation verifies that the carrier has indeed received the goods on board a specified vessel and that they will arrive in due course.

However, some forms of Bills of Lading will be notated as "received for shipment" or "received for carriage". Such a notation represents only that the carrier has taken the goods in charge but does not certify that they are placed on board a stipulated vessel for onward transport to the final destination. As there is a possibility that the goods may not be loaded on board, but may be awaiting another (later) vessel, this may put the buyer at a disadvantage and may not comply with the agreed terms of a Letter of Credit.

(d) An "On Deck" Bill

Implies that the goods are being carried on the deck of the vessel as opposed to "under the deck". Such Bills may not comply with a Letter of Credit as it implies additional risks of loss or damage.

Notwithstanding this, the following types of Bills are "received for shipment" by their very nature:

(i) *Common Short Form Bill* (See Appendix 4). Because it is a "common" form, i.e. a form for general use, it contains the printed words "received for carriage" upon it. However, it can be converted into an "on-board" document by the appropriate notation of the carrier. This has to be signed and dated by him.

(ii) *Combined Transport Bill* (See Appendix 4). Such a document is evidence of carriage by at least two modes of transport, e.g. road and ocean-going vessel. It is effective from the place of acceptance (say, the exporter's warehouse) to the place of delivery (say a port of destination). As a result it will be a "received for shipments" or an "accepted by the Carrier" Bill. Once again, it can be converted into an "on-board" Bill by the appropriate notation by the ship's master.

Under the *Uniform Rules for a Combined Transport Document* (ICC publication no. 298) the issuer of a combined transport document can either provide the transport, or part of it, or merely arrange for the provision of the transport. In either case he must be a principal or acting as an agent of a principal responsible for the carriage of the goods. The ICC Uniform Customs and Practice for Documentary Letters of Credit stipulates in article 25 that unless a credit calls for a marine Bill of Lading, banks will accept (unless otherwise specified in the credit) transport documents issued by a named carrier or his agent indicating dispatch or *taking in charge* of the goods. Thus a freight forwarder can issue such a document provided he is either responsible for at least part of the carriage or he is acting as agent for a carrier. (See Chapter 7 on Letters of Credit.)

It should be noted that a Combined Transport Bill of Lading is not quite the same thing as a Through Transport Bill of Lading. The former involves the issuer as principal for the entire multi-modal carriage; the latter makes the issuer principal only while the goods are in his care. Subsequently, he acts only as agent.

Other Forms of Bills of Lading

(a) Liner Bills (See Appendix 4)

Bills issued by liner carriers plying scheduled runs between ports on pre-announced dates and times. Such Bills are superior to tramp Bills which are issued by tramp carriers offering no certainty as to date, time or route schedules.

(b) Charterparty bills

Issued by charterers of vessels and not by the ship's owners, and must state "subject to charter party". As the terms of contract may differ from those available from shipowners they may not be acceptable under a Letter of Credit unless specifically permitted.

In addition to negotiable Bills of Lading there are other transport documents that act as receipts for goods entrusted to a carrier and which bear details of the terms of carriage but which *do not act as documents of title* and are not capable of being *negotiated* (i.e. transferred). These are:

(i) Sea Waybill (See Appendix 4)

Because of the advent of faster vessels, containerization and improved terminal facilities, the transit times of vessels have been greatly reduced. However, the time taken to process and deliver documents has not improved at the same rate and as a result it can happen that the goods arrive before the negotiable Bills of Lading. To solve this problem the Sea Waybill has evolved which – apart from its non-negotiability – has the same characteristics as the traditional Bill. The named consignee takes delivery of the goods subject to proof of identity without the need to present any document of title. Thus there is no need to delay the receipt of the goods just because the relevant documents have been delayed.

The SITPRO Sea Waybill is a common and short-form type. That is, there is no carrier logo and an incorporation clause on the front refers to the carrier's detailed conditions of carriage without setting them out on the back. Thus, it is a "Received for Carriage" Bill and it can be converted into a "Shipped on Board" Bill by the notation of the ship's master. As a "Received for Carriage" Bill it can be obtained by the shipper before the vessel sails. Because the Sea Waybill is not a document of title, the shipper (exporter) does not retain title to the goods prior to presentation to the buyer and therefore it will be inappropriate in much international trade. Currently it is used primarily in trade between multinational and associated companies and where open account trading is operated (see Chapter 6); in other words where the parties to the trade are happy to take each other on trust. Because of the speed of turnround of vessels on the North American and Scandinavian services, Sea Waybills are commonly used on these routes.

Because the Sea Waybill is non-negotiable, it cannot be issued "to order" but must be issued to a named consignee. This may make it unacceptable to a bank providing finance against documents as it fails to give them the control over the goods afforded by a traditional Bill. Although banks could be nominated as consignees, it would make them liable for receipt of the cargo and this they are not usually prepared to accept. However, it is possible to make the bank a "Notify Party" with a "no-disposal" clause which gives it the ability to prevent delivery to the buyer.

Unless there is a specific clause to the contrary in the Sea Waybill, it is only the shipper who can give the carrier instructions as to the delivery of the goods. The carrier has contracted only with the shipper and must carry out his instructions, which can theoretically, be altered while the goods are on the high seas. As a result, banks may not regard Sea Waybills as good security against the provision of finance because it is possible for the shipper to enforce a "stoppage in transitu" (prevent the goods reaching the consignee). However, the shipper can rescind this right or transfer it to a third party. By contrast a negotiable Bill of Lading is a contract with the carrier and the legitimate *holder* of the endorsed Bill. As a result, once the documents are presented to a bank the shipper loses the right to enforce a "stoppage in transitu".

(ii) Air Waybill (See Appendix 4)

Like the Sea Waybill the Air Waybill is not a document of title but acts only as a receipt for goods entrusted for carriage and carries the terms and conditions of such carriage. Like the Sea Waybill the Air Waybill is a contract between the shipper and the carrier; but the named consignee is *not* liable for proper receipt of goods. As a result banks *are* prepared to be named as consignees on Air Waybills. Also the likelihood of "stoppage in transitu" is much less as a result of the speed of transportation.

In relation to Freight Forwarders' liabilities under House Air Waybills there is uncertainty as to whether their functions as Forwarders Consolidators are to be viewed as agency or carrier-principal functions. To date there have been no decided cases under English law and, therefore, acting on legal advice to try to maximize the protection afforded to forwarders using the SITPRO Air Waybill format, SITPRO have included reference to the Warsaw Convention which limits carriers' liabilities in respect of loss, damage or delay. In addition SITPRO advises forwarders to consider taking out liability insurance to protect themselves further. Forwarders can also add their own terms and conditions on the back of the Air Waybill.

(iii) Rail Consignment Note; Road Waybill; Parcel Post Receipt

These transport documents also act only as receipts and terms of carriage documents. They are non-negotiable and cannot be issued "to order". Goods are surrendered only to the party offering proof of identity as the party named as consignee. Postal services are for parcels weighing up to 20 kilogrammes. Road transit delays can be minimized by obtaining a TIR (transport international routier) carnet. This is issued by HM Customs stating that they have inspected the goods and sealed the container or the vehicle. The vehicle is fitted with a TIR plate and this can speed customs formalities at foreign borders.

There are a number of other documents associated with the movement of goods. They are:

(a) Standard Shipping Note (See Appendix 4)

This is a form requesting ports and other receiving authorities to accept goods for carriage. It is made out by the shipper or his agent and accompanies the goods to the receiving authority.

(b) Dangerous Goods Note (See Appendix 4)

Has the same function as the standard shipping note except that it alerts the receiving authority to the receipt of cargo that may require special handling and/or storage.

(c) Export Consignment Note (See Appendix 4)

Again, the same function as the standard shipping note but applicable to goods transported by road or rail. It is accepted by British Rail and National Carriers Ltd.

(d) Export Cargo Shipping Instructions (See Appendix 4)

Made out by the shipper and contains a set of instructions to a Freight Forwarder as to the goods and means of forward transportation. It is on these instructions that the Freight Forwarder acts on behalf of the shipper. It can apply to any form of transportation.

(e) Container Inspection Report (See Appendix 4)

This document is completed by the truck driver as to the state of containers deposited or received.

(f) Weight Note and Packing List (See Appendix 4)

Issued by the shipper or a Freight Forwarder and contains details of the weights of individual items and packing numbers to identify specific pieces of cargo.

(g) Inspection Certificate (See Appendix 4)

This is issued by a reputable body and contains a certification of the quality of goods being shipped. This protects the buyer from purchasing goods of a quality not ordered. One such certifying organization is the *Société Générale de Surveillance* based in Switzerland.

(h) Blacklist Certificate (See Appendix 4)

A declaration by the shipper or the carrier as to the origin of the cargo or ownership and routing of the vessel. This document is especially required for transportation to Middle East countries.

(i) Certificate of Origin (See Appendix 4)

The main function of this document is to evidence the place of origin of the goods for the purposes of determining the tariff rate to be applied by the Customs authorities in the country of import. Some may be required to be authenticated by a Chamber of Commerce.

INVOICES

(a) Commercial Invoice (See Appendix 4)

This is another important document which can be defined as a document of information giving complete details of the goods, unit prices, terms of delivery and payments, etc. One major characteristic of the commercial invoice is that, when part of a set of documents to be presented under the terms of a Letter of Credit (see Chapter 7) must conform exactly to the descriptions in that Letter of Credit. The principal functions of this document is for accounting purposes, and to assist Customs and Excise authorities to determine the appropriate tariff (if any).

Apart from the commercial invoice there are a number of variants:

(b) Pro-forma Invoice

This document acts as an invitation to purchase the goods shown on it. It can be used in the following circumstances:

  (i) when goods are going on consignment, that is, when they are being exported with the expectation of a sale although no firm order has been received. This might be through an overseas agent (see Chapter 4) who can use the information supplied on it as the basis for sale;

 (ii) to effect a payment in advance of goods being despatched. On despatch of goods, a commercial invoice is prepared and supersedes the pro-forma document;

(iii) when overseas importers require a document evidencing a purchase of a foreign product in order to obtain an import licence and/or access to foreign exchange for payment purposes.

(c) Certified Invoice

This document (which can be an ordinary commercial invoice) carries the certification of the exporter of certain data called for by the overseas buyer; i.e. value, place of origin of the goods, etc.

(d) Legalized Invoice

Serving the same functions as a certified invoice except that the document must be verified by the embassy or consulate of the buyer's country in the country of export.

(e) Consular Invoice

Once again the purpose is to verify the data concerning goods going to certain countries but in this case the document is *issued in the exporter's country by the embassy or consulate of the importer's country*. Widely used by Latin American countries.

(f) Customs Invoice

As before, but used for sales to the US and Canada only. Special information is called for by these countries on goods worth more than a specified value and include the provision of discounts, rebates, use of importer's goods in the production of the exports, etc.

INSURANCE DOCUMENTS

One of the three major risks of international trade is the Marine Risk; i.e. loss of or damage to goods in transit. The other two risks are the Foreign Exchange Risk and the Credit Risk (these are covered in later chapters).

Now whether the goods are subject to Ex Works, FOB, CIF or DDP terms of shipment they will invariably be insured against the Marine Risk, if for no other reason than banks who offer finance against documents will insist upon it.

(a) The Insurance Policy (See Appendix 4)

This document forms the contract of insurance between the insurance company and the insured party. It contains all the details of, and exclusions to, the cover provided.

Regular exporters will normally have an "Open" or "Floating" policy to cover the whole of their overseas trade for a given period. Individual shipments will be covered by such a policy but as there is only one, the insurance document presented for any particular shipment will be a certificate of insurance (see Appendix 4). The only exception to this will be where the trade contract specifically calls for the presentation of the policy itself, in which case a copy will have to be obtained from the insurers.

Marine insurance is normally to cover the goods from the point of transportation from the seller's warehouse to the ultimate receipt by the buyer. Most policies are in standard form and follow the Lloyd's SG (Ships and Goods) format.

The risks covered should conform to the requirements of the trade contract and where a Letter of Credit is used, must be as detailed in the credit. For example, cover should be effected in the currency of the credit and should be for a value not less than the CIF value. Commonly, to be on the safe side insurance is effected to a value of CIF plus 10%. It is important that for cover to be properly arranged, the date of the commencement of the insurance must be on or before the date of the document evidencing despatch (e.g. Bills of Lading).

When cover is obtained by the exporter, say on a CIF or CIP contract, in order for the buyer to be able to make a claim in the event of loss or damage, the insurance document has to be endorsed over to him. This is done by the exporter signing the document on its reverse side. Like a Bill of Lading, an insurance policy is freely transferable by endorsement and delivery. When the buyer is responsible for insuring the goods, the exporter can obtain a seller's interest contingency insurance to cover him if the buyer fails to pay for the goods because of loss or damage. Such insurance would be appropriate for C and F, FOB and similar contracts.

The cover afforded by a policy will depend on the type of goods being transported. If the goods are not likely to be subject to damage or deterioration (e.g. mineral raw materials) then the minimum cover may suffice. Such cover is "free from particular average" (FPA) which excludes claims that have not resulted from the damage or loss to the vessel itself.

All cargo is covered for "general average", meaning loss or damage to goods as a result of efforts made to prevent or limit a hazard to the vessel or cargo in general. Examples of acts of general average are: where cargo is jettisoned to safeguard the crew, vessel and cargo; and where attempts to extinguish a fire on board causes damage to particular cargo.

If the goods are of a type that further cover is necessary, a "with particular average" (WPA) claused policy is called for. Such cover can include damage caused by docker's hooks, breakages and leakages.

Further cover can be obtained by an "all risks" policy. This covers most eventualities except strikes, war and piracy. However, even these can be covered by the payment of an additional premium.

As from December 1983 a new "Short-Form" Marine Insurance Policy came into use to cover both cargo and hull risks. The effect of this is to allow for the terms and conditions of the insurance (the clauses) to be written into each policy to reflect the degree of cover required by the insured. This format is illustrated in Appendix 4 by kind permission of Lloyds of London.

(b) Insurance Certificate (See Appendix 4)

This document is completed by the exporter either on forms supplied by the insurers or on common, short-form documents approved by Lloyds and The Institute of London Underwriters. The insurance certificate relates only to the goods shown on it and only for a specific shipment. It will accompany all other documents presented and is included in lieu of the insurance policy which it represents. It is therefore, subject to all of the terms of that policy. The certificate requires the signature of the insured party. The insurance document must be as called for under any Letter of Credit.

(c) Letter of Insurance (or Cover Note)

Such an insurance document is issued by a party other than the insurers and takes the form of a notification that insurance has been, or is being, effected while still awaiting the policy or certificate. It can be issued by an insurance broker or a bank. A letter of insurance may not be acceptable under a Letter of Credit as it is not issued by the insurers themselves and may, therefore, not carry the standard clauses of insurance.

Appendix 4

Examples of Forms

Liner Bill of Lading

Shipper DRESSER EUROPE S.A.	**BILL OF LADING**	UK Customs Assigned No. 13025	B/L No.
		Shipper's Ref. 3229-32	
		F/Agent's Ref. 2998	

| Consignee (If 'Order' state Notify Party and Address) |
| DRESSER EUROPE S.A. TUNISIAN BRANCH C/O COMPAGNIE TUNISIENNE D'ARMEMENT 10 RUE FARHAT HACHED, TUNIS, TUNISIA. |

It is agreed that no responsibility shall attach to the Carrier or his Agents for failure to notify the Consignee of the arrival of the goods.

Notify Party and Address (leave blank if stated above) M LUCQUET, DRESSER
EUROPE S.A. TUNISIAN BRANCH, P.O.BOX
252 IMMEUBLE FRIKIA K.M 2,5, ROUTE
DE SALTANIA, SFAX, TUNISIA.

ELLERMAN CITY LINERS
The Shipping Division of Ellerman Lines Ltd
12-20 CAMOMILE ST., LONDON EC3A 7EX
Telephone: 01-283 4311
Telegraphic Address: Buccaneer, London
Telex: 884771/2

PRINCE LINE LTD.
52 LEADENHALL ST., LONDON EC3A 2BJ
Telephone: 01-481 2020
Telegraphic Address: Spardeck, London
Telex: 888487

Pre-Carriage by*	Place of Acceptance*
Vessel WHITE COAST	Port of Loading LONDON
Port of Discharge TUNIS	Place of Delivery by On-Carrier*

Marks and Nos; Container No;	Number and kind of packages; description of goods	Gross Weight	Measurement
DESA 037/0681 3229-32 TUNIS	15 DRUMS SAID TO CONTAIN:- MAGCOLUBE	3060KLS	4.491M3
	10 DRUMS SAID TO CONTAIN:- PIPELAX	2180KLS	2.994M3

Particulars of goods are those declared by Shippers

Freight details, charges, etc.

Shipped either on board the above local vessel in or off the local port named to be transshipped direct or by transhipment and subject to the exceptions, terms and conditions of the bill of lading applicable tariff conditions (copies of which are available on request) to the extent that the latter do not conflict with the exceptions, terms and conditions of this bill of lading, to the above-named port of discharge or so near thereto as she may safely get, lie and discharge) and there to be delivered subject as aforesaid in the like good order and condition. Delivery to be made to the consignee named above or to his or their assigns.
Weights as shown in this bill of lading as declared by Shippers, and the Master is unable to check same. In accepting this bill of lading the Shipper, Consignee and Owners of the goods, and the holder of this bill of lading, agree to be bound by all of its conditions, exceptions and provisions whether written, printed or stamped on the front or back hereof. CONTAINER AND VEHICLE DEMURRAGE. Attention is drawn to the Carrier's Terms and Conditions for Container and Vehicle Demurrage which apply to this Contract and which may be obtained from the Carrier or their Agents.

| Ocean Freight Payable at LONDON | Place and date of issue |
| Number of Original Bs/L THREE | In witness whereof the Master, Owner or Agent of the ship has affirmed to the number of Bills of Lading stated above, all of this tenor and date one of which being accomplished, the others to stand void. |

ICS
B/L
1 Jan. 72
710 *Applicable only when document used as a Through Bill of Lading

Copy—not negotiable

CONDITIONS CONTINUED OVERLEAF

For the Master

Reverse of Liner Bill of Lading

DEFINITION OF GOODS — "Goods" means the cargo accepted from the Shipper and includes any container, transportable tank, flat or pallet not supplied by or on behalf of the Carrier.

1. CLAUSE PARAMOUNT IT IS MUTUALLY AGREED that this Bill of Lading shall take effect subject to the provision of the International Convention relating to Bills of Lading dated Brussels 25th August 1924 (here after called the Hague Rules) as set where legislation gives effect to the Hague Rules as amount by the Protocol signed in Brussels 23rd February 1968 (hereinafter called the Hague Visby Rules) in compulsorily applicable in which case this Bill of Lading shall have effect subject to the provisions of such legislation. To the same extent Hague Visby Rules shall apply where the goods...

2. RESPONSIBILITY FOR CONVEYANCE DISCHARGE AND DELIVERY
(a) The Carrier's obligations in respect of the goods shall begin when the goods are accepted at the ocean vessel's rail at the port of loading and shall continue until the goods are discharged at the ocean vessel's rail at the port of discharge...

3. DISCHARGE AND DELIVERY

OPTIONAL CARGO.

4. ACKNOWLEDGEMENT OF WEIGHT, QUALITY, MARKS, ETC.

5. THE CARRIER'S RIGHTS IF CONSIGNEE NOT READY.

6. LANDING. LANDING CHARGES.

VOYAGE.

8. DECK CARGO AND STOWAGE

9. CARRIER'S LIBERTIES IN THE EVENT OF BLOCKADE DELAY ETC

10. CARRIER'S LIBERTIES IN THE EVENT OF WAR, ETC.

11. CONTAINERS
(i) The Carrier has no responsibility whatsoever for the functioning of reefer containers or trailers, not owned nor leased by the Carrier
(ii) SHIPPER PACKED CONTAINERS.
(iii) INSPECTION OF GOODS.
(iv) REPOSITIONING OF CONTAINERS.

12. CONTAINER EQUIPMENT INTERCHANGE CONDITIONS.

12. PORT, CUSTOMS, CONSULAR AND OTHER REGULATIONS

13. DAMAGED PACKAGES, ETC.

14. TRANSHIPMENT CARGO.

15. TRANSHIPMENT AND FORWARDING.

16. DANGEROUS, INFLAMMABLE, RADIOACTIVE, DAMAGING OR CONTAMINATING GOODS

17. CLAIMS.

18. CALCULATION OF FREIGHT.

19. LIEN.

20. GENERAL AVERAGE AND SALVAGE
(a) General Average shall be payable according to York-Antwerp Rules 1974 and shall be adjusted at any port or place selected by the Carrier

21. BOTH TO BLAME COLLISION CLAUSE.

22. RIGHTS AND IMMUNITIES OF ALL SERVANTS AND AGENTS OF THE CARRIER

23. SURRENDER OF BILL OF LADING.

24. AGENCY CLAUSE.

25. JURISDICTION.

26. TUNIS.

27. ISTANBUL.

28. IZMIR.

29. OPORTO.

30. ALGERIAN PORTS.

TRANBY PRINTERS LIMITED   ANLABY   HULL

ECL 186 4.78

Bill of Lading

Shipper SITPRO EXPORT LIMITED HIGH STREET, BURTON ON TRENT, STAFFS DE15 1YZ ENGLAND INGLATERRA	**COMMON SHORT FORM BILL OF LADING**	UK Customs Assigned No. B/L No. 99999 Shipper's Reference 036-16418 F/Agent's Reference VE80-4740

Consignee (if 'Order' state Notify Party and Address)
LABORATORIOS FRANKENSTEIN S.A.
Rua Primera 1
Caracas, VENEZUELA

Name of Carrier
Transworld Containers Ltd

Notify Party and Address (leave blank if stated above)

The contract evidenced by this Short Form Bill of Lading is subject to the exceptions limitations conditions and liberties (including those relating to pre-carriage and on-carriage) set out in the Carrier's Standard Conditions applicable to the voyage covered by this Short Form Bill of Lading and operative on its date of issue.
If the carriage is one where the provisions of the Hague Rules contained in the International Convention for unification of certain rules relating to Bills of Lading dated Brussels on 25th August 1924 as amended by the Protocol signed at Brussels on 23rd February 1968 (the Hague Visby Rules) are compulsorily applicable under Article X the said Standard Conditions contain or shall be deemed to contain a Clause giving effect to the Hague Visby Rules. Otherwise except as provided below the said Standard Conditions contain or shall be deemed to contain a Clause giving effect to the provisions of the Hague Rules.
The Carrier hereby agrees that to the extent of any inconsistency the said Clause shall prevail over the exceptions limitations conditions and liberties set out in the Standard Conditions in respect of any period to which the Hague Rules or the Hague Visby Rules by their terms apply. Unless the Standard Conditions expressly provide otherwise neither the Hague Rules nor the Hague Visby Rules shall apply to this contract where the goods carried hereunder consist of live animals or cargo which by this contract is stated as being carried on deck and is so carried.
Notwithstanding anything contained in the said Standard Conditions the term Carrier in this Short Form Bill of Lading shall mean the Carrier named on the front thereof.
A copy of the Carrier's said Standard Conditions applicable hereto may be inspected or will be supplied on request at the office of the Carrier or the Carrier's Principal Agents.

Pre-Carriage by*	Place of Receipt by Pre-Carrier*
TWC Vehicle	Burton on Trent
Vessel	**Port of Loading**
Bebington	Liverpool
Port of Discharge	**Place of Delivery by On-Carrier***
La Guaira	Caracas

Marks and Nos. Container No.	Number and kind of packages; Description of Goods	Gross Weight	Measurement
FRANKENSTEIN ED1814 CARACAS VIA LA GUAIRA LCL in TWCU 1234564	2 Cartons Ethical Pharmaceuticals (Non-dangerous) Productos farmaceuticos I/L 80/9999999	160 kg	0.250 m3

Freight Details; Charges etc.

Freight (Flete)
£GBP 43.60
USD 97.23

RECEIVED FOR CARRIAGE as above in apparent good order and condition, unless otherwise stated hereon, the goods described in the above particulars.

IN WITNESS whereof the number of original Bills of Lading stated below have been signed, all of this tenor and date, one of which being accomplished the others to stand void.

GCBS
CSF
BL
1979

710

Ocean Freight Payable at	Place and Date of Issue
Origin	LIVERPOOL 15 SEPTEMBER 1980
Number of Original Bs/L	Signature for Carrier; Carrier's Principal Place of Business
1	TWC CUNARD BUILDING LIVERPOOL L3

Authorised and Licensed by the
General Council of British Shipping © 1979

SITPRO OVERLAYS 1979

Reproduced by kind permission of the General Council of British Shipping.

COMBINED TRANSPORT BILL OF LADING

Shipper		Bill of Lading Number
DEXION LIMITED, P.O. BOX 6 MAYLANDS AVE., HEMEL HEMPSTEAD, HERTS.		3137111A
		Shipper's Reference Number

Consignee	
TO ORDER	ARABIAN MIDDLE EAST LINE Cunard Steam-Ship Company Limited

Notify Party	Place and Date of Acceptance
ADHBAN TRADING CORPORATION, SANAA ST., P.O. BOX 3010, HODEIDAH, YEMEN ARAB REPUBLIC.	HEMEL HEMPSTEAD 5.5.81

Voyage No.		Place of Delivery
CB 313		
Vessel	Port of Loading	HODEIDAH QUAY
PETRA CROWN	FELIXSTOWE	
Port of Discharge		
HODEIDAH		

Marks and Nos. Container Nos:	Number and Kind of Packages, Description of Goods.	Gross Weight Kgs	Measurement Cu. M.
CNTR.NO.SCXU2849434 SEAL: 11558 861371 MATERIALS FOR NISSAN SUBARU RACKING ADHBAN (NISSAN STORE) HODEIDAH YEMEN ARAB REPUBLIC A-G 1/2	SUPPLIED BY THE CARRIER SAID TO CONTAIN: 6 CRATES & 1 CASE & 2 BUNDLES DEXION MATERIALS AND RACKING	4129	
861043 MATERIALS FOR SAVIEM BUILDING ADHBAN (SAVIEM STORE) HODEIDAH YEMEN ARAB REPUBLIC A-F	4 CRATES AND 2 CASES DEXION MATERIALS AND RACKING	5198	

CONTINUED ON FOUR SHEETS

Particulars above declared by the Shipper

Total No. of Containers/Packages (2) TWO CONTAINERS (20'S/L)	Endorsements	
Movement FCL/FCL		
Freight/Charges		

			Place and Date of Issue
Origin Zone	DUE U.K.		BARKING 26.5.81
Ocean Sector	DUE YEMEN		
Destination Zone	N/A	No. of Original Bills (3) THREE	IN WITNESS whereof TWO (2) original Bills of Lading have been signed, if not otherwise stated aside, one of which having been accomplished, the other(s) to be void.

ACCEPTED by the Carrier from the Shipper in apparent good order and condition (unless otherwise noted herein) the total number of containers or other packages or units indicated above stated by the Shipper to comprise the cargo specified above, for transportation subject to all the terms hereof (INCLUDING THE TERMS ON THE REVERSE HEREOF AND THE TERMS OF THE CARRIER'S APPLICABLE TARIFF) from the Place of Acceptance to the Place of Delivery. On presentation of this document (duly endorsed) to the Carrier, by or on behalf of the Holder, the rights and liabilities arising in accordance with the terms hereof shall (without prejudice to any rule of common law or statute rendering them binding upon the Shipper, Holder and Carrier) become binding in all respects between the Carrier and Holder as though the contract contained herein or evidenced hereby had been made between them.

As far as this Bill of Lading covers COMBINED TRANSPORT, it is based on the uniform rules for a Combined Transport document ICC Brochure No. 298.

For the Carrier

NON - NEGOTIABLE

Associated Container Transportation Services Ltd.

S 1.10.79

Reverse of Combined Transport Bill of Lading

CONDITIONS

1. DEFINITIONS

"Carrier" means the Carrier on whose behalf this Bill of Lading has been signed.

"Merchant" includes the Shipper, Holder, Consignee, Receiver of the Goods, any person owning or entitled to the possession of the Goods or of this Bill of Lading and anyone acting on behalf of any such person.

"Holder" means any person for the time being in possession of this Bill of Lading to whom the property in the Goods has passed on or by reason of the consignment of the Goods or the endorsement of this Bill of Lading or otherwise.

"Goods" means the cargo accepted from the Shipper and includes any Container not supplied by or on behalf of the Carrier.

"Container" includes any container, trailer, transportable tank, flat, or pallet or any similar article of transport used to consolidate goods.

"Carriage" means the whole of the operations and services undertaken by the Carrier in respect of the Goods.

"Combined Transport" arises when the Place of Acceptance and/or the Place of Delivery are indicated on the face hereof.

"Port to Port Shipment" arises where the Carriage called for by this Bill of Lading is not Combined Transport.

"Freight" includes all charges payable to the Carrier in accordance with the applicable Tariff.

2. CARRIER'S TARIFF

The terms of the Carrier's applicable Tariff are incorporated herein. Copies of the relevant provisions of the applicable Tariff are obtainable from the Carrier or his agents upon request. In the case of inconsistency between this Bill of Lading and the applicable Tariff, this Bill of Lading shall prevail.

3. WARRANTY

The Merchant warrants that in agreeing to the terms hereof he is, or has the authority of the person owning or entitled to the possession of the Goods and this Bill of Lading.

4. SUB-CONTRACTING

(1) The Carrier shall be entitled to sub-contract on any terms the whole or any part of the Carriage.

(2) The Merchant undertakes that no claim or allegation shall be made against any person by whom the Carriage or any part of the Carriage is performed or undertaken (other than the Carrier) which imposes or attempts to impose upon any such person or any vessel owned by any such person any liability whatsoever in connection with the Goods whether or not arising out of negligence on the part of such person and if any such claim or allegation should nevertheless be made to indemnify the Carrier against all consequences thereof. Without prejudice to the foregoing every such person shall have the benefit of all provisions herein benefiting the Carrier as if such provisions were expressly for his benefit; and in entering into this contract, the Carrier, to the extent of these provisions, does so not only on his own behalf, but also as agent and trustee for such persons.

5. CARRIERS RESPONSIBILITY

(A) Port to Port Shipment

Where the Carriage called for by this Bill of Lading is a port to port shipment then:

(1) The liability (if any) of the Carrier for loss of or damage to the Goods occurring from and during loading on to any sea going vessel up to and during discharge from that vessel or from another sea going vessel into which the Goods shall have been transhipped shall be determined in accordance with any national law making the Hague Rules or the Hague Rules as amended by the Protocol signed at Brussels on 23 February 1968 (Hague Visby Rules) compulsorily applicable to this Bill of Lading (including the UK Carriage of Goods by Sea Act 1924) or, if there be no such national law, in accordance with the Hague Rules contained in the International Convention for the unification of certain Rules relating to Bills of Lading, dated 25 August 1924. All the terms of this Bill of Lading (except (B) below) shall apply to such Carriage save that if any term in this Bill of Lading is inconsistent with or [illegible] repugnant to the Hague Rules or the Hague Visby Rules as the case may be it shall [illegible] the extent of such inconsistency or repugnance and no further be null and void. Notwithstanding the above, the Carriers liability, if any, shall be limited to loss of or damage to the Goods occurring from and during loading on to any sea going vessel up to and during discharge from that vessel.

(2) For the purpose of determining the extent of the Carriers liability for loss of or damage to the Goods, the sound value of the Goods is agreed to be the invoice value plus freight and insurance if paid.

(B) Combined Transport

Where the Carriage called for by this Bill of Lading is Combined Transport then, save as is otherwise provided in this Bill of Lading, the Carrier shall be liable for loss or damage occurring during Carriage to the extent set out below.

(1) Where the stage of Carriage where loss or damage occurred is not known

(a) Exclusions

Where the stage of Carriage where the loss or damage occurred is not known the Carrier shall be relieved of liability for any loss or damage if such loss or damage was caused by:

(i) an act or omission of the Merchant;

(ii) insufficiency of or defective condition of packing or marking;

(iii) handling, loading, stowing or unloading of the Goods by or on behalf of the Merchant;

(iv) inherent vice of the Goods;

(v) strike, lock-out, stoppage or restraint of labour the consequences of which the Carrier could not avoid by the exercise of reasonable diligence;

(vi) a nuclear incident if the operator of a nuclear installation or a person acting for him is liable for this damage under an applicable International convention or national law governing liability in respect of nuclear energy;

(vii) any cause or event which the Carrier could not avoid and the consequence whereof he could not prevent by the exercise of reasonable diligence.

(b) Burden of Proof

The burden of proving that the loss or damage was due to one or more of the causes or events specified in this sub-clause (B) (1) shall rest upon the Carrier. Save that, when the Carrier establishes that in the circumstances of the case, the loss or damage could be attributed to one or more of the causes or events specified in paragraphs (a) (ii), (iii) or (iv) above, it shall be presumed that it was so caused. The Merchant shall, however, be entitled to prove that the loss or damage was not, in fact, caused either wholly or partly by one or more of these causes or events.

(c) Amount of Compensation

(i) Compensation shall be calculated by reference to the value of such Goods at the place and time when they are delivered to the Merchant or at the [illegible] and time when they should have been delivered.

[illegible] the value of the Goods shall be determined according to the current [illegible]dity exchange price or, if there is no such price, according to the current market price, or, if there is no commodity exchange price or current market price, by reference to the normal value of goods of the same kind and quality.

(iii) Except as provided in sub-caluse (C) (3) below, compensation shall in no circumstances whatsoever and howsoever arising exceed U.S. $2·60 per kilo of the gross weight of the goods lost or damaged.

(2) Where the stage of Carriage where loss or damage occurred is known

Notwithstanding anything provided for in sub-clause (B) (1) above and subject to Clause 14 (Deck Cargo [and Livestock]), where it is known during which stage of Carriage the loss or damage occurred the liability of the Carrier in respect of such loss or damage shall be determined:

(a) by the provisions contained in any international convention or national law, which provisions—

(i) cannot be departed from by private contract to the detriment of the Merchant; and

(ii) would have applied if the Merchant had made a separate and direct contract with the Carrier in respect of the particular stage of Carriage where the loss or damage occurred and received as evidence thereof any particular document which must be issued in order to make such international convention or national law applicable.

Provided that an international convention or national law will determine the Carrier's liability as aforesaid only if it would have been applicable if the contract referred to in (ii) above were governed:

(A) where the loss or damage occurred between the time that the Goods were received by the Carrier for Carriage and the time that the Goods were loaded at the port of loading, by the internal law of the State of the place of receipt, or

(B) where the loss or damage occurred during carriage by sea, by the internal law of the state of the final port of discharge; or

(C) where the loss or damage occurred between the time that the Goods were discharged at the final port of discharge and the time that the Goods were delivered to the Merchant, by the internal law of the State of the place of delivery, or

(b) where no international convention or national law would apply by virtue of (a) above, by the Hague Rules contained in the International Convention for the unification of certain rules relating to Bills of Lading dated 25th August 1924 if the loss or damage is known to have occurred at sea or on inland waterways, or

(c) by the provisions of sub-clause (B) (1) in cases where the provisions of paragraphs (a) and (b) above do not apply.

Where under the provisions of this sub-clause (B) (2) the liability of the Carrier shall be determined by the provisions of any international convention or national law this liability shall be determined as though the Carrier were the carrier referred to in any such convention or national law;

References in this sub-clause (B) (2) to the internal law of a State shall be deemed to exclude all principles of private international law applied by that State.

For the purposes of this sub-clause (B) (2) references in the Hague Rules to carriage by sea shall be deemed to include references to carriage by inland waterways and the Hague Rules shall be construed accordingly.

(3) Special Provisions for Combined Tranport

(a) Notice of loss or damage

The Carrier shall be deemed *prima facie* to have delivered the Goods as described in this Bill of Lading unless notice of loss of, or damage to, the Goods, indicating the general nature of such loss or damage shall have been given in writing to the Carrier or to his representative at the place of delivery before or at the time of removal of the Goods into the custody of the person entitled to delivery thereof under this Bill of Lading, or, if the loss or damage is not apparent, within seven consecutive days thereafter.

(b) Time-bar

Subject to any provision of this Clause 6 to the contrary the Carrier shall be discharged of all liability under this Bill of Lading unless suit is brought and notice thereof given to the Carrier within nine months after delivery of the Goods or the date when the Goods should have been delivered.

(c) Exclusion of Limitation

The Carrier shall not be entitled to the benefit of the limitation of liability provided for in (B) (1) *(c)* above if it is proved that the loss or damage resulted from an act or omission of the Carrier done with intent to cause damage or recklessly and with knowledge that damage would probably result.

(C) General (applicable to both Port to Port Shipment and Combined Transport)

(1) Delay

The Carrier does not undertake that the Goods shall arrive at the port of discharge or place of delivery at any particular time or to meet any particular market or use and save as provided in sub-clause (B) (2) above the Carrier shall in no circumstances be liable for direct, indirect or consequential loss or damage caused by delay.

Where under the provisions of (B) (2) above the Carrier is liable for delay, liability shall be limited to the element of the freight applicable to the relevant stage of transport provided this is not contrary to the International convention or national law concerned.

(2) Supply of Containers

The terms of this Bill of Lading shall govern the responsibility of the Carrier in connection with or arising out of the supply of a Container to the Merchant, whether supplied before or after the Goods are received by the Carrier for Carriage or delivered to the Merchant.

(3) Ad Valorem

Higher compensation may be claimed only when, with the consent of the Carrier, the value of the Goods declared by the Shipper, which exceeds the limits laid down in this Clause, has been stated in this Bill of Lading and extra freight paid if required. In that case the amount of the declared value shall be substituted for those limits. Any partial loss or damage shall be adjusted *pro rata* on the basis of such declared value.

(4) Hague Rules Limitation

Subject to (3) above, whenever Hague Rules are applicable, otherwise than by national law, in determining the liability of the Carrier, the liability shall in no event exceed £100 sterling per package or unit.

(5) Scope of Application

Save as otherwise provided herein, the Carrier shall in no circumstances whatsoever or howsoever arising be liable for direct or indirect or consequential loss or damage. The defences and limits of liability provided for in this Bill of Lading shall apply in any action against the Carrier for loss or damage or delay whether the action be founded in Contract or in Tort.

6. SHIPPER-PACKED CONTAINERS

If a Container has not been stowed by or on behalf of the Carrier:—

(a) the Carrier shall not be liable for loss or for damage to the Goods caused by

(i) the manner in which the Container has been stowed; or

(ii) the unsuitability of the Goods for carriage in Containers; or

(iii) the unsuitability or defective condition of the Container provided that where the Container has been provided by or on behalf of the Carrier this paragraph (iii) shall only apply if the unsuitability or defective condition arose without any want of due diligence on the part of the Carrier or would have been apparent upon reasonable inspection by the Merchant at or prior to the time when the Container was stowed.

(b) the Merchant shall indemnify the Carrier against any loss, damage, liability or expense whatsoever and howsoever arising caused by one or more of the matters referred to in paragraph *(a)* (i), (ii) or (iii) above, save that where the loss, damage, liability or expense was caused by a matter referred to in paragraph *(a)* (iii) the Merchant shall not be liable to indemnify the Carrier in respect thereof unless both the provisions referred to in that paragraph apply.

7. INSPECTION OF GOODS

The Carrier or any person to whom the Carrier has sub-contracted the Carriage or any person authorised by the Carrier shall be entitled, but under no obligation, to open any Container or package at any time and to inspect the Goods.

8. CARRIAGE AFFECTED BY CONDITION OF GOODS

If it appears at any time that the Goods or any part thereof cannot safely or properly be carried or carried further, either at all or without incurring any additional expense or taking any measure(s) in relation to the Container or the Goods or any part thereof, the Carrier may without notice to the Merchant take any measure(s) and/or incur any reasonable additional expense to carry or to continue the Carriage thereof, and/or abandon the Carriage and/or store the same ashore or afloat under cover or in the open, at any place, which abandonment or storage shall be deemed to constitute due delivery under this Bill of Lading. The Merchant shall indemnify the Carrier against any reasonable additional expense so incurred.

9. DESCRIPTION OF GOODS

(1) This Bill of Lading shall be *prima facie* evidence of the receipt by the Carrier in apparent good order and condition, except as otherwise noted, of the total number of Containers, packages or other units or weight of other cargoes specified on the face hereof. Proof to the contrary shall not be admissible when this Bill of Lading has been transferred to a third party acting in good faith.

(2) Except as provided in sub-clause 9 (1) above, no representation is made by the Carrier as to the weight, contents, measure, quantity, quality, description, conditions, marks, numbers or value of Goods and the Carrier shall be under no responsibility whatsoever in respect of such description or particulars.

10. SHIPPER'S RESPONSIBILITY

(1) The Shipper warrants to the Carrier that the particulars relating to the Goods as set out overleaf have been checked by the Shipper on receipt of this Bill of Lading and that such particulars and any other particulars furnished by or on behalf of the Shipper are correct.

(2) The Shipper shall indemnify the Carrier against all loss, damage, fines and expenses arising or resulting from inaccuracies in or inadequacy of such particulars or from any other cause in connection with the Goods for which the Carrier is not responsible.

11 FREIGHT AND CHARGES

(1) Freight shall be deemed fully earned on receipt of the goods by the Carrier and shall be paid and non returnable in any event.

(2) The Merchant's attention is drawn to the stipulations concerning currency in which the freight is to be paid, rate of exchange, devaluation and other contingencies relative to freight in the applicable Tariff.

(3) The freight has been calculated on the basis of particulars furnished by or on behalf of the Shipper. The Carrier may at any time open any container or other package or unit in order to reweigh, remeasure or revalue the contents and if the particulars furnished by or on behalf of the Shipper are incorrect, it is agreed that a sum equal to either five times the difference between the correct freight and the freight charged or to double the correct freight less the freight charged, whichever sum is the smaller shall be payable as liquidated damages to the Carrier.

(4) Except as may be provided to the contrary in the applicable Tariff all unpaid charges shall be paid without any set off, counter claim, deduction or stay of execution.

(5) Freight and liquidation damages under sub-clause (11.3) above may be recovered by the Carrier from any person falling within the definition of Merchant in Clause 1 whether or not such person is the Shipper.

12 LIEN

The Carrier shall have a Lien on Goods and any documents relating thereto for all sums payable to the Carrier under this Contract and for general average contributions to whomsoever due and for the cost of recovering the same and for that purpose shall have the right to sell the Goods by public auction or private treaty without notice to the Merchant. Nothing in this clause shall prevent the Carrier from recovering from the Shipper, Consignee or Owner of the Goods the difference between the amount due from them or any of them to him and the amount retained by the exercise of the rights given to the Carrier under this Clause.

13. OPTIONAL STOWAGE

(1) The Goods may be stowed in poop, forecastle, deck house, shelter deck, passenger space, bunker space or any covered-in space commonly used in the trade for the carriage of goods.

(2) The Goods may be stowed by the Carrier in Containers.

(3) Goods stowed in Containers other than flats or pallets whether by the Carrier or the Merchant, may be carried on deck or under deck without notice to the Merchant. Such Goods (other than livestock) whether carried on deck or under deck shall participate in general average and shall be deemed to be within the definition of goods for the purposes of the Hague Rules (or where the Hague Visby Rules would be applicable to the Carriage under the provisions of Clause 5 (Carrier's Responsibility) hereof, for the purposes of the Hague Visby Rules).

14. DECK CARGO [AND LIVESTOCK]

[(1)] Goods (not being Goods stowed in Containers other than flats or pallets) which are stated herein to be carried on deck [and livestock, whether or not carried on deck] are carried without responsibility on the part of the Carrier for loss or damage of whatsoever nature arising during Carriage by sea whether caused by unseaworthiness or negligence or any other cause whatsoever.

[(2)] Livestock are carried at the sole risk of the Merchant. The Carrier shall be under no liability whatsoever for any injury, illness, death, delay or destruction howsoever arising even though caused or contributed to by the act, neglect or default of the Carrier or by the unseaworthiness or unfitness of any vessel, craft, conveyance, Container or other place existing at any time. In the event of the Master, in his sole discretion, [illegible] that any livestock is likely to be injurious to the health of any other [illegible] of any person on board or to cause the vessel to be delayed or [illegible] prosecution of the voyage such livestock may be destroyed and thrown overboard without any liability attaching to the Carrier. The Merchant shall indemnify the Carrier against all and any extra costs incurred for any reason whatsoever in connection with carriage of such livestock.]

15. METHODS AND ROUTE OF TRANSPORTATION

(1) The Carrier may at any time and without notice to the Merchant:—

(a) use any means of transport or storage whatsoever;

(b) transfer the Goods from one conveyance to another including transhipping or carrying the same on another vessel than that named on the face hereof or by any other means of transport whatsoever;

(c) unpack and remove Goods which have been stowed into a Container and forward the same in a Container or otherwise;

(d) proceed by any route in his discretion (whether or not the nearest or most direct or customary or advertised route) and proceed to or stay at any place or port whatsoever once or more often and in any order;

(e) load or unload the Goods at any place or port (whether or not any such port is named overleaf as the Port of Loading or Port of Discharge) and store the Goods at any such place or port;

(f) comply with any orders or recommendations given by any government or authority or any person or body acting or purporting to act as or on behalf of such government or authority or having under the terms of the insurance on the conveyance employed by the Carrier the right to give orders or directions;

(g) permit the vessel to proceed with or without pilots.

(2) The liberties set out in sub-clause (1) may be invoked by the Carrier for any purposes whatsoever whether or not connected with the Carriage of the Goods including undergoing repairs, towing or being towed, adjusting instruments, dry docking and assisting vessels in all situations. Anything done in accordance with sub-clause (1) or any delay arising therefrom shall be deemed to be within the contractual carriage and shall not be a deviation.

(3) By tendering Goods for Carriage without any written request for Carriage in a specialised Container or for Carriage otherwise than in a Container the Merchant accepts that the Carriage may properly be undertaken in a general purpose Container.

16. MATTERS AFFECTING PERFORMANCE

If at any time the Carriage is or is likely to be affected by any hindrance, risk, delay, difficulty or disadvantage of any kind (other than the inability of the Goods or any part thereof safely or properly to be carried or carried further) and howsoever arising (even though the circumstances giving rise to such hindrance, risk, delay, difficulty or disadvantage existed at the time this contract was entered into or the Goods were accepted for Carriage) and which cannot be avoided by the exercise of reasonable endeavours the Carrier (whether or not the Carriage is commenced) may either:—

(a) Without notice to the Merchant abandon the Carriage of the Goods and place the Goods or any part of them at the Merchant's disposal at any place or port which the Carrier may deem safe and convenient, whereupon the responsibility of the Carrier in respect of such Goods shall cease. The Carrier shall nevertheless be entitled to full Freight on Goods received for Carriage, and the Merchant shall pay any additional costs of Carriage to and delivery and storage at such place or port; or

(b) without prejudice to the Carrier's right subsequently to abandon the Carriage under *(a)*, upon notice to the Merchant suspend Carriage of the Goods or any part of them and store them ashore or afloat upon the terms of this Bill of Lading, against payment of such reasonable additional charges as the Carrier may determine. The Carrier undertakes to use best endeavours to forward Goods, the Carriage of which has been suspended, as soon as possible after the cause of hindrance, risk, delay, difficulty or disadvantage has been removed but makes no representations as to the maximum period between such removal and the forwarding of the Goods to the Place of Delivery named in the Bill of Lading.

17. DANGEROUS GOODS

(1) No goods which are or may become dangerous, inflammable or damaging (including radio-active materials), or which are or may become liable to damage any property whatsoever, shall be tendered to the Carrier for Carriage without his express consent in writing and without the Container or other covering in which the goods are to be transported and the goods being distinctly marked on the outside so as to indicate the nature and character of any such articles and so as to comply with any applicable laws, regulations or requirements. If any such articles are delivered to the Carrier without such written consent and marking or if in the opinion of the Carrier the articles are or are liable to become of a dangerous, inflammable or damaging nature, the same may at any time be destroyed, disposed of, abandoned, or rendered harmless without compensation to the Merchant and without prejudice to the Carrier's right to Freight.

(2) The Merchant undertakes that the Goods are packed in a manner adequate to withstand the ordinary risks of Carriage having regard to their nature and in compliance with all laws or regulations which may be applicable during Carriage.

(3) Whether or not the Merchant was aware of the nature of the goods the Merchant shall indemnify the Carrier against all claims, losses, damages or expenses arising in consequence of any breach of the provisions of this Clause.

(4) Nothing contained in this Clause shall deprive the Carrier of any of his rights otherwise provided for.

18. REGULATIONS RELATING TO GOODS

The Merchant shall comply with all regulations or requirements of customs, port and other authorities and shall bear and pay all duties, taxes, fines, imposts, expenses or losses incurred or suffered by reason thereof or by reason of any illegal, incorrect or insufficient marking, numbering or addressing of the Goods, and shall indemnify the Carrier in respect thereof.

19. NOTIFICATION AND DELIVERY

(1) Any mention herein of parties to be notified of the arrival of the Goods is solely for information of the Carrier, and failure to give such notification shall not involve the Carrier in any liability nor relieve the Merchant of any obligation hereunder.

(2) Where the Carriage called for by this Bill of Lading is a Port to Port Shipment the Carrier shall be at liberty to discharge the Goods or any part thereof without notice directly they come to hand at or on to any wharf, craft or place, on any day and at any time, whereupon the liability of the Carrier (if any) in respect of the Goods or that part thereof discharged as aforesaid shall wholly cease notwithstanding any custom of the port to the contrary and notwithstanding that any charges, dues or other expenses may be or become payable. If craft are used, other than at the request of the Merchant, in circumstances where the Goods or that part thereof so discharged could have been discharged ashore without additional delay, the Goods (or that part thereof, as the case may be) shall nevertheless not be deemed to be discharged for the purposes of this Clause and of Clause 5 until they are discharged from such craft. The Merchant shall take delivery of the Goods upon discharge. All expenses incurred by reason of the Merchant's failure to take delivery of the Goods as aforesaid shall be for the Merchant's account.

(3) Where the Carriage called for by this Bill of Lading is Combined Transport, the Merchant shall take delivery of the Goods within the time provided for in the Carrier's applicable Tariff (see Clause 2).

(4) If delivery of the Goods or any part thereof is not taken by the Merchant at the time and place when and where the Carrier is entitled to call upon the Merchant to take delivery thereof, whether the carriage called for by this Bill of Lading is a Port to Port Shipment or Combined Transport, the Carrier shall be entitled without notice to unstow the Goods or that part thereof if stowed in Containers and/or to store the Goods or that part thereof ashore, afloat, in the open or under cover at the sole risk of the Merchant. Such storage shall constitute due delivery hereunder, and thereupon the liability of the Carrier in respect of the Goods or that part thereof stored as aforesaid (as the case may be) shall wholly cease and the cost of such storage (if paid or payable by the Carrier or any agent or subcontractor of the Carrier) shall forthwith upon demand be paid by the Merchant to the Carrier.

(5) If the Merchant fails to take delivery of the Goods within thirty days of its becoming due under sub-clause (2) or (3) above or if in the opinion of the Carrier they are likely to deteriorate, decay, become worthless or incur charges whether for storage or otherwise in excess of their value, and whether the Carriage is a Port to Port Shipment or Combined Transport, the Carrier may, without prejudice to any other right which he may have against the Merchant, without notice and without any responsibility whatsoever attaching to him, sell or dispose of the Goods and apply the proceeds of sale in reduction of the sums due to the Carrier from the Merchant in respect of this Bill of Lading.

20. BOTH-TO-BLAME COLLISION

If the (carrying) ship comes into collision with another ship as a result of the negligence of the other ship and any act, neglect or default in the navigation or the management of the carrying ship, the Merchant undertakes to pay the Carrier, or, where the Carrier is not the owner and in possession of the carrying ship, to pay to the Carrier as trustee for the owner and/or demise charterer of the carrying ship, a sum sufficient to indemnify the Carrier and/or the owner and/or demise charterer of the carrying ship against all loss or liability to the other or non-carrying ship or her owners insofar as such loss or liability represents loss of or damage to, or any claim whatsoever of the Merchant, paid or payable by the other or non-carrying ship or her owners to the Merchant and set-off, recouped or recovered by the other or non-carrying ship or her owners as part of their claim against the carrying ship or her owner or demise charterer of the Carrier. The foregoing provisions shall also apply where the owners, operators, or those in charge of any ship or ships or objects, other than, or in addition to the colliding ships or objects, are at fault in respect to a collision, contact, stranding or other accident.

21 GENERAL AVERAGE

General Average shall be adjusted according to York Antwerp Rules 1974 save and except that no loss of or injury sustained by live animals whether by jettison or otherwise shall be recoverable. Adjustments shall be prepared at such port as shall be selected by the Carrier supplemented by the practice of English Average Adjusters on all points on which such Rules contain no provision. [illegible] Carrier, salvage shall be paid for as fully as if the [illegible] vessel or vessels belonged to strangers. Such [illegible] his Agents may deem sufficient to cover the estimated contribution of the [illegible] and any salvage and special charges thereon shall, if required, be made by the [illegible] Shippers, Consignees or Owners of the Goods to the Carrier before delivery. [illegible] adjustment is made in accordance with the law and practice of the United States of America [illegible] following clauses shall apply.

New Jason Clause: (a) In the event of accident, danger, damage or disaster before or after the commencement of the voyage resulting from any cause whatsoever, whether due to negligence or not, for which, or for the consequence of which, the Carrier is not responsible by statute, contract or otherwise, the Goods, Shippers, Consignees or Owners of the Goods shall contribute with the Carrier in general average to the payment of any sacrifices, losses or expenses of a general average nature that may be made or incurred and shall pay salvage and special charges incurred in respect of the Goods.

[illegible] vessel is owned or operated by the Carrier, salvage shall be paid for as fully as if the said salving vessel or vessels belonged to strangers. Such deposit as the Carrier or his Agents may deem sufficient to cover the estimated contribution of the Goods and any salvage and special charges thereon shall, if required, be made by the Goods, Shippers, Consignees or Owners of the Goods to the Carrier before delivery.

23 LAW AND JURISDICTION

Any claim or dispute arising under this Bill of Lading shall be determined by the courts of the country where the Carrier has its principal place of business and according to the law of those courts.

Shipper SITPRO Export Limited High Street Burton on Trent, DE15 1YS England VAT No. 241 8235 77	NON-NEGOTIABLE SEA WAYBILL Shipper's Reference 862 - 12381 CD F/Agent's Reference 12479

Consignee

Laboratorios Frankenstein S.A.
Rua Primera 1
Caracas, Venezuela

Name of Carrier

Lennon Line Limited

Notify Party and Address (leave blank if stated above)

The contract evidenced by this Waybill is subject to the exceptions, limitations, conditions and liberties (including those relating to the storage and stowage) set out in the Carrier's Standard Conditions of Carriage applicable to the voyage covered by this Waybill and operative on the date of issue. If the carriage is one where no Bill of Lading been issued the provisions of the Hague Rules contained in the International Convention for unification of certain rules relating to Bills of Lading dated Brussels 25th August 1924 as amended by the Protocol signed at Brussels on the 23rd February 1968 (the Hague Visby Rules) would have been compulsorily applicable under Article X, the said Standard Conditions contain or shall be deemed to contain a Clause giving effect to the Hague Visby Rules. Otherwise the said Standard Conditions contain or shall be deemed to contain a Clause giving effect to the provisions of the Hague Rules. In neither case shall the proviso to the first sentence of Article X of the Hague Rules or the Hague Visby Rules apply. The Carrier hereby agrees (i) that to the extent of any inconsistency the said clause shall prevail over the said Standard Conditions in respect of any period so which the Hague Rules or the Hague Visby Rules by their terms apply, and (ii) that for the purpose of the terms of this Contract of Carriage this Waybill falls within the definition of Article 1(b) of the Hague Rules and the Hague Visby Rules.
The Shipper accepts the said Standard Conditions on his own behalf and on behalf of the Consignee and the owner of the goods and warrants that he has authority to do so. The Consignee by presenting this Waybill and/or requesting delivery of the goods further undertakes all liabilities of the Shipper hereunder, such undertaking being additional and without prejudice to the Shipper's own liability. The benefit of the contract, evidenced by this Waybill shall thereby be transferred to the Consignee or other persons presenting this Waybill.
Notwithstanding anything contained in the said Standard Conditions, the term Carrier in this Waybill shall mean the Carrier named on the front thereof.
A copy of the Carrier's said Standard Conditions applicable hereto may be inspected or will be supplied on request at the office of the Carrier or the Carrier's Principal Agents.

Pre-Carriage by*	Place of Receipt by Pre-Carrier*
Lennon Vehicle	Burton-on-Trent
Vessel	Port of Loading
Voyager	Liverpool
Port of Discharge	Place of Delivery by On-Carrier*
La Guaira	Caracas

Marks and Nos. Container No.	Number and kind of packages; Description of Goods	Gross Weight	Measurement
FRANKENSTEIN ED1814 CARACAS VIA LA GUAIRA	2 Cartons Ethical Pharmaceuticals (Non-dangerous) Productos farmaceuticos I/L 80/9999999	160 kg	0.250 m3

(These **invoice** details can be masked out of
shipping documents (see SITPRO Overlay for C273(1)).

123456	Pocion:	Gutrot potion, 100ml bottles
234567	Calcetinos:	Athletes foot socks
345678	Ampullas:	Airfilled ampoules, 25cc
456789	Grasa:	Elbow Grease, 250G tins
678901	Pros. Electricos:	Monster Electrodes, pairs
789012	Azadas:	Exhuming spades
890123	Pros. Adhesivos:	"Joincorpse" patent glue
901234	Martillos:	Hammers to start migraine
012345	Tabletas:	"Costalot" Migraine relief tablets

Freight to Caracas (flete)
Insurance (seguro)

Freight Details; Charges etc.

RECEIVED FOR CARRIAGE as above in apparent good order and condition, unless otherwise stated hereon, the goods described in the above particulars.

Ocean Freight Payable at	Place and Date of Issue
Origin	
	Signature for Carrier; Carrier's Principal Place of Business

GCBS
SV.3
1979

711

Authorised and Licensed by the
General Council of British Shipping © 1979

SITPRO OVERLAYS 1982

Reproduced by kind permission of the General Council of British Shipping.

INCORPORATION CLAUSE FOR THE SEA WAYBILL

1 "Received for carriage as above in apparent good order
2 and condition, unless otherwise stated hereon, the
3 goods described in the above particulars. The contract
4 evidenced by this Waybill is subject to the exceptions,
5 limitations, conditions and liberties (including those
6 relating to pre-carriage and on-carriage) set out in
7 the Carrier's Standard Conditions of Carriage applicable
8 to the voyage covered by this Waybill and operative on
9 its date of issue; if the carriage is one where had a
10 Bill of Lading been issued the provisions of the Hague
11 Rules contained in the International Convention for
12 unification of certain rules relating to Bills of Lading
13 dated Brussels, 25th August 1924 as amended by the
14 Protocol signed at Brussels on the 23rd February 1968
15 (The Hague Visby Rules) would have been compulsorily
16 applicable under Article X, the said Standard Conditions
17 contained or shall be deemed to contain a Clause giving
18 effect to the Hague Visby Rules. Otherwise the said
19 Standard Conditions contain or shall be deemed to contain
20 a Clause giving effect to the provisions of the Hague
21 Rules. In neither case shall this proviso be the first
22 sentence of Article V of the Hague Rules or the Hague
23 Visby Rules apply. The carrier hereby agrees: (i) that
24 to the extent of any inconsistency the said Clause shall
25 prevail over the said Standard Conditions in respect of
26 any period to which the Hague Rules or the Hague Visby
27 Rules by their terms apply, and (ii) that for the purpose
28 of the terms of this Contract of Carriage this Waybill
29 falls within the definition of Article 1(b) of the Hague
30 Rules and the Hague Visby Rules.

31 The Shipper accepts the said Standard Conditions on his
32 own behalf and on behalf of the Consignee and the owner
33 of the goods and warrants that he has authority to do
34 so. The Consignee by presenting this Waybill and/or
35 requesting delivery of the goods further undertakes all
36 liabilities of the Shipper hereunder, such undertaking
37 being additional and without prejudice to the Shipper's
38 own liability. The benefits of the contract evidenced
39 by this Waybill shall thereby be transferred to the
40 Consignee or other persons presenting this Waybill.

41 Notwithstanding anything contained in the said Standard
42 Conditions, the term Carrier in this Waybill shall mean
43 the Carrier named on the front thereof.
44 A copy of the Carrier's Standard Conditions of Carriage
45 Applicable hereto may be inspected or will be supplied
46 on request at the office of the Carrier or the Carrier's
47 Principal Agents."

Air Waybill

777-1234 5675				777-1234 5675

Airport of Departure	Execution date Day/Mth/Year	TC	CHGS Code	Cur'cy Code	for carrier use only		
LGW	80.09 12	x	x	x	Flight/Day	Flight/Day	

Airport of departure (address of first carrier) and requested routing	Airport of Destination	Flight/Day	Flight/Day
London Gatwick	CAPACAS	BR675/12	
			Booked

1 Routing and Destination
To CCS | by first carrier BR | to | by | to | by

Not negotiable

Air Waybill
(Air Consignment note)
Issued by
(PRINT NAME OF ISSUING CARRIER HERE)
(Print address of issuing carrier here)

AIRLINE SYMBOL
Member of International
Air Transport Association

2 Consignee's account number | Consignee's name and address

BRITISH INTERNATIONAL BANK LTD
(para la cuenta de Labos.Frankenstein SA)
Box 9999, Caracas
TELEPHONE 12 34 56

Copies 1, 2 and 3 of this Air Waybill are originals and have the same validity

It is agreed that the goods described herein are accepted in apparent good order and condition (except as noted) for carriage SUBJECT TO THE CONDITIONS OF CONTRACT ON THE REVERSE HEREOF. THE SHIPPER'S ATTENTION IS DRAWN TO THE NOTICE CONCERNING CARRIERS' LIMITATION OF LIABILITY. Shipper may increase such limitation of liability by declaring a higher value for carriage and paying a supplemental charge if required.
Carrier is not liable for the goods until they are received at its town terminal or airport office.

3 Shipper's account number | Shipper's name and address

SITPRO EXPORT LTD
High St
Burton on Trent
Staffs DE15 1YZ

Shipper certifies that the particulars on the face hereof are correct and that insofar as any part of the consignment contains restricted articles, such part is properly described by name and is in proper condition for carriage by air according to the International Air Transport Association's Restricted Articles Regulations.

Signature of Shipper or his Agent

J. Martin-Smith

4 Issuing carrier's agent, account no. 123456 | Issuing carrier's agent, name and city

BURTON FORWARDING LTD, GATWICK

Agent's IATA Code
999999

Signature of Issuing Carrier or its Agent

J. Martin-Smith

Date 12 Sep 80   Place LGW

5

Currency	Declared value for carriage		Declared value for customs	Amount of insurance	INSURANCE—If shipper requests insurance in accordance with conditions on reverse hereof, indicate amount to be insured in figures in box marked amount of insurance
GBP	NVD		720	NVD	

WEIGHT CHARGE AND VALUATION CHARGE		ALL OTHER CHARGES AT ORIGIN		Accounting information
PREPAID	COLLECT	PREPAID	COLLECT	
X		X		

6

No of packages RCP	Actual gross weight	kg lb	Rate class Commodity item no.	Chargeable weight	Rate/Charge	Total	Nature and quantity of goods (incl. dimensions or volume)
2	160	k		150	1.00	160.00	2 cartons Ethical Pharmaceuticals (Non-dangerous) Productos farmaceuticos I/L 80/9999999 0.250 m3

prepaid 7

Prepaid weight charge	Prepaid valuation charge	Due carrier	Total other prepaid charges	Due agent	Total prepaid	For carrier's use only at destination
160.00				5.00	165.00	

R Other charges (except weight charge and valuation charge) | Collect charges in destination currency

S | COD amount

T | Total charges

collect 8

Collect weight charge	Collect val. charge	Due carrier	Total other collect charges	Due agent	COD amount	Total collect

9 Handling information

Reproduced with the kind permission of Midland Bank Ltd.

© SITPRO 1981

STANDARD SHIPPING NOTE

IMPORTANT. USE THE DANGEROUS GOODS NOTE IF THE GOODS ARE CLASSIFIED AS DANGEROUS ACCORDING TO APPLICABLE REGULATIONS SEE BOX 10A	Exporter	1	Veh. Bkg Ref.	2	Customs Reference Status	3

Exporter [1]
SITPRO Export Ltd
High Street
Burton on Trent DE15 1YZ
England

Veh. Bkg Ref. [2]

Customs Reference Status [3]
PRE-ENTRY (C273)

Exporter's Reference [4]
036-12345-24

[X] Exporter / Freight Forwarder / Other (Name and Address) — Port Charges Payable by* [5]

Fd's Ref. [6]

SS Co Bkg. No. [7]
SYD427-05

Name of Shipping Line or CTO [8]
Transworld Containers Ltd

Port Account No.

Freight Forwarder [9]
SITPRO Export Ltd
High Street
Burton on Trent DE15 1YZ

For use of Receiving Authority Only

Receiving Date(s) / Berth/Dock/Containerbase etc. [10]
Collect 6 Oct 81   Birmingham C Base

[10A] The Company preparing this note declares that the goods have been accurately described, their quantities, weights and measurements are correct and at the time of despatch they were in good order and condition; that the goods are not classified as dangerous in any UK, IMCO, ADR, RID or IATA/ICAO regulation applicable to the intended modes of transport.

Vessel / Port of Loading [11]
Bebington   London

TO THE RECEIVING AUTHORITY — Please receive for shipment the goods described below subject to your published regulations & conditions (incl. those as to liability).

Port of Discharge / Destination Depot [12]
Sydney   Sydney

Name of Receiving Authority [13]
Containers Ltd

Marks & Numbers; No. & Kind of Packages, Description of goods	[14] Receiving Authority Use	Gross Wt (kg) of goods [15]	Cube (m³) of goods [16]
ED1814 1/16	1 x 20 ft container holding 16 cases machine tools automatic lathes		18000	17.920

SPECIAL STOWAGE * [17]	For use of shipping company only	Total Gross weight of goods	Total Cube of goods
		18000	17.920

PREFIX & Container/Trailer Number(s) [18]	Seal Number(s)	Container/Trailer Size(s) & Type(s) [19A]	[18B] Tare wt (kg) as marked on contr.	[18C] Wt of container and goods (kg) [18D]
AEXU 2128835	GH20540	1 x 20ft	1845	19845

Received the above number of packages/containers/trailers in apparent good order and condition unless stated hereon.
RECEIVING AUTHORITY REMARKS

Haulier's Name

Vehicle Reg. No.

DRIVER'S SIGNATURE | SIGNATURE AND DATE

Name of Company preparing this Note [19]
SITPRO Export Ltd
0283-41835
H J Helliar Chief Clerk

Date
Burton 5 Oct 1981

DANGEROUS GOODS NOTE

DG

& CONTAINER/VEHICLE PACKING CERTIFICATE
© SITPRO 1982

Special
Information
is required
for (a)
Dangerous
Goods in
Limited
Quantities
(b)
Radioactive
Substances
(class 7)
(c) Tank
Containers
and
(d) In certain
circumstances
a weathering
certificate
is required

SHADED
AREAS
NEED NOT
BE SHIPPER
COMPLETED
FOR SHORT
SEA, RO. RO/
RAIL

Exporter	1	Veh. Bkg. Ref.	2	Customs Reference/Status	3
SITPRO Export Limited High Street Burton-on-Trent DE15 1YZ England		6-002		PRE-ENTRY C273	

Exporter's Reference 4
036-123456-24

Exporter Freight Forwarder	Port Charges 5 Payable by*	Fwdr's Ref. 6	SS Co Bkg No. 7
Other (Name & Address) 8A			SYD429-05

Consignee	Name of Shipping Line or CTO	8	Port Account No.
SITPRO Australia (Pty) Limited P O Box 102 Sydney Cove NSW 2000, Australia	Transworld Containers Limited		

Freight Forwarder	9	For Use of Receiving Authority Only
SITPRO Export Limited High Street Burton-on-Trent DE15 1YZ		

Receiving Date(s)	Berth/Dock/Containerbase etc	10
TWC Vehicle		

Consecutive no. or DG reference allocated by shipping line or C.T.O. 10A
(if any)

Vessel	Port of Loading	11
Bebington	London	

TO THE RECEIVING AUTHORITY
Please receive for shipment the goods described below subject to your published regulations & conditions (including those as to liability)

Port of Discharge	Destination Depot	12
Sydney	Sydney	

Name of Receiving Authority 13
Containers Limited

SHADED
AREAS (black circle)

Marks & Numbers; No. & Kind of Packages; Description of goods.† 14 INDICATE: HAZARD CLASS, UN NUMBER, FLASHPOINT °C.	Receiving Authority Use	Gross Wt(kg) 15 of goods	Cube (m³) 16 of goods
SITPRO ED1814 SYDNEY 1/200	1 x 20ft container holding 200 x 50kg net polythene lined steel drums ANTIMONY TRICHLORIDE Class 8 UN No. 1733		1) 10540 kg 2) 7650 kg	13.180 m³ 9.6 m³
201/500	300 x 25kg polythene drums HYDROFLUORIC ACID SOLUTION 50% w/w Class 8 UN No. 1790			

Net Wt(kg) 16A of goods
1) 10000
2) 7500

IN BLACK AND WHITE FOR PHOTOCOPYING
CONVENIENCE.

MUST BE
COMPLETED
FOR FULL
CONTAINER/
VEHICLE
LOADS:—

†CORRECT TECHNICAL NAME, PROPRIETARY NAMES ALONE ARE NOT SUFFICIENT.

CONTAINER/VEHICLE PACKING CERTIFICATE 17 It is declared that the packing of the container has been carried out in accordance with the provisions shown overleaf —	DANGEROUS GOODS DECLARATION I hereby declare that the contents of this consignment are fully and accurately described above by the correct technical name, is correctly marked / numbered, that the shipment is packaged in such a manner as to withstand the ordinary risks of handling and transport by sea, having regard to the proper stow of goods to be carried, and that the quality is classified, packaged, marked and labelled in accordance with the requirements of the Merchant Shipping (Dangerous Goods) Regulations 1981 as currently amended. I further declare that if appropriate the goods are classified, packaged and marked to comply with the requirements of the European Agreement concerning the International Carriage of Dangerous Goods by Road, with and of Annex I-IRD to the International Convention concerning the Carriage of Goods by Rail (CIM) or special arrangements made between the contracting parties to these Agreements	Total Gross weight of goods	Total Cube of goods
Name of Company SITPRO EXPORT LIMITED Signature 9. Parker of person responsible for packing container Date 9/10/81	The shipper must complete and sign box 19	18190kg	22.780m³

Prefix & Container/Vehicle Number 18	Seal Number(s)	Container Vehicle Size & Type 18A	18B Tare wt (kg) as marked on container	Total Net and goods
ABCU 2128835	GH 20540	1 x 20ft	1724	19914

Received the above number of packages, containers, trailers in apparent good order and condition unless stated hereon.
RECEIVING AUTHORITY REMARKS

Haulier's Name

Vehicle Reg No

DRIVER'S SIGNATURE | SIGNATURE & DATE

Name of Shipper preparing this note & tel no
SITPRO Export Ltd 0283 41835
NAME/STATUS OF DECLARANT

H J Helliar, Chief Clerk
DATE

Burton 6 Oct 1981
Signature of declarant
H J Helliar

Reverse of Dangerous Goods Note

CONTAINER/VEHICLE PACKING CERTIFICATE (see box 17 overleaf)

It is certified that:-

1   The container/vehicle was clean, dry and appeared fit to receive the goods.

2   No incompatible substances have been packed within the freight container/ vehicle except where this is permitted by the Merchant Shipping (Dangerous Goods) Regulations 1981 as currently amended.

3   Where packages or receptacles have been packed into a container/vehicle they were in sound condition.

4   All packages have been properly stowed and secured and where necessary suitable securing materials used.

5   The packages are clearly marked with a distinctive label or stencil of the label and the container/vehicle is clearly marked with labels to indicate the nature of the danger to which the goods give rise. Where the vehicle is a road tank vehicle or the goods are contained in a portable tank or tank container the label or marking shall in addition indicate the correct technical name of the goods.

6   The Dangerous Goods in this container/vehicle are those accepted by the carrier against the reference as identified in box 7 overleaf.

7   Where this Dangerous Goods Note is used as a Container/Vehicle Packing Certificate only, not a combined document, a Dangerous Goods Declaration signed by the shipper or supplier has been issued/received to cover each dangerous goods consignment packed in the container.

8   Where the dangerous Goods Note applies to a road tank vehicle, or tank container, closures and valves have been properly closed and the correct ullage space left.

THE SIGNATURE GIVEN OVERLEAF IN BOX 17 MUST BE THAT OF THE PERSON CONTROLLING THE LOADING OPERATION, AFTER THE CONTAINER/VEHICLE HAS BEEN PACKED AND IS TO BE GIVEN TO THE DRIVER ON COLECTION OR PRESENTED TO THE CONTAINER/VEHICLE OPERATOR ON DELIVERY OF THE CONTAINER/VEHICLE.

DECLARATION

The company preparing this note declares that the quantities, weights and measurements of the goods are correct, and at the time of despatch the goods were in good order and condition.

© SITPRO 1976 EXAMPLE

EXPORT CONSIGNMENT NOTE

Exporter/Shipper (Name and Address)	[1] Vehicle Bkg Ref	[2] CAN/Pre-Entry No./Other Customs Ref.
SITPRO EXPORT LIMITED HIGH STREET BURTON ON TRENT STAFFS., DE15 1YZ, ENGLAND	0415	99999 (108 v)

Exporter's Ref.
364/B205/190

Port-Handling charges to be paid by *	F/Agent's Ref.	S.S. Co. Bkg. No.
☐ Exporter ☐ Agent	IR76-4740	BU64
Other (Name and Address)		

Name of Shipping Line or CTO (if required)	[6] Port Account N
	12742

Forwarding Agent/Merchant (Name and Address) [7]

Burton Forwarding Ltd.
210 Station St.
Burton on Trent, Staffs., DE15 4ZY

Receiving Date(s)	Berth & Dock/Container base Etc. [8]
4 - 9 Nov 76	SE3 Canada Dock

Ship	Port of Loading [9]
Bebington	Liverpool

TO THE HAULIER/CARRIER

Please Receive/Collect, for delivery as indicated, the goods described below, subject to your published Regulations and Conditions (including those as to liability.)

Port of Discharge	Destination Depot (LCL only) [10]	Name of Receiving Authority (if required):—
Bushire	Shiraz	British Line

[12] Marks and Numbers; No. and Kind of Packages; Description of Goods; Nature of Hazard (if any) ** Pack. dimensions in cm (if required) [13] Gross Weight (Kg) [14] Cube (M³)

Marks/Numbers; Description	Gross Weight (Kg)	Cube (M³)
SITPRO ED1814A SHIRAZ VIA BUSHIRE Nos. 1-3	3 Cases: Refills for ballpoint pens (Cat. no. 43-746)	1) 186	0.126
		2) 213	0.369
SITPRO ED1814B SHIRAZ VIA BUSHIRE No. 4	1 Case: Electronic duplicator stencils (Cat. no. 42-648)	3) 26	0.042
		4) 67 kg	0.175
SITPRO ED1814C SHIRAZ VIA BUSHIRE No. 5	1 Carton: Self-adhesive labels size 70mm x 50mm boxed in packs of 1000 (Cat. no. 40-070)		
SITPRO ED1814D SHIRAZ VIA BUSHIRE No. 6	1 Case: Self-inking hand operated rubber date stamps (Cat. no. 44-101)		

Cargo Status*	X	Customs Free Status	Special Stowage [16]		Total Gross Wt.	Total Cube
		Customs Pre-Entry			492	0.712

Note: For Dangerous Goods, Indicate the
Correct Technical Name
IMCO Class
UN Number
Flashpoint (if applicable) in °C.

To be completed by Haulier/Carrier

Carrier.....................................Vehicle Reg. No....................

Number of Packages Received ....

Condition ....

Signature and Date

343   *Mark 'X' as appropriate.

Name of Company preparing this Note
Sitpro Export Ltd/0283-41835
H J Helliar, Chief Clerk
Date
Burton, 1 November 1976
(Indicate Name and Telephone No. of Contact).

© SITPRO 1976 Example (Approved by IFF)

EXPORT CARGO SHIPPING INSTRUCTIONS

Exporter/Shipper (Name and Address)	Ⓐ For F/Agent's Use	CAN/Pre-Entry No./Other Customs Ref.
SITPRO EXPORT LIMITED HIGH STREET BURTON ON TRENT STAFFS., DE15 1YZ, ENGLAND		99999 (103w) **Exporter's Reference** 364/B205/190 **F/Agent's Ref.** IR76-4740 **S.S. Co. Bkg. No.** BU64

Consignee (If 'Order', state Notify Party and Address)	Ⓑ Other Address	
SITPRO IRAN LTD. Khiaban Takhte Shiraz IRAN	SITPRO IRAN LTD. Avenue Ferdowsi Tehran, IRAN	Ⓓ

TO ▷

Forwarding Agent (Name and Address) Ⓒ	(If required, this space may be used for other addresses, e.g. Buyer, Place of Acceptance/Delivery, additional Notify Party)	
Burton Forwarding Ltd. 210 Station St. Burton on Trent, Staffs., DE15 4ZY	**Country of Origin of Goods** United Kingdom	**Country of Final Destination** Iran

Receiving Date(s)	Berth & Dock/Container base Etc.		Ⓔ
4 - 9 Nov 76	SE3 Canada Dock		
Despatched By	**Place of Acceptance**	(If required, this space may be used for extra addresses or other information)	
Our vehicle			
Vessel/Aircraft etc.	**Port of Loading**	Please insure against all risks plus war	
Bebington	Liverpool		
Port of Discharge	**Place of Delivery**	**for**	(N.B. Insurance will not be effected unless instructed in writing)
Bushire	Shiraz	Stg £2660.00	

Marks and Numbers; No. and Kind of Packages; Description of Goods (Specify Hazard if any*)		Tariff/Trade Code No.	Gross Weight (Kg)	Cube (M³)
SITPRO ED1814A SHIRAZ VIA BUSHIRE Nos. 1-3	3 Cases: Refills for ballpoint pens (Cat. no. 43-746)		1) 186 2) 213	0.126 0.369
			3) 26	0.042
SITPRO ED1814B SHIRAZ VIA BUSHIRE No. 4	1 Case: Electronic duplicator stencils (Cat. no. 42-648)		4) 67 kg	0.175

		Quantity 2 for U.K. Customs	Net Weight	FOB Value for U.K. Customs (£)
SITPRO ED1814C SHIRAZ VIA BUSHIRE No. 5	1 Carton: Self-adhesive labels size 70mm x 50mm boxed in packs of 1000 (Cat. no. 40-070)		1) 154 2) 180	
SITPRO ED1814D SHIRAZ VIA BUSHIRE No. 6	1 Case: Self-inking hand operated rubber date stamps (Cat. no. 44-101)	Quantity 3 for U.K. Customs	3) 24 4) 50 kg	

*NB. DANGEROUS GOODS
Indicate the Correct Technical Name
IMC ass, UN Number, and Flashpoint (if applicable) in °

Cargo Status	X	Customs Free Status		Special Stowage	Charges to FOB Payable by Ⓐ	Invoice Price
		Customs Pre-Entry				£ 2416.68

Please Prepare/ Attend To		Certificate of Shipment	Port/Terminal charges Payable by Ⓐ	Special Instructions
		Air, Ocean or other Waybill		1. See attached Invoice for values and quantities
	X	Bill of Lading	Insurance Payable by Ⓐ	
	X	H.M. Customs Formalities		2. Also Notify Ⓓ
	X	Consular Formalities	Freight/Haulage to BUSHIRE Payable by Ⓐ	
		'T' Forms where appropriate		

These Goods are/are not in Free Circulation within the E.E.C.
Make out documents as indicated and dispose of as follows:

Deliver all documents to Ⓐ By hand

Ocean Freight Payable at Liverpool	Name of Contact and Telephone Number Sitpro Export Ltd/0283-41835
No. of Bills of Lading Required 2 Original 4 Copy	H J Helliar, Chief Clerk
I/We hereby declare that the above particulars are correct and agree to your published Regulations and Conditions, (including those as to Liability)	Date Burton, 1 November 1976 Signature H. J. Helliar

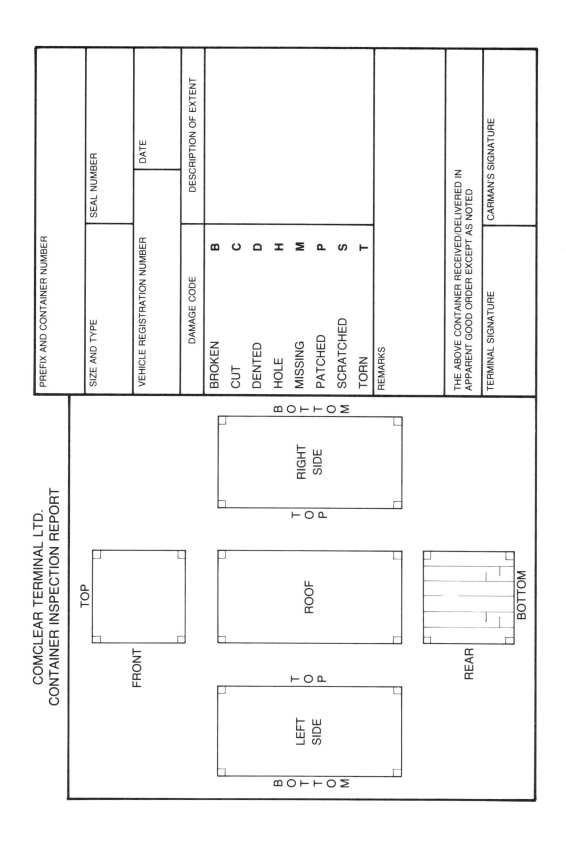

COMCLEAR TERMINAL LTD.
CONTAINER INSPECTION REPORT

PREFIX AND CONTAINER NUMBER

SIZE AND TYPE

SEAL NUMBER

VEHICLE REGISTRATION NUMBER

DATE

DAMAGE CODE

DESCRIPTION OF EXTENT

BROKEN   B
CUT   C
DENTED   D
HOLE   H
MISSING   M
PATCHED   P
SCRATCHED S
TORN   T

REMARKS

THE ABOVE CONTAINER RECEIVED/DELIVERED IN APPARENT GOOD ORDER EXCEPT AS NOTED

TERMINAL SIGNATURE

CARMAN'S SIGNATURE

TOP

FRONT

RIGHT SIDE

ROOF

LEFT SIDE

REAR

BOTTOM

B.S. CHEMICALS LIMITED — Packing/Weight List

B.S. CHEMICALS LIMITED
Prince-Rupert House
P.O. Box No. 163, London, EC4
Telephone No. 01 236 3319
Telex No. 893311 BSGRP
VAT No. 243 1144 06
Registered in England No. 597949

Packing/Weight List.

Invoice No. & Date	Sale Contract No. & Date
BS/1397 7.3.83	BSC52012 22.12.82

Customer Reference
P9412 9.12.82

Customer
East Asiatic Trading Co. Ltd.
(Toa Boeki Kabushiki Kaisha),
2-2-1100, Umeda 1-Chome,
Kitaku, OSAKA, JAPAN

Notify Party (Other Invoice Address)

Licence Number

Country of Origin of Goods	Country of Final Destination
UNITED KINGDOM	JAPAN

Vessel/Aircraft Etc—	Port of Loading
EVER VIGOR	FELIXSTOWE

Port of Discharge	Place of Delivery
OSAKA, JAPAN	OSAKA

Packages Marked	Number & Kind of Packages	TT Code No.	Gross Wt. (Kgs.)	Cube (M³)
T.B.K. OSAKA 9412	EVODE PRODUCTS.		16892	26.72
			Net Wt. (Kgs.) 14887	

PACKING SPECIFICATION

Package Number(s)	Item	Code	Quantity	Measurements (M³)	Net Kilos	Gross Kilos
1–350		RDM 2073 Sealant	350 drums each 1 x 25 kgs	49 x 30 x 30 cms.	8750	9800
351–385		BLACK 505 STD	35 W/cases each 10 x 5 litre	59 x 37 x 32 cms.	1575	1960
386–445		SUPAPROOF BLACK	60 Drums each 1 x 25 litre	49 x 30 x 30 cms	1500	1680
446–515		SUPAPROOF GREY	70 drums each 1 x 25 litre	49 x 30 x 30 cms	1750	1960
516–517		F/BAND ALUM. 50 mm.	2 W/cases each 50x6x50 mm.	94 x 94 x 88 cms.	656	746
518–519		F/BAND GREY 100 mm.	2 W/cases each 50x3x100 mm	94 x 94 x 88 cms.	656	746
				26.72 M3	14,887	16,892

Certificate of Inspection

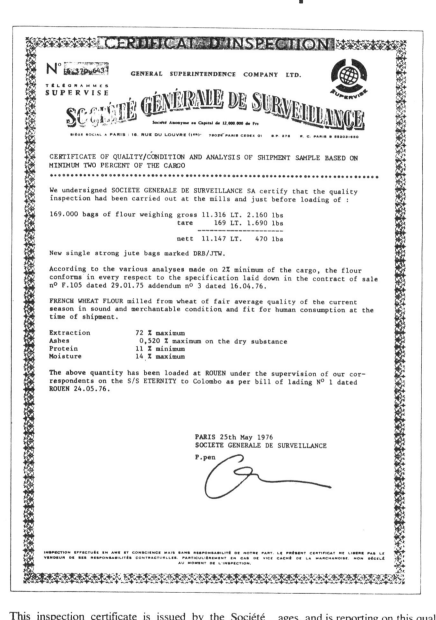

This inspection certificate is issued by the Société Générale de Surveillance.

This body has examined a shipment characterized by its identification marks, weight, and number of packages, and is reporting on this qualitative and analytical examination performed through checking at least two percent of the tonnage.

ACT Services

Head Office:
Associated Container Transportation Services Ltd. Registered Number 1021141 England.
Richmond House, Terminus Terrace, Southampton SO9 1GG. Telephone 0703-34433.
Telex: 477822. Telegraphic Address: Inland/Overseas: Actrans Soton.

CUNARD ARABIAN MIDDLE EAST LINE

TO WHOM IT MAY CONCERN

We confirm that the M.V. "HODEIDAH CROWN" is not scheduled or intended to
call at any Israeli ports whilst on her current voyage to Piraeus -Greece:
Jeddah - Saudi Arabia: Hodeidah - Yemen Arab Republic: Aqaba - Jordan
and Port Sudan - Sudan.

We are advised by the owners that this vessel is not Israeli owned, is not
more than 15 years old and the cargo handling equipment is suitable for
discharging at Jordanian, Y.A.R., Saudi Arabian and Sudanese ports.

We further confirm that the "HODEIDAH CROWN" is owned by Ernst Willner GMBH
and Co Cosuina Reederei KG, is West German registered and is chartered by
Cunard Brocklebank who are members of the U.K./Jordan Conference, U.K./Jeddah
and Yembo Conference and the U.K./Hodeidah and Mocha Conference.

The intended itinerary of the current sailing of the M.V. "HODEIDAH CROWN"
subject to terms and conditions laid down in the Bill of Lading is as follows:

             HAMBURG - West Germany
             ROTTERDAM - Netherlands
             LE HAVRE - France
             FELIXSTOWE - United Kingdom
             PIRAEUS - Greece
             JEDDAH - Saudi Arabia
             AQABA - Jordan
             HODEIDAH - Yemen Arab Republic
             PORT SUDAN - Sudan

To the best of our knowledge and belief, this vessel is not included in the
Arabian boycott or Israeli blacklist.

ASSOCIATED CONTAINER TRANSPORTATION SERVICES LIMITED
AS FREIGHT AGENTS

Registered Office: Richmond House, Terminus Terrace, Southampton, SO9 1GG. Registered Number 1021141 England.

CERTIFICATE OF ORIGIN

Consignor: المرسل : [1]	CONTROL COPY C 151688
DEXION LIMITED MAYLANDS AVENUE HEMEL HEMPSTEAD HERTFORDSHIRE	Consignor's ref. [4]

Consignee: المرسل اليه : [2]

ABDULAZIZ ABDUL MOHSIN ALRASHED
PO BOX SAFAT 241
KUWAIT
STATE OF KUWAIT

شهادة منشأ
CERTIFICATE OF ORIGIN

تشهد السلطة الموقعة بأن البضائع الوارد بيانها أدناه
The undersigned authority certifies that the goods shown below
originated in: منشأها : [5]

EUROPEAN COMMUNITIES — UNITED KINGDOM

Consigned by: مرسلة بواسطة : [3]

SEA ROUTE

غرفة التجارة العربية البريطانية
ARAB-BRITISH CHAMBER OF COMMERCE

Marks and Numbers: الأرقام والعلامات	Quantity and Kind of Packages: كمية ونوع الطرود	Description of Goods: مواصفات البضاعة	Weight (gross & net): الوزن (الصافي والاجمالي) [6]
861128 ALRASHED 65/80 KUWAIT, 1-393, 395 761	1 x 20' CONTAINER NO: CTIU 035356/7 SAID TO CONTAIN 20 M/BUNDLES, 374 PKGS & 1 CASE DEXION ANGLE		GROSS WEIGHT 15,443 KLS
861129 ALRASHED O/N 65/80 KUWAIT 633-824 MADE IN ENGLAND	192 PKS DEXION ANGLE		

MANUFACTURED BY: DEXION LIMITED, MAYLANDS AVENUE, HEMEL HEMPSTEAD, HERTFORDSHIRE

LCCI
[12 DEC 1980   Mrs. M. P. PALMER

EDGBRIDGE SHIPPERS LTD.
390/398, HIGH ROAD
ILFORD, ESSEX IG1 1UH
TEL. 478 6911

861

Arab-British Chamber of Commerce

B.S. CHEMICALS LIMITED

Prince Rupert House
P.O. Box No. 168, London, EC4

Telephone No. 01 236 3319   Telex No. 893311 BSGRP
VAT No. 243 1144 06   Registered in England No. 597949

Export Invoice Original

Invoice No. & Date	Sale Contract No. & Date
BS/1397 7.3.83	BSC52812 22.12.82

Customer Reference
P9412 9.12.82

Customer	Notify Party (Other Invoice Address)
East Asiatic Trading Co. Ltd. (Toa Boeki Kabushiki Kaisha), 2-2-1100, Umeda 1-Chome, Kitaku, OSAKA, JAPAN	

Licence Number

Country of Origin of Goods	Country of Final Destination
UNITED KINGDOM	JAPAN

Terms of Delivery & Payment   CANDF OSAKA. Paymnt:
120 Days D/A thro Kyowa Bank Ltd. plus int
from date B/L to date arrival proceeds
London plus 1% financing charge. Dlvry: Erlist

Vessel/Aircraft etc:-	Port of Loading
EVER VIGOR	FELIXSTOWE
Port of Discharge	Place of Delivery
OSAKA, JAPAN	OSAKA

Packages Marked	Number & Kind of Packages	TT Code No.	Gross Wt. (Kgs.)	Cube (M³)
			16892	26.72
T.B.K. OSAKA 9412	EVODE PRODUCTS		Net Wt. (Kgs.) 14887	

Item	Description of Goods	Quantity Supplied	Unit Price	Amount
		Drums	pr drum	
	Evode RDM 2073 25k drums	350	£18.45	£6457.50
	Evode Black 505 Std. Grade 51 tins	350	4.33	1515.50
	Evode Supaproof 251 Drums -			
	Black	60	15.33	919.80
	Grey	70	17.09	1196.30
	Evode Flashband Alum. 10m Rolls 5cm	Carton	pr ctn	
	(2 standard cases)	100	11.40	1140.00
	Evode Flashband Spec. Gray 10m rolls			
	10cm (2 standard cases)	100	11.30	1130.00
				12359.10
	PLUS FINANCING CHARGE @ 1%			123.59

CERTIFIED CORRECT

Invoice Currency	Invoice Total
Sterling	£12,482.69

Signed

E & OE   Dated   -7 MAR 1983

Insurance Policy

(No.   )

Any person not an Underwriting Member of Lloyd's subscribing this Policy, or any person uttering the same if so subscribed, will be liable to be proceeded against under Lloyd's Acts.

S.G.

£ 4520.00

Printed at Lloyd's, London, England.

INSTITUTE DANGEROUS DRUGS CLAUSE.

"It is understood and agreed that no claim under this Policy will be paid in respect of drugs to which the various International Conventions relating to Opium and other dangerous drugs apply unless

(i) the drugs shall be expressly declared as such in the Policy and the name of the country from which, and the name of the country to which they are consigned shall be specifically stated in the Policy

and

(ii) the proof of loss is accompanied either by a licence, certificate or authorisation issued by the Government of the country to which the drugs are consigned showing that the importation of the consignment into that country has been approved by that Government, or, alternatively, by a licence, certificate or authorisation issued by the Government of the country from which the drugs are consigned showing that the export of the consignment to the destination stated has been approved by that Government;

and

(iii) the route by which the drugs were conveyed was usual and customary."

No Policy or other Contract dated on or after 1st Jan., 1924, will be recognised by the Committee of Lloyd's as entitling the holder to the benefit of the Funds and/or Guarantees lodged by the Underwriters of the Policy or Contract as security for their liabilities unless it bears at foot the Seal of Lloyd's Policy Signing Office.

Be it known that

Speirs and Wadley Ltd.

as well in   *their*   own name as for and in the name and names of all and every other person or persons to whom the same doth, may, or shall appertain, in part or in all, doth make assurance and cause   *themselves* and them, and every of them, to be insured, lost or not lost, at and from

Warehouse Hackney via London to Warehouse New York

Upon any kind of goods and merchandises, and also upon the body, tackle, apparel, ordnance, munition, artillery, boat, and other furniture, of and in the good ship or vessel called the   Rail and/or

Conveyance and S.S. Ionian or substitute

whereof is master under God, for this present voyage, or whosoever else shall go for master in the said ship, or by whatsoever other name or names the same ship, or the master thereof, is or shall be named or called ; beginning the adventure upon the said goods and merchandises from the loading thereof aboard the said ship, *as above* upon the said ship, &c., *as above* and so shall continue and endure, during her abode there, upon the said ship, &c. And further, until the said ship, with all her ordnance, tackle, apparel, &c., and goods and merchandises whatsoever shall be arrived at *as above* upon the said ship, &c., until she hath moored at anchor twenty-four hours in good safety ; and upon the goods and merchandises, until the same be there discharged and safely landed. And it shall be lawful for the said ship, &c., in this voyage, to proceed and sail to and touch and stay at any ports or places whatsoever *and wheresoever for all purposes* without prejudice to this insurance. The said ship, &c., goods and merchandises, &c., for so much as concerns the assured by agreement between the assured and assurers in this policy, are and shall be valued at

£4520.00 on 5 cases electric drills.
With average in accordance with the terms and
conditions of the Institute Cargo Clauses
(All Risks) including Warehouse to Warehouse.

Touching the adventures and perils which we the assurers are contented to bear and do take upon us in this voyage : they are of the seas, men of war, fire, enemies, pirates, rovers, thieves, jettisons, letters of mart and countermart, surprisals, takings at sea, arrests, restraints and detainments of all kings, princes, and people, of what nation, condition, or quality soever, barratry of the master and mariners, and of all other perils, losses, and misfortunes, that have or shall come to the hurt, detriment, or damage of the said goods and merchandises, and ship, &c., or any part thereof. And in case of any loss or misfortune it shall be lawful to the assured, their factors, servants and assigns, to sue, labour, and travel for, in and about the defence, safeguard, and recovery of the said goods and merchandises, and ship, &c., or any part thereof, without prejudice to this insurance ; to the charges whereof we, the assurers, will contribute each one according to the rate and quantity of his sum herein assured. And it is especially declared and agreed that no acts of the insurer or insured in recovering, saving, or preserving the property insured shall be considered as a waiver, or acceptance of abandonment. And it is agreed by us, the insurers, that this writing or policy of assurance shall be of as much force and effect as the surest writing or policy of assurance heretofore made in Lombard Street, or in the Royal Exchange, or elsewhere in London.

1. *Warranted free of capture, seizure, arrest, restraint or detainment, and the consequences thereof or of any attempt thereat; also from the consequences of hostilities or warlike operations, whether there be a declaration of war or not ; but that warranty shall not exclude collision, contact with any fixed or floating object (other than a mine or torpedo), stranding, heavy weather or fire unless caused directly (and independently of the nature of the voyage or service which the vessel concerned or, in the case of a collision, any other vessel involved therein, is performing) by a hostile act by or against a belligerent power ; and for the purpose of this warranty "power" includes any authority maintaining naval, military or air forces in association with a power.*
Further warranted free from the consequences of civil war, revolution, rebellion, insurrection, or civil strife arising therefrom, or piracy.

2. *Warranted free of loss or damage*
   (a) *caused by strikers, locked-out workmen, or persons taking part in labour disturbances, riots or civil commotions ;*
   (b) *resulting from strikes, lock-outs, labour disturbances, riots or civil commotions.*

3. (a) *Should the risks excluded by Clause 1 (F.C. & S. Clause) be reinstated in this Policy by deletion of the said clause, or should the risks or any of them mentioned in that clause or the risks of mines, torpedoes, bombs or other engines of war be insured under this Policy, Clause (b) below shall become operative and anything contained in this contract which is inconsistent with Clause (b) or which affords more extensive protection against the aforesaid risks than that afforded by the Institute War Clauses relevant to the particular form of transit covered by this Insurance is null and void.*
   (b) *This Policy is warranted free of any claim based upon loss of, or frustration of, the insured voyage or adventure caused by arrests restraints or detainments of Kings Princes Peoples Usurpers or persons attempting to usurp power.*

And so we, the assurers, are contented, and do hereby promise and bind ourselves, each one for his own part, our heirs, executors, and goods to the assured, their executors, administrators, and assigns, for the true performance of the premises, confessing ourselves paid the consideration due unto us for this assurance by the assured, at and after the rate of

27p %

IN WITNESS whereof we, the assurers, have subscribed our names and sums assured in *LONDON, as hereinafter appears.*

N.B.—Corn, fish, salt, fruit, flour, and seed are warranted free from average, unless general, or the ship be stranded ; sugar, tobacco, hemp, flax, hides and skins are warranted free from average under five pounds per cent., and all other goods, also the ship and freight, are warranted free from average under three pounds per cent. unless general, or the ship be stranded.

Now know Ye that We, the Assurers, members of the Syndicate(s) whose definitive Number(s) in the attached list are set out in the Table overleaf, or attached overleaf, hereby bind Ourselves, each for his own part and not one for another, and in respect of his due proportion only, to pay or make good to the Assured all such Loss and/or Damage which he or they may sustain by any one or more of the accidents stated and so that the due proportion for which each of Us the Assurers is liable shall be ascertained by reference to his proportion as ascertained according to the said list of the Amount, Percentage or Proportion of the total Sum assured which is in the said Table set opposite the definitive Number of the Syndicate of which such Assurer is a member.

IN WITNESS whereof the Manager of Lloyd's Policy Signing Office has subscribed his Name on behalf of each of Us.

LLOYD'S POLICY SIGNING OFFICE,

M.E. Wallington

MANAGER.

Dated in London, the   30th July, 19..

LP.O. 60

(In the event of loss or damage which may result in a claim under this Insurance, immediate notice should be given to the Lloyd's Agent at the port or place where the loss or damage is discovered in order that he may examine the goods and issue a survey report.)

Reproduced with kind permission of Barclays Bank International.

Lloyd's Marine Policy

We, The Underwriters, hereby agree, in consideration of the payment to us by or on behalf of the Assured of the premium specified in the Schedule, to insure against loss damage liability or expense in the proportions and manner hereinafter provided. Each Underwriting Member of a Syndicate whose definitive number and proportion is set out in the following Table shall be liable only for his own share of his respective Syndicate's proportion.

In Witness whereof the General Manager of Lloyd's Policy Signing Office has subscribed his Name on behalf of each of Us.

LLOYD'S POLICY SIGNING OFFICE
General Manager

This insurance is subject to English jurisdiction.

MAR
LPO 62A (1.1.82) Printed by The Cardon Berry Co. Ltd

Royal Insurance (U.K.) Limited

HEAD OFFICE:
NEW HALL PLACE, LIVERPOOL L69 3EN

REGIONAL MARINE CENTRE:
ROSEBERY HOUSE, 41 SPRINGFIELD ROAD,
CHELMSFORD, ESSEX CM2 6RA

Exporter's Reference

EA 1305

CERTIFICATE No.   JP02472/ 02431

THIS IS TO CERTIFY that **ROYAL INSURANCE (U.K.) LIMITED** has insured under an Open Policy the Goods specified below, valued at sum insured, for the insured transit and on the conditions stated in this certificate.

Assured   MOONBRIDGE SHIPPERS LIMITED

Local Vessel	From (Local Port of Loading)	
	UK WAREHOUSE	
Ocean Vessel/Aircraft. etc.	Sea/Air Port of Loading	
DECAS	FELIXSTOWE	
Sea/Air Port of Discharge	Final Destination (if On-Carriage)	Insured Value/Currency (£7,100.00)
PORT LOUIS	MAURITIUS WAREHOUSE	SEVEN THOUSAND ONE HUNDRED POUNDS STERLING ONLY

Marks and Numbers

Interest

LAI TUNG
MAURITIUS

1360 CARTONSPROCESSED PEAS

Notwithstanding that the description of the insured transit in this Certificate may state only the port or place of shipment, the insurance shall attach from the time of leaving warehouse or place of storage in the interior, if goods are at the assured s risk and if in accordance with the Open Contract.
Claims to be adjusted according to the conditions of the Policy which contains, *inter alia*, the following clauses:—

This insurance covers all risks of loss of or damage to the subject matter insured as provided in the :—

Institute Cargo Clauses (A) and/or Institute Cargo Clauses (Air) (excluding sendings by Post) as applicable, but subject to the exclusions contained therein.

Institute War Clauses (Cargo) and/or Institute War Clauses (Air Cargo) (excluding sendings by Post) Institute War Clauses (sendings by Post) as applicable. Institute Strikes Clauses (Cargo) and/or Institute Strikes Clauses (Air Cargo) as applicable. Institute Classification Clause.

Institute Replacement Clause.

Notwithstanding anything contained herein to the contrary the liability under this policy in respect of any destruction of or damage to the subject matter of this policy shall not exceed its rateable proportion having regard to other insurances whether Marine or Fire and whether or not such other insurances are exempted from contributing either by the existence of this policy or any other.

In the event of loss or damage for which the Company may be liable under this certificate immediate notice must be given

to:—   HARDY REGGARY LTD, 6TH FLR, LABATA HSE, 35 SIR WILLIAM NEWTON ST, PORT LOUIS
"SURVEYS MUST BE HELD BEFORE GOODS ARE REMOVED FROM PORT OR DOCKS AREAS
Claims payable at:—   AT PORT LOUIS" AS ABOVE   SEE SPECIAL INSTRUCTIONS OVERLEAF

by:—
This insurance is subject to English jurisdiction.
For ROYAL INSURANCE (U.K.) LTD.

COPY

This Certificate is not valid unless countersigned by or on behalf of
MOONBRIDGE SHIPPERS LIMITED-

Dated 18.5.83

Signed

GENERAL MANAGER

This Certificate represents and takes the place of the original Policy and conveys, subject to the terms of that Policy, all the rights of the original Policy Holder (for the purpose of collecting claims) as fully as if the property

Chapter 6

Bank Finance for Exporters Short-Term: With Recourse

We now turn our attention to another major theme of international commerce namely –the *financing* of trade. By this term we refer to facilities made available to traders to bridge the gap between buyers who need time before making payment and sellers who need to be paid on shipment of the goods (or before).

For the purposes of this chapter we shall ignore all Export Credits Guarantee Department (ECGD) facilities which, because of their importance, are treated in a separate chapter (see Chapter 10).

While in practice the difference between short and medium-term financial facilities may be blurred, it is convenient to deal with them separately; likewise, it is useful to differentiate *with recourse* from *without recourse* finance even though any one facility may carry either condition.

WITH RECOURSE AND WITHOUT RECOURSE FINANCE

These terms refer to whether or not the recipient of a financial facility is under any liability to reimburse the lender in the event that something goes wrong; e.g. the buyer defaults on the debt. A facility is said to be without recourse to the exporter when funds which have been advanced to him cannot be taken back provided he has conformed to the conditions under which the finance had been made available. It goes without saying that exporters prefer without recourse finance.

Finally, it is also useful to treat *export* finance separately from *import* finance, even though, as we shall see, some facilities may apply to both.

BANK EXPORT FINANCE – SHORT-TERM; WITH RECOURSE

Let us begin by looking first at export finance, which is both short-term and with recourse. Short-term finance can be said to be where a debt is due for repayment anywhere between a few days and up to several months (perhaps one year). In world trade three or six months are typical periods of short-term credit granted by sellers to their buyers.

BANK OVERDRAFT OR LOAN

Obviously, it is possible for an exporter to arrange for a bank overdraft or loan to cover his working capital requirements just as any other business-man might do. An overdraft is a *general* facility and need not be specific either to the customer's overseas business or to any one contract. The bank will make such a facility available in the light of the general trading and financial position of the customer. Overdrafts are convenient because they need not be fully drawn, in which case interest costs are minimized, and they are available for general expenditure. However, even if they are not drawn at all, a bank charge will be incurred, and the rate of interest is likely to be high although it will vary with the status of the customer.

A bank loan is another possibility. Here the exporter arranges for a loan for a specific amount for a given period and at a fixed rate of interest. For example a bank may be prepared to offer a loan facility where it is handling documents going abroad as a collection of funds from a buyer. However, as with an overdraft, interest costs are likely to be unattractive (except where an ECGD facility is available).

Both these possibilities are common where traders are operating their financial arrangements on an *open account* basis. That is, where goods are shipped but payment is delayed for some weeks or months on a basis of *trust* between the parties. For example, the arrangement could be that the buyer will pay for the goods (say) two months after delivery, or alternatively, where large sums are involved, payment could be spread over a period of months with remittances on the first of each month after a grace period of (say) three months.

Because of the risk that payment may not be forthcoming, open account trading tends to be restricted to inter-related companies and those firms who, from past experience, consider the risks, if any, to be small. In such circumstances a bank overdraft or loan could be made available with little risk to the bank. Nevertheless, such bank facilities are with recourse in the sense that when default by the buyer occurs the exporter is not relieved of his obligation to repay his debt to the bank. Although such facilities are usually described as short-term, it is quite possible for them to be *revolving*, i.e. renewed on a continuous basis, albeit on adjusted terms. Loans can be in domestic or foreign currency. The latter is useful where the exporter's receipts are in currency because the risk of currency exposure is eliminated. (But see *Foreign Exchange; Covered Interest Arbitrage*, Chapter 9.)

BILLS OF EXCHANGE

Where exporters are rather less certain of the credit risks they can use a *Bill of Exchange* (see page 149). As we shall now see, the use of this financial document reduces (but does not eliminate) the possibility of default by the buyer.

It is "an unconditional order in writing addressed by one person to another, signed by the person giving it, requiring the person to whom it is addressed to pay on demand, or at a fixed or determinable future time, a sum certain in money to, or to the order of, a specified person or bearer". (Bills of Exchange Act, 1882.)

In other words, it is a document by which a debtor pays, or agrees to pay in the future a certain sum of money. When a Bill is so worded that payment is required on presentation and therefore carries with it no time delay for payment the Bill is said to be a *Sight Bill*. That is payment is required on *sight* of the *Bill*. In this case the document is little more than a demand for payment. However, in the context of trade credit we need to consider the Bill which *does* carry with it the right of the debtor to delay making payment. Such a Bill is referred to as a *Time, Tenor, Term* or *Usance Bill*. For the sake of simplicity we shall refer to such Bills as *Time Bills*.

By definition there must be at least two parties to a Bill; the *Drawer* and the *Drawee*.

Drawer

The drawer of a Time Bill is the party who establishes it (the exporter/creditor).

Drawee

The drawee of a Time Bill is the party upon whom the document is drawn (the importer/debtor).

Thus a typical draft Bill[1] used in international financing consists of one drawn by the exporter on the importer asking him to *accept* its terms by signing across the face of the document. Once it has been accepted the drawee is bound by its terms. The Bill is now referred to as *an acceptance*. (See *Discounting* on page 134.) Bills can be drawn in copies or just singly in which case it is called a *Sola Bill*.

---

[1] A draft bill is one not yet accepted by the drawee.

Once accepted the Bill is likely to be held by a bank in the importer's country awaiting its maturity (the date of payment) when it will be re-presented to the drawee for payment. Alternatively it could be returned to the drawer who will re-present it on maturity.

A Bill offers an exporter a certain security in that if it is dishonoured either by (i) non-payment of a Sight Bill or (ii) non-acceptance of a Time Bill or (iii) non-payment of an Accepted Time Bill, legal action can be taken in many countries to recover monies and using the Bill as evidence of debt. (See *Collections* on page 129).

Nevertheless a man of straw cannot meet his financial liabilities even when they are embodied in a Bill of Exchange and therefore the risk of non-payment is still present.

Apart from the drawer and the drawee there can be other parties to a Bill, e.g.

Acceptor

We have already seen that a drawee can accept a draft Bill and thus become an *acceptor*. However, in addition to this it is possible for a party to accept a draft drawn upon him where he is not the trader/debtor. For example, drafts can be drawn on *banks* under Letters of Credit, and also in other circumstances. (See *Acceptance Credits*, later in this Chapter.)

Negotiator

It is possible for a bank to *negotiate* (i.e. purchase) a draft Bill *where it is not* named as a drawee. It will then present the draft for payment or acceptance *in its own right*. (See Collections, page 129.)

Discounter

Once a draft Bill is accepted it can be *discounted*, i.e. purchased with recourse to the acceptor. (See *Discounting*, page 134.)

Payee

This is the party to receive payment on maturity of the Bill. It can be the exporter drawer, or bank negotiator, or discounter.

Endorser

An endorser of a Bill transfers his rights to receive payment by signing his name on the back. Thus a drawer is also an endorser when he offers a draft Bill to a negotiator. Draft Bills presented for payment to the drawee must also be endorsed. An endorsement can be in favour of a named *endorsee* (a special endorsement) or it can be endorsed *in blank* making it a *bearer* document. A Bill of Exchange is always negotiable unless it expressly states to the contrary. A Bill of Lading is *only* negotiable it if is made out "to order". (See Chapter 5.)

Bills of exchange may carry certain clauses relating to the rate of exchange between the currencies of the drawer and drawee and also to the party to incur collection charges, foreign stamp duty and rate of interest.

When an exporter draws a Bill in a foreign currency he will receive the proceeds on maturity less foreign stamp duty (if applicable) and collection charges. However, both these items may be for the drawee's account if the words "plus collection charges" are added to the Bill. The *domestic* currency receipts will be the proceeds of selling the foreign currency at the spot rate on the day it is received. Alternatively, these proceeds could have been sold in the forward market to yield a pre-determined domestic currency sum. (See Chapter 9.) Another possibility is for the exporter to receive the foreign currency proceeds and place them to the appropriate currency account (if he has one).

When an exporter draws a Bill in his own currency he will, of course, receive the agreed amount less any charges (unless specified to the contrary). However, the cost to the drawee in terms of *his* own currency will depend on the rate of exchange used.

"Drawn in sterling, payable at the collecting bank's selling rate on day of payment for sight drafts on London"

The drawer receives sterling (his own currency) less charges (unless specified to the contrary) and the drawee will have to pay a sufficient amount of his own currency at the rate of exchange existing on the day that the collecting bank remits sterling to the exporter's bank.

"Drawn in sterling, payable at the collecting bank's selling rate on day of payment for sight drafts on London with interest at . . . per cent per annum from the date hereof until the approximate date of arrival of the proceeds in London"

This type of clause fixes the date for exchange rate purposes and also includes an interest payment. Although the appropriate interest figure is inserted in the gap provided, the fact that date of arrival of proceeds in London is approximate makes the total interest sum indeterminate. In theory this offends against the Bills of Exchange Act 1882 which requires that all sums are "certain in money". However, in practice this clause is still used. If the draft Bill is drawn in another currency, then the financial centre will be that of the specified currency, e.g. US dollars, New York etc.

"Drawn in sterling, payable in English pounds, sterling effective"

This clause is frequently used on draft Bills drawn on European drawees and confirms that they have (or will have) exchange control approval to freely remit sterling on the due date. (See Chapter 6, *Uniform Rules for Collections*, Articles 11 and 12.)

"Drawn in sterling, payable with exchange and stamps as per endorsement"

This clause can be used when the drawer wishes to negotiate (see later in this chapter) the draft drawn on the drawee. It allows for the drawer to receive the full sterling value of the draft but the drawee has to pay in his own currency at the London buying exchange rate to include charges and interest from the time negotiation is effected to the time the drawee makes payment. Such clauses are mainly used in trade between the UK and Australia, New Zealand, East and South Africa. This clause may not appear on the draft Bill but can be stipulated in the Collection order (see later in this Chapter). All clauses, must of course, be agreed beforehand with the overseas buyer.

An alternative financial document to the Bill of Exchange is the Promissory Note.

PROMISSORY NOTE

"An unconditional promise in writing made by one person to another signed by the maker, engaging to pay, on demand or at a fixed or determinable future time, a sum certain in money, to, or to the order of, a specified person or to bearer" (Bills of Exchange Act 1882).

As the definition makes clear, this financial document also permits for a period of time to elapse between its establishment and the due date for payment. However, unlike a Bill of Exchange it is drawn up by the *debtor* who is called a *maker* and it is in favour of the *creditor* who is called the *payee* or *beneficiary* to whom it is sent. Prior to receipt by the beneficiary the note is said to be *inchoate*, i.e. incomplete. Once delivered it is a bona fide note. A Bill of Exchange can sometimes also be *inchoate* (see *Refinance Credits* – Chapter 7). Promissory Notes are mainly used in *Forfaiting* arrangements (see Chapter 8). When due for payment it is presented to the maker by the holder who may be the original beneficiary or someone to whom the Note has been negotiated (see later in this Chapter). As a general consideration the status of the parties may be important in determining which type of financial instrument is used. For example, a small UK exporter may benefit by negotiating his buyer's Promissory Note if the latter is a large, well-known international organization as this could well be at a lower cost. A major disadvantage of this document is that it cannot be re-discounted by the Bank of England and therefore it will carry a higher (ineligible) rate of discount.

From time to time in this chapter reference has been made to the possibility that commercial banks might be involved in the handling of Bills of Exchange. It is now time to be more specific about the role of banks in this regard but before we do so it should be pointed out that it is quite possible for traders to conduct their financial and trading arrangements without the special assistance of banks.

Diagram 6.1

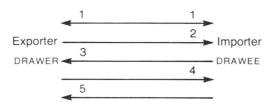

Example of the Use of a Bill of Exchange without Bank Involvement

1 Contract of sale to include three months credit facilitated by a 91 day trade Bill of Exchange. (A trade Bill is one drawn on a non-bank.)

2 Exporter remits a draft Bill for acceptance by the importer. If this is clean, i.e without accompanying commercial documents, then the importer's acceptance binds him to a legal contract to pay on maturity *irrespective* of the proper fulfilment of the underlying sales contract.

It is unlikely that an importer would wish to commit himself to such a liability *before the receipt of the goods* and clearly the exporter would be unwise to release any document of title to the goods *before the importers' acceptance*.

If the draft Bill is accompanied by the commercial documents then this is referred to as a documentary presentation. However, as already mentioned, this involves the risk to the exporter that the goods may be accepted but the draft Bill ignored. As with a clean Bill, acceptance by the importer binds him to a financial contract.

3 Assuming that the importer accepts the draft Bill, it is then returned to the exporter to hold until maturity. Alternatively, he may be able to discount the Bill but because it is a trade Bill it will not attract the finest (cheapest) discount rates.

4 On the due date (the 91st day) the payee presents the Bill to the importer for settlement.

5 Payment is made to the payee.

It is obvious from the foregoing that considerable risks attach to such operations. With a documentary presentation the importer can receive title to the goods without accepting his liability to pay, or the exporter can receive a confirmation of liability by the importer and fail to deliver proper goods.

It is to reconcile these differences that banks offer a collections service.

BANK COLLECTIONS

The use of commercial banks in the handling, despatch and presentation of documents gives certain advantages.

(1) Banks operate within a well-defined set of rules called "Uniform Rules for Collections", International Chamber of Commerce Publication No. 322 (1978). These rules (shown in Appendix 5 at the end of the chapter) contain a set of Articles outlining the duties and responsibilities of all the parties involved and therefore gives both the importer and the exporter greater confidence that, providing they conform to their obligations, goods will be received and payment will be forthcoming.

(2) A financial facility can be associated with the collection allowing the exporter to receive funds on shipment of goods even though he has advanced credit to his buyer.

(3) The procedure is more convenient and less expensive than other methods of financing trade credit.

There may be four or five parties to a collection. They are shown in Diagram 6.2.

The procedure is as follows:

1 Goods are despatched.

2 Documents are sent to the Exporter's bank (the Remitting Bank). This is immediately after 1. The documents are accompanied by a collection order. This will detail all the information the bank will need to know in order to carry out its functions properly.

Collection Order (See Page 150)

This is completed by the principal usually on a blank form available from his bank. Apart from the names of the parties involved it will give details of:

(a) all commercial and financial documents;

(b) whether collection charges are to be for the drawee's account;

(c) the value, date and tenor of the Bill of Exchange (if any);

Diagram 6.2
A Bank Collection

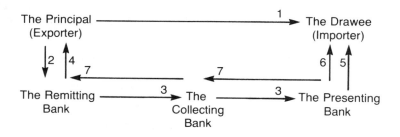

(d) the required release of the commercial documents. If there are no commercial documents then the procedure is called a clean collection. In this case the financial document will be presented to the drawee or maker for payment or acceptance.

If a Sight Bill is presented then the collection order will specify "payment". If a Time Bill is presented then "acceptance" will be specified.

Apart from a Bill or Note it is possible to present a cheque drawn by the buyer in which case it must be presented to the overseas bank on which it is drawn. It is also possible to present a Traveller's Cheque (see Chapter 11). Again, it will have to be presented to the issuing bank for payment.

If commercial documents are involved then instruction as to their release must be given. If they are to be released to the drawee against the payment of a Sight Bill, "a documents against payments (D/P) collection" must be indicated. If they are to be released against acceptance of a Time Bill (a documents against acceptance or D/A collection) then this must be indicated in the order.

(e) the steps the bank must take in the event of non-payment or non-acceptance. This involves the action of protesting.

Protesting

The act of protesting a Bill involves the use of a notary public who will attempt to obtain payment or acceptance on behalf of the principal. In the event of his failure to achieve this he will record all relevant facts of the case in a deed of protest which can be presented as legal evidence of failure to meet a contract. The act of protesting is thus a prerequisite for legal action which may be taken at a later stage. Protesting is also necessary to protect the right of recourse by a payee against the drawer.

Protesting is viewed as a serious step as it can have grave implications for the credit rating of the drawee.

The collection order must specify whether or not the bank should proceed with protesting in the event of default.

(f) the method of advising the principal in the event of default; e.g. by cable or air-mail;

(g) whether the proceeds should be remitted by cable or air-mail;

(h) someone to act as a case of need. This is an agent of the principal in the drawee's country who can investigate any problem and communicate with the principal. The collection order must specify whether the banks must accept the instructions of the case of need or whether the latters' function is simply an advisory one. (See Uniform Rules for Collection, Article 18.)

(i) whether the bank is to warehouse and insure the goods in the event of non-payment or non-acceptance.

It is essential to understand that the banks involved in a collection do so entirely on the authority of the collection order and of the Uniform Rules for Collection. In general the collection order is the *principal* authority and the Uniform Rules act as a back-up in cases where the order itself is silent or ambiguous. The exporter should therefore be sure that he completes it to include all the relevant conditions under which he wishes to proceed.

3 If the documents appear to be in order the Remitting bank will despatch them to its correspondent bank in the importer's country (referred to as the Collecting bank), who, in turn, will remit them to the importer's own bank (called the Presenting bank). Alternatively, the Remitting bank can despatch documents directly to the Presenting bank. The method used will depend on whether the principal has instructed the Remitting bank to remit to a named overseas bank or not.

4 At the same time as 3 the Remitting bank may credit the principal's account with all or most of the expected proceeds depending on the type of facility agreed (see later in this chapter).

5 The Presenting bank may wish to see that the collection order conforms to the accompanying documents and if so, they will then release the documents to the drawee.

(a) If there are no commercial documents (a clean collection) and the Bill of Exchange is a Sight Bill, then it will be presented for payment; if it is a Time Bill, it will be presented for acceptance.

(b) If there are no financial documents and no immediate payment required, the commercial documents will be released to the importer.

In both (a) and (b) the exporter is operating his business similar to open account trade except that in (a) the drawee is reminded that he has an immediate or future liability in the form of a Bill of Exchange, and in (b) the banks are being utilized to safeguard the importer against incorrect documentation (and therefore inferior delivery of goods). However, as payment is not linked to the presentation of the documents this is likely to be less of a problem to the importer.

(c) If there are both commercial and financial documents – a documentary collection – and the financial document consists of a Sight Bill, then the commercial documents will be released only on the payment of the Sight Bill (a documents against payment or D/P collection). If there is a Time Bill then the commercial documents will be released only against the acceptance of the Time Bill (a documents against acceptance or D/A collection).

Naturally, the exporter prefers a D/P to a D/A collection while the importer will prefer a D/A collection. This will have to be agreed in the contract of sale and be stipulated in the collection order.

6 The acceptance (Accepted Bill) is usually retained by the Presenting or Collecting bank until maturity and then re-presented for payment.

7 The funds from 6 will be remitted to the Remitting bank, who if it has negotiated the draft Bill will be the payee entitled to receipt of the proceeds.

(The methods of transmitting funds and inter-bank settlements are dealt with in Chapter 11.)

Earlier in this chapter we noted that an exporter can obtain an overdraft or loan from his bank to finance the granting of credit to his overseas buyer. We are now in a position to examine other forms of bank finance, in particular, those linked or associated with a collection:

(1) An Advance

A bank may be prepared to offer an exporter an advance of a proportion of the value of the goods without itself becoming a party to the Bill of Exchange. The proportion may be up to about 85% of the value of the Bill which, together with the other documents will be sent for collection in the manner already described. Where the Bill of Lading is made out "to order" the bank has effective control over the goods until the documents are presented to the importer. (See Chapter 5.) To this degree the bank has an element of security against the advance but in addition, the bank can call on the exporter to provide a pledge or letter of hypothecation. (Hypothecation is another word for pledge or mortgage.) Such a pledge allows the bank to hold the proceeds of the goods and any or all Bills and other financial documents to be remitted for presentation to the bank's account as security for the advance in the event that the exporter cannot meet his recourse liabilities to the bank.

Such a facility will be cheaper than arranging finance for the whole value of the Bill. Naturally an advance is offered with recourse to the exporter; i.e. in the event of the buyer defaulting on the Bill, the bank will recover from the exporter.

(2) Negotiation

Where the full value of the Bill is required the exporter can arrange to have it negotiated. It is possible for this facility to be arranged even though there is no financial document to be remitted. In such a case the *commercial documents* are negotiated.

Thus, either the bank buys the rights to the proceeds of any draft Bill sent for collection, in which case the bank *will present the Bill for payment in its own right*; or the bank buys the rights to the commercial documents and will await payment by the importer in its own right.

For a Bill of Exchange to be negotiated it must first be endorsed by the drawer on the back, thus transferring the status of payee to the bank.

The bank will credit the exporter's account with the value of the Bill less the negotiating charge. This represents the interest cost to the exporter of not having to wait for his money until the Bill matures. In practice this charge will not be debited until the Bill is presented for payment because the time element involved is not precisely determinable. This is because the drawee may delay making payment and also because of the time taken for the banks to remit the proceeds. As a result the value of the rate of interest will not be precisely known at the time of negotiation.

Before a bank would be willing to grant such a facility it would want to check the credit-worthiness of its customer/exporter in the same way it would do so under any lending operation. Providing the customer is deemed to be credit-worthy the bank may be prepared to grant a negotiation line of credit for an overall value. The exporter is then able to present documents for collection and receive negotiation finance up to that agreed revolving value.

Holder for Value and Holder in Due Course. These terms refer to the rights of the bank to the proceeds of a Bill. When an advance is made, the bank will be a holder for value; i.e it will have a lien on the Bill giving it the right to retain the proceeds of the Bill. When a Bill is negotiated, the bank is a holder for value and may also become a holder in due course; i.e. a legal right of action against the exporter in the event of the importer's default. The Bills of Exchange Act lays down that if a dishonoured Bill is not protested within 24 hours of default the bank loses this right, and therefore, to protect themselves they will require the exporter to sign a recourse agreement allowing them to recover monies advanced to the exporter in the event of default. Thus, negotiation is a "with recourse" facility.[2]

If a Bill is drawn in foreign exchange and it is negotiated in sterling at the spot rate current when documents are remitted overseas and the importer defaults, the exporter will have to repay the bank the then current sterling value of the value of the Bill. This could result in either an exchange loss or gain. (See Chapter 9.)

Negotiation under a collections procedure is not to be confused with a "negotiations letter of credit" (see Chapter 7).

(3) Discounting

In theory it is conceivable that a Bill drawn on an overseas buyer (a Trade Bill) could be discounted by the Remitting bank. As this facility involves the purchase of the right to an acceptance, i.e. an *accepted* Bill, it follows that discounting cannot be effected at the time of the exporter's presentation of documents to the Remitting bank. For this reason (and others specified below) this is an unlikely arrangement under a collections procedure.

---

[2]Strictly speaking, a holder of a Bill has the right of recourse against the drawer, immediately on dishonour, provided that it is noted or protested not later than the next business day after dishonour (Bills of Exchange Act).

Other Reasons Why Discounting is Unlikely:

(a) Only Bills of Exchange can be discounted. Not all collection orders include a Bill.

(b) Only Time Bills can be discounted. This is because the discounting of Bills is an *investment medium*. The discounter invests in a short-term financial instrument by parting with cash for a period of time for which he receives the discount rate. In addition, in London there is a *secondary market* in discount paper allowing for Bills to be re-discounted, perhaps, several times. A Sight Bill cannot, therefore, be discounted.

(c) Only Accepted Bills can be discounted. Thus, under a collections procedure, the exporter will have to wait for the importer's acceptance before he can have it discounted.

(d) Bills must be payable in the country of discount. In other words, it will have to be discounted *in the importer's country*. Not all countries will have such facilities.

In practice therefore, it is most unlikely that such a facility will be available under a collections procedure.

However, this point is somewhat qualified under an inward collections (as opposed to an outward collections). These terms refer to the *direction* in which the documents are flowing from the point of view of an involved bank.

Outward Collections
Here a Remitting bank will be involved in the presentation of documents and obtaining payment. It acts as a *collector* of funds.

Inward Collections
Here, the bank acts as a Collecting or Presenting bank receiving documents for presentation to the importer and *remitting* funds. Now, when a London bank acts in this capacity, it may be possible for the overseas exporter to draw a draft Bill on the UK importer and have it discounted in London. Providing that the exporter has a prime name the cost of this arrangement may be lower than with a negotiations facility abroad. However, as before, the drawer overseas will have to wait for the proceeds of the Bill.

(4) Acceptance Credits (or Accommodation Finance)

Yet another way in which an exporter can acquire finance on presentation of documents is to arrange with his own bank, or with a merchant bank to allow him to draw a Time Bill on them which they accept. An Acceptance Commission is charged, depending on the drawer's credit-worthiness, but usually lies between ⅛% and 3% per annum.

The bank will then discount the Accepted Bill to one of the Discount Houses in the London Money Market and the proceeds, less the discount charge and the commission, are available to the exporter. The bank will usually require the exporter to allow them to handle the collections procedure and it is these documents which provide them with a degree of security, but, in any event, should the Trade Bill be dishonoured the discounter will have recourse to the acceptor (the collecting bank) who, in turn, will have recourse on the drawer/exporter. So, once again, this is an example of *with recourse* finance.

In order to allow the exporter time to receive the proceeds under the *Trade* Bill before he becomes liable under the *Bank* Bill, the latter will be drawn for a period somewhat longer than the former.

Calculating the Cost of Discounting

We have already noted that the cost of negotiating documents cannot be exactly determined at the outset because of the extra time it will take for proceeds to arrive. However, this is not the case with discounting. Both the acceptance commission and the discount rate are known and are "front-ended", i.e. deducted on day 1.

We can illustrate the cost by reference to a hypothetical exporter in the UK who has drawn a Bill on his bank for £100,000 with a 100 day maturity. The underlying Trade Bill has a maturity of 91 days. Let us assume that the discount rate is 15% per annum.

Thus; $\quad £100,000 \times \dfrac{15}{100} \times \dfrac{100}{365} = £4,109.59 =$ Discount charge.

In addition, if the Acceptance commission is 2% per annum it will amount to a further cost of:

$$£100,000 \times \dfrac{2}{100} \times \dfrac{100}{365} = £547.95 = \text{Acceptance commission.}$$

The UK exporter's net receipts on day 1 is therefore £100,000 less £4,109.59, less £547.95 = £953,342.46.

This *net* receipt should be compared with the *gross* receipt the exporter would have obtained if he had negotiated his Trade Bill instead. Thus, an *additional* cost of discounting lies in the fact that the exporter has the use of *less* money during the trade credit period than he would have with a negotiations facility.

We can therefore arrive at the *true cost* of discounting by applying the following formula:

$$\dfrac{365}{\text{no. of days}} \times 100 \left(\dfrac{\text{value of the bill}}{\text{proceeds}} - 1 \right) = \text{real annual \%rate}$$

This has to be applied to both the discount charge and to the acceptance commission:

$$\textit{Discount charge} \quad \dfrac{365}{100} \times 100 \left(\dfrac{£100,000}{£95,890.41} - 1 \right) = 15.64\%$$

$$\begin{array}{l} \textit{Acceptance} \\ \textit{commission} \end{array} \quad \dfrac{365}{100} \times 100 \left(\dfrac{£100,000}{£99,452.05} - 1 \right) = 2.01\%$$

Thus the *true* cost is 17.65% per annum, which is somewhat greater than the combined discount rate and Acceptance commission because it allows for the fact that the charges are "front-ended" compared with a negotiation where costs are deducted at the end of a maturity period. However, a negotiations fee may be charged on day 1.

It should be noted that for sterling Bills a 365 day year is taken; while for currency Bills a 360 day year is taken.

The actual discount rate will of course depend on current short-term rates of interest as well as the status of the accepting bank and the exporter.

Since August 1981 the cheapest (finest) discount rates are reserved for Bills which are:

(a) drawn on and accepted by a bank that the Bank of England defines as "eligible";

(b) drawn in sterling. A Currency Bill will attract the appropriate Euro-rate for that currency. (This could be more or less than the sterling rate);

(c) not in excess of a maturity period of 187 days including all holidays and weekends;

(d) self-liquidating, i.e. Bank Bills backed by Trade Bills evidencing the eventual receipt of funds.

Bills which the Bank of England are not prepared to re-discount are termed "ineligible" Bills and carry a higher discount rate.

Summary of Export Finance with a Collection

Finance that can be available to an exporter who presents documents to a bank under a collections procedure are therefore:

1 Overdraft or loan;
2 Advance against documents sent for collection;
3 Negotiation of documents;
4 Discounting of Trade Bill (unlikely);
5 Acceptance credit.

In considering which type of finance to obtain the exporter must take the following factors into account:

(a) Availability
(b) Cost
(c) Convenience

(a) Availability

Not all these facilities may be offered to the exporter. For example his bank may not be prepared to negotiate documents because of the uncertain status of the overseas buyer in which case an advance facility for a lesser value may be the alternative.

(b) Cost

The lowest cost facility is likely to be the Acceptance credit but this will depend on the status of the exporter which will determine the Acceptance commission, and also the discount rate.

(c) Convenience

This will depend on whether the exporter is operating on an Open Account basis or is utilizing Bills of Exchange. In the former case a general overdraft facility would be the simplest while in the latter a negotiations facility might be more convenient. Where an exporter is conducting his trade on a continuous basis a revolving negotiations facility might be appropriate and where, in addition, the values are large an acceptance credit might prove the most apt facility, especially a revolving one.

Remember that these financial facilities have been discussed in the context of a collections procedure and it is now time to look at and examine the Uniform Rules for Collections (reproduced at end of chapter, Appendix 5).

Let us now look at the things that banks are, and are not, responsible for in a collection.

Banks' Responsibilities[3]

1. *Good Faith.* Banks must act in good faith.   (Article 1)

2. *Verification of Documents.* Banks must examine the documents to see that they conform with the collection order and advise the principal (or his agent) if there are inconsistencies or errors.   (Article 2)

3. *Proper Presentation of Documents.* Banks must present documents as received except for any necessary additions in the form of stamps, etc.   (Article 7)

4. *No Delay in Presenting Documents, or in Transferring Payment or in Advising Fate.* Banks must: (i) present documents without delay; (ii) remit proceeds without delay; (iii) advise the remitting bank of payment or non-payment, acceptance or non-acceptance by quickest mail, or if urgent by cable, etc.   (Articles 9, 14 and 20)

5. *Payment Subject to Control Limits.* The presenting bank must only accept payment which can be immediately remitted and not subject to exchange control limitations unless otherwise instructed in the collections order.   (Articles 11 and 12)

6. *Partial Payments.* With a *clean collection* partial payments can be accepted subject to local laws but documents must not be released until full payment is made.   (Article 13)

[3]See also article by Brian White in *Banking World*, May 1985.

With a *documentary collection* partial payments are accepted only if permitted in the collection order. Documents are to be released on full payment unless otherwise authorised in the collection order.

7. *The Acceptance of Bills of Exchange.* Banks must see that (Article 15) the way in which a bill is accepted appears to be complete and correct.

8. *Reasons for Non-Payment or Non-Acceptance.* The pre- (Article 20) senting bank should try to discover the reason for non-payment or non-acceptance and advise the remitting bank.

9. *Further Instructions on Non-Payment or Non-Acceptance.* (Article 20) The remitting bank must give further instructions on advice of non-payment or non-acceptance within 90 days of receipt of that advice. Failing this the documents may be returned to the remitting bank.

10. *Payment of Interest.* Where the financial document con- (Article 21) tains an instrument clause banks must not deliver documents to the drawee if he refuses to pay or accept interest unless the collection order allows interest to be waived.

If there is no financial document, or if there is but it does (Article 21) not contain an interest clause, the banks can deliver documents to the drawee even if he refuses to pay or accept interest unless the collection order specifies otherwise.

11. *Collection Charges.* If the drawee refuses to pay or accept (Article 22) collection charges the documents may be delivered to him unless the collection order specifies otherwise.

Banks Are Not Responsible For:

1. *The Validity of Documents.* Banks have no obligation to (Article 2) ensure that presented documents are as required by the buyer.

2. *Services Provided by Other Banks.* For example, the (Article 3ii) remitting bank is not liable for the service (or misservice) of the collecting and presenting banks.

3. *Foreign Laws.* Banks are not responsible for costs and (Article 3ii) delays caused by laws or usages in the buyer's country.

4. *Delays, Acts of God, etc.* Banks have no liability for delay, (Articles 4 loss, mistranslations or misinterpretations of instruc- and 5) tions etc.; or for Acts of God, wars, etc., caused beyond their control.

5. *Goods Despatched to a Bank*. Unless agreed beforehand,   (Article 6)
   banks have no liability if goods are delivered to their
   premises.

6. *Incorrect Addresses*. If documents carry incomplete or   (Article 8)
   incorrect addresses liability remains with the principal.

7. *Absence of Information in the Collection Order*. In the   (Article 10)
   absence of instructions in the collection order as to
   whether the documents are to be released to the drawee
   against acceptance (D/A) or against payment (D/P)
   banks will release only against payment.

8. *The Genuineness or Authority of Signatures*. The pre-   (Article 16)
   senting bank is not responsible for the genuineness or
   authority of the signature of acceptance of a Bill of
   Exchange or of the signature on a Promissory Note.

9. *Protesting without Authority*. Without specific instruc-   (Article 17)
   tions in the collection order, banks have no authority to
   proceed with protesting for non-payment or non-
   acceptance.

10. *Unclear Powers of a Case of Need*. If the collection order   (Article 18)
    fails to make clear the powers of a nominated case of
    need, banks are not to accept instruction from them.

11. *Goods*. Banks have no obligation to take action in respect   (Article 19)
    of goods relating to a collection.

12. *Collection Charges and Expenses*. Banks are not liable for   (Article 23)
    any costs of collection, expenses incurred, etc., but can
    recover these from the principal regardless of the fate of
    the collection.

It is clear from these points that the main purposes of the Uniform Rules for
Collection are:

(1) To define terms and parties to a collection.

(2) To limit the liabilities and responsibilities of banks engaged in a col-
    lection.

(3) To specify responsibilities and actions where the collection order is sil-
    ent or unclear.

By adherence to these Rules then, all parties are aware of the terms under
which the arrangements to present documents are being made.

It must be pointed out however, that banks will, in the normal course of
events, draw their customers' attention to any point they consider to be a
possible cause of conflict or misinterpretation, even though they are not
under any contractual liability to do so. When a Bill of Lading is made out
"to order" and blank endorsed, thus giving the banks constructive control

over the goods, they will be further motivated to ensure that they are properly insured, warehoused, etc.

Advantages and Disadvantages of a Collection

Advantages for the Exporter

(1) Where a "To Order" Bill of Lading is used or where the goods are consigned to the collecting bank with its approval, control of the goods does not pass to the buyer until he pays or accepts a Bill of Exchange.

(2) He may be able to raise finance by any of the methods already noted.

(3) Banks may be able to spot any oversight or error in his documents that could cause the buyer to refuse to accept them.

(4) The Rules for Collection are applicable to all the parties including the buyer, and therefore mis-understandings are less likely.

(5) The collecting bank may be able to press for payment and thus avoid protesting measures.

(6) A collections procedure is cheaper than a Letter of Credit.

Disadvantages for the Exporter

(1) Any finance obtained will be *with recourse* to the exporter.

(2) The exporter will not receive finance until the remitting bank receives payment unless he obtains a financial facility noted above. These facilities could be expensive.

(3) If the buyer fails to take up the goods the exporter will incur re-shipping charges, warehouse charges, demurrage charges.

Advantages to the Importer

(1) Under a clean collection, where he has already received the commercial documents, he is trading on terms similar to Open Account.

(2) With documents against acceptance, he has the chance to examine the goods without making payment.

(3) If a Time Bill is used the buyer is given time to pay.

(4) It is a cheaper system than a Letter of Credit.

(5) He may be able to obtain finance from his own bank (see Chapter 8).

Disadvantages to the Importer

(1) With a documents against payment collection, the importer must pay before he receives the goods.

(2) Default on an accepted Bill of Exchange can result in legal action against him irrespective of any discrepancies in the sales contract.

Appendix 5

ICC Uniform Rules for Collections, 1978 Revision No. 322

GENERAL PROVISIONS AND DEFINITIONS

A. These provisions and definitions and the following articles apply to all collections as defined in (B) below and are binding upon all parties thereto unless otherwise expressly agreed or unless contrary to the provisions of a national, state or local law and/or regulation which cannot be departed from.

B. For the purpose of such provisions, definitions and articles:

1. i. "Collection" means the handling by banks, on instructions received, of documents as defined in (ii) below, in order to

    a) obtain acceptance and/or, as the case may be, payment, or

    b) deliver commercial payments against acceptance and/or, as the case may be, against payment, or

    c) deliver documents on other terms and conditions.

    ii. "Documents" means financial documents and/or commercial documents:

    a) "financial documents" means bills of exchange, promissory notes, cheques, payment receipts or other similar instruments used for obtaining the payment of money;

    b) "commercial documents" means invoices, shipping documents, documents of title or other similar documents, or any other documents whatsoever, not being financial documents.

iii. "Clean collection" means collection of financial documents not accompanied by commercial documents.

iv. "Documentary collection" means collection of

a) financial documents accompanied by commercial documents;

b) commercial documents not accompanied by financial documents.

2. The "parties thereto" are:

i. the "principal" who is the customer entrusting the operation of collection to his bank;

ii. the "remitting bank" which is the bank to which the principal has entrusted the operation of collection;

iii. the "collecting bank" which is any bank, other than the remitting bank, involved in processing the collection order;

iv. the "presenting bank" which is the collecting bank making presentation to the drawee.

3. The "drawee" is the one to whom presentation is to be made according to the collection order.

C. All documents sent for collection must be accompanied by a collection order giving complete and precise instructions. Banks are only permitted to act upon the instructions given in such collection order, and in accordance with these Rules.

If any bank cannot, for any reason, comply with the instructions given in the collection order received by it, it must immediately advise the party from whom it received the collection order.

LIABILITIES AND RESPONSIBILITIES

Article 1
Banks will act in good faith and exercise reasonable care.

Article 2
Banks must verify that the documents received appear to be as listed in the collection order and must immediately advise the party from whom the collection order was received of any documents missing.

Banks have no further obligation to examine the documents.

Article 3
For the purpose of giving effect to the instructions of the principal, the remitting bank will utilize as the collecting bank:

i. the collecting bank nominated by the principal, or, in the absence of such nomination,

ii. any bank, of its own or another's choice, in the country of payment or acceptance, as the case may be.

The documents and the collection order may be sent to the collecting bank directly or through another bank as intermediary.

Banks utilizing the services of other banks for the purpose of giving effect to the instructions of the principal do so for the account of and at the risk of the latter.

The principal shall be bound and liable to indemnify the banks against all obligations and responsibilities imposed by foreign laws or usages.

Article 4

Banks concerned with a collection assume no liability or responsibility for the consequences arising out of delay and/or loss in transit of any messages, letters or documents, or for delay, mutilation or other errors arising in the transmission of cables, telegrams, telex or communication by electronic systems, or for errors in translation or interpretation of technical terms.

Article 5

Banks concerned with a collection assume no liability or responsibility for consequences arising out of the interruption of their business by Acts of God, riots, civil commotions, insurrections, wars, or any other causes beyond their control or by strikes or lockouts.

Article 6

Goods should not be dispatched direct to the address of a bank or consigned to a bank without prior agreement on the part of that bank.

In the event of goods being dispatched direct to the address of a bank or consigned to a bank for delivery to a drawee against payment or acceptance or upon other terms without prior agreement on the part of the bank, the bank has no obligation to take delivery of the goods, which remain at the risk and responsibility of the party dispatching the goods.

PRESENTATION

Article 7

Documents are to be presented to the drawee in the form in which they are received, except that remitting and collecting banks are authorized to affix any necessary stamps, at the expense of the principal unless otherwise instructed, and to make any necessary endorsements or place any rubber stamps or other identifying marks or symbols customary to or required for the collection operation.

Article 8

Collection orders should bear the complete address of the drawee or of the domicile at which presentation is to be made. If the address is incomplete or incorrect, the collecting bank may, without obligation and responsibility on its part, endeavour to ascertain the proper address.

Article 9

In the case of documents payable at sight the presenting bank must make presentation for payment without delay.

In the case of documents payable at a tenor other than sight the presenting bank must, where acceptance is called for, make presentation for acceptance without delay, and where payment is called for, make presentation for payment not later than the appropriate maturity date.

Article 10

In respect of a documentary collection including a bill of exchange payable at a future date, the collection order should state whether the commercial documents are to be released to the drawee against acceptance (D/A) or against payment(D/P).

In the absence of such statement, the commercial documents will be released only against payment.

PAYMENT

Article 11

In the case of documents payable in the currency of the country of payment (local currency), the presenting bank must, unless otherwise instructed in the collection order, only release the documents to the drawee against payment in local currency which is immediately available for disposal in the manner specified in the collection order.

Article 12

In the case of documents payable in a currency other than that of the country of payment (foreign currency), the presenting bank must, unless otherwise instructed in the collection order, only release the documents to the drawee against payment in the relative foreign currency which can immediately be remitted in accordance with the instructions given in the collection order.

Article 13

In respect of clean collections partial payments may be accepted if and to the extent to which and on the conditions on which partial payments are authorized by the law in force in the place of payment. The documents will only be released to the drawee when full payment thereof has been received.

In respect of documentary collections partial payments will only be accepted if specifically authorized in the collection order. However, unless otherwise instructed, the presenting bank will only release the documents to the drawee after full payment has been received.

In all cases partial payments will only be accepted subject to compliance with the provisions of either Article 11 or Article 12 as appropriate.

Partial payment, if accepted, will be dealt with in accordance with the provisions of Article 14.

Article 14

Amounts collected (less charges and/or disbursements and/or expenses where applicable) must be made available without delay to the bank from which the collection order was received in accordance with the instructions contained in the collection order.

ACCEPTANCE

Article 15

The presenting bank is responsible for seeing that the form of the acceptance of a bill of exchange appears to be complete and correct, but it is not responsible for the genuineness of any signature or for the authority of any signatory to sign the acceptance.

PROMISSORY NOTES, RECEIPTS and OTHER SIMILAR INSTRUMENTS

Article 16

The presenting bank is not responsible for the genuineness of any signature or for the authority of any signatory to sign a promissory note, receipt, or other similar instrument.

PROTEST

Article 17

The collection order should give specific instructions regarding protest (or other legal process in lieu thereof) in the event of non-acceptance or non-payment.

In the absence of such specific instructions the banks concerned with the collection have no obligation to have the documents protested (or subjected to other legal process in lieu thereof) for non-payment or non-acceptance.

Any charges and/or expenses incurred by banks in connection with such protest or other legal process will be for the account of the principal.

CASE-OF-NEED (PRINCIPAL'S REPRESENTATIVE) and PROTECTION OF GOODS

Article 18

If the principal nominates a representative to act as case-of-need in the event of non-acceptance and/or non-payment the collection order should clearly and fully indicate the powers of such case-of-need.

In the absence of such indication banks will not accept any instructions from the case-of-need.

Article 19
Banks have no obligation to take any action in respect of the goods to which a documentary collection relates.

Nevertheless in the case that banks take action for the protection of the goods, whether instructed or not, they assume no liability or responsibility with regard to the fate and/or condition of the goods and/or for any acts and/or omissions on the part of any third parties entrusted with the custody and/or protection of the goods. However, the collecting bank must immediately advise the bank from which the collection order was received of any such action taken.

Any charges and/or expenses incurred by banks in connection with any action for the protection of the goods will be for the account of the principal.

ADVICE of FATE, etc.

Article 20
Collecting banks are to advise fate in accordance with the following rules:

i. *Form of advice.* All advices or information from the collecting bank to the bank from which the collection order was received, must bear appropriate detail (including, in all cases, the latter bank's reference number of the collection order.

ii. *Method of advice.* In the absence of specific instructions, the collecting bank must send all advices to the bank from which the collection order was received by quickest mail but, if the collecting bank considers the matter to be urgent, quicker methods such as cable, telegram, telex, or communications by electronic systems, etc. may be used at the expense of the principal.

iii. a) *Advice of payment.* The collecting bank must send without delay advice of payment to the bank from which the collection order was received, detailing the amount or amounts collected, charges and/or disbursements and/or expenses deducted, where appropriate, and method of disposal of the funds.

b) *Advice of acceptance.* The collecting bank must send without delay advice of acceptance to the bank from which the collection order was received.

c) *Advice of non-payment or non-acceptance.* The collecting bank must send without delay advice of non-payment or advice of non-acceptance to the bank from which the collection order was received.

The presenting bank should endeavour to ascertain the reasons for such non-payment or non-acceptance and advise accordingly the bank from which the collection order was received.

On receipt of such advice the remitting bank must, within a reasonable time, give appropriate instructions as to the further handling of the documents. If such instructions are not received by the presenting bank within 90 days from its advice of non-payment or non-acceptance, the documents may be returned to the bank from which the collection order was received.

INTEREST, CHARGES, and EXPENSES

Article 21

If the collection order includes an instruction to collect interest which is not embodied in the accompanying financial document(s), if any, and the drawee refuses to pay such interest, the presenting bank may deliver the document(s) against payment or acceptance as the case may be without collecting such interest, unless the collection order expressly states that such interest may not be waived. Where such interest is to be collected the collection order must bear an indication of the rate of interest and the period covered.

When payment of interest has been refused the presenting bank must inform the bank from which the collection order was received accordingly.

If the documents include a financial document containing an unconditional and definitive interest clause the interest amount is deemed to form part of the amount of the documents to be collected. Accordingly, the interest amount is payable in addition to the principal amount shown in the financial document and may not be waived unless the collection order so authorizes.

Article 22

If the collection order includes an instruction that collection charges and/or expenses are to be for account of the drawee and the drawee refuses to pay them, the presenting bank may deliver the document(s) against payment or acceptance as the case may be without collecting charges and/or expenses unless the collection order expressly states that such charges and/or expenses may not be waived. When payment of collection charges and/or expenses has been refused the presenting bank must inform the bank from which the collection order was received accordingly. Whenever collection charges and/or expenses are so waived they will be for the account of the principal, and may be deducted from the proceeds.

Should a collection order specifically prohibit the waiving of collection charges and/or expenses then neither the remitting nor collecting nor presenting bank shall be responsible for any costs or delays resulting from this prohibition.

Article 23

In all cases where in the express terms of a collection order, or under these Rules, disbursements and/or expenses and/or collection charges are to be borne by the principal, the collecting bank(s) shall be entitled promptly to recover outlays in respect of disbursements and expenses and charges from the bank from which the collection order was received and the remitting bank shall have the right promptly to recover from the principal any amount so paid out by it, together with its own disbursements, expenses and charges, regardless of the fate of the collection.

Examples of Bills of Exchange

£4,108   London
                                                          11th August 19..

AT 90 DAYS AFTER DATE OF THIS FIRST OF EXCHANGE (SECOND OF THE SAME

TENOR AND DATE BEING UNPAID) PLEASE PAY TO OUR ORDER THE SUM OF

STERLING POUNDS FOUR THOUSAND ONE HUNDRED AND EIGHT ONLY FOR VALUE

RECEIVED

Drawn under Irrevocable Credit of Barclays Bank International Ltd.,

168 Fenchurch Street, London No. FDC/2/6789 dated 20th July 19..

To: Barclays Bank International Ltd   For and on behalf of
      168 Fenchurch Street   SPEIRS AND WADLEY LTD
      London EC3

                                               W. H. Speirs
                                               Director

£4,108   London
                                                          11th August 19..

AT SIGHT OF THIS SOLA OF EXCHANGE PAY TO OUR ORDER THE SUM OF

STERLING POUNDS FOUR THOUSAND ONE HUNDRED AND EIGHT ONLY FOR

VALUE RECEIVED

Drawn under Irrevocable Credit of Barclays Bank International Ltd.,

168 Fenchurch Street, London No. FDC/2/6789 dated 20th July 19..

To: Barclays Bank International Ltd   For and on behalf of
      168 Fenchurch Street   SPEIRS AND WADLEY LTD
      London EC3

                                               W. H. Speirs
                                               Director

FOREIGN BILL AND/OR DOCUMENTS FOR COLLECTION

Drawer/Exporter
SITPRO EXPORT LIMITED
HIGH STREET
BURTON ON TRENT
STAFFS., DE15 1YZ, ENGLAND

Drawer's/Exporter's Reference(s) (to be quoted by Bank in all correspondence)
16418   1 Nov 1976   364/B205/190

Consignee
SITPRO IRAN LTD.
Khiaban Takhte
Shiraz
IRAN

Drawee (If not Consignee)
SITPRO IRAN LTD.
Avenue Ferdowsi
Tehran, IRAN

To (Bank)
BRITISH INTERNATIONAL BANK LTD.
HIGH STREET,
BURTON ON TRENT,
STAFFS., DE15 1ZZ

For Bank use only

FORWARD DOCUMENTS ENUMERATED BELOW BY AIRMAIL. FOLLOW SPECIAL INSTRUCTIONS AND THOSE MARKED X

Bill of Exchange	Comm'l. Invoice	Cert'd./Cons. Inv.	Cert. of Origin	Ins'ce Pol./Cert.	Bill of Lading	Parcel Post Rec'pt.	Air Waybill
1	2			1	2/2		

Combined Transport Doc. | Other Documents and whereabouts of any missing Original Bill of Lading

RELEASE DOCUMENTS ON	ACCEPTANCE	PAYMENT	If unaccepted →	Protest	Do Not Protest
		X			
If documents are not taken up on arrival of goods	Warehouse Goods X	Do Not Warehouse	and advise reason by	Cable	Airmail
	Insure Against Fire	Do Not Insure X	If unpaid →	Protest	Do Not Protest X
Collect ALL Charges			and advise reason by	Cable X	Airmail
Collect Correspondent's Charges ONLY		X	Advise acceptance and due date by	Cable	Airmail
Return Accepted Bill by Airmail			Remit Proceeds by	Cable X	Airmail

In case of need refer to
SITPRO SALES LTD, 3742 AVE. FERDOWSI, TEHRAN

For Guidance | **Accept their Instructions** X

SPECIAL INSTRUCTIONS: 1. Represent on arrival of goods if not honoured on first presentation.

2. Please present through British International Bank, Tehran

Date of Bill of Exchange 1 Nov 1976

Tenor of Bill of Exchange Sight

Bill of Exchange Clausel:—

Bill of Exchange Value/Amount of Collection
£   2416.68

Please collect the above mentioned Bill and/or Documents subject to the Uniform Rules for the Collection of Commercial Paper, ICC Brochure No. 254 (July 1967). I/We agree that you shall not be liable for any loss, damage, or delay however caused which is not directly due to the negligence of your own officers or servants.

Date and Signature

Burton, 1 November 1976
H. J. Hellier

Chapter 7

Bank Finance for Exporters Short-term: Without Recourse

In the last chapter we considered ways in which exporters may be able to enlist the help of commercial banks to provide them with finance on presentation of documents so as to avoid their having to wait for payment where they are offering the buyer time to pay. We also noted that these financial services are *with recourse* to the exporter. It is now time to consider a major bank facility which can, in most circumstances, provide the exporter with finance on presentation of documents *without the bank having recourse to him in the event of default by the overseas buyer.*

DOCUMENTARY LETTERS OF CREDIT

A bank's letter of credit is simply a document issued by a bank giving its authority to another bank or banks in an overseas country to provide funds to the named holder of the letter (who is called the *beneficiary*) against the reimbursement by the issuing bank. It is therefore a bank's promise to pay and can take more than one form. (See for example Traveller's letter of Credit – Chapter 11).

In this chapter however, we are concerned with that type of credit which is used to finance international trade. It is called a *documentary* credit because it usually calls for the presentation of specific commercial and financial documents as a pre-condition of the granting of funds under the credit.

As with collections there are internationally agreed rules as to the conditions under which banks may be prepared to issue such credits. They are called "Uniform Customs and Practice for Documentary Credits", International Chamber of Commerce Publication No. 400 (1983). These are reproduced at the end of this chapter. Although they do not have legislative force their acceptance is virtually universal with the notable exception of the People's Republic of China. They have been revised on several occasions, the latest being in 1983, which came into effect in October 1984. There are usually four parties to such a financial facility although there could sometimes be three or five. They are:

The Applicant. The applicant is the party to the credit who is seeking to provide a party overseas (with whom he is conducting trade) finance made available by, or through, his own bank. Thus the applicant is usually an importer who wishes his bank to undertake to arrange for payment or promise to pay to an overseas exporter on proper presentation of documents.

The Issuing Bank. The issuing bank is that bank which is requested by the applicant to open a credit in favour of an overseas supplier. As the applicant is likely to be a customer of the bank it is in a good position to note his credit-worthiness overall and the risks it may be taking in any one credit in particular. By opening a credit the issuing bank is making itself liable to meet the payment of monies transferred to the overseas supplier, but may not be able to obtain payment from its customer/applicant if the latter runs into financial difficulties. Therefore this bank is at the centre of a Documentary Letter of Credit as it is the party taking the principal credit risk.

The Beneficiary. The beneficiary is the party named in the credit to receive the results of the facility, usually receipt of payment on the proper presentation of documents called for in the credit. Once in receipt of the credit the beneficiary has a bank's promise to pay on certain conditions, which may or may not also carry with it the right to payment at the time of presentation of documents. He is therefore in a much less risky position in terms of the credit risk than he might be if he arranged to present documents under a collections facility, which as we have seen, leaves him liable to recourse by the banks in the event of a default by the drawee. As a result, the receipt of such a credit allows the beneficiary to deliver goods in the expectation that he will be paid.

The Advising or Confirming Bank. When an issuing bank arranges for a Letter of Credit it will normally enlist the support of a bank in the beneficiary's country. That bank can be the beneficiary's own bank if the applicant to the credit has specified it as such. Otherwise it will tend to be a bank nominated by the issuing bank and with whom an account in the currency of the credit is maintained. The role of this bank can be to:

(a) Advise the Credit

In this case the bank in the beneficiary's country, on receipt of the notification of the credit from the issuing bank, passes on to (advises) the beneficiary the details of the credit. This is usually done by passing on one of the two copies of the credit received from the issuing bank. An advising bank is not itself under any liability to the beneficiary.

In the case of credits issued in the UK (an import or outward credit), the credit is normally addressed directly to the overseas beneficiary, although a bank in his country may be used to "hand-on" the credit to him. Where a bank is used in this way it will be sent a separate instruction in connection with reimbursements relating to any payment it may be authorized to make to the beneficiary.

Where no advising or "hand-on" bank is used, or where the latter is used but not for the provision of finance, the beneficiary will not receive payment or a promise to pay by the issuing bank until that bank has itself received the required documents under the credit.

(b) Confirming the Credit

An issuing bank may authorise or request a bank in the beneficiary's country to *confirm* the credit. By doing this, the confirming bank adds its own promise to pay, accept or negotiate documents presented to it by the beneficiary. The advantages of a confirmed credit to the beneficiary are:

(1) he deals with a local bank;

(2) that bank's promise will stand even if the issuing bank cannot or will not make good its own promise;

(3) bills accepted can be discounted.

Such confirmed credits are clearly useful where the issuing bank is likely to be subject to exchange control regulations which restrict its ability to honour its own credits. In such circumstances, the confirming bank's reimbursement will be delayed until the restrictions are lifted. Naturally, a bank must look carefully at a credit made available to one of its customers or one of its nationals (an export or *inward* credit) to see whether the request to add its confirmation can be accepted.

The credits issued by the major banks do not usually call for confirmation, simply because of their unrivalled standing. As confirmation carries with it an additional cost, it follows that credits issued by the major banks possess a cost advantage over credits of other banks.

An exporter may wish to be a beneficiary under a confirmed credit where he believes that a bank acting merely in an advising capacity will not, in fact, pay, accept or negotiate documents presented, perhaps because it is aware of the likelihood of late reimbursement from the issuing bank. In such circumstances the exporter would be wise to insist on a confirmed credit as part of the conditions of the contract of sale. A bank may only agree to confirm a credit if the issuing bank makes a cash deposit with it beforehand, thus partly or wholly eliminating the risk of non-reimbursement. In many developing countries regulations require that an applicant for a credit provides the issuing bank with a cash deposit as a prerequisite of the credit.

Because, as we shall see, Documentary Letters of Credit are commonly without recourse to an exporter, and also because finance is usually provided by a bank in his own country on the presentation by him of proper documents, and finally, because of the promise to pay by a bank or banks rather

Diagram 7.1
A Letter of Credit

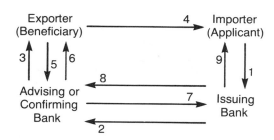

than by an overseas buyer, such credits are far superior than documents sent for collection and negotiated by a bank with recourse to the exporter.

So let us examine how credits are opened and issued. This is shown in outline in Diagram 7.1.

Diagram 7.1 sets out the parties to a credit and their relationships to each other.

1. The Application

The importer requests his bank to issue a credit in favour of a named overseas beneficiary (the exporter). This may be because exchange control regulations require all imports to be financed in this way to enable the authorities to maintain stricter control over funds moving out of the country. In any case it will have been one of the conditions in the contract of sale agreed to between the two trading parties. (See benefits of credits to applicants later in this chapter.)

When a bank is approached for a credit to be opened it will treat the request just like any other request for finance by one of its customers. Once the credit has been issued the bank will be under a liability to honour it by reimbursing the overseas bank who may have parted with money in favour of the beneficiary. However, if the applicant's financial position deteriorates in the meantime and the issuing bank is unable to extract payment, the debt may have to be written off. *It cannot be over-emphasised that the party accepting the credit risk is the issuing bank.*

Revolving (or Line of) Credit

Although a single credit for the purchase of one (or several) shipments of goods can be established it is also possible (and more usual when the importer is conducting continuous business over time), to arrange for a revolving credit, sometimes called a line of credit. This allows the applicant to make purchases over time from one or more overseas suppliers who could all be beneficiaries under the credit arrangement. Usually, the issuing bank will specify a ceiling value per time period; say £10,000 per month and the applicant is able to arrange for purchases under the credit up to that value each month. There is normally an overall ceiling (say £200,000) after which the credit arrangements will have to be re-established.

Security

The issuing bank may require the applicant to place monies in a special account to meet drawings under the credit. It is also usual for the applicant to offer the bank a letter of pledge giving it the right to hold the proceeds of goods and documents in the event of default by the applicant. (See Collections in Chapter 6). This pledge can be for just one credit or for all transactions entered into by the customer.

2. The Credit Issued

When the bank is assured that it is not taking on an undue risk it will issue the credit as requested by the customer. This will take the form of a credit notification usually addressed to a correspondent bank in the beneficiary's country, authorizing them to pay, accept or negotiate on their behalf, against specified documents to be presented by the beneficiary. The notification will also specify:

(a) whether the credit is to be confirmed or unconfirmed;

(b) whether there is to be a Bill of Exchange and if so upon whom it is to be drawn;

(c) whether the draft Bill (if any) is to be a sight or time one;

(d) which commercial documents are called for;

(e) brief description of goods and where to be shipped to and from. If the goods are going by combined transport the credit must *not* specify ports of shipment and destination but merely places of taking in charge and delivery;

(f) latest shipment date;

(g) whether partial shipments are permitted;

(h) the last date by which documents must be presented to the correspondent bank;

(i) the value of the credit;

(j) whether the credit is *revocable* or *irrevocable*.

Revocable and Irrevocable Credits

An irrevocable credit is one to which amendments cannot be made, nor can the credit be cancelled, without the full consent of all the parties to the credit.

Thus an exporter who is in receipt of an irrevocable credit can proceed to ship the goods and deliver the documents called for in the knowledge that, providing he adheres to the terms of the credit it will be honoured by the issuing bank. A revocable credit on the other hand is open to unilateral alteration or termination at any time by either the issuing bank or the applicant.

However, where the amendment or cancellation is received by the advising bank *after* it has made payment to, or promised to pay, the beneficiary, the issuing bank *is* liable to the advising bank.

It is clear from the exporter's viewpoint a revocable credit is inferior to an irrevocable one because it is possible for goods to be made ready for despatch only to receive an amendment from the applicant calling for some change that may be difficult or impossible to meet. For example, bringing forward of the date of shipment or a change in the quantity or type of product, or a demand for a particular document that might be difficult to obtain; e.g. a blacklist certificate.

On the other hand a revocable credit favours the applicant and can be used when he feels that the supplier has a questionable record, especially in connection with the *quality* of the goods he supplies. If the applicant becomes aware from his agent in the exporter's country that the supplier's goods are lacking in quality in some respect a revocable credit allows him to cancel the financial arrangement unilaterally thus ensuring that his liability under the credit is terminated. However, the underlying contract of sale still stands and the importer's liability under that is in no way affected by the cancellation of the credit. Nevertheless, a revocable credit may, in these circumstances, prove to be a factor motivating the supplier to ensure good delivery of proper goods.

Revocable credits are uncommon because few exporters are prepared to engage in transactions that can be so unilaterally terminated or adjusted. However, where the overseas buyer has undoubted integrity and is not likely to capriciously amend or cancel the credit, or where trade is between inter-related companies forming part of an international or multinational group, such credits may be acceptable. In any case it may well be that a supplier is offered only a revocable credit and must decide whether to accept or reject such terms on the basis of a status report he may be able to obtain from his bank, a chamber of commerce or a professional agency.

Confirmed and Irrevocable Credits

It is possible for a credit to be:

(a) revocable and unconfirmed;
(b) irrevocable and unconfirmed;
(c) irrevocable and confirmed.

However, there is no such thing as a revocable confirmed credit.

This is simply because no correspondent bank would be prepared to offer its own confirmation to a credit which is capable of being cancelled unilaterally. If confirmation *were* given to such a credit it would leave the confirming bank with a liability to the beneficiary without any assurance of re-imbursement from the issuing bank. Without doubt the most superior form of credit from an exporter's point of view is *the confirmed and irrevocable credit*. Not only is he assured of payment or promise to pay by a local bank, but he is protected from changes in the terms of the credit to which he has not himself concurred. It should be pointed out that amendments to irrevoc-able credits are quite common and are usually agreed to by the beneficiary. Indeed, he may himself request such an amendment – perhaps an extension in the date of the expiry of the credit – in order to more properly meet the contract of sale conditions.

3. The Credit Advice

The correspondent bank must now advise the beneficiary of the credit to which it may itself have added its own confirmation. It is possible for the credit to be advised to the beneficiary directly by the overseas issuing bank, in which case this step no. 3. does not occur. This is uncommon as exporters prefer to deal with a bank in their own country. On the other hand, the bank authorized to act as advising or confirming bank may not be conveniently near to the beneficiary and providing that the credit is a *negotiations credit* (see later in this chapter) and is designated, *freely negotiable* then the expor-ter's own bank can provide finance against documents and seek re-imbursement from the issuing bank.

When a bank advises a credit it does so as an agent of the issuing bank and unless it adds its own confirmation has no liability to the beneficiary.

4. Despatch of Goods

On receipt of the advice of the credit the exporter/beneficiary must examine its terms to see they are as agreed and that he is able to conform to them. He will know that any unilateral divergence from those terms will result in at least a delay in receipt of payment, and at worst the cancellation of the order. If there are any problems he must request the appropriate amend-ments which may or may not be acceptable to the applicant. Assuming that there are no foreseeable problems or that the irrevocable credit has been amended by agreement he can now arrange to ship the goods called for under the credit. He must ensure that the date of shipment is not later than that specified in the credit and the terms of shipment are also as specified; i.e. CIF, DCP, etc. (See Chapter 5.)

5. Presentation of Documents

The beneficiary will want to present documents to the correspondent bank as quickly as possible after despatching the goods in order to obtain his finance. In any case presentation must not be later than the expiry date of the credit itself (Article 46). In addition to this time limit for presentation of documents, the beneficiary is under an obligation to present them not later then 21 days after the issuance of the Bills of Lading or other shipping documents unless the credit itself specifies otherwise (Article 47a).

It is the responsibility of the correspondent bank to examine documents presented to it to ensure that they conform to the terms of the credit (Article 15). Should it accept irregular documents and release monies against them it may find that it will not be reimbursed by the issuing bank who may refuse to accept the documents (Article 16b). However, it must be stressed that banks have no liability or responsibility for the *accuracy* or genuineness of the documents. *Their function is only to ensure that they are as called for in the credit.* (Article 17.)

If the correspondent bank believes the documents are irregular they can:

(a) return them to the beneficiary for re-presentation but this must be within the time limit set by the credit; or

(b) advise the beneficiary to request an amendment to the terms of the credit thus making the documents acceptable; or

(c) arrange for the documents to be remitted on a documentary collections basis; or

(d) pay or promise to pay against the original documents after obtaining an indemnity either from the beneficiary or from his own bank. Such indemnities will list the discrepancies in the documents and give the bank some protection in the form of recourse against the beneficiary in the event of non-reimbursement by the issuing bank; or

(e) negotiate *under reserve*, i.e. where the credit calls for the correspondent bank to negotiate the documents, they will be accepted *with recourse* even though the credit has been confirmed; or

(f) pay the beneficiary in spite of the discrepancies if they believe them to be of little importance and likely to be ignored by the issuing bank and the applicant.

It is interesting to note that in August 1982 SITPRO reported that up to 60% of sets of documents lodged under documentary letters of credit were rejected by banks on first presentation because they were either incomplete or incorrect; and that one in five of these sets of documents were rejected for reasons of:

(a) expiry of the credit;

(b) late presentation of documents;

(c) late shipment.

Exporters who fail to comply with the terms of the credit undermine one of the major advantages they can achieve, namely, non-recourse finance on shipment. If some of them have difficulty in meeting these credit terms then either they should negotiate terms that they will be able to honour or they should find other means of financing their operation. (See Chapter 8.)

Apart from timing discrepancies referred to above, other items a beneficiary must note are:

(a) that the description of the goods in the commercial invoice corresponds with the description in the credit (Article 41c);

(b) the goods are not under-insured (Article 37b);

(c) documents are properly signed;

(d) documents must not differ in respect to details;

(e) no missing documents;

(f) insurance documents must be dated at least from day of despatch of the goods;

(g) insurance cover not less than required in the credit;

(h) no claused (dirty) Bills of Lading;

(i) non-payment of freight when trade terms call for the payment to be made by the exporter;

(j) no unacceptable type of Bills of Lading.

6. Bank Finance

We now come to what must be, from the exporter's point of view at least, the *raison d'être* of the whole exercise, namely the receipt of payment or the promise of payment on the proper presentation of documents.

Assuming that the correspondent bank finds the documents to be as called for in the credit they must now comply with whatever financial undertaking they have agreed to provide to the beneficiary (if any). There are three possibilities:

(a) *To Pay Against Submitted Documents*. This is called a *Payments Credit*. The presented documents will either include a Sight Bill of Exchange drawn on the correspondent bank or no Bill of Exchange at all. Under the new UCP for Documentary Credits, ICC Publication No. 400, a payments credit can also be defined as a *deferred* payments credit where the paying bank agrees to make payment at a point in time *after* it has received the documents; e.g. when it has itself received payment. If the credit has been confirmed then the confirming bank is under an obligation to credit the beneficiary with the value of the credit either by payment against a Sight Bill drawn on it or by payment against presentation of the commercial documents. This is without recourse to the beneficiary.

If the credit has not been confirmed the advising bank is not under an obligation to make payment but in normal circumstances will do so. Confirmed or not, once payment has been made, it is without recourse to the beneficiary. However, if the advising bank has some doubt that reimbursement by the issuing bank is likely to be delayed it may decide not to pay the beneficiary if it has not confirmed the credit, in which case the exporter will have to wait for payment until the issuing bank is in receipt of the documents.

With a payments credit there is no machinery within the credit itself for the applicant to receive time to pay. Should he require time to pay he must arrange for a separate facility with his own bank. (See Chapter 8.)

(b) *To Accept a Time Bill of Exchange Drawn on the Confirming Bank.* This is called an *Acceptance Credit.* In this case the terms of the credit calls for a time draft Bill of Exchange to be drawn on, and presented to the confirming bank together with the other required documents. As the correspondent bank has agreed to accept draft Bills of Exchange drawn upon it by the beneficiary it is not likely that it will refuse to confirm the credit. To do so would be tantamount to dishonouring its own Bills. Once accepted the Time Bill can now be discounted and the proceeds credited to the beneficiary. (See Chapter 6.) Once again this provides non-recourse finance to the exporter but in addition, as the confirming bank has not parted with funds itself (except where it has discounted its own acceptance) there is no call for reimbursement by the issuing bank (and thus the applicant) until the maturity of the Bill of Exchange. In this way the importer too has received credit even though the exporter receives payment on shipment. Where the acceptance is discounted by a first class bank in London it will attract a fine discount rate and thus release a greater proportion of the face value of the Bill of Exchange than if the Bill had been a trade one drawn on the overseas buyer. It is possible, however, for the terms of the credit to authorize the confirming bank to pay the face value of the Bill to the beneficiary and pass on all costs to the issuing bank and ultimately to the applicant.

Without doubt a confirmed acceptance credit provides a UK exporter with an excellent low cost, non-recourse source of finance.[1]

(c) *To Negotiate Presented Documents with a Draft Bill of Exchange Drawn on the Applicant, the Issuing Bank or a Third Bank.* This is called a *Negotiations Credit.* Note that a major distinction between this and the acceptance credit is that whoever *is* to be the drawee, it will *not* be the correspondent bank, who may or may not add its own confirmation.

---

[1]See section on calculation of the cost of discounting compared to negotiating in Chapter 6.

Thus whether the presented documents include a sight or time draft Bill of Exchange it is not possible for the negotiating bank (as it is now called) to *accept* the draft. This can only be done by the party named as drawee; e.g. the issuing bank.

Another very important distinction is that when a negotiations credit is unconfirmed, funds made available by the negotiating bank will be *with recourse* to the exporter. *An unconfirmed negotiations documentary letter of credit, is in fact, the only variety that is with recourse to the beneficiary.*

A confirmed negotiations credit is, of course, without recourse to the exporter.

When, under a confirmed Negotiations Credit, a Sight Bill is called for, the negotiating bank will pay the exporter immediately. When the credit is unconfirmed the bank may not wish to pay at this stage but to wait until it has received reimbursement from the issuing bank.

If the credit calls for a Time Bill to be negotiated then it is possible that the issuing bank may be able to raise finance itself by having it drawn on them and then discounting it. In this way it can raise funds to offset its reimbursement to the overseas negotiating bank. Note that in this case the discounting takes place in the country of the *issuing bank* while in the case of the acceptance credit the discounting is effected in the country of the *confirming bank*. However, as with the acceptance credit this affords the applicant time before he has to pay.

Summary

To summarize then, a Documentary Credit can be by payments, acceptance or negotiations on the part of the correspondent bank who may or may not add its own confirmation to an irrevocable credit. It usually allows for non-recourse shipment finance for the exporter and can also provide the importer with time to pay.

7. Remittance of Documents

When the issuing bank receives the documents from its overseas correspondent bank it will examine them to ensure that they appear to be as required by the terms of their credit. Article 4 of the UCP for Documentary Credits has it that ". . . all parties concerned deal in documents and not in goods", and provided the remitted documents are in order the issuing bank is obliged to honour whatever commitment it has promised. This is so even if, in the meantime, the applicant's financial position has deteriorated. If the issuing bank believes that the documents are not in order they have a duty to contact the correspondent bank within a reasonable time to say that the documents are being held by them at the disposal of the correspondent bank or alternatively to say that they are being returned for re-presentation. It should be remembered that the issuing bank may be reluctant to delay passing on the documents to their applicant customer as this will also delay the latter in obtaining delivery of the goods. However, it is unlikely that a significant error would be present, seeing that the documents have (or should have) been vetted already by the correspondent bank.

8. Bank Reimbursement

We shall be looking at the mechanism by which banks settle payments between themselves in a later chapter (see Chapter 11), but clearly when a bank has been paid funds to an exporter under a Letter of Credit it will seek to be reimbursed by the overseas issuing bank. This assumes, of course, that it has not already received a partial or total advance payment from the issuing bank prior to paying the beneficiary.

The *timing* of reimbursement will depend on the type of the credit. For example a payments credit will call for immediate reimbursement, unless it is a Deferred Payments Credit (see UCP Article 10a(ii)) while an acceptance credit which involves the discounting of a Bank Bill of exchange will require reimbursement on the date of the maturity of the Bill. In all cases the issuing bank has a clear liability to the paying, accepting or negotiating bank to meet its outgoings to the beneficiary.

In the event that exchange restrictions are applied so as to prevent the issuing bank from meeting its liabilities, and where the credit is of the confirmed, non-recourse variety, the correspondent bank will have to await the lifting of the exchange restrictions for its reimbursement.

9. Release of Documents

Once the documents have been received and vetted by the issuing bank they will be released to the applicant on the terms agreed between them. This may call for immediate payment by the applicant, especially where the credit was a payments one or where a Sight Bill of Exchange had been drawn under a Negotiations Credit. However, in most cases the importer/applicant will require some time to pay, but it should be realized that such credit arrangements fall outside the boundaries of the credit itself and are separate terms agreed to between the issuing bank and its customer. Once the documents (including a Bill of Lading), have been released to the importer he can obtain possession of the goods (see Chapter 5).

We have now outlined the basic mechanism by which Letters of Credit offers both finance and protection to the trading parties; however, we shall make a more detailed reference to the benefits and drawbacks later in this chapter. In the meantime we need to consider other varieties of credits.

(A) CLEAN REIMBURSEMENT CREDITS

Sometimes a bank acting in an advising or confirming capacity will not have an account in the currency of the credit with the issuing bank. In such cases a third bank will be authorized by the issuing bank to make payment to the

Diagram 7.2
A Reimbursement Credit

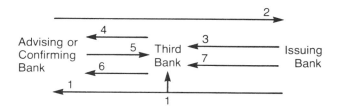

advising or confirming bank. Diagram 7.2 illustrates the operation for a clean reimbursement credit.

1. The issuing bank authorises the third bank to meet a claim made by the advising or confirming bank who is advised of their right to claim on the third bank. This would be the case where neither of the principal banks have accounts with each other in the currency of the credit but both have such accounts with the third bank.

2. The advising or confirming bank requests the issuing bank to authorize the third bank to issue a "confirmation of payment".

3. The authorization to the third bank.

4. The confirmation.

5. The claim by the advising or confirming bank.

6. Settlement by the third bank.

7. Reimbursement by the issuing bank.

Under the UCP requirements Article 11 lays down that credits must nominate the bank to pay, accept or negotiate, i.e. the *Nominated Bank*. Where this bank is not the issuing or advising or confirming bank, such nomination does not constitute any undertaking by that nominated bank, although it may be authorized by the issuing bank to pay, accept or negotiate against documents which appear on their face to be in order. The issuing bank is bound to make reimbursement.

(B) STANDBY CREDITS

A Standby Credit is issued by a bank on behalf of a customer and in favour of an overseas beneficiary in the same manner as a documentary credit except that it will *not* call for payment, acceptance or negotiation by it or an advising or confirming bank. Indeed it is an *unconditional* liability of the issuing bank to the beneficiary against the default of the applicant. It is effected by the beneficiary presenting a sight draft drawn on the issuing bank with a statement of non-performance of the applicant. It is thus a payment on *non-performance* as opposed to a payment on *performance*. The UCP for Documen-

Diagram 7.3
A Transit Credit

(a) *Issuing Bank in London*

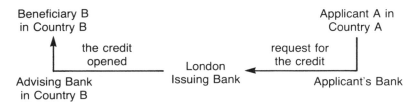

Diagram 7.4
A Transit Credit

(b) *Confirming Bank in London*

tary Credits makes standby credit subject to the same rules as other credits (Article 2).

(C) TRANSIT CREDITS

Sometimes a credit can be issued by a bank in a country other than that of the applicant and the beneficiary. This is especially the case where there is a problem of the two countries effecting business directly, and where the standing of the advising or issuing bank in the third country is of the highest integrity and not likely to be subject to exchange controls. A further factor concerns the possibility of discounting accepted Bills of Exchange at the least possible cost. London is frequently the centre of the issuing or advising a transit credit. Diagrams 7.3 and 7.4 illustrate the relationships.

(D) RE-FINANCE CREDITS

In some cases an applicant to a credit may wish to obtain time to pay via an acceptance facility but the prospective beneficiary insists on a sight payments credit. In these circumstances it may be possible to establish a sight payments credit incorporating an *inchoate* Bill of Exchange drawn by the applicant on the confirming bank. Such a Bill contains no date or value as these items will not be known accurately prior to presentation of documents.

Diagram 7.5
A Re-finance Credit

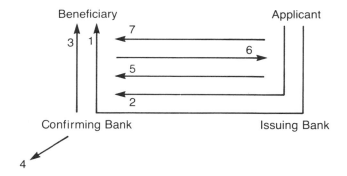

1 The credit issued; 2 The inchoate Bill of Exchange; 3 Payment against presented documents;
4 Bill completed and discounted; 5 Issuing bank reimburses confirming bank; 6 Proceeds of
discounting credited to issuing bank; 7 Issuing bank pays on maturity of the Bill and debits the
applicant.

When these are presented, the confirming/accepting bank makes a sight payment to the beneficiary and completes the details on the Bill which is then discounted. This bank receives reimbursement from the issuing bank but then credits the latter with the proceeds of the discounting, effectively giving them – and the applicant – time to pay. On maturity of the Bill the issuing bank is debited and it in turn will debit the applicant. None of these details need to be revealed to the beneficiary whose principal concern is to receive payment on shipment. A re-finance credit is illustrated in Diagram 7.5.

So far in the outline of letters of credit we have only dealt with arrangments whereby finance is made available to a beneficiary on shipment of goods. It is possible, however, for special arrangements to be made whereby the beneficiary is in receipt of payment, or promise to pay, *before* he effects shipment or presents his own invoices. This can be referred to as *Pre-Shipment Finance*.

(E) PRE-SHIPMENT FINANCE

(a) Red Clause Credits

In some types of trade, e.g. the Australian wool business, it is customary for the exporter of the wool to be granted a special clause in the credit of which he is the beneficiary, enabling him to draw funds from the advising or confirming bank *before* he presents his documents. This is to enable him to meet payments to the farmer supplying the wool. The advance payment will be deducted from the eventual payment against presented documents, and can be for part or all of the value of the credit.

Diagram 7.6
A Red Clause Credit

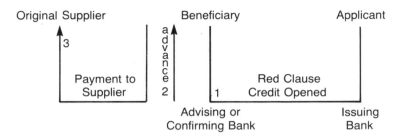

Such a credit must be arranged by the applicant and approved by the issuing bank who is liable to the paying bank in all circumstances; e.g. where an advance has been made but the documents, when presented, are out of order. The advance is without recourse to the beneficiary and its name derives from the past practice of printing the clause in red ink. Interest payment on the advance will be taken out of the residual proceeds of the credit. Diagram 7.6 illustrates a red clause credit.

After transaction 3, documents are presented in the usual way. A variant of the red clause credit is one where the issuing bank itself provides the funds for the advance made to the beneficiary by making a reimbursement immediately the advising bank credits the beneficiary's account. In both cases the beneficiary is provided with funds to assist him in the purchase of raw materials, etc., and processing costs before he ships the products and submits documents. In the event of default by the beneficiary, e.g. failure to on-ship the goods, the paying bank has recourse to the issuing bank who will turn to the applicant for reimbursement. The applicant, of course, can take action against the beneficiary for failure to comply with the terms of the credit.

(b) Transferable Credits

Another method whereby a beneficiary can obtain funds to meet payments against purchases before he presents documents is to ask his buyer to open a transferable Documentary Letter of Credit. This would be called for in the case where the beneficiary is a merchant buying goods in one centre and reselling them in another centre. The credit can only be transferred once (Article 54e). However, they can be divided into segments each transferable to different parties provided that partial shipments are allowed for in the credit. The credit is transferable only on the terms and conditions in the credit itself, except for the transferred values, the unit price of the goods and the period of validity of the transferred credit or credits. These exceptions are to permit the merchant to earn the difference between the receipts he expects from the original credit and his payments under the transferred credit or credits. Also, he will want to limit the time period of the transferred credit so as to ensure that he receives documents from the original supplier in good time before his own credit expires. One other permitted change is that the name of the beneficiary can be substituted for that of the applicant so as to protect the former's position. The credit is transferable to a supplier in the same country or in another country unless the credit states otherwise. An illustration of a transferable credit is shown in Diagram 7.7.

Once documents have been received by Advising Bank (1) the first beneficiary will be informed and he will then present his own invoice for the full value of the credit to substitute the invoices of the other beneficiaries which will total a lower value. The difference between the values represents the first beneficiary's gross profit. The substituted invoices and the other documents are now remitted in the usual way for the completion of the operation. If for any reason the first beneficiary fails to provide his own invoices, the advising bank may elect to despatch the other invoices without liability. Of course, if the second beneficiaries fail to supply documents within the time limit set by the applicant to the original credit then the term of that credit will have been breached and the applicant could refuse to allow an extension. Note that in a transferable credit there is only one issuing bank which is liable under the credit as long as its terms are adhered to.

Transferable credits are always irrevocable in practice to protect the first beneficiary from entering into a contract to purchase goods which he may find that he will not be able to pay for if the credit is revoked before the second beneficiaries are themselves paid. Of course these latter beneficiaries will themselves probably be unwilling to ship goods on the basis of a revocable credit.

It should be noted that the goods themselves can be shipped directly from the second beneficiaries to the applicant; only the invoices will be substituted. Such an arrangement is therefore very suitable for a trader who is able to obtain supplies on superior terms (perhaps because of the volume of orders or the relationship with the supplier); these terms being better than the applicant himself may be able to obtain, assuming he is even aware of the best source of supply of the goods he requires.

The International Chamber of Commerce (ICC) Banking Commission in its meetings to discuss actual problems raised by the use of Letters of Credit

Diagram 7.7
A Transferable Credit

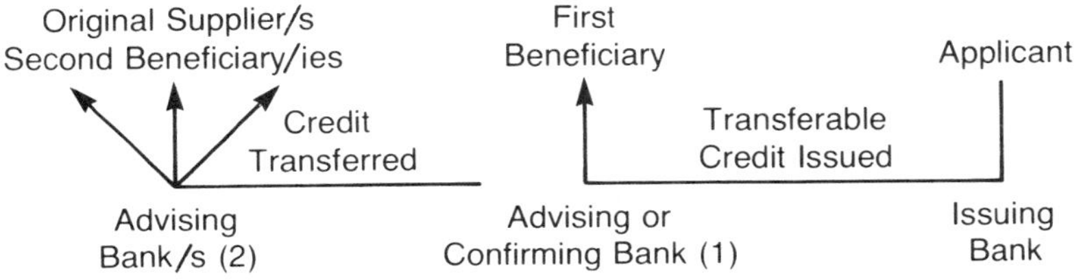

considered an aspect of transferable credits concerning the disclosure of the name of a second beneficiary and the amount made available to him by the transferring bank to the issuing bank.

The transferring bank's reply to the protestations of the first beneficiary was to the effect that it was standard practice on its part. On 8 March 1976 the Commission put out a statement saying that while it was reasonable for the issuing bank to be informed of the transfer of the credit, it was not customary practice to give that bank further details, and in any case, it would be "quite abnormal if the issuing bank, in turn, were to notify the applicant" (of further details).

At another of its sessions the Commission was asked to declare its views on a case where an advising bank refused to transfer a credit. On 1 December 1978 the decision was that the bank is entitled to make such a refusal on the basis of Article 54c, but it should at least give reasons for its refusal.

(c) Back to Back Credits

A third method by which funds can be obtained by a beneficiary under a credit before he needs to submit documents (pre-shipment finance), is to arrange a second credit as applicant, using the first credit as security. Diagram 7.8 illustrates a back to back credit.

It may be that, as with a transferable credit, the exporter is a merchant or middleman buying goods from another supplier and on-selling them to an ultimate buyer. However, it may not be possible to arrange for a transferable credit either because the ultimate buyer refuses to offer this or because the terms of a possible transferable credit are unacceptable to the original supplier.

In such cases the beneficiary under the first credit requests the bank advising that credit to issue a second credit in favour of the ultimate supplier (the beneficiary under the second credit). As that bank is to be in receipt of reimbursement from the issuing bank of the first credit it is in possession of good security for the issuance of the second credit. However, in order to protect its own position the bank issuing the second credit should not offer one superior to that of the first credit; otherwise it may find that for reasons beyond its control the first credit is aborted even though its liability under the second credit remains intact. For example, it may have parted with funds under a *sight payments* second credit while awaiting reimbursement under a *deferred payments* first credit. If the issuing bank of the first credit refuses to accept the documents on the basis of their disorder, a dispute could arise between these two banks causing delay in final reimbursement. However, it may be possible to vary them in order to allow a customer/merchant to obtain the order. For example, it may be that while the ultimate *buyer* incorporates a credit arrangement for himself in the first credit by way of a time Bill of Exchange drawn by the beneficiary on the confirming bank, the ultimate *supplier* may insist on receiving a sight payments credit. The

Diagram 7.8
A Back to Back Credit

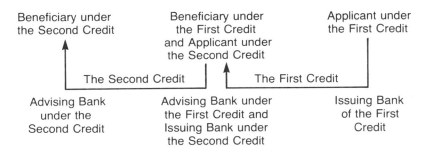

bank issuing the second credit will look for reimbursement out of the funds arising from the discounting of the accepted Bill drawn by their customer on themselves as the confirming bank of the first credit.

Another difference can be in the insured values for each credit. If the goods are supplied by the original supplier on a CIF basis through to the final destination, the insurance cover will be based on the value in the second credit which because that will be less than in the first credit, may result in under-insurance. To avoid this the middleman can be permitted to substitute his own insurance document for the one supplied by the original supplier.

As with a transferable credit certain exceptions are permitted, namely, the substitution of invoices by the middleman; a reduction in the value of the second credit to allow for his profits; and a reduction in the time allowed for the expiry of the second credit to give time for the invoice substitution and examination of documents. In addition the names of the original supplier and the ultimate buyer can be kept from each other.

Note that with a back to back credit there are *two* issuing banks and that each credit stands separately. It is conceivable that the second credit could be carried out yet the first credit could be aborted. This is quite different to a transferable credit which is *one* credit with *one* issuing bank. However, as with a transferable credit the goods can be dispatched directly to the ultimate buyer; also the middleman is relieved of the need to provide working capital prior to receipt of funds under the first credit.

Note also, that although the credits were designated "first" and "second" in relation to the timing of their issuance, they are completed in reverse order. That is, the second credit is completed *before* the first credit.

It may be that the bank advising the first credit refuses to issue the second credit; in this case the middleman can approach his own bank for this service. If approved the arrangement is referred to as a Counter Credit. This is illustrated in Diagram 7.9.

Diagram 7.9
A Counter Credit

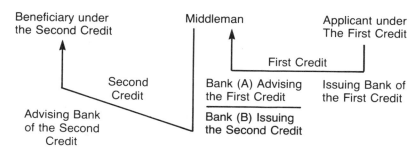

All that has been said about a back to back credit also applies to a counter credit except that in the latter case the merchant's own bank is prepared to offer the second credit on the security of the first credit. There is a slight disadvantage here in that there will be a further time delay in connection with the receipt of documents by the merchant under the second credit and the re-presentation of documents to the advising bank under the first credit. The issuing bank under the second credit will grant its customer/merchant a financial facility related to the payment to the beneficiary under the second credit, which will be repaid out of the receipts to be obtained under the first credit.

Summary of Pre-Shipment Credits

There are then three kinds of letters of credit which allow the beneficiary a facility to pay for goods before himself receiving payment on presentation of documents. They are:

(a) Red clause credits;
(b) Transferable credits;
(c) Back to back or counter credits.

They are either specific to certain kinds of trade (red clause) i.e. commodities, or they can be diverted to original suppliers (transferable), or one credit can act as security for another (back to back). Their use therefore, will depend on:

 (i) custom;
 (ii) availability;
(iii) bank's willingness to accept a credit as security.

However, before we leave the topic mention should be made of one further possibility, namely the ASSIGNMENT of credits.

(F) THE ASSIGNMENT OF LETTERS OF CREDIT

Article 55 states that a beneficiary has the right to assign the proceeds of a credit. An assignment of the proceeds of an asset gives the assignee (the party receiving the asset), the same rights as had the assignor (the party assigning the proceeds). It is possible therefore that a beneficiary under a credit wishing to use its value to make payment to an original supplier, can assign part of the value of the credit in order to make payment before he presents his own documents. An assigned credit is illustrated in Diagram 7.10.

1. Notification of irrevocable assignment of part of the value of the credit in favour of the supplier.

2. Advice of assignment to supplier and that value will be paid to him on behalf and for account of the beneficiary as and when the latter is entitled to payment and on the adherence of the term of the credit.

The assignee, being in receipt of an asset which depends on the good presentation of documents by the assignor will be paid as and when such presentation is made or when otherwise provided in the credit.

This method is inferior from the supplier's viewpoint in that his receipts will depend on the proper completion of the terms of the credit and is usually only resorted to if the assignee and assignor are well known to each other. For example, if the assignor presents documents outside the validity of the credit neither they nor the assignee will be paid. At a meeting on 1 December 1978 the ICC Banking Commission was asked to give an opinion on a situation where a bank refused to honour its undertaking to pay an assignee of an irrevocable credit. The Commission said that the solution was to be found in the law applicable to the transaction and was not covered by the UCP for Documentary Credits.

Charges

Provided there are no stipulations to the contrary all commissions and expenses have to be borne by the applicant. These costs will normally be a percentage of the value of the credit (say 0.5%). They will comprise:

(a) the issuing commission;
(b) the notifying or confirmation commission;

Diagram 7.10
An Assigned Credit

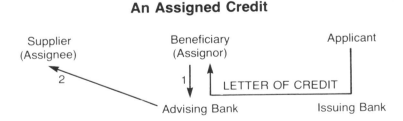

Table 7.1
Advantages and Disadvantages of Letters of Credit

Advantages	Disadvantages
To the exporter	
1. Assured shipment or pre-shipment finance.	1. Not as good as an advanced payment.
2. Generally finance is without recourse.	2. There may be problems in presenting proper documents.
3. He deals with a local bank.	3. An unconfirmed negotiations credit will be with recourse.
	4. He may have to reduce his quoted price of the goods in return for the credit.
To the importer	
1. Payment only made if the documents (and hopefully also the goods) are in order.	1. Cost of arranging the credit.
2. Receipt of the documents is assured once they have been released by the exporter.	2. He may be called on to deposit funds in a special account to cover the credit.
3. Goods likely to be delivered on time otherwise the exporter may not receive payment.	3. An irrevocable credit cannot be cancelled even if he wishes to cancel the contract of sale.
4. He can receive time to pay by use of a deferred payment or acceptance credit.	

(c) documentary examination commission;

(d) advising bank's commission;

(e) cables, airmail postage and other charges.

All commissions and charges which have been debited are not usually refundable even if the credit is unutilized in part or in whole.

Where a credit is of the acceptance type it should specify which party is to bear the discount charges. The credit may allow the beneficiary to receive the full value of the Bill of Exchange in which case, the issuing bank will meet them for the applicant's account. If there is no such reference to the credit, the beneficiary will receive the proceeds of the Bill net of the discount charges.

The Uniform Customs and Practice for Documentary Credits

The Articles contained in this document do not have the force of law but most banks in 165 countries operate letters of credit under them. They were first published in 1933 and have been revised four times, the latest being in 1983 with effect from October 1984 (ICC Publication No. 400, 1983). The Articles relevant to the period up to October 1984 are in the ICC Publication No. 290, 1974.

Prior to reproducing these Articles it would be useful to examine the main changes made by the 1983 revision.

Changes Made by UCP No. 400.

Articles 1 and 2, Standby Credits. Now may be subject to the UCP rules.

Article 10 (a) (ii), Deferred Payments. Introduced as an alternative to a sight payment. Thus there are now four possibilities; a sight payment, a deferred payment, an acceptance, a negotiation.

Article 11 (b), Nominated Bank. This new term refers to a bank which has been nominated by the issuing bank to pay at sight or not (paying bank), to accept draft Bills of Exchange (accepting bank), or to negotiate (negotiating bank).

The nominated bank can be the advising or confirming bank but if it is not, the nominated bank is under no obligation to pay, accept or negotiate (Article 11(c)). Should it do so however, the issuing bank must reimburse it provided documents are presented which appear to be in order. The introduction of a nominated bank allows for the situation where a credit has been advised to a bank not in the locality of the beneficiary. The issuing bank then can nominate a bank near to the beneficiary who may or may not be prepared to act in this capacity. However, the new Article provides for reimbursement if it does so, provided it accepts proper documents.

Article 22 (c), Reprographic Documents. Banks are authorized to accept cable, telegram or telex and it is intended to be the operative instrument it should state clearly that it is issued subject to UCP for Documentary Credits 1983 revision, ICC Publication No. 400 (Article 12(c)).

Article 22 (c), Reprographic Documents. Banks are authorised to accept documents produced as a result of automated or computerised data transmission systems provided that they are either signed by their issuer or are authenticated by some other method. Carbon copies marked as originals and authenticated by signature are also acceptable.

Article 23, Issuance of "Other" Documents. The 1974 UCP required that the description of the goods in the commercial invoice must correspond with that in the credit itself (old Article 32c). This provision is retained in the new UCP in Article 41c, but in addition there is a reference to documents other than transport, insurance and invoice documents in a new Article 23. This lays down that the credit should specify which party is to supply the other documents; e.g. certificate of origin, inspection certificates, etc. Also, the credit should stipulate the wording and data content of these other documents. If there is no such stipulation in the credit, banks can accept these documents provided they can relate the details in them to the commercial invoice.

By introducing this new Article, the UCP attempts to ensure that where the applicant to a credit wishes to obtain certain kinds of other documents he must say so in the credit. Where he fails to make this clear banks are relieved of liability if they accept these documents provided – like the credit itself – they correspond with the commercial invoice.

Articles 25 and 26. Transport Documents. If the credit calls for a Marine Bill of Lading *then Article 26 applies*. This requires that the Bill indicates that the goods have been *loaded on board the vessel* (Article 26(a)).

However, if the credit does *not* require a Marine Bill of Lading then Article 25 applies. This allows for the presentation of transport documents issued by a named carrier or his agent, indicating dispatch, or *taking a charge of the goods*, or loading on board as the case may be, provided it is not otherwise stipulated in the credit (Article 25(a)).

Further, such documents will not be rejected if they are "Combined Transport Bill of Lading" or "Combined Transport Document" or "Port to Port Bill of Lading", or a similar combination of titles, unless otherwise specified in the credit (Articles 25(b) and 26(b)).

In addition, *short-form documents* and documents *indicating the place of taking in charge* which is different from the port of loading; documents relating *to cargoes in containers or pallets* (Articles 25(b) and 26(b)); documents including the word "intended" in relation to the vessel or other means of transport and/or the port or loading and/or the port of discharge, are all acceptable if the credit does not reject them (Article 25(b)(v)).

However, banks *will* reject transport documents that indicate carriage by a charter party or by a vessel propelled only by sail; and those issued by a freight forwarder unless acting for the carrier or as a carrier in their own right, again unless otherwise shown in the credit (Articles 25 (c and d), and 26(c)).

The effect of Articles 25 and 26 is to make it clear that if goods are being transported by ocean-going vessels and the buyer wishes to ensure that the goods are loaded on board a named vessel then the credit must stipulate this and it is covered by Article 26.

However, Article 25 now makes it plain that banks can accept other forms of transport documents that relate to modern methods of packing and transportation, subject to the terms of the credit. For example, a transport document indicating only that the goods have been "taken in charge" is acceptable. Up to the time of the implementation of these new Articles exporters have had to face the problem of shipping goods in the most effective way and yet to comply within a credit calling for "a Bill of Lading". If the goods are in fact delivered to a carrier at the premises of the exporter and a combined transport document is received, the advising bank can reject such a document as not being within the terms of the credit. The new Articles are an attempt to limit these problems by putting the onus on the applicant to specify exactly his requirements in the credit which, of course, have to be accepted by the exporter; and if he fails to so specify then the exporter is permitted to present transport documents of his choice.

Apart from the changes in the latest revision, the other Articles remain as before, except of course that they are re-numbered.

Generally speaking the Articles are an attempt to achieve the following:

(a) To Define Terms

The parties to a credit including the banks are defined as to their functions and the various types of credit, revocable, irrevocable, confirmed, unconfirmed, transferable, etc., are spelled out.

(b) To Specify Bank Liabilities

It is indicated on what terms banks are liable to pay on sight or deferred terms, to accept or to negotiate; the duties of an issuing bank and a nominated bank. The proper examination of documents.

(c) To Specify Limits on Bank Liabilities

Banks are not concerned with the underlying sales contract; they deal in documents and not in goods. They are not responsible for accuracy or genuineness of documents or of any delay in their transmission.

(d) To Determine the Acceptability of Presented Documents

They must either be as specified in the credit or conform to the UCP.

(e) To Determine the Expiry Date of Credits

Old Article 37 laid down that credits must stipulate an expiry date and old Article 41 called for the credit to also stipulate the period of time after the date of the issuance of the transport documents after which documents will be refused by the banks. If no such time limit is indicated then 21 days is the maximum permitted. New Articles 46 and 47(a) repeat these requirements.

Appendix 6

UCP No. 400 (1983)

A. General provisions and definitions

Article 1

These articles apply to all documentary credits, including, to the extent to which they may be applicable, standby letters of credit, and are binding on all parties thereto unless otherwise expressly agreed. They shall be incorporated into each documentary credit by wording in the credit indicating that such credit is issued subject to Uniform Customs and Practice for Documentary Credits, 1983 revisions, ICC Publication No. 400.

Article 2

For the purposes of these articles, the expressions "documentary credit(s)" and "standby letter(s) of cre-

dit" used herein (hereinafter referred to as "credit(s)"), mean any arrangement, however named or described, whereby a bank (the issuing bank) acting at the request and on the instructions of a customer (the applicant for the credit),

i is to make a payment to or to the order of a third party (the beneficiary), or is to pay or accept bills of exchange (drafts) drawn by the beneficiary,

or

ii authorizes another bank to effect such payment, or to pay, accept or negotiate such bills of exchange (drafts),

against stipulated documents, provided that the terms and conditions of the credit are complied with.

Article 3

Credits, by their nature, are separate transactions from the sales or other contract(s) on which they may be based and banks are in no way concerned with or bound by such contract(s), even if any reference whatsoever to such contract(s) is included in the credit.

B. Form and notification of credits

Article 4

In credit operations all parties concerned deal in documents, and not in goods, services and/or other performances to which the documents may relate.

Article 5

Instructions for the issuance of credits, the credits themselves, instructions for any amendments thereto and the amendments themselves must be complete and precise.

In order to guard against confusion and misunderstanding, banks should discourage any attempt to include excessive detail in the credit or in any amendment thereto.

Article 5

A beneficiary can in no case avail himself of the contractual relationships existing between the banks or between the applicant for the credit and the issuing bank.

Article 7

a. Credits may be either
   i revocable, or
   ii irrevocable.

b. All credits, therefore, should clearly indicate whether they are revocable or irrevocable.

c. In the absence of such indication the credit shall be deemed to be revocable.

Article 8

A credit may be advised to a beneficiary through another bank (the advising bank) without engagement on the part of the advising bank, but that bank shall take reasonable care to check the apparent authenticity of the credit which it advises.

Article 9

a. A revocable credit may be amended or cancelled by the issuing bank at any moment and without prior notice to the beneficiary.

b. However the issuing bank is bound to:

   i reimburse a branch or bank with which a revocable credit has been made available for sight payment, acceptance or negotiation, for any payment, acceptance or negotiation made by such branch or bank prior to receipt by it of notice of amendment or cancellation, against documents which appear on their face to be in accordance with the terms and conditions of the credit.

ii reimburse a branch or bank with which a revocable credit has been made available for deferred payment, if such branch or bank has, prior to receipt by it of notice of amendment or cancellation, taken up documents which appear on their face to be in accordance with the terms and conditions of the credit.

Article 10

a. An irrevocable credit constitutes a definite undertaking of the issuing bank, provided that the stipulated documents are presented and that the terms and conditions of the credit are complied with:

i if the credit provides for sight payment – to pay, or that payment will be made;

ii if the credit provides for deferred payment – to pay, or that payment will be made, on the date(s) determinable in accordance with the stipulations of the credit;

iii if the credit provides for acceptance – to accept drafts drawn by the beneficiary if the credit stipulates that they are to be drawn on the issuing bank, or to be responsible for their acceptance and payment at maturity if the credit stipulates that they are to be drawn on the applicant for the credit or any other drawee stipulated in the credit;

iv if the credit provides for negotiation – to pay without

recourse to drawers and/or bona fide holders, draft(s) drawn by the beneficiary, at sight or at a tenor, on the applicant for the credit or on any other drawee stipulated in the credit other than the issuing bank itself, or to provide for negotiation by another bank and to pay, as above, if such negotiation is not effected.

b. When an issuing bank authorizes or requests another bank to confirm its irrecovable credit and the latter has added its confirmation, such confirmation constitutes a definite undertaking of such bank (the confirming bank), in addition to that of the issuing bank, provided that the stipulated documents are presented and that the terms and conditions of the credit are complied with:

i if the credit provides for sight payment – to pay, or that payment will be made;

ii if the credit provides for deferred payment – to pay, or that payment will be made, on the date(s) determinable in accordance with the stipulations of the credit;

iii if the credit provides for acceptance – to accept drafts drawn by the beneficiary if the credit stipulates that they are to be drawn on the confirming bank, or to be responsible for their acceptance and payment at maturity if the credit stipulates that they are to be drawn on the applicant for the credit or any other drawee stipulated in the credit;

iv if the credit provides for negotiation – to negotiate without recourse to drawers and/or bona fide holders, draft(s) drawn by the beneficiary, at sight or at a tenor, on the issuing bank or on the applicant for the credit or on any other drawee stipulated in the credit other than the confirming bank itself.

c. If a bank is authorized or requested by the issuing bank to add its confirmation to a credit but is not prepared to do so, it must so inform the issuing bank without delay. Unless the issuing bank specifies otherwise in its confirmation authorization or request, the advising bank will advise the credit to the beneficiary without adding its confirmation.

d. Such undertakings can neither be amended nor cancelled without the agreement of the issuing bank, the confirming bank (if any), and the beneficiary. Partial acceptance of amendments contained in one and the same advice of amendment is not effective without the agreement of all the above named parties.

Article 11

a. All credits must clearly indicate whether they are available by sight payment, by deferred payment, by acceptance or by negotiation.

b. All credits must nominate the bank (nominated bank) which is authorized to pay (paying bank), or to accept drafts (accepting bank), or to negotiate (negotiating bank), unless the credit allows negotiations by any bank (negotiationg bank).

c. Unless the nominated bank is the issuing bank or the confirming bank, its nomination by the issuing bank does not constitute any undertaking by the nominated bank to pay, to accept, or to negotiate.

d. By nominating a bank other than itself, or by allowing for negotiation by any bank, or by authorizing or requesting a bank to add its confirmation, the issuing bank authorizes such bank to pay, accept or negotiate, as the case may be, against documents which appear on their face to be in accordance with the terms and conditions of the credit, and undertakes to reimburse such bank in accordance with the provisions of these articles.

Article 12

a. When an issuing bank instructs a bank (advising bank) by any teletransmission to advise a credit or an amendment to a credit, and intends the mail confirmation to be the operative credit instrument, or the operative amendment, the teletransmission must state "full details to follow" (or words of similar effect), or that the mail confirmation will be the operative credit instrument or the operative amendment. The issuing bank must forward the operative credit instrument or the operative amendment to such advising bank without delay.

b. The teletransmission will be deemed to be the operative credit instrument or the operative amendment, and no mail confirmation should be sent, unless the teletransmission states "full details to follow" (or words of similar effect), or states that the mail confirmation is to be the operative credit instrument or the operative amendment.

c. A teletransmission intended by the issuing bank to be the operative credit instrument should clearly indicate that the credit is issued subject to Uniform Customs and Practice for Documentary Credits, 1983 revision, ICC Publication No. 400.

d. If a bank uses the services of another bank or banks (the advising bank) to have the credit advised to the beneficiary, it must also use the services of the same bank(s) for advising any amendments.

e. Banks shall be responsible for any consequences arising from their failure to follow the procedures set out in the preceding paragraphs.

Article 13

When a bank is instructed to issue, conform or advise a credit similar in terms to one previously issued, confirmed or advised (similar credit) and the previous credit has been the subject of amendment(s, it shall be understood that the similar credit will not include any such amendment(s) unless the instructions specify clearly the amendment(s) which is/are to apply to the similar credit. Banks should discourage instructions to issue, confirm or advise a credit in this manner.

Article 14

If incomplete or unclear instructions are received to issue, confirm, advise or amend a credit, the bank requested to act on such instructions may give preliminary notification to the beneficiary for information only and without responsibility. The credit will be issued, confirmed, advised or amended only when the necessary information has been received and if the bank is then prepared to act on the instructions. Banks should provide the necessary information without delay.

C. Liabilities and responsibilities

Article 15

Banks must examine all documents with reasonable care to ascertain that they appear on their face to be in accordance with the terms and conditions of the credit. Documents which appear on their face to be inconsistent with one another will be considered as not appearing on their face to be in accordance with the terms and conditions of the credit.

Article 16

a. If a bank so authorized effects payment, or incurs a deferred payment undertaking, or accepts, or negotiates against documents which appear on their face to be in accordance with the terms and conditions of a credit, the party giving such authority shall be bound to reimburse the bank which has effected payment, or incurred a deferred payment undertaking, or has accepted, or negotiated, and to take up the documents.

b. If, upon receipt of the documents, the issuing bank considers that they appear on their face not to be in accordance with the terms and conditions of the credit, it must determine, on the basis of the documents alone, whether to take up such documents, or to refuse them and claim that they appear on their face not to be in accordance with the terms and conditions of the credit.

c. The issuing bank shall have a reasonable time in which to examine the documents and to determine as above whether to take up or to refuse the documents.

d. If the issuing bank decides to refuse the documents, it must give notice to that effect without delay by telecommunication or, if that is not possible, by other expeditious means, to the bank from which it received the documents (the remitting bank), or to the beneficiary, if it received the documents directly from him. Such notice must state the discrepancies in respect of which the issuing bank refuses the documents and must also state whether it is holding the documents at the disposal of, or is returning them to, the presentor (remitting bank or the beneficiary, as the case may be). The issuing bank shall then be entitled to claim from the remitting bank refund of any reimbursement which may have been made to that bank.

e. If the issuing bank fails to act in accordance with the provisions of paragraphs (c) and (d) of this article and/or fails to hold the documents at the disposal of, or to return them to, the presentor, the issuing bank shall be precluded from claiming that the documents are not in accordance with the terms and conditions of the credit.

f. If the remitting bank draws the attention of the issuing bank to any discrepancies in the documents or advises the issuing bank that it has paid, incurred a deferred payment undertaking, accepted or negotiated under reserve or against an indemnity in respect of such discrepancies, the issuing bank shall not be thereby relieved from any of its obligations under any provision of this article. Such reserve or indemnity concerns only the relations between the remitting bank and the party towards whom the reserve was made, or from whom, or on whose behalf, the indemnity was obtained.

Article 17

Banks assume no liability or responsibility for the form, sufficiency, accuracy, genuineness, falsification or legal effect of any documents, or for the general and/or particular conditions stipulated in the documents or superimposed thereon; nor do they assume any liability or responsibility for the description, quantity, weight, quality, condition, packing, delivery, value or existence of the goods represented by any documents, or for the good faith or acts and/or omissions, solvency, performance and standing of the consignor, the carriers, or the insurers of the goods, or any other person whomsoever.

Article 18

Banks assume no liability or responsibility for the consequences arising out of delay and/or loss in transit of any messages, letters or documents, or for delay, mutilation or other errors arising in the transmission of any telecommunication. Banks assume no liability or responsibility for errors in translation or interpretation of technical terms, and reserve the right to transmit credit terms without translating them.

Article 19

Banks assume no liability or responsibility for consequences arising out of the interruption of their business by Acts of God, riots, civil commotions, insurrections, wars or any other causes beyond their control, or by any strikes or lockouts. Unless specifically authorized, banks will not, upon resumption of their business, incur a deferred payment undertaking, or effect payment, acceptance or negotiation under credits which expired during such interruption of their business.

Article 20

a. Banks utilising the services of another bank or other banks for the purpose of giving effect to the instructions of the applicant for the credit do so for the account and at the risk of such applicant.

b. Banks assume no liability or responsibility should the instructions they transmit not be carried out, even if they have themselves

taken the initiative in the choice of such other bank(s).

c. The applicant for the credit shall be bound by and liable to indemnify the banks against all obligations and responsibilities imposed by foreign laws and usages.

Article 21

a. If an issuing bank intends that the reimbursement to which a paying, accepting or negotiating bank is entitled shall be obtained by such bank claiming on another branch or office of the issuing bank or on a third bank (all hereinafter referred to as the reimbursing bank) it shall provide such reimbursing bank in good time with the proper instructions or authorization to honour such reimbursement claims and without making it a condition that the bank entitled to claim reimbursement must certify compliance with the terms and conditions of the credit to the reimbursing bank.

b. An issuing bank will not be relieved from any of its obligations to provide reimbursement itself if and when reimbursement is not effected by the reimbursing bank.

c. The issuing bank will be responsible to the paying, accepting or negotiating bank for any loss of interest if reimbursement is not provided on first demand made to the reimbursing bank, or as otherwise specified in the credit, or mutually agreed, as the case may be.

D. Documents

Article 22

a. All instructions for the issuance of credits and the credits themselves and, where applicable, all instructions for amendments thereto and the amendments themselves, must state precisely the document(s) against which payment, acceptance or negotiation is to be made.

b. Terms such as "first class", "well known", "qualified", "independent", "official", and the like shall not be used to describe the issuers of any documents to be presented under a credit. If such terms are incorporated in the credit terms, banks will accept the relative documents as presented, provided that they appear on their face to be in accordance with the other terms and conditions of the credit.

c. Unless otherwise stipulated in the credit, banks will accept as originals documents produced or appearing to have been produced:

i by reprographic systems;

ii by, or as the result of, automated or computerized systems;

iii as carbon copies,

if marked as originals, always provided that, where necessary, such documents appear to have been authenticated.

Article 23

When documents other than transport documents, insurance documents and commercial invoices are called for, the credit should stipulate by whom such documents are to be issued and their wording or data content. If the credit does not so stipulate, banks will accept such documents as presented, provided that their data content makes it possible to relate the goods and/or services referred to therein to those referred to in the commercial invoice(s) presented, or to those referred to in the credit if the credit does not stipulate presentation of a commercial invoice.

Article 24

Unless otherwise stipulated in the credit, banks will accept a document bearing a date of issuance prior to that of the credit, subject to such document being presented within the time limits set out in the credit and in these articles.

D1. Transport documents (documents indicating loading on board or dispatch or taking in charge)

Article 25

Unless a credit calling for a transport document stipulates as such document a marine bill of lading (ocean bill of lading or a bill of lading covering carriage by sea), or a post receipt or certificate of posting:

a. banks will, unless otherwise stipulated in the credit, accept a transport document which:

i appears on its face to have been issued by a named carrier, or his agent, and

ii indicates dispatch or taking in charge of the goods, or loading on board, as the case may be, and

iii consists of the full set of originals issued to the consignor if issued in more than one original, and

iv meets all other stipulations of the credit.

b. Subject to the above, and unless otherwise stipulated in the credit, banks will not reject a transport document which:

i bears a title such as "Combined transport bill of lading", "Combined transport document", "Combined transport bill of lading or port-to-port bill of lading", or a title or a combination of titles of similar intent and effect, and/or

ii indicates some or all of the conditions or carriage by reference to a source or document other than the transport document itself (short form/blank back transport document), and/or

iii indicates a place of taking in charge different from the port of loading and/or a place of final destination different from the port of discharge, and/or

iv relates to cargoes such as those in Containers or on pallets, and the like, and/or

v contains the indication "intended", or similar qualification, in relation to the vessel or other means of transport, and/or the port of loading and/or the port of discharge.

c. Unless otherwise stipulated in the credit in the case of carriage by sea or by more than one mode of transport but including carriage by sea, banks will reject a transport document which:

i indicates that it is subject to a charter party, and/or

ii indicates that the sailing vessel is propelled by sail only.

d. Unless otherwise stipulated in the credit, banks will reject a transport document issued by a freight forwarder unless it is the FIATA Combined Transport Bill of Lading approved by the International Chamber of Commerce or otherwise indicates that it is issued by a freight forwarder acting as a carrier or agent of a named carrier.

Article 26

If a credit calling for a transport document stipulates as such document a marine bill of lading:

a. banks will, unless otherwise stipulated in the credit, accept a document which:

i appears on its face to have been issued by a named carrier, or his agent, and

ii indicates that the goods have been loaded on board or shipped on a named vessel, and

iii consists of the full set of originals issued to the consignor if issued in more than one original, and

iv meets all other stipulations of the credit.

b. Subject to the above, and unless otherwise stipulated in the credit, banks will not reject a document which:

i bears a title such as "Combined transport bill of lading", "Combined transport document", "Combined transport bill of lading or port-to-port bill of lading", or a title or a combination of titles or similar intent and effect, and/or

ii indicates some or all of the conditions of carriage by reference to a source or document other than the transport document itself (short form/blank back transport document), and/or

iii indicates a place of taking in charge different from the port of loading, and/or a place of final destination different from the port of discharge, and/or

iv relates to cargoes such as those in Containers or on pallets, and the like.

---

c. Unless otherwise stipulated in the credit, banks will reject a document which:

i indicates that it is subject to a charter party, and/or

ii indicates that the carrying vessel is propelled by sail only, and/or

iii contains the indication "intended", or similar qualification in relation to

● the vessel and/or the port of loading — unless such document bears an on board notation in accordance with article 27(b) and also indicates the actual port or loading, and/or

● the port of discharge — unless the place of final destination indicated on the document is other than the port of discharge, and/or

iv is issued by a freight forwarder, unless it indicates that it is issued by such freight forwarder acting as a carrier, or as the agent or a named carrier.

Article 27

a. Unless a credit specifically calls for an on board transport document, or unless inconsistent with other stipulation(s) in the credit, or with article 26, banks will accept a transport document which indicates that the goods have been taken in charge or received for shipment.

---

b. Loading on board or shipment on a vessel may be evidence either by a transport document bearing wording indicating loading on board a named vessel or shipment on a named vessel, or, in the case of a transport document stating "received for shipment", by means of a notation of loading on board on the transport document signed or initialled and dated by the carrier or his agent, and the date of this notation shall be regarded as the date of loading on board the named vessel or shipment on the named vessel.

Article 28

a. In the case of carriage by sea or by more than one mode of transport but including carriage by sea, banks will refuse a transport document stating that the goods are or will be loaded on deck, unless specifically authorized in the credit.

b. Banks will not refuse a transport document which contains a provision that the goods may be carried on deck, provided it does not specifically state that they are or will be loaded on deck.

Article 29

a. For the purpose of this article transhipment means a transfer and reloading during the course of carriage from the port of loading or place of dispatch or taking in charge to the port of discharge or place of destination either from one conveyance or vessel to another conveyance or vessel within the same mode of transport to another mode of transport.

b. Unless transhipment is prohibited by the terms of the credit, banks will accept transport documents which indicate that the goods will be transhipped, provided the entire carriage is covered by one and the same transport document.

c. Even if transhipment is prohibited by the terms of the credit, banks will accept transport documents which:

i incorporate printed clauses stating that the carrier has the right to tranship, or

ii state or indicate that transhipment will or may take place, when the credit stipulates a combined transport document, or indicates carriage from a place of taking in charge to a place of final destination by different modes of transport including a carriage by sea, provided that the entire carriage is

covered by one and the same transport document, or

iii state or indicate that the goods are in a Container(s), trailer(s), "LASH" barge(s), and the like and will be carried from the place of taking in charge to the place of final destination in the same Container(s), trailer(s), "LASH" barge(s), and the like under one and the same transport document.

iv state or indicate the place of receipt and/or of final destination as "C.F.S." (container freight station) or "C.Y." (container yard) at, or associated with, the port or loading and/or the port of destination.

Article 30

If the credit stipulates dispatch of goods by post and calls for a post receipt or certificate of posting, banks will accept such post receipt or certificate of posting if it appears to have been stamped or otherwise authenticated and dated in the place from which the credit stipulates the goods are to be dispatched.

Article 31

a. Unless otherwise stipulated in the credit, or inconsistent with any of the documents presented under the credit, banks will accept transport documents stating that freight or transportation charges (hereinafter referred to as "freight") have still to be paid.

b. If a credit stipulates that the transport document has to indicate that freight has been paid or prepaid, banks will accept a transport document on which words clearly indicating payment or repayment of freight appear by stamp or otherwise, or on which payment of freight is indicated by other means.

c. The words "freight payable" or "freight to be prepaid" or words of similar effect, if appearing on transport documents, will not be accepted as constituting evidence of the payment of freight.

d. Banks will accept transport documents bearing reference by stamp or otherwise to costs additional to the freight charges, such as costs of, or disbursements incurred in connection with, loading, unloading or similar operations, unless the conditions of the credit specifically prohibit such reference.

Article 32

Unless otherwise stipulated in the credit, banks will accept transport documents which bear a clause on the face thereof such as "shippers load and count" or "said by shipper to contain" or words of similar effect.

Article 33

Unless otherwise stipulated in the credit, banks will accept transport documents indicating as the consignor of the goods a party other than the beneficiary of the credit.

Article 34

a. A clean transport document is one which bears no superimposed clause or notation which expressly declares a defective condition of the goods and/or the packaging.

b. Banks will refuse transport documents bearing such clauses or notations unless the credit expressly stipulates the clauses or notations which may be accepted.

c. Banks will regard a requirement in a credit for a transport document to bear the clause "clean on board" as complied with if such transport document meets the requirements of this article and of article 27(b).

D2. Insurance documents

Article 35

a. Insurance documents must be as stipulated in the credit, and must be issued and/or signed by insurance companies or underwriters, or their agents.

b. Cover notes issued by brokers will not be accepted, unless spe cifically authorised by the credit.

Article 36

Unless otherwise stipulated in the credit, or unless it appears from the insurance document(s) that the cover is effective at the latest from the date of loading on board or dispatch or taking in charge of the goods, banks will refuse insurance documents presented which bear a date later than the date of loading on board or dispatch or taking in charge of the goods as indicated by the transport document(s).

Article 37

a. Unless otherwise stipulated in the credit, the insurance document must be expressed in the same currency as the credit.

b. Unless otherwise stipulated in the credit, the minimum amount for which the insurance document must indicate the insurance cover to have been effected is the CIF (cost, insurance and freight ... "named port of destination") or CIP (freight/carriage and insurance paid to "named point of destination") value of the goods, as the case may be, plus 10%. However, if banks cannot determine the CIF or CIP value, as the case may be, from the documents on their face, they will accept as such minimum amount the amount for which payment, acceptance or negotiation is requested under the credit, or the amount of the commercial invoice, whichever is the greater.

Article 38

a. Credits should stipulate the type of insurance required and, if any, the additional risks which are to be covered. Imprecise terms such as "usual risks" or "customary risks"

should not be used; if they are used, banks will accept insurance documents as presented, without responsibility for any risks not being covered.

b. Failing specific stipulations in the credit, banks will accept insurance documents as presented, without responsibility for any risks not being covered.

Article 39

Where a credit stipulates "insurance against all risks", banks will accept an insurance document which contains any "all risks" notation or clause, whether or not bearing the heading "all risks", even if indicating that certain risks are excluded, without responsibility for any risk(s) not being covered.

Article 40

Banks will accept an insurance document which indicates that the cover is subject to a franchise or an excess (deductible), unless it is specifically stipulated in the credit that the insurance must be issued irrespective of percentage.

D3.   Commercial invoice

Article 41

a. Unless otherwise stipulated in the credit, commercial invoices must be made out in the name of the applicant for the credit.

b. Unless otherwise stipulated in the credit, banks may refuse commercial invoices issued for amounts in excess of the amount permitted by the credit. Nevertheless, if a bank authorised to pay, incur a deferred payment undertaking, accept, or negotiate under a credit accepts such invoices, its decision will be binding upon all parties, provided such bank has not paid, incurred a deferred payment undertaking, accepted or effected negotiation for an amount in excess of that permitted by the credit.

c. The description of the goods in the commercial invoice must correspond with the description of the credit. In all other documents, the goods may be described in general terms not inconsistent with the description of the goods in the credit.

D4. Other documents

Article 42

If a credit calls for an attestation or certification of weight in the case of transport other than by sea, banks will accept a weight stamp or declaration of weight which appears to have been superimposed on the transport document by the carrier or his agent unless the credit specifically stipulates that the attestation or certification of weight must be by means of a separate document.

E. Miscellaneous provisions

Quantity and amount

Article 43

a. The words "about", "circa" or similar expressions used in connection with the amount of the credit or the quantity or the unit price stated in the credit are to be construed as allowing a difference not to exceed 10% more or 10% less than the amount or the quantity or the unit price to which they refer.

b. Unless a credit stipulates that the quantity of the goods specified must not be exceeded or reduced, a tolerance of 5% more or 5% less will be permissible, even if partial shipments are not permitted, always provided that the amount of the drawings does not exceed the amount of the credit. This tolerance does not apply when the credit stipulates the quantity in terms of a stated number of packing units or individual items.

Partial drawings and/or shipments

Article 44

a. Partial drawing and/or shipments are allowed, unless the credit stipulates otherwise.

b. Shipments by sea, or by more than one mode of transport but including carriage by sea, made on the same vessel and for the same voyage, will not be regarded as partial shipments, even if the transport documents indicating loading on board bear different dates of issuance and/or indicate different ports of loading on board.

c. Shipments made by post will not be regarded as partial shipments if the post receipts or certificates of posting appear to have been stamped or otherwise authenticated in the place from which the credit stipulates the goods are to be dispatched, and on the same date.

d. Shipments made by modes of transport other than those referred to in paragraphs (b) and (c) of this article will not be regarded as partial shipments, provided the transport documents are issued by one and the same carrier or his agent and indicate the same date of issuance, the same place of dispatch or taking in charge of the goods, and the same destination.

Drawings and/or shipments by instalments

Article 45

If drawings and/or shipments by instalments within given periods are stipulated in the credit and any instalment is not drawn and/or shipped within the credit allowed for that instalment, the credit ceases to be available for that and any subsequent instalments, unless otherwise stipulated in the credit.

Expiry date and presentation

Article 46

a. All credits must stipulate an expiry date for presentation of documents for payment, acceptance or negotiation.

b. Except as provided in Article 48(a), documents must be presented on or before such expiry date.

c. If an issuing bank states that the credit is to be available "for one month", "for six months" or the like, but does not specify the date from which the time is to run, the date of issuance of the credit by the issuing bank will be deemed to be the first day from which such time is to run. Banks should discourage indication of the expiry date of the credit in this manner.

Article 47

a. In addition to stipulating an expiry date for presentation of documents, every credit which calls for a transport document(s) should also stipulate a specified period of time after the date of issuance of the transport document(s) during which presentation of documents for payment, acceptance or negotiation must be made. If no such period of time is stipulated, banks will refuse documents presented to them later than 21 days after the date of issuance of the transport document(s). In every case, however, documents must be presented not later than the expiry date of the credit.

---

b. For the purpose of these articles, the date of issuance of a transport document(s) will be deemed to be:

i in the case of a transport document evidencing dispatch, or taking in charge, or receipt of goods for shipment by a mode of transport other than by air — the date of issuance indicated on the transport document or the date of the reception stamp thereon whichever is the later.

ii in the case of a transport document evidencing carriage by air — the date of issuance indicated on the transport document or, if the credit stipulates that the transport document shall indicate an actual flight date, the actual flight date as indicated on the transport document.

iii in the case of a transport document evidencing loading on board a named vessel — the date of issuance of the transport document or, in the case of an on board notation in accordance with article 27(b), the date of such notation.

iv in cases to which Article 44(b) applies, the date determined as above of the latest transport document issued.

Article 48

a. If the expiry date of the credit and/or the last day of the period of time after the date of issuance of the transport document(s) for presentation of documents stipulated by the credit or applicable by virtue of Article 47 falls on a day on which the bank to which presentation has to be made is closed for reasons other than those referred to in article 19, the stipulated expiry date and/or the last day of the period of time after the date of issuance of the transport document(s) for presentation of documents, as the case may be, shall be extended to the first opening business day on which such bank is open.

---

b. The latest date for loading on board, or dispatch, or taking in charge shall not be extended by reason of the extension of the expiry date and/or the period of time after the date of issuance of the transport document(s) for presentation of document(s) in accordance with this article. If no such latest date for shipment is stipulated in the credit or amendments thereto, banks will reject transport documents indicating a date of issuance later than the expiry date stipulated in the credit or amendments thereto.

---

c. The bank to which presentation is made on such first following business day must add to the documents its certificate that the documents were presented within the time limits extended in accordance with Article 48(a) of the Uniform Customs and Practice for Documentary Credits, 1983 revision, ICC Publication No. 400.

Article 49

Banks are under no obligation to accept presentation of documents outside their banking hours.

Loading on board, dispatch and taking in charge (shipment)

Article 50

a.   Unless otherwise stipulated in the credit, the expression "shipment" used in stipulating an earliest and/or a latest shipment date will be understood to include the expressions "loading on board", "dispatch" and "taking in charge".

b.   The date of issuance of the transport document determined in accordance with article 47(b) will be taken to be the date after shipment.

c.   Expressions such as "prompt", "immediately", "as soon as possible", and the like should not be used. If they are used, banks will interpret them as a stipulation that shipment is to be made within thirty days from the date of issuance of the credit by the issuing bank.

d.   If the expression "on or about" and similar expressions are used, banks will interpret them as a stipulation that shipment is to be made during the period from five days before to five days after the specified date, both end days included.

Date terms

Article 51

The words "to", "until", "till", "from", and words of similar import applying to any date term in the credit will be understood to include the date mentioned. The word "after" will be understood to exclude the date mentioned.

Article 52

The terms "first half", "second half" of a month shall be construed respectively as from the 1st to the 15th, and the 16th to the last day of each month, inclusive.

Article 53

The terms "beginning", "middle", or "end" of a month shall be construed respectively as from the 1st to the 10th, the 11th to the 20th, and the 21st to the last day of each month, inclusive.

F.   Transfer

Article 54

a.   A transferable credit is a credit under which the beneficiary has the right to request the bank called upon to effect payment or acceptance or any bank entitled to effect negotiation to make the credit available in whole or in part to one or more other parties (second beneficiaries).

---

b. A credit can be transferred only if it is expressly designated as "transferable" by the issuing bank. Terms such as "divisible", "fractionable", "assignable", and "transmissible" add nothing to the meaning of the term "transferable" and shall not be used.

---

c. The bank requested to effect the transfer (transferring bank), whether it has confirmed the credit or not, shall be under no obligation to effect such transfer except to the extent and in the manner expressly consented to by such bank.

---

d. Bank charges in respect of transfers are payable by the first beneficiary unless otherwise specified. The transferring bank shall be under no obligation to effect the transfer until such charges are paid.

---

e. A transferable credit can be transferred once only. Fractions of a transferable credit (not exceeding in the aggregate the amount of the credit) can be transferred separately, provided partial shipments are not prohibited, and the aggregate of such transfers will be considered as constituting only one transfer of the credit. The credit can be transferred only on the terms and conditions specified in the original credit, with the exception of the amount of the credit, or any unit prices stated therein, of the period of validity, of the last date for presen-

tation of documents in accordance with Article 47 and the period for shipment, any or all of which may be reduced or curtailed, or the percentage for which insurance cover must be effected, which may be increased in such a way as to provide the amount of cover stipulated in the original credit, or these articles. Additionally, the name of the first beneficiary can be substituted for that of the applicant for the credit, but if the name of the applicant for the credit is specifically required by the original credit to appear in any document other than the invoice, such requirement must be fulfilled.

---

f. The first beneficiary has the right to substitute his own invoices (and drafts if the credit stipulates that drafts are to be drawn on the applicant for the credit) in exchange for those of the second beneficiary, for amounts not in excess of the original amount stipulated in the credit and for the original unit prices if stipulated in the credit and upon such substitution of invoices and drafts) the first beneficiary can drawn under the credit for the difference, if any, between his invoices and the second beneficiary's invoices. When a credit has been transferred and the first beneficiary is to supply his own invoices (and drafts) in exchange for the second beneficiary's invoices (and drafts) but fails to do so on first demand, the paying, accepting or negotiating bank has the right to deliver to the issuing bank the documents received under the credit, including the second beneficiary's invoices (and drafts) without further responsibility to the first beneficiary.

---

g. Unless otherwise stipulated in the credit, the first beneficiary of a transferable credit may request that the credit be transferred to a second beneficiary in the same country, or in another country. Further, unless otherwise stipulated in the credit, the first beneficiary shall have the right to request that payment or negotiation be effected to the second beneficiary at the place to which the credit has been transferred, up to and including the expiry date of the original credit, and without prejudice to the first beneficiary's right subsequently to substitute his own invoices and drafts (if any) for those of the second beneficiary and to claim any difference due to him.

Assignment of proceeds

Article 55

The fact that a credit is not stated to be transferable shall not affect the beneficiary's right to assign any proceeds to which he may be, or may become, entitled under such credit, in accordance with the provisions of the applicable law.

The Uniform Customs and Practice for Documentary Credits were proposed by the ICC Commission on Banking Technique and Practice. This Commission brings together bankers from throughout the world with the object of:

● defining, simplifying and harmonizing the practices and terminology used in international banking;

● expressing the views of bankers before relevant international organizations, in particular the United Nations Commission on International Trade Law (UNCITRAL);

● serving as a forum for bankers to discuss common problems.

Each ICC National Committee may appoint members of the Banking Commission, and of the twenty other ICC Commissions covering most subject areas of interest to international business.

Seminars and conferences on practical aspects of the application of the UCP are also held every year in numerous countries: details on application from National Committees.

ICC publication no. 400, *Uniform Customs and Practice for Documentary Credits*, copyright © 1983.

This and other ICC publications are available from the International Chamber of Commerce, 38 Cours Albert 1er, 75008 Paris, from ICC UNITED KINGDOM, Centre Point, 103 New Oxford Street, London, WC1A 1QB and from other ICC National Committees in over fifty countries.

The ICC is the representative organisation for International business and is supported through membership subscriptions. Although a private organisation without legal backing, its rules for the facilitation of trade and payments are accepted worldwide because they are sensible and practical.

Chapter 8

Other Trade Finance

In the previous two chapters we looked at ways in which banks can provide finance for exporters. In this chapter we are concerned with other forms of trade finance which are both with and without recourse and can range from the short-term to the medium-term period. As before we shall be ignoring the facilities of the Export Credits Guarantee Department (ECGD) for they will be dealt with in a special chapter (see Chapter 10).

This chapter comprises the following:

(A) Non-Bank Export Finance

(1) Export Houses facilities
(2) Hire Purchase
(3) Leasing
(4) Credit Factoring
(5) Invoice Discounting
(6) Forfaiting

(B) Import Financing

(1) Bank facilities
(2) Non-bank facilities

(A) NON-BANK EXPORT FINANCE

(1) EXPORT HOUSES

We start by looking at ways in which UK exporters can finance their overseas trade other than from the banking sector, although as we shall see, many of these facilities are in fact provided by bank subsidiary companies.

When we looked at intermediaries in Chapter 4 we saw that there were a number of them that were in the business of providing finance. For example:

(a) *Export Merchants*. Purchase goods from the supplier for cash and can give credit to overseas buyers;

(b) *Export Distributors/Managers*. May be prepared to pay cash on shipment and offer the overseas buyer better credit terms than could the supplier.

(c) *The Confirming House*. May be able to confirm an order placed with an exporter and possibly open a documentary letter of credit in his favour with credit extended to the buyer. As the Confirming House acts as agent for the buyer this is very like a UK bank issuing a letter of credit in favour of a UK supplier but on behalf of an overseas client. Documents are presented to the house who will add its own invoice for its fees which could be 3% to 4% of the contract value.

The Confirming House can have these documents negotiated by its bank with the interest cost being met by passing them to on to the buyer. In so doing it ceases to be a *provider* of finance and becomes instead a *risk taker*. That is, its prime function is to take the risk that the overseas buyer may not meet his obligations to pay. It should be noted here that many of these intermediary finance houses are themselves covered by credit insurance from the Export Credits Guarantee Department. A variant of the Confirming House is the *Buying House* (see Chapter 4). They too will pay a supplier on shipment. Both tend to offer short-term credit facilities; usually up to six months.

(d) *The Export Finance House*. These specialist finance institutions can, in fact, provide a wide variety of financial facilities including hire-purchase, leasing and direct loans. The first two are dealt with separately later on in this chapter. Here we are concerned with their export credit services.

Some of the largest are subsidiaries of UK banks. For example, the British Overseas Engineering and Credit Company (BOECC) is a subsidiary of Midland Bank and Barclays Export Services (BES) is a subsidiary of Barclay's Bank.

Whereas the Confirming House acts on behalf of the overseas buyer, the Export Finance House acts on behalf of the exporter. They give credit of up to five years to the overseas buyer and pay the exporter on shipment on a without recourse basis. They can be responsible for the administrative work including collecting payments, buyer information and overseas trade requirements. Exports which qualify for the longer-term credit periods include machine tools, commercial vehicles, printing machinery, etc. However, for these types of goods requiring (say) five years credit, the buyer must pay 15% in advance to the seller and repays the House in six-monthly instalments.

For consumer goods, raw materials and semi-finished goods there is no advance payment required but the credit period extended to the buyer is limited to 180 days. As with many Confirming Houses, Export Finance Houses tend to be covered by Export Credits Guarantee Department credit insurance. Because of this they can usually offer low rates of interest both short- and medium-term. In addition they charge a service fee. The availability and terms of their services depend on the credit-worthiness of the overseas buyer and the political and economic conditions in the buyer's country. They can supply both sterling and currency loans.

The advantages to an exporter are:

  (i) Non-recourse finance;
 (ii) Low cost finance (although a similar facility may be available direct from ECGD);
(iii) Loans made direct to overseas buyers.

The disadvantages are:

  (i) Service fees;
 (ii) Limit may be placed on the credit value and/or period, or indeed, the House may not offer credit at all.

(2) HIRE PURCHASE

This arrangement allows for the exporter to be paid in full by the Hire Purchase Company who obtains instalment payments from the buyer overseas. However, because hire purchase restrictions vary from country to country it is not usual for the credit to be made available from the country of export. Instead the exporter can either:

  (i) approach a Hire Purchase Company (usually a bank subsidiary) who will contact one of its overseas offices to arrange the facility for the buyer. Alternatively an Export Finance House can be used who will also put the business in the hands of one of its overseas offices, or

 (ii) ask a Hire Purchase Company or Export Finance House to put the business the way of a member of one of the International Credit Unions resident in the buyer's country. There are a number of these Unions, for example The Amstel Club with The United Dominions Trust as its British member, or Eurocredit with Lloyds and Scottish as their British member. Members have reciprocal arrangements to provide credit to each other's importer customers.

The outcome of either method is for the exporter to receive full non-recourse payment on shipment and the buyer receives credit from a local Finance House in the form of instalment payments over an agreed period of time, although the terms of the credit will depend on the limitations imposed on this form of finance in the importer's country. In addition to these limitations, the interest rate cost is likely to be higher than provided directly by the bank.

(3) LEASING

Leasing differs from Hire Purchase in that the latter provides for the ownership of the goods to be passed to the buyer at the outset of the arrangement whereas the former provides for the *use* of a capital good by an overseas user, who is called the lessee, and who pays a leasing rental to the Leasing Company who is called the lessor, but who does not have ownership of the goods which is in the hands of the lessor. The arrangements can be effected in the same way as for Hire Purchase, namely, through an overseas network of offices or through an International Credit Union.

There are two major reasons for the growth of Leasing; they are:

(i) Overseas buyers of expensive, high-obsolescence capital goods may find that an outright purchase is too costly even when credit is advanced. Leasing the goods instead gives immediate use of the products and the chance to switch to a newer, more productive alternative at the end of the leasing period without incurring large capital outlays.

(ii) Because ownership of the goods is retained by the Leasing Company (again subsidiaries of banks) they attract depreciation allowances against tax that they are able to pass on to the user in the form of lower rentals.

Goods that are commonly leased are plant, machinery, computers, vehicles, ships. On the termination of the leasing period, which is usually for three years or more, the property reverts to the Leasing Company. In the UK there is no provision for the user to become the owner but in overseas countries this may be permitted.

There are various forms of Leasing but the more common are:

(i) Finance Leasing

Here the Leasing Company will determine a rental based on the life of the product. At the end of the agreed rental period the lessee may be permitted to act as an agent to on-sell the equipment and to retain a large proportion of the proceeds. If the lessee wishes to continue using the equipment then the rental charges are reduced to a small level.

(ii) Operating Leasing

In this case the Leasing Company calculates its leasing rentals according to the period of the rental which is usually shorter than the life of the product. So, for example, if a machine has a possible ten-year life but a lessee only wants to lease it for three years due perhaps to the likelihood of a newer model coming on the market, then the rental charged will relate to only a percentage of the total value of the machine. In effect, the Leasing Company is taking a view about its residual value in terms of re-leasing it to another user.

(iii) Cross-border Leasing

This is where the overseas lessee deals directly with a UK Leasing Company. This is mostly used for large transactions, say, an entire plant where there would be a need for very close consultation between the supplier, the Leasing Company and the lessee.

(iv) Local Leasing

Here, the overseas user is in contact with a local Leasing Company introduced by the Leasing Company in the supplier's country through a credit club or union. The advantages to a lessee is that he gets 100% "delivered cost" finance and pays in local currency. This is more common for lower value items.

Advantages and Disadvantages of Leasing

Advantages for the lessee

  (i) Low rentals due to tax benefits accrued by the Leasing Company;
 (ii) Tax relief on rentals;
(iii) No capital outlay;
 (iv) Rental terms can be adjusted to suit the needs of the lessee.

Disadvantages for the Lessee

  (i) Leasing normally available for certain types of products only;
 (ii) The goods may never be owned by the lessee.

Advantages for the Supplier

  (i) Non-recourse shipment finance;
 (ii) Possible increase in overseas marketing due to attractive financial arrangements for the buyer;
(iii) No currency risks.

Disadvantages for the Supplier

  (i) Leasing Company may require a price discount;
 (ii) Cross-border leasing can involve considerable co-operation with both the Leasing Company and the lessee.

(4) CREDIT FACTORING

This first started in the UK by US subsidiaries who were accustomed to open account trading on an inter-state basis at home and who were familiar with the facilities offered by Factors. Later the UK clearing banks took an interest and purchased controlling shares of UK Factoring Companies, as did some Confirming Houses. An example is that of Griffin Factors who are part of the Midland Bank Group. They are also members of an international body of Factors called Factors Chain International (FCI).

Export factoring can provide a useful service to an exporter trading on an open account basis as it offers a number of facilities which can be categorized in two headings:

(a) A Management Service

The exporter (called the client) sells his sales receivables (invoices) to the Factor. When invoices are despatched a copy goes to the Factor. The buyer (called the customer) is required to pay the Factor. The Factor becomes responsible for:

  (i) All sales ledger work;
 (ii) Despatch of statements usually on a monthly basis;
(iii) Collection of payments;
(iv) Payment to the client at agreed periods, usually on agreed maturity dates.

The export Factor (with whom the exporter has entered into a factoring agreement) will co-operate with his counterpart in the buyer's country (the import Factor) who will be responsible for:

  (i) Credit rating of customer;
 (ii) Remitting payments;
(iii) Passing on customers' enquiries to the exporter.

The import Factor deals with the customer in his own language and is therefore in a good position to obtain payment and to pass on market information to the client. Both Factors will be members of an international factoring group.

(b) A Financial Service

The Factor can also provide a financial service consisting of:

  (i) Allowing the client to draw money at the time of invoicing of up to 80% of the invoice value on a *non-recourse* basis. This would be only for so-called "approved debts"; i.e. debts that the Factor has designated as such after receiving credit rating reports on the customer. The only stipulation is that the exporter is required to honour his export sales contract. Factors are not prepared to be drawn into trade disputes;
 (ii) Allowing the client to draw money at the time of invoicing on a *with recourse* basis. This would be for "unapproved debts", i.e. debts on which the Factor is not prepared to carry the credit risk as a result of information he has obtained on the overseas buyer. Debt from one buyer could fall into both categories; the Factor may be prepared to approve debt up to a given value after which it may only be able to provide finance on a with recourse basis.

Export factoring is not suitable for the smaller exporting company (say, with an export turnover of much below £100,000 p.a.) because the cost of the service could be relatively high in comparison with other types of export finance. These costs comprise a discount charge above bank base rates for finance plus a factoring charge of 1 to 2% of the total invoice value, although it could be as high as 3%. This depends on:

  (i) Average invoice size;
 (ii) Expected sales volume;
(iii) Credit rating of buyer.

Factors insist on their role being made known to the customer (called notification) in the belief that overdue payments will be reduced as a result. However, legal action against the customer will not be taken without first consulting the client. In order to protect themselves Factors limit their business to those companies offering no more than 180 days credit to their overseas buyers.

Advantages and Disadvantages of Credit Factoring

Advantages of Export Credit Factoring to an Exporter

  (i) The entire burden of keeping a sales ledger is taken away;

 (ii) Likewise both credit control and debt collection is transferred to the Factor;

(iii) A change from a multitude of debtors is just one (the Factor) can improve the possibilities of additional bank finance;

(iv) Discounts to buyers to induce them to pay quickly can be reduced;

 (v) The Factor carries the foreign exchange risk;

(vi) Offering "open account" terms could increase sales;

(vii) Analysis of sales statistics is provided by the Factor.

Disadvantages

  (i) It could be expensive for the smaller exporter or one with low credit-rated buyers;

 (ii) Factors could influence the client's sales by encouraging "approved" sales and discouraging "unapproved" sales. This could be a problem if the Factor takes a short-term view of a customer's credit-worthiness.

(5) INVOICE DISCOUNTING

Where an exporter believes that a full factoring service, which includes the disclosure of the Factor's name to the overseas buyer, is likely to be detrimental to his business, he can opt for a lesser facility called Invoice Discounting. This is also known by the titles of Confidential or Undisclosed Factoring. In such an arrangement the Factor appoints the exporter/client as an agent to collect the debts due, and as a result the buyer is not aware of the intervention of the Factor whose proper title is Invoice Discounting House. Although the House is prepared to offer up to 80% of the values of the invoices on presentation to the buyer it is on a *with recourse* basis. The proceeds of the debt collection are then remitted to the House on their receipt from the buyer. Apart from the financial service provided, no other facility is offered and thus, the exporter has to maintain his own sales ledger facility and, of course, has to meet any bad debts.

(6) FORFAITING

Where an exporter is selling high value capital goods on medium-term credit, say up to eight years, and is unable to obtain a revolving Documentary Letter of Credit from his buyer, he can turn to Forfaiting as an alternative method of *without recourse* shipping finance. The mechanics are described in Diagram 8.1.

1. The traders come to an arrangement whereby a financial instrument is established in favour of the exporter. This could be:

(a) A Time Bill of Exchange; or
(b) A Promissory Note.

Alternatively the exporter could use his book receivables or deferred payments Letter of Credit.

The last two are less common because they tend to involve more complicated supporting documents and a separate guarantee of the indebtedness of the importer, and in any case, the first two are well known and understood and facilitate ease of transaction.

In comparing Bills of Exchange with Promissory Notes it should be understood that the former involves the liability of the drawer (exporter) under the Bills of Exchange Act 1882 even when it is claused "without recourse". As a result he would need to record his *contingent* liability on

Diagram 8.1
Forfaiting

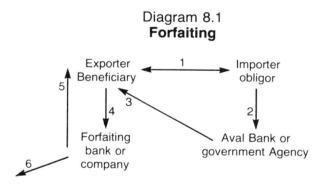

his balance sheet even though the likelihood of it becoming an *actual* liability is remote. In addition, as we shall see, the *Avalization* process is not recognised in English law; there is no reference to it in the Bills of Exchange Act.

Promissory Notes on the other hand, do not suffer from these problems. Under the Bills of Exchange Act, a Promissory Note being a financial instrument established by the maker (importer) promising to pay a certain sum of money at a certain date in the future to, or to the order of the beneficiary (exporter), involves no liability on the part of the beneficiary under the Bills of Exchange Act. In addition the "International Conventions for Commercial Bills" lays down that the endorser of a Promissory Note (the beneficiary) has the legal right to absolve himself from liability by adding the words "without recourse". Although a forfaiter will provide a written undertaking to the beneficiary not to take proceedings against him in the event of default by the drawee under a Bill of Exchange, this could be overturned by a court of law if the forfaiter chooses to act against the beneficiary.

For our purposes therefore we shall incorporate Promissory Notes into the diagram of a forfaiting arrangement. However, should Bills of Exchange be used they will have to be presented to the drawee for acceptance. In the case of Notes or Bills, these are made out in an agreed number, each for a specified value and maturing at such times as to spread the maturities over the life of the agreed credit period. Although it is possible for each Note or Bill to be of a different value to the others and also for them to be spread over the life of the credit period in an irregular manner, it is usual for this not to be the case. A typical situation would be where Notes (or Bills) are drawn up for (say) 80% of the total value of the goods to be supplied (with the remaining 20% being paid as cash on delivery) and each of the instruments being for an identical value, the total of which equals the total value of the credit. Moreover, each Note or Bill would have such maturities that one of them matures at regular intervals of (say) six months. In effect, the importer is agreeing to pay a certain sum of money regularly every six months for (say) eight years, until his debt has been settled by way of sixteen financial instruments.

Let us assume that the notes have been drawn up by the importer (who is referred to as an *Obligor*) in the agreed form. If he is a trader of first class standing there may be no need for the Notes to be guaranteed or avalized but this is the exception to the rule. In order to protect himself, the forfaiter will usually require a bank in the importer's country to provide security in one or other of these forms.

2. The obligor therefore will need to present the Notes to the bank in his country or an agency of his government nominated by the forfaiter for:

   (a) *A Guarantee.* This takes the form of a separate document signed by the guarantor. This can be a time consuming matter as it has to specify a number of details; for example, each maturity date with its corresponding repayment, its complete transferability, and it must not be dependent on the underlying commercial contract, i.e. it must not be subject to the proper fulfilment of the exporter's contract to deliver. In the event that the guaranteeing bank cannot meet these requirements, the forfaiter will offer the beneficiary a *with recourse* facility.

(b) *Avalization*. This is a much simpler act of security and consists merely of the Aval Bank writing on the back of each Note or Bill the words "per aval" and signing it together with the name of the obligor. Avalization is regarded in international practice as an irrevocable and unconditional guarantee to pay on the due date as if the Aval Bank is the obligor. However, in some countries, notably the UK and the US, avalization is not a legally recognised concept and therefore a guarantee would be preferred. Whichever form it takes, the guarantee effectively puts the Aval Bank into a position similar to that of an Issuing Bank under a Letter of Credit, namely, the party to whom the provider of finance can have recourse. Like the Issuing Bank therefore, the Aval Bank will need to be one which has access to the credit rating of the obligor upon whom it will have recourse in the event of the obligor's default.

3. The Aval Bank now remits the avalized papers to the beneficiary who needs to endorse them on the back in favour of the forfaiter, adding the words "without recourse". They are then presented to the forfaiter, who could be a bank, a finance house or discount house, who discounts them.

It should be noted at this point that while the description of the mechanism of forfaiting has left the operation of the forfaiter to the end, in fact, he will have been aware of and party to these operations from the start.

The exporter will need to contact him at an early stage in order to ascertain the possibility of such finance and its terms. Although the forfaiter will not be in a position to give specific detailed information at this stage due to lack of knowledge about discount costs in the future, nevertheless a rough indication would be provided – enough to allow the exporter to either consider it a possibility or not – and to allow him to load his quoted price to the buyer with the associated estimated costs. If the exporter wishes the forfaiter to make a firm offer which allows for some months to pass before being taken up, then an "option fee" is payable by the exporter.

The period between the forfaiting agreement and the *act* of forfaiting the Bills or Notes can be several months. However, once the agreement is in force the forfaiter is bound by its terms. As a result, to protect his position he charges a "commitment fee" comprising the cost of holding money ready for the exporter and also the costs of adverse movements in discount and exchange rates. Such fees are usually around ¾% per annum to ⅛% per month paid monthly in advance, depending on the length of the period and the value of the deal. In addition a "penalty" fee may become payable if the exporter fails to deliver the paper.

4. When the Notes or Bills are presented to the forfaiter for discounting the latter takes up the entire responsibility of presenting them to the obligor on maturity. Further, he takes up the risk of default subject only to the guarantee of the Aval Bank. As we have seen in connection with Letters of Credit, conditions may prevail to prevent their honouring their liabilities, at least for a time. Thus the forfaiter – like a confirming bank – does take some risk.

   The forfaiter, in effect, buys the presented paper from the beneficiary by exchanging them for their total cash value less fees and *a discount charge at a fixed rate for the entire credit period without recourse to the beneficiary*.

5. This then is the central, most significant aspect of forfaiting. The forfaiter will provide the exporter on presentation of his Bills and Notes properly endorsed:

   (a) The entire value of all the paper less charges mentioned above;
   (b) Without recourse;
   (c) At a pre-agreed fixed discount rate for the entire credit period;
   (d) In his domestic currency with the forfaiter carrying the foreign exchange risk;
   (e) With no responsibility on the exporter to present matured paper to the obligor.

   In the event of default, the forfaiter will look to the Aval Bank for reimbursement who in turn will look to the obligor.

6. The forfaiter need not, in fact, carry the paper to maturity but can invite investors to participate in a large deal in order to spread the risk. In some cases the forfaiter acts merely as a broker by on-selling all paper to other investors. In effect, investors are buying a fixed rate instrument, the profitability of which will depend on the way in which interest rates fluctuate during the life of the paper. Most forfaiting is done in currencies in which re-financing is convenient, i.e. US dollars, Deutsche marks and Swiss francs although other currencies are sometimes used.

   Forfaiters may give investors a choice between a participation agreement and a placement.

Participation

Under a participation agreement the forfaiter supplies the investor with a letter setting out the terms agreed upon but retaining the financial instruments and responsibility for presentation on maturity. The investor can ask to see copies for his own perusal.

Placement

In this case the investor is an outright purchaser of the financial paper. The forfaiter will endorse them "without recourse" and remit them to the new owners who, in effect, become the new forfaiters. Investors will have to decide whether the higher return this allows is sufficient reward for the extra risk and inconvenience.

The term "forfaiting" derives from the French term "à forfait" meaning "the surrendering of rights"; those rights, of course, being those of the exporter expecting to receive payment in the future from his buyer. The facility developed in central Europe during the late 1950s when a seller's market for capital goods developed into a buyer's market motivating exporters to offer more attractive credit terms. At this time also trade between Eastern and Western Europe grew rapidly as did exports of capital goods to developing countries. Forfaiting became an attractive method of financing such trade where the governments (or their agencies) of the buyer were prepared to guarantee the debt. Switzerland was a natural centre for such operations and in 1965 Credit Suisse Bank established a forfaiting subsidiary, Finanz AG Zurich. In 1974 they opened a London subsidiary Finanz AG London. Other banks also offer a forfaiting facility.

Another factor leading to the development of this facility came when the Export Credits Guarantee Department (ECGD) ceased to offer preferential medium-term, fixed interest guarantees for exports to the European Community countries. (See Chapter 10.) As a result, forfaiting became the *only* facility to offer fixed interest terms for medium-term credits for sale to EEC countries.

Advantages and Disadvantages of Forfaiting to an Exporter

Advantages

(a) Medium-term non-recourse finance;

(b) A contingent liability on the balance sheet is converted into cash;

(c) No exchange rate risk;

(d) Fixed interest rates permit the exporter to adjust his selling prices to take all his costs into account;

(e) Fixed interest rates may prove to be cheap if rates rise;

(f) Exporter bears no part of any loss due to default.

Disadvantages

(a) No preferential interest rates;

(b) Fixed rates may prove to be expensive if rates fall;

Table 8.1
Forfaiting and Letters of Credit

Term	Forfaiting	Letters of Credit
Initiating party	Arranged by exporter	Arranged by importer on exporter's behalf
Cost	Borne by the exporter but can be loaded into the quoted selling price	Borne by the importer unless the credit stipulates otherwise. Discount charges usually for the exporter's account
Term of maturity	Up to about 8 years	Not likely to be for more than several months (on a revolving basis)
Preferential interest rates	No	No
Fixed interest rates	Yes	No
Discounting facility	Yes	Only with an Acceptance Credit
Recourse to exporter	No	Only with an Unconfirmed Negotiations Credit
"Proper documents" qualification	No. Documents are presented at intervals over the extended delivery period and after forfaiting has been effected	Yes. Credit is invalidated by improper documentation
Exporter to present Bills or Notes on maturity	No. Responsibility of the forfaiter	Usually performed by the bank acting for the exporter
Pre-shipment finance	Only insofar as delivery of the goods is over a period of time after forfaiting	Only with special arrangements
Importer's credit	Yes	Only with a Time Bill of Exchange or with a Promissory Note

(c) The "option fee" is payable even if the facility is not taken up;

(d) The "commitment fee" is payable at the outset and a "penalty fee" may become payable if paper is not delivered or delivered late;

(e) Discounting charges are effectively higher than the nominal rate suggests because they are "front ended"; i.e. deducted at the outset. (See Discounting in Chapter 6.)

Finally, let us make a comparison between forfaiting and Letters of Credit as set out in Table 8.1.

(B) IMPORT FINANCE

It is now time to turn our attention away from the viewpoint of export finance to consider ways in which buyers of goods can arrange for credit terms. In fact much has already been said of this in passing when discussing export finance. However, it is useful to bring them together in one section and add those facilities which are special to the importer.

One point must be made clear at the beginning. Import finance is always with recourse to the importer! This may be an obvious, even a trite point, but making it highlights the fact that the importer is the party receiving the credit in the last resort, even where the exporter receives it in the first resort! Or to use a familiar expression "the buck stops here".

We can divide import finance into those facilities offered by banks and those offered outside the banking sector.

(1) BANK FACILITIES

(a) Bank Loan or Overdraft

As we saw when bank loans and overdrafts were discussed in Chapter 6 these facilities may be available to traders on an unsecured basis. The same principles would apply when offered to an importer as to an exporter.

(b) Produce or Merchandise Loan

However, as the importer is going to use the proceeds of a facility for the purpose of purchasing goods which, hopefully, will ultimately yield a profit to him, the bank may be prepared to provide him with an advance based on the security of the goods themselves. Indeed, insofar as an exporter also needs to purchase goods from overseas for the purpose of producing the exports, he may too, qualify for a produce or merchandise loan or advance. Of course, the proceeds of the sale of the exports, or in the case of the importer, the proceeds of the sale of the goods, will provide the funds to meet the repayment of the loan.

These loans are normally available for periods up to three months and are usually provided for customers who import seasonal goods and have insufficient capital to finance the carrying of stocks. They will be offered to the importer on a separate loan account, and can be a one-off arrangement or on a revolving basis over an agreed period of time.

Under such arrangements, the bank will pay for the imports on their customers' behalf and take title to the goods as security in the form of Negotiable Bills of Lading endorsed in blank (see Chapter 5) if shipped by sea, or the goods should be consigned to the bank if shipped by air; however, in practice the kinds of goods for which such loans are made are unlikely to move by air because of their bulk. The bank will be anxious to ensure that the marine insurance cover is valid and for the full value of the goods.

Once the goods arrive in the importer's country the documents of title need to be transferred to the importer for him to turn the goods into cash as quickly as possible. It is therefore not in the interest of the bank to withhold them unduly.

However, if the importer does not have an immediate customer for the goods or if they need to be used for processing purposes, then the bank will arrange to warehouse them in its own name and also to arrange for insurance; both costs are to the importer's account. The bank will obtain a Warehouse Receipt as evidence of ownership or alternatively it could receive a Warehouse Warrant. A Warehouse Receipt is not negotiable and rights to the goods cannot be transferred under it. Therefore when the bank requires to deliver the goods into the control of the importer they must issue a Delivery Order which authorises the warehouse to release the goods to the named importer. Where a Warehouse Warrant has been issued to the bank, it can arrange for the release of the goods to the importer by endorsing the Warrant in his favour.

In order to protect the bank it will require that its customer provides it with a Trust Receipt, being an undertaking by the customer that it accepts the goods for value in the bank's name and to agree that the proceeds are utilized for the purpose of extinguishing the bank loan. In effect, the customer holds the goods as agent for the bank; the customer becomes a trustee for the bank. In addition, the bank can call for an assignment of the debt to the bank; the ultimate buyer of the goods is notified of the assignment and will be required to make payment direct to the bank. The use of Trust Receipts provide banks with only a limited form of security. For example, the value of the goods may fall while a buyer is awaited or their use in processing for re-sale may not result in the value anticipated by the customer. Again, once the goods have been released to the importer, even though constructive possession is retained by the bank, it is possible for them to be used by the importer as security for another loan. In the UK, the courts will uphold the right of the second lender to the value of the goods.

Letter of Pledge/Hypothecation

Another method whereby the bank can protect its position is to ask the importer to provide a letter of pledge and/or hypothecation. Under a letter of pledge the customer gives the bank the right to sell the goods if they remain unsold and if they have not received the repayment of their loan. A letter of hypothecation gives the bank the right to dispose of the goods even before asking the customer for repayment of the loan. A *general* letter of hypothecation covers all the advances to the customer and expected receipts. (See also Chapter 6, *Advances*.)

(c) Accommodation Finance

In Chapter 6 we saw that one way in which exporters could obtain with recourse finance was by way of an Acceptance Credit, otherwise known as Accommodation Finance. Banks may be prepared to allow their importer customers to draw Time Bills of Exchange on them, usually for sixty to ninety days, which are then discounted and the proceeds, net of interest and charges, being credited to the customer to allow him to meet the cost of the goods. On the maturity of the Bill the customer's account is debited with its face value. In order to permit the customer to have enough time to on-sell the goods the time period of the Bill of Exchange will be slightly longer than the anticipated time it will take to receive the sale proceeds. Because it is a Bank Bill it will be discounted at more favourable rates than would a Trade Bill. As with a Produce Loan the bank will want to take security in the form of a Letter of Pledge and a Trust Receipt.

(d) Loans by the Exporter's Bank under an ECGD Buyer Credit Guarantee

Although we shall be dealing in detail with the ECGD in Chapter 10, it is worth pointing out at this stage that it is possible for overseas buyers of UK exports of capital goods to receive a medium-term loan from a bank in the UK for the purpose of meeting the cost of the goods. See also Lines of Credit in the same chapter.

(e) Letters of Credit

Where it is agreed between the parties to a Letter of Credit that an exporter can draw Time Bills of Exchange on either the Issuing Bank or Confirming Bank (a Negotiation Credit and Acceptance Credit respectively) the importer's account will not be debited for the cost of the goods until the maturity of the Bills. The availability and cost of such a facility will be factors determinings its utilization.

(f) A Refinance Credit

A variant of a Letter of Credit is a Refinance Credit which allows the importer to draw an inchoate Bill of Exchange on the bank in the exporter's country but where the exporter himself is in receipt of a Sight Payments Credit. (See Chapter 7 for details.)

(2) NON-BANK FINANCE

(a) Open Account Trading

As mentioned in an earlier chapter, importers may be able to obtain credit directly from their suppliers by means of open account trading. Payment to the exporter will be at agreed intervals after the receipt of the goods. Although no direct charge will be made, the exporter will have to load his quoted prices to include the cost to him of financing this service. Sometimes the importer will be offered an incentive to pay early by way of a discount on the quoted price; say 2½% for payment within two weeks. He will then have to compare the benefits of paying early (the discount) with the cost of raising the money to do so (interest rate). This topic is referred to again in the next chapter (see *Interest Arbitrage*).

(b) Time Bills of Exchange

Another method whereby an importer can receive credit from his supplier is to accept a Time Bill of Exchange drawn on him by the exporter in exchange for the receipt of the documents relating to the goods. Once again cost is a factor as the exporter will have to pass on the cost of the finance in any of the methods outlined in Chapter 6 on export finance.

(c) Forfaiting

It is clear from the section on forfaiting earlier in this chapter that the importer is able to obtain medium-term finance by way of Time Bills of Exchange or Promissory Notes in favour of the exporter. Moreover, the interest cost will be fixed for the period of the credit. The problem from the importer's viewpoint is that such interest will form an integral part of the price of the goods and that this could prove expensive were interest rates to fall. On the other hand it does enable him to spread his payments over several years, perhaps to match his expected cash receipts.

(d) Hire Purchase and Leasing

As we have already considered these facilities earlier in this chapter, suffice it to say that these are yet other ways in which medium-term credit can be made available to an importer. Note that with Leasing the goods may never become the user's property depending on the laws of the country, and with Hire Purchase, property passes only on the final payment. Were payments to be delayed the goods could be reclaimed by the Hire Purchase Company.

(e) Intermediary Finance

Merchants, Agents, Confirming Houses and Finance Houses may all be able to offer a buyer time to pay on his purchased imports. See earlier in this chapter. In effect, the situation as seen by the importer is as if he were receiving credit from the supplier himself, except that the intermediary being a specialist organization and possibly offsetting its risks with an ECGD credit insurance policy, can offer more attractive terms to the importer than could the exporter himself. In addition, the Confirming House may also be able to act as agent for the purpose of obtaining the goods from a potential supplier at a competitive quote.

Chapter 9

Foreign Exchange

In previous chapters reference has been made from time to time to the use of foreign currencies in financing international trade and payments. In this chapter we consider the markets in foreign currencies called the "foreign exchange markets".

THE FOREIGN EXCHANGE MARKETS

Like any other market for, say, commodities or manufactures, buyers and sellers come together to determine both the volume of traded business they agree to perform per time period and also the prices at which such trade will be carried on. An analogy can be drawn with a street market where traders offer their goods at prices each day which they are prepared to accept in order to perform an acceptable volume of business. The customer either buys or does not buy at the quoted price – or more usually – will buy *more* or *less* depending on need and the price itself.

COMPETITIVE VERSUS NON-COMPETITIVE MARKETS

A street market is competitive in the sense that prices are displayed and can be compared by the buyer who can decide on where to make a purchase consistent with the quality of the goods. However, some markets are less competitive. For example, where there are only a few sellers or a few buyers a state of monopoly and monopsony respectively, can exist. In such conditions, the sellers or the buyers can agree to fix prices at a rate above or below the rate which would otherwise prevail. Examples include prices for foodstuffs under the Common Agricultural Policy of the European Community, the OPEC price cartel and other international agreements to determine prices. An example of a monopsony would be where traders at an auction agree among themselves to a maximum bid price. The markets for foreign exchange are competitive in the sense that they are world-wide and comprise very many participants, not one of which is so large relative to the market that it has the ability to fix prices. However, central banks and governments have attempted in the past to so fix currency prices by way of international agreements and indeed still do so today either by agreement or unilaterally (see Chapter 12). This latter operation is usually to offset unacceptable changes occurring in the rate for a particular currency.

Apart from intervening in the foreign exchange markets, governments can have similar effects by limiting trade. For example, restricting imports will tend to limit the domestic demand for foreign exchange, and the same result is likely when overseas investment is controlled. In both cases the exchange rate is likely to change to one more acceptable to the authorities. In addition it is possible for exchange controls to be imposed to maximize an inflow of foreign exchange and minimize the outflow. A currency is said to be "inconvertible" when residents and non-residents are not permitted to sell the domestic currency in an open market and where the central bank is not obliged to purchase the domestic currency from residents and non-residents at a known market exchange rate. Currencies which are not controlled in this way are said to be "convertible". It is possible for the degree of convertibility to vary from time to time and from country to country but there are fifteen major currencies which can be said to be more or less convertible.

What then is the foreign exchange market and where is it to be found? The latter question may be answered first.

WHERE IS THE MARKET TO BE FOUND?

The answer is nowhere and everywhere! Nowhere, in the sense that there is no one site or building where it can be said that the market operates, like the Commodities Markets or the Stock Exchange. Everywhere, in the sense that the market is world-wide and operates in most of the major financial centres around the world.

There has been no meeting of buyers and sellers for trading in the London markets since before the First World War but in many Western European countries the main participants have a brief daily meeting where rates for certain transactions are agreed. However, even in these markets, trading goes on throughout the day outside such meetings.

In fact, the markets (plural, for there are markets for different currencies and for different types of transactions e.g. spot and forward) are to be found in the dealing rooms of the commercial banks around the world who communicate with each other by telephone and telex, and whose deals are later confirmed by letter.

It has been estimated that for 1982 there were world-wide transactions in foreign exchange worth more than $200 billion each day and that London performed some $60 billion of this. This makes London the largest single market and this is due not only to the historical role of sterling but also to the fact that its geography means that it can deal with the Far East and New York on the same day. There are also markets in Singapore, Hong

Hong, Tokyo, Zurich, Frankfurt, Paris, San Francisco, Amsterdam, Milan, Toronto, Brussels and Bahrain. Because of this a market is open for trading somewhere virtually twenty-four hours a day. In the UK all deals are done at the London offices of the banks and other participants. There are 300 recognised banks in London offering a foreign exchange service, and also twelve brokers. These latter firms are involved in providing data and matching buyers and sellers, for which they receive a brokerage fee. Brokers are also in business to match currency borrowers and lenders (this is part of the Euro-currency market – see Chapter 12).

WHAT IS THE FOREIGN EXCHANGE MARKET/MARKETS?

Like all other markets, the foreign exchange market is in business to assist buyers to buy and sellers to sell. However, unlike other markets where money exchanges for goods or for services, in this one money exchanges for money! The motives for such exchanges arise, of course, from the needs of traders, investors and others who have currencies they wish to dispose of and/or seek currencies to acquire. To be more precise they can be categorized as:

(a) Traders in goods and services;
(b) Investors and dis-investors;
(c) Recipients and payers of dividends, interest, profits and royalties, gifts and loans;
(d) Speculators;
(e) Arbitrageurs;
(f) Central banks.

As the vast majority of traded currencies are maintained as bank deposits, the market is actually one of selling a deposit of one currency in exchange for a deposit of another currency. The price at which these deposits are exchanged is called "the exchange rate". Although an exchange rate is another term for "price", it can be expressed in a manner not usual for other markets. For example, we can say that the price of £1 is $1.2950. However, we can reverse the equation to read the price of $1.2950 is £1. By analogy with, say, the market for carpets we could say that the price of carpet x is £500 and also *that the price of £500 is carpet x*! Although there is logic in this type of expression it is not usually resorted to except in the foreign exchange market.

The reason for this is simply that money is exchanging for money and the position of the two currencies in the equation depends on usage and the convenience of traders. In London it is the practice to quote all the major currencies in relation to the US dollar with the exception of sterling itself!

Thus, US$1 = Deutsche mark 2.6885–2.6895
and   US$1 = Japanese yen   243.95–244.05 etc.

while sterling would be quoted:

    £1   = US$1.2925–1.2935.

Note that currency rates are expressed in spread form; i.e. two rates are quoted. The left-hand rate is the one offered by banks to *sell* and the right-hand rate is the one offered by banks to *buy* the currency *expressed in the spread*.

It is of course, possible to reverse the equations and also to express them by using the other currency as the unit of measurement. This is done simply by finding the reciprocal of the first expression.

Thus, if US\$1 = Deutsche mark 2.6885

then Deutsche mark 1 = US\$$\frac{1}{2.6885}$ = US\$0.3719546.

Again, if £1 = US\$1.2925

then   US\$1 = £$\frac{1}{1.2925}$ = £0.7736943

Indirect Method or Currency Rate Expression

When currencies are expressed as equivalent to one unit of domestic currency (as with the £/\$ expression) this is called the Indirect Method or Currency Rate.

Direct Method or Pence Rate Expression

When the domestic currency is expressed as equivalent to one unit of foreign currency as it is done in the vast majority of the world's markets (e.g. in Frankfurt the expression would be US\$1 = Deutsche mark 2.6885), this is called the Direct Method or Pence Rate.

The size of the US economy, the level of her world trade and investments and the relative stability and availability of her currency are the factors that have led to the US dollar becoming the predominant unit of currency against which to measure other currencies. The anomaly of sterling is due to its historical role as the major world currency earlier in the century. An advantage of quoting against the US dollar is that this reduces the number of possible quotes. Non-dollar expressions (called cross rates) can be calculated from the dollar expression. For example:

  let   US\$1 = Spanish peseta 152
  and US\$1 = Italian lira 1594

then, by calculation, Spanish peseta 1 = Italian lira $\frac{1594}{152}$ = 10.486.

In this way any two currencies can be expressed against each other by reference to the US dollar acting as a common denominator. (See section on cross rates later on in this chapter.)

THE OPERATIONS OF THE MARKET

As we have seen, the foreign exchange markets are essentially concerned with the exchange of bank deposits and banks are the principal participants. Banks act both on behalf of their customers and on their own behalf. The customers include:

(a) Central banks;
(b) Foreign banks;
(c) Governments;
(d) Companies;
(e) Individuals,

who for one reason or another wish to dispose of or acquire a bank deposit in a particular currency or currencies. However, of the total volume of daily business only a very small fraction is on behalf of customers wishing to finance their trading and capital flows. The vast bulk of all business is, in fact, done *between* the banks themselves. This is called inter-bank business and consists of banks contacting each other directly or through brokers to exchange currency deposits not just to meet their own customers' requirements but to maintain what they regard as adequate balances. "Adequate" in this context is determined by such factors as:

(a) Likely changes in interest rates;
(b) Likely changes in exchange rates;
(c) Differences in rates around the world.

Simple Arbitrage

The latter factor (c) gives rise to the process of simple arbitrage, where banks are constantly on the look-out for minor differences in exchange rate quotations in different markets around the world. If for example £1 trades for US$1.2923 in London while at the same time £1 trades for US$1.2925 in New York, there will be a demand by UK banks to purchase dollars in New York and to sell them in London. Of course by the process of arbitrage itself, the differences in the rates will be ironed out. The £1 will fall to (say) US$1.2924 in New York and rise to that level in London. Although such operations tend to be self-limiting, the differences in market conditions, however fractional, will always cause rate differentials. This is particularly so when conditions are hectic and delays occur in operating arbitrage deals. Note also that because of the "spread" in the rates, the profitability of simple arbitrage is further limited. (See later in this chapter.)

Inter-bank dealings are very important to the smooth running of the market. Customers' needs tend to be uneven in timing and amount, and if deals were done only on their behalf, rates would tend to be more volatile. By operating on a larger scale on their own behalf, banks in effect, "make the market", i.e. their own dealings determine exchange rates. Moreover, because of arbitrage, rates tend to be the same world-wide. Banks give depth to the market. A thin market is one where there are a few traders who deal only intermittently. The result tends to be rates which change direction frequently. By adding their own deals, banks give "depth" and make rates less volatile than they otherwise would be.

Because the bulk of dealings are done between the banks on their own behalf, it follows that they will be holding currencies, at any one time, above or below levels needed to service their customers' requirements. Indeed, the desk managers in charge of currency dealings have to work each day to a policy laid down for them by the banks so that by the end of each day's operations they are holding the required positions in each unit. Thus, they may need to "go long" or "go short" in various currencies; i.e. to hold more or less respectively than is needed to match customer needs. The motive for such positions are views about exchange rates and interest rate changes. The latter expectation will determine the maturity of the currency assets they are buying or selling.

Retail and Wholesale Business

A bank's currency dealing can be said to be:

(a) Wholesale inter-bank business at Head Office;
(b) Retail customer business at branch level buying and selling foreign currency denominated financial instruments from customers and buying and selling foreign currency deposits from and to customers;
(c) Purchase and sale of banknotes for travellers.

It is possible that where a customer requires a particularly large deal (say, over £100,000) then business can be done in category (a), in which case the exchange rate for wholesale business would apply. Like in most other markets there is a "rate for the market", meaning that retail rates are at "higher" prices than at wholesale level. In effect, there is a range of exchange rates, each one relevant to a particular type of business. The most disadvantageous rate from a customer's point of view applies to the purchase and sale of currency notes (as advertised by travel agencies). This is done by widening the spread between the rate at which the bank is prepared to buy a currency and the rate at which it is prepared to sell it.

For example, in London the French franc could be quoted:

(a) £1 = FF12.07–12.08
(b) £1 = FF12.00–12.15
(c) £1 = FF11.93–12.22

each quote being applicable to the aforementioned types of business. Thus a customer wishing to purchase francs would receive FF11.93 for banknote trading, FF12.00 for commercial trading and FF12.07 at the level of wholesale trading. The difference between the bank's selling and buying rate is called a "turn" or "spread" and it fluctuates according to the level of stability in the market, the currency in question, and the volume of business. Thus, if there is a degree of volatility in an exchange rate, and if business is "thin", and if rumours persist about the currency that cause traders to believe that the current exchange rate is unsustainable, banks will protect themselves by widening their quote from say:

£1 = FF12.07–12.08 to
£1 = FF12.06–12.09

that is, they will offer *less* currency when selling but require *more* currency when buying. The spread represents the gross return to the dealer for the risks inherent in "making a market".

Note that it is common practice to express rates by quoting the bank's *selling* rate first and *buying* rates second. These are referred to as the "offer" and "bid" rates respectively. Because dealers are frequently engaged in hectic business they save time by quoting only a small portion of the whole rate. Thus, for the US dollar, an exchange rate of:

£1 = US$1.2925–1.2935

would not be quoted in its entirety but only by reference to the last two digits; i.e. 25–35. These are referred to as "points". In US dollar terms a "point" is $\frac{1}{10,000}$ part of the unit. Thus one point = US$0.0001.

A "pip" is one further decimal place to the right, i.e. US$0.00001 and represents $\frac{1}{100,000}$ part of a dollar.

Most quoted currencies are expressed to four decimal places but Italian lire and Japanese yen are usually expressed only to two decimal places because of the low value of those currencies relative to others.

In the London market the volume of business fluctuates according to the time of day. For example, in the early afternoon there can be considerable business because New York, Frankfurt and Chicago are open. A large order placed at this time of day will have less influence on rates than, say, from midnight to early morning (London time) when San Francisco is closing and Hong Kong has not yet opened. When central banks wish to influence rates they stand a better chance of success at this time of day.

When banks quote rates over the telephone they are deemed to be good for an agreed period of time, for up to a certain volume of business, depending on the counter-party (the other party to the possible deal). When brokers present clients with the best available offer and bid rates they will be aware of the underlying terms.

Spot Transactions

A spot transaction is defined as one where currencies are exchanged on *the second working day* after the agreement to make the deal. This allows time for paperwork to be completed and for the appropriate transfer of funds to be made. Such transfers to and from banks will be effected when their overseas currency accounts (i.e. those held to their credit by foreign banks) are either credited or debited, depending on whether the bank is buying or selling. (See Chapter 11 on Nostro and Vostro Accounting.)

About two-thirds of all deals are for spot transactions. The remaining deals are called "Forward". (See later in this chapter.)

"Contract" Date and "Value" Date

The date of the agreed deal on the telephone is called the "contract" date; the "value" date is the one when the deposit is credited or debited.

Table 9.1
Borrowing Currency as an Alternative to Buying It

US importer		US exporter		UK merchant trader	
$ debit	$ credit	$ debit	$ credit	$ debit	$ credit
					(a) dollars borrowed
				(b) dollars paid	
			(c) dollars received		
(d) dollars paid					
					(e) dollars received
				(f) dollar loan repaid	

(a) The UK trader borrowers dollars (instead of buying them);
(b) These are paid over to the US exporter;
(c) Who receives them into his own account;
(d) A US importer pays dollars to the UK trader;
(e) Who receives them into his dollar account;
(f) And who uses them to repay the original dollar loan.

Not all Foreign Commerce Involves a Foreign Currency Deal

From what has been said it may appear that all international trade and payments necessarily involve either buying or selling a foreign currency. This is not so.

For example, companies who need to make a payment in a foreign currency may – if they maintain such currency balances – merely instruct their bank to debit their currency accounts. Equally, receipts of currency can be credited to such accounts. If a company is doing business where it both pays and receives a particular currency, the debiting and crediting can maintain a steady balance without any need to buy or sell the unit. Where there is a time gap between payments and receipts the trader can *borrow* the necessary currencies. This is illustrated in Table 9.1.

In this manner two sets of trade can be paid for without any resort to the foreign exchange market by the traders concerned, except perhaps for a small amount representing the interest cost of borrowing dollars. It is this interest cost which is one of the factors that helps to determine whether or not the market for *borrowing* foreign exchange – the Euro-currency market – is a more profitable one or not than *buying* the same currency – the foreign exchange market. This topic is dealt with more fully later in this chapter.

Appreciation/Depreciation

When a unit buys less of a currency it is said to have depreciated against that currency; of course by the same token, the latter currency is said to have appreciated against the first. For example:

US$1 = Dutch Guilder 3.0050–3.0070

but then changes to

US\$1 = Dutch Guilder 3.0025–3.0045

The dollar is said to have depreciated and the guilder appreciated. It is changes such as this which give rise to *Foreign Exchange Risk*: i.e. the loss (or gain) resulting from a currency *receipt* becoming worth less (or more) than originally expected or a currency *payment* costing more (or less) than originally expected, both results in terms of the domestic currency. See section on Forward Rates.

Apart from one currency changing its value against another currency it is also possible to estimate its change against several currencies which can comprise some that have appreciated and some which have depreciated against it. This is referred to as a change in the currency index or against a basket of currencies. (See Chapter 12.)

Determination of Spot Rates

Because exchange rates are prices of one currency in terms of another they are determined by the strength of the demand for them and supply of them.

If at any given rate the demand for a currency suddenly increases, then other things being equal, that currency will tend to appreciate against others. Diagram 9.1 illustrates this.

In Diagram 9.1 the quantity of sterling is measured along the horizontal axis and the price of sterling (its rate against the US dollar) is measured along the vertical axis.

The demand to purchase sterling is shown as falling to the right indicating that at lower exchange rates demand volume *increases*. The supply of sterling is shown as increasing to the right indicating that at higher exchange rates supply *increases*. This is consistent with normal market behaviour. At some price level, in this case where £1 exchange for \$1.50 at price P, volume demanded and supplied are equal at point Q.

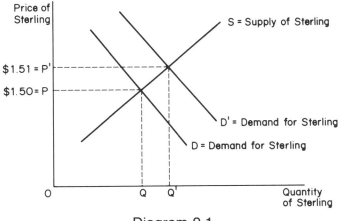

Diagram 9.1

Should the demand for sterling now rise with all other variables remaining constant, the demand curve moves to the right to D′ and a new equality is reached at £1 = $1.51 at point P′ and a new volume at Q′.

The increase in demand for sterling has caused an appreciation against the US dollar from $1.50 to $1.51. Other changes of demand and supply can be illustrated using the same diagram.

Factors Determining the Demand for and Supply of a Currency

Earlier in this chapter we noted the various participants using the foreign exchange markets, namely customers of banks and banks themselves. The factors that determine the level of demand for and supply of any one currency must therefore be these participants and their changing requirements over time.

To give some examples:

(a) An increase in imports will tend to cause an increase in demand for foreign exchange;

(b) An increase in domestic interest rates will tend to increase the supply of foreign exchange as overseas residents will usually try to sell their currencies to buy the domestic unit in order to gain a higher rate of interest;

(c) An increase in domestic inflation rates may cause both residents and non-residents to increase their demand for foreign exchange in order to maintain the value of their financial assets;

(d) Attractive investment opportunities abroad will tend to increase the supply of the domestic unit to purchase the foreign currency with which to buy the overseas investment asset.

Note that the *supply* of any one currency is the same thing as the *demand* for the currency it is being exchanged for. A basic principle that is said to operate in determining rates is called Purchasing Power Parity.

The Purchasing Power Parity Theory

This theory holds that prices of traded goods and services world wide are interlinked through exchange rates. Thus the rates between any two currencies will be heavily influenced by the prices of traded goods, services and assets in these countries.

For example if a representative sample of such goods and services in one country is priced at (say) $200 and in another country at (say) £100, then the exchange rate will tend to be at $2 = £1.

Should the rate move away from this level, then goods, services and assets become cheaper (or dearer) to buy from one country's point of view. This would cause people to buy more (or less) of the goods, services and assets of the other country and this would, by itself, bring about a change in the rate by a process of changing demand for a currency.

Of course, other factors will play their part too. For example, changing rates of interest, anticipated inflationary levels and political considerations will all help to push rates one way or another. In addition, central banks can influence rates by buying or selling currency in the market. Note however, that an outflow of capital from one country to another will cause an increase in demand for foreign currency which will push the rates down for the domestic unit. This effect will, in turn, help to make the exports of the capital supplying country more attractive and export volume should rise.

Cross rates

Earlier in this chapter we defined a cross rate as any rate which excluded the US dollar. We can now qualify this statement to read "any rate between two currencies which excludes the currency of the country where the rate is offered". Thus, in London, a cross rate is any exchange rate which excludes sterling, e.g. French franc/Deutsche mark, or US dollar/Italian lira, etc.

Bearing in mind that dealers express rates for buying and selling, how do they arrive at a cross rate?

Let us take as our example:

US$1 = Deutsche mark 2.6885–2.6895
US$1 = French franc 8.0875–8.0925

Question: What is the cross rate between marks and francs?

The answer is *not* to be found simply by dividing units *on the same side* into each other! The reason for this is that cross rate calculations are found by a process of hypothetical transactions between the *three* currencies. For example to find the French franc value of one Deutsch mark:

(a) buy one dollar for DM2.6895 (bank buying DMs)
(b) sell one dollar for FF8.0875 (bank selling FFs)

Thus DM2.6895 = FF8.0875

Therefore $DM1 = \dfrac{8.0875}{2.6895} = FF3.0070$

Note that we have divided the DM (bank buying) rate into the FF (bank selling) rate.

However, we have only found *one* rate and we need *two* to give us a bank selling and a bank buying expression. This is done by simply using the remaining two rates:

(a) buy one dollar for FF8.0925 (bank buying FFs)
(b) sell one dollar for DM2.6885 (bank selling DMs)

Thus DM2.6885 = FF8.0925

Therefore $DM1 = \dfrac{8.0925}{2.6885} = FF3.010$

Cross rates are DM1 = FF3.0070–3.0100.

That is banks will *sell* francs for marks at FF3.0070 per one mark, and *buy* francs for marks at FF3.0100 per one mark.

To find the Deutsche mark value of one franc simply divide the mark values by the franc values.

The Forward Markets

It has already been noted that the spot markets – the markets for delivery of a currency by two working days – comprise the major portion of the total foreign exchange markets. However, the remaining portion – the forward markets – is very important because it affords anyone engaged in overseas business who is going to have to wait for currency receipts to arrive, or who is given time before making currency payments, the opportunity to *offset the risk that they will receive less (or more) domestic currency if they are waiting for receipts, or the risk that they will pay more (or less) domestic currency if they are waiting to make a payment, because of exchange rate changes between the signing of the contract of sale and the eventual transmission of payment.*

This risk is called the "Foreign Exchange Risk" and must be faced by at least one of the two parties to an international transaction.

Either the currency of the importer or of the exporter is used and whichever of these two agrees to make payment in, or take payment in, the other's currency, accepts this risk. This is so even where payment is made from balances of foreign currency held by the importer, for eventually those balances will need to be replenished and the exchange rate may then be more (or less) unfavourable.

When (as sometimes happens) both parties agree to use a third currency – say, the US dollar then *both* are open to the foreign exchange risk.

A "Delay in Payment" Risk

It should be emphasized that the risk arises when there is any time gap between the acceptance of a contract to supply goods and the time of actual payment. Even a few days could cause traders to incur significant losses (or gains). How much more important is the risk then when traders agree to three or six months credit from the date of shipment!

The Forward Market – A Definition

The forward market/markets for foreign exchange can be defined as:

> "a market where buyers and sellers of currency arrange deals at agreed exchange rates for delivery of the currency beyond two working days".

Although it is possible to arrange "tailor-made" periods for forward delivery it is usual for them to be for one and three months because these are the typical periods for which trade credit on a short-term basis tends to be arranged. In theory, there is no limit on the forward delivery period; there have been contracts for ten years! In practice such long-term periods are unusual, largely because there may be no market available, or if there is, the cost could be prohibitive.

As with the spot markets, forward deals are handled by the commercial banks who may be prepared to quote selling and buying rates for customers who wish to buy or sell currency for delivery in the future.

The markets are to be found around the world although London and New York are the main centres followed by Frankfurt, Tokyo and Zurich. The major currency of transaction is, of course, the US dollar, but most other major currencies are also quoted.

Determination of Forward Rates

Just as in the spot market, there are parties who wish to either buy or sell currencies for forward delivery. We have already noted the case of traders wishing to avoid the foreign exchange risk. This operation is called "Hedging" but there are other motives for forward deals. Apart from:

(a) Hedging;

there is also

(b) Speculating;
(c) Interest arbitraging;
(d) Central Bank intervention.

We shall be dealing with these types of transactions in detail later in this chapter but at this stage it should be understood that there are a number of reasons why there is a demand for, or a supply of foreign exchange for forward delivery. The exchange rates in the forward markets are, therefore, determined by demand and supply factors just as in any other markets. However, because these factors are not necessarily going to be identical to those in the spot market a gap is usual between spot and forward rates. This gap is called a "swap margin" and is expressed as so many points away from the spot rate itself. For example:

If the spot rate is . . . . £1 = US$1.2815–1.2825
and the one month forward quote is . . . . . 0.07c–0.12c discount
the forward discount is *added* to the
  spot rate to give . . . . £1 = US$1.2822–1.2837

Note that the forward quote is expressed as "points". The invariable rule is simple – *discounts are added to spot and premiums are deducted from spot*.

Thus, forward rates are said to be:

(a) At a discount against spot;
(b) At a premium against spot;
(c) At par (with spot).

(a) *Discount* means that the currency in question buys *more* of the quoted currency forward than at spot (as above).

(b) *Premium* means that the currency in question buys *less* of the quoted currency forward than at spot.

(c) *Par* means that the currency in question buys *the same* of the quoted currency forward as at spot.

Fixing "Points" in a Forward Quote

It may appear difficult to determine just where to place the forward "points" against spot. The general rule is:

always place the last digit of the "points" expression against the last digit of the spot rate, except where a fractional expression is used, in which case apply the $\frac{1}{100}$ part of the forward currency unit to the $\frac{1}{100}$ part of the spot rate.

For example:

Spot Rate = £1 = Canadian $1.8320–1.8330
One Month Forward = 0.05c pm–0.05c dis

Note: the abbreviations "pm" = premium, and "dis" = discount.

In both cases the "5" of the forward quote is placed against the "0" of the spot quote; i.e.

Spot £1 =	Can$1.8320–1.8330
1 month forward	0.05– 0.05
= Forward rate	1.8315–1.8335

The bank *selling* rate for Canadian dollars forward is at a *premium* of 0.05 cents (that is $\frac{5}{100}$ of one cent), and so it is *deducted* from the equivalent part of spot quote.

The bank *buying* rate for Canadian dollars forward is at a *discount* of 0.05 cents and so it is added to the equivalent part of the spot quote.

Note: the decimal point in the forward expression is *not* to be confused with the decimal point in the spot quote. The latter distinguishes *parts* of a whole currency unit from the *whole* currency unit while the former distinguishes parts of a *subdivision* of a whole currency unit from the *whole* subdivision.

Thus: 0.05c = $\frac{5}{100}$ part of a *cent*,
while: $0.8320 = 83 cents and $\frac{20}{100}$ part of a cent.
Therefore, *never match these decimal points*.

Note also that in the case of the above example, sterling buys (exchanges for) *fewer* Canadian dollars forward at the bank *selling* rate but *more* at the bank *buying* rate, than at spot.

While this is not common, it is by no means rare. In effect, the spread in the forward rate is thus larger than in the spot rate than it would have been had both sides been the same. In other words, while spreads are generally wider than for spot, in this case the gap is even larger. This probably reflects the feelings of uncertainty over likely spot changes in the near future.

Where rates are expressed in terms of *fractions* as opposed to decimals the same principle applies.

For example: where the spot £1 =   DM3.79½–3.80½
and the forward quote for one month is   3¼pf–3pf pm
then clearly the forward rate is   DM3.76¼–3.77½

Note: DM = Deutsche mark and pf = pfennig.

Fraction expressions are usual for:

Danish kroner   (100 ore to one kroner)
German mark   (100 pfennig to one mark)
Portuguese escudo   (100 cents to one escudo)
Italian lira (lire, plural) (no quoted subdivision)
Norwegian krone   (100 ore to one krone)
French franc   (100 centime to one franc)
Swedish krona   (100 ore to one krona)
Austrian schilling   (100 groschen to one schilling)
Swiss franc   (100 centimes to one franc).

Fixed and Option Forward Deals

Fixed Forward

A fixed forward deal is one where delivery of the currency is to take place on an agreed, specified, date in the future.

For example: if the customer is an exporter who has a currency Time Bill of Exchange in his favour which matures in exactly three months time, he can arrange a *forward* contract with his bank in which he agrees *now* to sell the proceeds of the Bill to the bank in exchange for domestic currency at an exchange rate determined by either deducting the forward premium or adding the forward discount, from and to the spot rate.

Thus, if the domestic currency is sterling and the Bill of Exchange is expressed in Belgian francs and the rates are:

                  Spot £1 = BF80.70–80.80
3 months spot forward   13–   3c pm
Then the forward rates are   80.57–80.77

Note: that if there is some doubt whether the forward expression of 13–3 represents a premium or a discount, the answer will always be found by reference to the calculated forward quote. This must always be such that the bank selling rate (the left-hand rate) is always lower than the bank buying rate (the right-hand rate). In the above example, the forward expression must represent a premium because if it were a discount then the result would be 80.83–80.83! Clearly a nonsense quote.

As our exporter wishes to sell Belgian franc receipts to the bank in three months time he will be given the rate of BF80.77 being the bank's buying rate. *That is, the bank will credit his sterling account in three months time with £1 for every BF80.77 he delivers to the bank.*

Assuming he makes the deal with the bank on 12 May for BF500,000 in three months time, then on 12 August he will be expected to deliver the currency. His sterling receipt will be:

$$\frac{500,000}{80.77} = £6190.42$$

Because the contract is a fixed one, he will not be able to deliver the currency on a date prior to or after 12 August.

Bank Charges

This can vary from bank to bank, depending on the sums involved and the status of the customer. This will be deducted from receipts to the exporter and added to payments from him.

Benefits of Forward Cover

Because the exporter expects to receive Belgian francs in three months time and because the sterling/BF rate can be expected to change in that period, he faces the risk that were he simply to wait till the Bill matures and then sell his francs at the then spot rate, his sterling receipts will be less (or more) than he anticipated. In fact, he will sustain a loss if the Belgian franc *depreciates* against sterling, and make a gain if it *appreciates* against sterling.

By not entering into a forward deal he will, effectively become a *speculator*, hoping that, at least, the Belgian franc will not depreciate. Although reference to speculation will be made later in this chapter, it is useful to note in this connection that it can arise *when no specific activity is entered into*.

That is to say that by doing nothing at all, the exporter is speculating, because he is taking a chance (risk) that currency rates will not move against him. This non-activity can be called "passive speculation" as opposed to "active speculation".

It can now be seen that use of the forward market to counter possible movements in rates is an antidote to speculation because the forward rate *is known at the outset* and can be used for the purposes of calculating predetermined costs and receipts.

Hedging

This process is referred to as "hedging" and is commonly used by those who engage in international transactions and do not wish to be exposed to the foreign exchange risk. Recipients of currency will sell forward, and payers of currency will buy forward.

However, if the market is to be used to best effect, it should be referred to as early as possible when the contract of sale is being drawn up. For example, if a UK manufacturer receives a request to deliver goods in one month's time and is asked to provide a quote in (say) Swiss francs, it would be prudent if he first obtained the forward rate to enable him to make the sterling profit he regards as necessary. If he wishes to receive (say) £100,000 and the forward rate is £1 = SF3.25–3.26, then he should offer a quote of SF326,000. This, when sold one month fixed forward will yield the required £100,000.

Of course, it is impossible to be absolutely precise because the contract of sale may take time to conclude and in that time rates could alter. The exporter could, if he wished, put a time limit on the importer's acceptance of the quote after which a new one would be required.

In this way the exporter achieves two, major benefits:

(a) He makes a quote in the buyer's currency (or in the one the buyer wishes to have);

(b) He protects himself from exchange rate fluctuations.

Note: that if sterling buys fewer Swiss francs forward than at spot (the SF is at a forward premium) then the quote to the buyer will be lower than if the payment was to be made at the outset; while if the Swiss franc was at forward discount the quote will be higher. Thus, the exporter effectively passes on the forward margin to his buyer. However, as this is hidden in the total price it will not be seen as an additional cost or reduction. Nevertheless the buyer is at liberty to accept or reject the quote as he pleases.

On the other hand, the exporter may be able to keep any forward advantage to himself. That is, if the Swiss franc is at a forward premium at (say) SF3.23, he may still be able to quote SF326,000 and eventually receive £100,928–79 making an additional profit of £928–79. This will depend on the buyer's awareness of forward rates and the availability of competitive quotes. Of course, if the Swiss franc is at a forward discount at (say) SF3.30, then SF326,000 will yield £98787–88 – a loss of £1212–13. It will be the exporter who will have to decide whether to bear this loss or load the quoted price to offset it.

By the same token a UK importer who is to pay foreign exchange in the future, will seek rates in the forward market to calculate his sterling costs exactly. By so doing, he is able to compare competitive quotes coming from overseas suppliers with those available from local sources.

Forward cover is not the only method to offset the foreign exchange risk. Other methods are dealt with later in this chapter.

Option Forward

We have seen that traders (and others) can buy or sell currencies with a specified date in the future for delivery. However, it is more usual for traders to be uncertain as to exactly when they expect to pay or receive foreign exchange. In these circumstances a fixed contract would not be suitable and the alternative, an option forward deal, would be relevant.

An option forward contract can be defined as "an agreement to buy or sell foreign exchange with delivery in the future *between* agreed, specified dates, at exchange rates determined at the outset".

For example, suppose a UK importer places an order for goods to be delivered and paid for within six weeks of placing the order (on say) 3 October. Payment is to be in Dutch guilders and the rates are:

3 October Spot £1 =   DG4.51 –4.52
          1 month forward 1½–1c pm
          2 months forward 2½–2c pm
          3 months forward 4⅛–3⅝ pm.

If the importer knew that he would pay in (say) two months time he could buy guilders, two months fixed forward at DG4.48½ (after deducting 2½c from the spot bank selling rate of DG4.51).

However, all he knows is that he may be called upon to pay at *any* time from 3 October to 14 November (six weeks). In order to ensure that the bank will release guilders to him as and when he will need them, he can buy guilders six weeks *option* forward, or, as our rates show only one, two and three months, he can buy guilders two months option forward, between 3 October and 3 December. *This deal gives the importer the flexibility of obtaining guilders any time between the two aforementioned dates.*

Suppose, for example, that actual payment is called for on the 28 October; he can ask his bank to sell him the guilders *on that day* as it is within the option period. However, should he not require the currency until *after* the last day of the option period then he will suffer the same fate as if he had purchased a fixed forward deal – namely, a close-out (see later in this chapter).

Option Exchange Rates

But what rate will the bank quote for an option deal? The answer is simple –

"banks will quote the worst rate from the customers' point of view selected from all the rates within the option period".

Look at the guilder rates again. If the importer buys guilders two months option forward the relevant bank selling rates are:

3 October spot   DG4.51
          1 month   DG4.49½
          2 months DG4.48½

By giving him the right to acquire guilders anytime during this period the bank will have to protect itself by quoting the rate which would have applied if the customer had purchased guilders two months fixed forward; namely DG4.48½. That is, the *least* number of guilders.

However, unlike a fixed deal, the importer can receive guilders from the bank at this exchange rate, at any time up to two months from 3 October. These forward rates are at a premium on spot. Does it make a difference if they were at a discount? The answer is yes.

For example, suppose the bank selling rates were:

3 October spot   DG4.51
            1 month DG4.52
            2 months DG4.53

The importer wishing to buy guilders two months option forward will now be quoted DG4.51. Once again, the *least* number of guilders.

The same principle applies; the customer could ask for the guilders almost at once (spot) and the bank protects itself by quoting the rate that applies to its most exposed position.

Principle One:

When banks are selling currency and forward rates are at a premium, option deals will tend to be at rates at the furthest end of the time range; when rates are at a discount, option deals will tend to be at spot rates.

The examples so far have been of customers wishing to *buy* currency forward. What is the case when they wish to *sell* currency forward?

Let us suppose that the *bank buying rates* are:

3 October spot   DG4.52
            1 month forward DG4.51
            2 months forward DG4.50.

Note that forward rates are at a *premium* on spot. If the customer wishes to *sell* guilders two months option forward, the bank will quote DG4.52. The *most* number of guilders.

If the rates were at a discount, for example:

3 October spot   DG4.52
            1 month DG4.53
            2 months DG4.54

then the bank will quote DG4.54 for selling guilders to a customer two months option forward. Again, the *most* number of guilders.

Principle Two:

When banks are buying currency and forward rates are at a premium, option deals will tend to be at rates nearest to spot; when rates are at a discount, option deals will tend to be at the furthest end of the time range.

Note that Principle Two is a mirror image of Principle One.

The best way to ensure the correct option forward quote is to remember that the bank will compare the rates at the beginning and the end of the option period and select the one *least advantageous* from the customer's point of view.

Unfortunately, there is one qualification to this. It sometimes happens that within the time span of an option period, rates can move from premium to discount or vice versa.

For example: Let spot be £1 = DG4.51 (bank selling)
>   1 month forward DG4.50   „   „
>   2 months forward DG4.52   „   „
>   3 months forward DG4.54   „   „

Let us suppose that an importer wishes to buy guilders three months option forward. The rate at the beginning of the option period is DG4.51 and at the end is DG4.54. As the bank is selling guilders the rate of DG4.51 (spot) seems applicable. However, this is not so because there is an even more disadvantageous rate from the importer's point of view within the time span of the option period, namely, the one month rate of DG4.50. This will be the rate quoted to the exporter. The principle remains the same; the customer always gets the worse rate because he has the opportunity to activate delivery at any time during the option period.

Combined Fixed and Option Deals

Finally, we have to consider cases where currencies need to be bought and sold forward where:

(a) an option is called for and
(b) the option period starts *after* day 1.

For Example: Suppose an exporter knows that he will receive Dutch guilders not later than in three months time, but he also knows that they will not arrive within the first month. This is shown in Diagram 9.2.

Diagram 9.2 illustrates that the option period starts *after* the end of the first month; thus, using our principle again, we have to select the rate at the beginning of the option period, namely, the one month's rate, and at the end of the option period, namely, the three month rate.

If the rates are:

Day 1   Spot   DG4.47½–4.48½
>   1 month forward   4.45⅞   4.47⅜
>   2 months forward   4.44   4.46½
>   3 months forward   4.42⅛   4.44⅝

Diagram 9.2
Determination of forward rates with a part fixed and part option contract

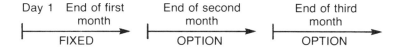

Thus, the selection will be from DG4.47⅜ and DG4.44⅝ with the *former rate being quoted*.

Note that this is a better rate for the exporter than he would receive if he wanted a *full* three months option deal; this would have been at DG4.48½.

However, had the rates all been at a forward *discount*, or had the customer been *buying* forward currency, then this advantage would not apply.

It is a matter for the trader's own decision whether to go for a fixed or option deal, and if the latter, whether to have a full or part option and part fixed contract. His decision will depend on:

(a) The expected timing of his receipts or payments;
(b) The forward rates;
(c) His willingness to speculate.

Note: within the time span of a forward contract there can be variations of the combinations of part fixed and part option.

For Example: given a six months forward deal there can be:

  (i) one month fixed and five months options
 (ii) two   ,,   ,,   ,,   four   ,,   ,,
(iii) three ,,   ,,   ,,   three ,,   ,,
(iv) four ,,   ,,   ,,   two   ,,   ,,
 (v) five ,,   ,,   ,,   one   ,,   ,,

Each of these combinations will command a unique exchange rate.

In addition to bank forward options described above a new facility is now available from UK banks called "Currency Options". This facility originated in the United States. It allows a trader to make a "put" or "call" option (to sell a currency at a fixed exchange rate in the future and to buy a currency at a fixed exchange rate in the future, respectively).

The purchaser is called a "taker" and he must pay a premium on taking the contract. Unlike a forward option, the taker need not exercise his option to sell or buy and if not so exercised all he loses is the premium.

He will only wish to exercise the option if the rates of exchange move in a favourable direction; e.g. if he makes a put option in dollars at $1.3655 and the spot rate moves to $1.3665 he will exercise his option by buying dollars at $1.3665 and selling them to his put option at $1.3655 making a gain of 10 points per £1. A call option would be exercised if the rates move the other way.[1]

Close-outs

We now turn to the question of what happens to a forward contract when events occur to prevent its proper completion. The first point to note is that a forward contract is legally binding on both parties. If a trader agrees to buy forward, buy he must! If a bank agrees to sell forward, sell it must! *There is no "option" to the honouring of this contract.*

But what happens when a customer *cannot* honour his forward deal? Suppose for example, a customer agrees to sell a currency forward but due to matters beyond his control, he is unable to deliver the currency in the forward period (option or fixed). This could be due to the receipts failing to arrive as planned perhaps because of a dispute with the party remitting the funds.

In *all* cases where a customer cannot meet his forward liabilities he will suffer what is called a "close-out".

Definition of a Close-out. A close-out is defined as "an effective honouring of a forward commitment by use of a spot transaction". In other words, to take our example of a customer not having the currency to deliver as planned, he will have to purchase that currency in the then spot market at the then current rate, and deliver the same under his forward contract.

Let us take an example. Suppose an exporter has agreed to sell Portuguese escudos two months fixed forward, and at the end of the two months he has not received the escudos from his Portuguese buyer. He is locked into a forward rate of £1 = PE185.25. He will then have to purchase escudos in the spot market (say) at £1 = PE181.75 and deliver them as per his forward agreement, losing PE3.5 for every £1's worth of business. This is illustrated in Table 9.2.

His loss has been due to the new spot £1 being at a *depreciated* level relative to his forward rate.

Had the £1 moved the other way (say) to PE187.50 then a gain of PE2.25 per £1 would have been made.

This puts a close-out into proper perspective. It is a situation where the customer can lose or gain, in complete contrast to the hedging concept of a forward deal.

In other words, a closed-out forward contract is a *negated* contract, leaving the customer in a *speculative* position as if he had never covered forward at all! A close-out is hedging in reverse.

In a situation where an importer buys forward currency and then for one reason or another finds that he has no need for the currency in the time span

[1]For further details see *A Businessman's Guide to the Foreign Exchange Market* by Brian Kettell (Graham & Trotman Ltd) 1985.

Table 9.2

| | | U.K. Exporter's Account | | | |
| | | Sterling | | Escudos | |
		D	C	D	C
1 June.	UK Exporter sells Escudos 500,000 2 months forward @ 185.25 = £2699.05 expected receipt.				
1 August.	Forward contract matures – no payment of Escudos received. Bank "closes-out" customer by making him buy Escudos 500,000 spot @ 181.75 = £2751.03 cost.	2751.03			500,000
	The Escudo proceeds of the close-out are then used to meet the exporter's forward liability.		2699.05	500,000	
	Net loss =	£51.98	—	—	—

Although Table 9.2 is set out as if the exporter had an Escudo account, this need not be the case. Instead, the bank will simply credit or debit his sterling account for the difference between the sterling receipt from the forward sale and the sterling cost of the spot purchase.

of the forward deal, he can close-out himself, i.e. he can take delivery and then sell it spot making a gain or loss as in the previous example.

Under UK Exchange Control Regulations which were put into abeyance in October 1979, currencies purchased forward had to be for acceptable commercial purposes (like buying imports). If they were not in fact needed, they *had* to be sold spot.

However, it is now quite legal for UK residents to hold foreign currency accounts and therefore close-outs are no longer binding. The alternative in this last case is simply to put the currency receipts to the credit of the existing currency account, or to open a new currency account.

In the case of the UK exporter, he can now borrow the relevant currency in the Euro-market, and deliver that to his forward contract.

In other words, the alternative to a close-out is:

(a) Lending currency (a currency account), instead of selling it spot;
(b) Borrowing currency, instead of buying it spot.

The factors that will determine whether to select a close-out are:

 (i) Expectations of future exchange rates;
 (ii) Current and future rates of interest;
(iii) Commercial need to hold currency balances.

These factors are discussed in detail later in this chapter. (See Interest Arbitrage.)

Extensions and New Contracts

What happens when a "close-out" has occurred and the customer still wants further forward cover? The answer is that he can obtain either an Extension to his previous contract or a completely new contract.

A New Contract

Quite simply the customer enters into a new forward deal for the same or different value to that of the first, but of course, at current forward rates.

For Example: Suppose a customer sells $200,000 one month fixed forward.

The rates are: spot   £1 = $1.5230–1.5240
                  1 month forward   0.05–0.10c dis.
                  giving forward rates of $1.5235–1.5250

He will be quoted $1.5250 for the one month deal giving a sterling receipt of £131,147-54.

At the end of one month he does not have the dollars to deliver so he is closed-out. The following new rates apply:

New spot $1 = $1.5325–1.5335
1 month forward   0.50–   1.00c dis.
giving forward rates $1.5375–1.5435

The close-out rate is $1.5325 (bank selling spot dollars). That is he buys $200,000 spot at $1.5325 giving a sterling cost of £130,505–76.

He now enters into a new forward contract to sell $200,000 for one month fixed at $1.5435 yielding a sterling receipt of £129,575–63. The results are summarised in Table 9.3.

Table 9.3
Customers' Forward Transactions

| | Customers' Bank Account | | | |
| | Debit | | Credit | |
	$s	£s	$s	£s
Original forward contract at maturity				
Close-out. Customer buys $200,000		130,505–70	200,000	
$200,000 delivered as per original contract	200,000			131,147–54
New forward contract at maturity				
$200,000 received from abroad			200,000	
$200,000 delivered as per new contract	200,000			129,575–63
Net receipts	—		—	£130,217–47

In fact, his final sterling receipt is £930–07 less than his original forward contract if completed would have yielded, and this is because although the close-out spot rate is *favourable*, this is more than offset by the *unfavourable new forward rate*.

Extensions

Where a bank regards a customer highly, or where the volume of business warrants it, a customer may receive a special new forward exchange rate which is more favourable than under a *new contract*. This would apply when a bank is prepared to offer a customer an extension of his existing forward contract to cover problems of the timing of the delivery of the currency, as an alternative to a new contract.

For Example: Using the above rates, instead of the bank quoting $1.5435 as it did under the new contract method, it will quote a more favourable rate which is found as follows:

New Spot £1 = 1.5325–1.5335
1 month forward   0.50–   1.00c dis.

The customer wishes to extend by *selling* $200,000 one month forward. The rate is calculated by taking the spot bank selling rate of $1.5325 *and adding the bank buying discount of 1.00 cents*.

This gives a 1 month rate of $1.5325
plus   100
gives $1.5425

This is a more favourable rate for the customer as he now sells $200,000 one month fixed forward at $1.5425 giving a sterling receipt of £129,659–64 which is £84–01 more than under the new contract method.

Note: this concession is achieved by "crossing-over" from the bank *selling* spot rate and adding the bank *buying* forward discount. Of course, the method works just as well if the customer is buying forward or if the forward rates are at a premium. Extension rates *always* give more favourable results to the customer. A useful way to understand this is by reference to the "cross-over" arrows shown in the following example.

Customer original forward sale of dollars $\begin{cases} \text{SPOT } \$1.5230\text{--}1.5240 \\ \text{FWD(DIS) } 005\text{--} \quad 010 \end{cases}$

close-out $\begin{cases} \text{SPOT } \$1.5325\text{--}1.5335 \\ \text{FWD(DIS) } 050\text{--} 100 \end{cases}$

In fact, although in theory both methods involve new forward contracts, the bank will, actually, simply increase or decrease the sterling credit or debit accordingly at the end of the day. The customer will have been *deemed* to have carried out these deals.

Covered Interest Arbitrage

Earlier in this chapter we saw that a process called "simple arbitrage" occurs when banks buy and sell spot currencies to profit from tiny variations in exchange rates around the world.

Interest Arbitrage is the term given to the process whereby banks (and others) seek to profit by holding high *interest rate* currencies instead of low interest rate ones.

For example: If a three month sterling deposit attracts the following rates 11¾%–11⅞% p.a. and the appropriate Swiss franc deposit yields 4³⁄₁₆%–4⁵⁄₁₆% p.a. it would profit an interest arbitrageur to withdraw funds from his Swiss franc deposit account which yields 4³⁄₁₆% per annum (for three months deposit) and invest in a sterling deposit yielding 11¾% on the same terms. (Interest spreads are shown to differentiate deposits from borrowing.)

This operation is called *Uncovered* Interest Arbitrage because it leaves the investor facing the exchange risk that sterling might depreciate during the three months and that a net loss could obtain.

To avoid this possibility the interest arbitrageur can cover himself by a *forward swap deal*. A swap is defined as "a simultaneous purchase and sale (or sale and purchase) of a certain amount of currency for two different value dates".

In the context of an arbitrageur selling Swiss francs spot for sterling, the swap would be:

(a) *Sell* Swiss francs for sterling *spot*;
(b) *Buy* Swiss francs for sterling *three months forward*.

Let us take an example based on the following exchange rates and using the above interest rates.

Day 1   spot £1 = Swiss francs 3.26¼–3.27¼
        3 month forward   4⅝– 4⅛c pm
        giving forward rates of 3.21⅝–3.23⅛.

Let us suppose that the investor withdraws Swiss francs 500,000 thereby foregoing 4¹⁄₁₆% p.a. interest fixed.

He *sells* SF500,000 spot at SF3.27¼ = £152,788–38 receipts.

This is invested in a three month sterling instrument giving a fixed interest return of 11¾% p.a.

It is assumed throughout that apart from currency changes there are no capital gains or losses and that interest rates are fixed for three months. (See *Financial Futures* later in this chapter.) To cover himself the investor also sells three months fixed forward his £152,788–38 asset together with the predetermined interest yield, i.e.:

11¾% on £152,788–38 = £17,952–63 interest p.a. For simplicity, assume the three month yield is one quarter of that = *£4,488–16 interest.*

Total known sterling receipts will therefore be: £152,788–38 capital
                                                                        plus   4,488–16 interest
                                                                                     £157,276–54 total receipts

This £157,276–54 is, therefore, sold three months fixed forward at SF3.21⅝ which yields SF505,840–67.

This, however, is a *gross* figure because it does not take into account the interest foregone on the Swiss franc deposit. This would have been at 4³⁄₁₆% per annum.

Thus, find 4³⁄₁₆% per annum for three months on SF500,000

$$= \frac{4.1875}{4} \times \frac{500,000}{100} = \text{SF5234–38 cost.}$$

In other words, had the investor left his money in a Swiss franc asset he would have received a profit of SF5,234–36.

By switching to a sterling asset and covering forward his profits are:

SF5,840–67.

It has paid him to move to a higher interest rate currency on a covered basis. Of course, he need not have covered the deal with a forward contract, but that would have left him with a foreign exchange risk and made him a *speculator*, although his actual profit would have been higher in this case. *Covered* Interest Arbitrage eliminates the speculative aspect but in this case it drastically reduces profitability.

Although the non-speculative gain is small, banks and other arbitrageurs are constantly on the look-out for such interest rate/exchange rate discrepancies on which guaranteed, non-risk gains may be made.

By the very process of Covered Interest Arbitrage, the gains themselves are eliminated because buying a currency spot to gain its higher rate of interest will tend to cause that currency to appreciate, thus causing further pur-

Table 9.4
Cost of Forward Cover and Interest Rate Differential

$$\text{Interest Rate Differential (IRD)} = \frac{r^o - r^d}{t}$$

$$\text{Cost of Forward Cover (CFC)} = \frac{S - F}{F} \times 100$$

$$\text{or} = \frac{F - S}{S} \times 100.$$

where r^d = domestic rate of interest
r^o = overseas rate of interest
t = time period
S = spot exchange rate
F = forward exchange rate

chases to become more expensive. Likewise, funds moving into a foreign asset are likely to push down the rate of interest on that asset.

The whole process can be summarised into a formula called the Cost of Forward Cover and Interest Rate Differential formula. This is illustrated in Table 9.4.

Applying this formula to our example, we have:

$$\text{IRD} = \frac{r^o - r^d}{t} = \frac{\overset{(\pounds s)}{11.75\%} - \overset{(SFs)}{4.1875\%}}{4} = 1.8906\% = \text{Gain}$$

(Note: three months is deemed to be ¼ of a year.)

$$\text{CFC} = \frac{F - S}{S} \times 100 = \frac{\overset{(\text{Buy SF fwd.})}{3.21625} - \overset{(\text{Sell SF spot})}{3.2725}}{3.2725} \times 100 = 1.7189\% = \text{Cost}$$

The IRD *gain* is not entirely offset by the CFC *cost*. There is a *net gain* of 0.1717%.

The cause of the CFC cost is that the investor *sells Swiss francs spot @ 3.2725* and *buys them back forward @ 3.21625*.

Determination of the Use of Either the Spot (S) or the Forward (F) Rate as the Divisor. This will depend on whether the *direct* or the *indirect* method of expression is being employed (see page 216).

In the above illustration the Swiss investor views the expression of £1 = SF3.26¼–3.27¼ as a *direct* expression and thus uses the formula

$$\frac{F - S}{S} \times 100.$$

However viewed from a UK vantage point the same currency expression is considered an *indirect* one. In this case the appropriate formula is

$$\frac{S - F}{F} \times 100.$$

Readers who wish to pursue the logic of this are directed to Appendix 7 at the end of this chapter.

Because of the activities of covered interest arbitrageurs, currencies which have high relative rates of interest will tend to have forward rates which are at a *discount* on the spot rate. That is, the high interest rate currency will buy fewer units of foreign exchange forward than it buys spot.

Were this not so, then not only could a profit be made on the interest differential but also on the forward differential! Such a situation is unlikely to be available for long because of the impact of huge flows of funds into that currency.

It should not be assumed from the foregoing that Covered Interest Arbitrage is the prerogative of the investor or non-trader. For example, importers who are given time to pay but who are also offered a reduced price (a discount) if payment is made early, have to decide whether it would be cheaper to:

(a) Buy currency spot at once and obtain the price discount; or

(b) Delay payment as allowed for and buy the currency forward without a price discount.

In effect, the importer is considering the IRD, being in this case, the interest lost by purchasing spot currency, against the "interest" gain of the price discount, and the CFC, being the exchange rate spot against forward.

Likewise, an exporter who provides his buyer with credit will have to consider whether to offer him a price discount for immediate payment.

Interest Rate Parity

The foregoing has shown that funds will move from currency to currency as long as there is a difference between the IRD and the CFC but that the movements themselves will tend to bring these into equality or near equality (to allow for transactions costs). This concept of equality is called Interest Rate Parity. However, in practice, this is seldom achieved in totality. Reasons for this are:

(a) *Transactions Costs*. I.e. bank charges, etc.

(b) *Exchange Restrictions*. These limit the permitted flows.

(c) *Inequality of Comparable Assets*. I.e. the Treasury Bills available in one country may not be viewed as identical in terms of risk or default as those issued in another country.

(d) *Inelastic Supply of Funds*. Although arbitrage profits may be available, banks may be reluctant to tie up funds which could be used to provide customers with credit facilities. "Inelastic" in this context means that arbitrageurs will need a fairly large arbitrage profit to motivate them to shift their funds into such activities.

(e) *Speculation*. I.e. the purchase or sale or spot or forward currencies with a view to making a *capital gain* from an anticipated appreciation or depreciation.

Such speculative operations can play havoc with interest rate parities. For example, in the latter half of October 1976 when sterling was under pressure, one month financial instruments in London were 9% to 10% points higher than in the US. Yet in spite of this, sterling was at a forward premium against the US dollar. That is, sterling bought more dollars forward than at spot. In these circumstances interest arbitrageurs could obtain both an interest differential gain *and* a *negative* cost of forward cover – a gain.

Table 9.5
Effect of Speculation on Interest Rate Parity

	Original rates		*Likely subsequent rates*	
	Spot	Forward	Spot	Forward
Arbitrageur	buys £s at $1.52	sells £s at $1.50	$1.53	$1.49
Speculator	sells £s at $1.52	sells £s at $1.50	$1.46	$1.49
		Net	$1.47	$1.49

However, because speculators believed that sterling was likely to depreciate against the dollar their volume of *selling* spot and forward sterling (not necessarily in equal volumes) more than offset covered interest arbitrageurs' transactions of *buying* spot sterling and selling it forward, causing the cost of forward cover to become *negative*.

An illustration of this effect is shown in Table 9.5.

The net result is that the new spot rate is *lower* than the new forward rate because the volume of speculative spot *selling* of sterling more than offsets the volume of arbitrage *buying* of sterling.

Buy/sell rates are ignored for the purpose of this illustration.

"Active" Speculation

This speculative process can be called "active" as opposed to the "passive" variety dealt with earlier in this chapter. Readers are reminded that the latter type involves not covering forward to meet a possible currency exposure (risk).

In practice, a transaction can be a mix of arbitrage and speculation where a currency is purchased to acquire its interest benefit without an associated sale of that currency forward.

Central Bank Intervention

Although Central Banks rarely intervene in the forward foreign exchange markets there have been occasions when it has happened on a large scale. Such occasions were in the period 1964 to 1967 when the Bank of England *purchased* substantial amounts of forward sterling with a view to increasing the dollar value of sterling in the forward market. The hope was that this would limit speculation against sterling and encourage arbitrageurs to *buy spot sterling* and gain advantage from the improved forward rate.

This support for sterling was essentially counter-speculative and its principal advantage was that it did not deplete the official dollar reserves at the outset as support for spot sterling would have done.

However, the disadvantages of such forward intervention are:

(a) At the maturity of the forward contracts to purchase sterling, dollars will *have* to be released (although they could be repurchased spot in the right circumstances);

(b) the intervention could be (and was) unsuccessful if the volume of speculation exceeds that of official intervention.

Another example of official intervention came in the 1970s when the Bank of England bought spot and sold forward sterling. This had the same effect as arbitrage, namely, to widen the forward discount of sterling against spot. See Table 9.5. In effect, the authorities acted to support arbitrageurs against speculators. If the latter would have been able to borrow sterling and *sell* it spot, hoping for a sterling depreciation, this would have undone the effects of intervention. However, controls were in force and UK non-bank residents were not permitted to act in this way. UK banks were restricted within tight limits and non-UK residents were not allowed access to the UK sterling market. This strategy has proved useful to the authorities on occasions.

Summary of Forward Transactions

To summarize the classes of operators in the forward markets, we have:

(a) Hedgers – who cover expected receipts or payments;
(b) Arbitrageurs – who seek small covered gains;
(c) Speculators – who seek capital gains;
(d) Central Banks – who seek to offset speculation.

Between them they will influence the forward rates, and by implication the spot rates too. In addition, interest rates are going to be affected.

Note: All references to speculation are made throughout without any implication of its desirability or otherwise. The term is used merely in its neutral and technical sense. However, as seen above, Central Banks may regard it as undesirable and take steps to offset it in its destabilising form. It is therefore necessary to distinguish destabilising from stabilising speculation.

Stabilising Speculation

This can be defined as "taking an uncovered position in a currency which seeks to profit from exchange rate changes moving in the *opposite direction* from current movements".

Thus if spot rates are £1 = $1.50 moving to $1.49, the stabilising speculator will *buy* sterling, because he believes that it is likely to swing back to $1.50 or more.

Destabilising Speculation

This can be defined as "taking an uncovered position in a currency which seeks to profit from exchange rate changes moving further *in the same direction* as current movements".

244 FINANCE OF INTERNATIONAL TRADE

Thus, using the above rates, the destabilising speculator believes that they are likely to move from $1.49 to $1.48 or less.

The net impact of all speculation will depend on the volume of business of these two types of traders. Only one of these can emerge with speculative profits.

Other Ways to Avoid the Foreign Exchange Risk

Apart from covering forward, it is possible to cover the risk of currency changes in other ways. For example:

(a) Interest Arbitrage

I.e. suppose an exporter expects to receive currency in the future; instead of selling it forward he can borrow the currency, sell it spot for domestic money and repay his currency loan out of his expected currency proceeds.

Likewise an importer given time to pay, need not buy currency forward but buy it spot and hold it on deposit until needed. Both traders will have to consider the interest rate differential (IRD) and the cost of forward cover (CFC).

(b) Limit to Credit

If no trade credit is granted (or if it is limited) the exchange risk is eliminated or possibly reduced. Such a policy however could limit an exporter's market and might call for a more competitive price for his goods.

(c) Invoice in Domestic Currency

As noted earlier in this chapter, invoicing in domestic currency merely transfers the risk to the overseas buyer. Again, this could call for a price reduction.

(d) Invoice in Foreign Exchange but Stipulate that the Amount must be Equivalent to a Specific Domestic Currency Value

For example, a UK exporter can agree to accept Italian lire (LIT) so long as on the day of eventual payment it is worth (say) £10,000. Thus, the Italian importer will not know how much lire it will cost to be equivalent to £10,000 until the day that payment is effected.

Although the UK exporter receives lire, he knows that it will be worth £10,000; no risk is attached. The Italian importer has the advantage in that he pays in his own currency but, of course, there is the big disadvantage that his costs will depend on the movements of the £/LIT rate. In effect, he is carrying the exchange risk. For this, he may require a price discount if he is willing to do business at all!

(e) Invoice in Foreign Exchange but Link Payment to a Currency "Basket"

A currency "basket" is a compilation of several currencies each with a specific "weight" (see Chapter 12). As long as the "basket" contains some currencies that are likely to appreciate and some that are likely to depreciate, the net change of the "basket" unit against one particular currency is likely to be less than the change of any one currency against that particular currency.

For example: the Special Drawing Right (SDR) can be used (see Chapter 12). Suppose a UK exporter agrees to payment in Italian lire but specifies that he must receive lire worth (say) SDR 15,000. On the day of payment the exporter will receive his lire, but if that currency has depreciated sharply against sterling, but less sharply against the SDR because the latter contains some weak currencies which have also depreciated against sterling, then the exchange risk may be shared between buyer and seller depending on their own currency changes against the SDR. This is illustrated in Table 9.6.

The SDR has depreciated by 12% against sterling;
The SDR has appreciated by 10% against lire;
Lire have depreciated by 20% against sterling;
Lire have depreciated by 9.1% against the SDR;
Sterling has appreciated by 25% against lire;
Sterling has appreciated by 13.75% against the SDR.

When the contract of sale is agreed the Italian importer accepts that he will make payment in lire worth SDR 15,000.

To the UK exporter this is worth at the time $15,000 \times 0.625 = £9,375$.

To the Italian importer this is worth at the time $15,000 \times 1,500 = \text{LIT22.5}$ million.

When payment falls due the Italian importer must pay $15,000 \times 1650 = \text{LIT24.75}$ million.

To the UK exporter this is worth $\dfrac{24.74\,\text{m}}{3000} = £8,250$

Summary. The Italian importer pays LIT2.25 m more, equal to a 10% *increase in cost.* The UK exporter receives £1,125 less, equal to a 12% *reduction in receipts.*

Table 9.6
Hypothetical Example of Invoicing in an SDR-Linked Currency

Rates at start of credit period	Rates at end of credit period
SDR1 = £0.625 = LIT 1500	SDR1 = £0.55 = LIT 1650
SDR1.6 = £1.00 = LIT 2400	SDR1.82 = £1.00 = LIT 3000

In this way the risk has been shared between them. Of course there is no guarantee that the risk will be divided more or less equally between the parties or that they will even be divided at all! This will depend on the degree to which both currencies fluctuate against each other and against the "basket" unit itself.

(f) Matching Currency Receipts to Currency Payments

Where a trader or investor is expecting to pay *and* receive currencies it may be possible to match forthcoming receipts and payments to avoid a currency exposure.

For example, if $300,000 is expected in three months time and $200,000 is to be paid in four months time, then the transactor can hold $200,000 of his receipts (if they arrive) to meet his dollar outgoings. The remaining $100,000 can be sold forward at the outset. Alternatively, the remaining $100,000 can be borrowed at the outset and sold for spot sterling, using the expected dollar receipts to repay the loan. This is, of course, yet another reference to Covered Interest Arbitrage and its use will depend on the factors already dealt with in this chapter.

Banks Covering their Customer's Forward Deals

We need to consider how banks pass on to the market the liabilities they enter into when they agree to buy or sell currencies from or to customers for delivery in the future. Let us assume they need to cover a purchase of currency from a customer. There are two ways in which they can do this:

1. (a) The bank borrows the currency for the period of the customer's forward deal;

   (b) The bank sells the currency for spot sterling;

   (c) The sterling is invested by the bank for the same time period;

   (d) At the maturity of the customer's forward deal the bank pays over the sterling to him;

   (e) The currency received in return is used to repay the original currency loan.

   Attentive readers will have noticed that this behaviour by banks is nothing less than our old friend, Covered Interest Arbitrage! Its occurrence will depend on interest rates and exchange rates.

2. *The Bank Undertakes a "Swap" Transaction.* A swap has already been defined as a purchase and sale of currency for two different time periods, normally one spot and one forward. A swap should be differentiated from an "outright" transaction which can be defined as "a single spot or forward deal having no association with any other deal". An example of an outright deal is that of an importer or exporter buying or selling currency forward.

How a Swap Works

(a) The bank buys spot sterling;

(b) The bank enters into a swap arrangement with the market (other banks) in which it:

  (i) sells sterling *spot* for currency;

  (ii) buys it back for the same *forward period* as the customer's forward deal.

The swap comprises items (i) and (ii). However, the first leg (i) cancels out the original spot purchase (a) leaving the bank with item (ii) which is a forward deal by the bank to buy sterling forward (sell currency forward). This forward sale of currency thus matches (and offsets) the forward purchase of currency from the bank's customer.

In effect, in method (ii) the bank is really passing the deal with its customer to the market as a whole.

One final aspect of a swap should be noted. Swaps are quoted in the forward leg at exchange rates calculated in the same way as for "extensions". (See earlier in this chapter.) An outright forward deal, however, is quoted in the same way as a "new contract". Swaps, therefore, give banks a better forward exchange rate than they themselves give their customers. Or to put it another way, inter-bank spreads are less than retail spreads. In fact, there is no inter-bank market in outright forward deals.

THE CURRENCY FUTURES MARKET (FINANCIAL FUTURES)

There are several centres for currency futures trading; the largest is in Chicago, USA, where the International Monetary Market (IMM) has been operating for several years. The London market opened in September 1982 at the Royal Exchange Building opposite the Bank of England. Its name is the London International Finance Futures Exchange, otherwise referred to as LIFFE. LIFFE itself is a limited company which sells seats on the floor of the exchange to traders. Separate from LIFFE but complimentary to its operations is the Clearing House whose functions are to protect clients by guaranteeing all deals and also by offering a bank deposit facility whereby clients' accounts may be debited and credited for initial and variation margins.

In addition to these, there are markets in Toronto, Sidney, New York, and Singapore; Hong Kong and Brazil are soon to open their own markets.

At first sight these markets appear to duplicate the work of the bank forward exchange markets and the futures commodity markets. But, of course, differences exist. They are:

(a) Financial futures are traded on an organized exchange (fixed site) by open outcry and not over the counter or over the telephone.

(b) Futures contracts are standardized to a few specific currencies and time periods; they are not "tailored" to meet users' requirements as in the bank markets.

(c) Futures contracts have no buy-sell spreads. Instead there is an explicit brokerage fee.

(d) Futures contracts are rarely allowed to go to maturity. Instead, transactors sell or buy back prior to maturity in order to gain a speculative profit or limit a speculative loss.

(e) Settlement in the futures market is with the Clearing House itself and not with another trading party.

(f) Unlike the forward markets, an initial margin is required to be placed and a variation margin is levied daily in relation to the price fluctuations until the transaction is closed-out or taken to delivery.

(g) Unlike the forward markets, currency futures contracts are at exchange rates which do not vary with the size of the deal. Thus, a relatively small deal might be available at a more attractive exchange rate than for a forward contract. However, the minimum deal for a sterling futures contract is £25,000.

From an exporter or importer's viewpoint the currency futures market may be advantageous insofar as the broker's fee is less than the bank's buy/sell spread, and trade can be for smaller values than permitted in the bank markets. However, the degree of flexibility in terms of forward maturities and currencies is limited. In practice, the futures market is really for those who wish to take up positions in certain currencies and not so much for hedgers.

There are currency contracts in:

(a) Sterling;
(b) Swiss franc;
(c) Deutsche mark;
(d) Yen.

All currencies are traded against the US dollar.

Apart from currency features, the market in London trades in Interest Rate Contracts in:

(a) three month Eurodollars;
(b) three month Sterling;
(c) twenty-year Gilt (based on a notional 12% stock);
(d) FT-SE 100 index;
(e) US Treasury Bond 8%.

Before we conclude, it would be useful to illustrate the facilities offered by LIFFE to customers who have an interest rate problem.

For Example: Suppose a UK company has an outstanding bank overdraft which it will be drawing down by £100,000 over the next three months. It will incur interest currently at 14% per annum subject to movements up or down.

Problem: Because rates may change, the company is unable to calculate its total interest costs over the next three months.

Solution: Contact a member of the LIFFE Clearing House and offer to sell a three months sterling interest rate contract say for 18% p.a. At this rate of interest the receipt will be:

$$S/(1 + i) = P$$

where S = Future sum (£100,000)
i = Rate of interest (18% per annum)
P = Present value (to be found)

Thus, $£100,000 \Big/ \left(1 + \dfrac{4.5\%}{100}\right) = \dfrac{100,000}{1.045} = £95,693.78$

Therefore the sale of the sterling three month interest rate contract will yield £95,693.78.

At the end of the three months the company "closes-out" its position by buying the same instrument and delivering it as per its original agreement.

Rates Remaining Constant

If interest rates have not changed in the three months the "close-out" will be at the same cost as the original receipts (£95,693.78) apart from known brokerage fees. However, the bank overdraft is also likely to be at the same interest charge, so interest costs have been fixed.

Rates Increasing

If interest rates have risen then the cost of "closing out" will have fallen. For example, suppose rates rise to 20% per annum. Using the above formula we get:

$$£100,000 \Big/ \left(1 + \dfrac{5\%}{100}\right) = \dfrac{100,000}{1.05} = £95,238.09$$

The company will therefore make an overall gain of £455.69. However, this will be offset by an equivalent increase in the bank overdraft cost. So once again, interest costs have been fixed.

Rates Decreasing

If interest rates fall, then the cost of "closing-out" will rise. For example, suppose rates fall to 16% per annum, then:

$$£100,000\bigg/\left(1+\frac{4\%}{100}\right)=\frac{100,000}{1.04}=£96,153.85.$$

The company will, therefore, make an overall loss of £460–07. However, bank overdraft rates will also fall to offset this loss to give fixed rates once again.

It will be seen therefore, that the effect of trading in interest rate futures is to lock-in a given rate of interest for a specific period of time. Like trading in the bank forward market for foreign exchange it enables traders to exchange *uncertainty* for *certainty*.

Of course, this concept is applicable only to "hedgers" as just described. However, there is nothing to stop traders acting as speculators in the futures markets by "closing-out" their futures purchase or sale at any time prior to the maturity of the contract.

Note: Readers are reminded that these calculations are based on the fact that *rising* rates of interest are accompanied by *falling* prices of financial assets and vice versa.

International traders who offer or receive credit on which interest rates fluctuate over the period of the credit can take advantage of the futures market to lock-in a given rate. This will enable them to more easily calculate real rates of receipts and payments in the future.

For example, importers who receive a bank overdraft or produce loan subject to fluctuating interest rates, or where payment is delayed under a Negotiations Letter of Credit, or where an inchoate Bill of Exchange is drawn under a Refinance Credit, or where a Time Bill of Exchange is accepted, can benefit from trading in the financial futures market to lock-in the cost of the credit. (See Chapter 8.)

Exporters who offer credit terms to their buyers on the basis of variable interest rates can also lock-in the interest receipt for the maturity of the credit. Exporters can also benefit in their capacity as borrowers, e.g. bank overdrafts, etc.

TRADED CURRENCY OPTIONS

One other currency market is the Traded Currency Option (TCO) market which is based in the Chicago Mercantile Exchange and available through brokers in the UK such as Eastern Capital Corporation Ltd.

A TCO contract can be defined as "a purchase which gives the right – but *not* the obligation – to receive or deliver currency within 3 months at fixed rates of exchange". The option can be traded (sold) at any time within this period but terminates at the end of it. The major difference then, between this and the bank option forward market and the UFFE market is that there *is no obligation* to take or deliver currency unless one wishes to do so within the time period.

Currently, each contract is for £25,000 and is available against dollars only. There is a brokerage commission payable, usually $50 per contract.

Using the TCO Market for Hedging

(1) A UK importer wishes to cover $33,750 payable in 3 months time. He buys a Sterling Put Option which gives him the right to receive these dollars within that time. Assume a spot rate of $1.3500 with a 3 month premium of 3.25 cents. He must pay 25,000 times 3.25 cents = $812.50 as an initial margin at $1.3500 = £601.85 cost.

If the £1 moves to $1.2500 within the next 3 months (a sterling depreciation), the importer can take delivery of his $33,750 for £25,000 giving a total cost of £25,601.85.

If the £1 moves to $1.4500 (a sterling appreciation), the importer can allow his TCO to expire because he can buy $33,750 more cheaply. Total cost is $33,750 at 1.4500 = £23,275.86 plus the margin of £601.85 = £23,877.71.

With a bank option forward contract, the importer would be *bound* to take delivery of $33,750 within the 3 months.

(2) A UK exporter expects to receive $33,750 within 3 months. He buys a Sterling Call Option which gives him the right to deliver these dollars within that time. Assuming the same rates as before, he will pay an initial margin of (say) 3.55 cents = 25,000 at 3.55 cents = $887.50. At spot this costs £657.40.

If the £1 moves to $1.2500 he will allow his TCO to expire because he can sell $33,750 at a more attractive rate at spot. I.e. $33,750 at $1.2500 = £27,000 receipt. Deduct cost of £657.40 gives £26,342.60 net.

If the £1 moves to $1.4500 he will take delivery of £25,000 under his TCO contract giving net receipts of £24,342.60.

With a bank option forward contract, the exporter would be *bound* to deliver $33,750 within the 3 months.

Assuming that the above quoted rates would apply to bank forward contracts (and this would not necessarily be so) the TCO offers the possibility of a lower cost or higher receipt at the cost of losing the initial premium.

The same analysis can be made in connection with speculation. In this case, TCO contracts are purchased for their own right and not to cover expected receipts or expenditures in currency.

For further reading see *A Businessman's Guide to the Foreign Exchange Market* by Brian Kettell (Graham & Trotman), 1985.

Appendix 7

Determination of spot (S) and forward (F) rates as divisors in calculating the percentage Cost of Forward Cover (CFC)

Throughout the world, with the exception of the UK, rates are quoted in terms of the US dollar. For example, $1 = Swiss francs 2.1275–2.1353.

Such an expression is viewed in New York as an *indirect* one. However, from Zurich, it is seen as a *direct* expression.

In the UK, currencies are measured against sterling. Thus, £1 = Swiss francs 3.26¼–3.27¼. Viewed from the UK this is an *indirect* expression but from Zurich it is a *direct* expression.

Let us suppose that the following are the spot and forward rates (and cross-rates) for dollars, sterling and Swiss francs.

In New York (*indirect*)

Spot $1 = SF2.1275–2.1354; and £0.6521–0.6525
3 months forward = SF2.0837–2.1016; and £0.6479–0.6504

In London (*indirect*)

Spot £1 = SF3.26¼–3.27¼; and $1.5325–1.5335
3 months forward = SF3.21⅝–3.23⅛; and $1.5375–1.5435

In Zurich (*direct*)

Spot $1 = SF2.1275–2.1354; and £0.6521–0.6525
3 months forward = SF2.0837–2.1016; and £0.6479–0.6504.
Cross-rates £1 spot = SF3.2605–3.2746.
Cross-rates £1
   3 months forward = SF3.2037–3.2312.

Arbitraging from New York

For example, sell $100,000 spot @ SF2.1275 gives SF212,750,
and sell SF212,750 3 months forward @ SF2.1016 gives $101,232–39.

The CFC (gain) is $1,232–39 or *1.23239%** on $100,000.

The formula then is: $\dfrac{2.1275(S) - 2.1016(F)}{2.1016(F)} \times 100 = 1.23239\%*$

*Reconciliation.
The forward (F) rate is here used as the divisor because the expression is
seen as an *indirect* one.

Again, sell $100,000 spot @ £0.6521 gives £65,210,
   and sell £65,210 3 months forward @ £0.6504 gives $100,261–37.

The CFC (gain) is $261–37 or *0.26137%*‡ on $100,000.

The formula is again: $\dfrac{0.6521(S) - 0.6504(F)}{0.6504(F)} \times 100 = 0.26137\%‡$

‡Reconciliation.
Again the forward (F) rate is used as the divisor because the expression is
seen as an *indirect* one.

Had the spot (S) rate been used as the divisor then there would be no
reconciliation between the percentage results derived from the value
calculation and the formula calculation.

Arbitraging from London

For example, sell £100,000 spot @ SF3.26¼ gives SF326,250,
and sell SF326,250 3 months forward @ SF3.23⅛ gives £100,967–11.

The CFC (gain) is £967–11 or *0.96711%** on £100,000.

The formula is: $\dfrac{3.2625(S) - 3.23125(F)}{3.23125(F)} \times 100 = 0.96711\%*$

*Reconciliation.
Once again, the forward (F) rate is used as the divisor because the expression
is seen as an *indirect* one.

Again, sell £100,000 spot @ $1.5325 gives $153,250,
   and sell $153,250 3 months forward @ $1.5435 gives £99,287–33.

The CFC (loss) is £712–67 or *0.71267%*‡ on £100,000.

The formula is: $\dfrac{1.5325(S) - 1.5435(F)}{1.5435(F)} \times 100 = -0.71267\%$‡

‡ Reconciliation.
The forward (F) rate is used as the divisor because the expression is seen as an *indirect* one.

Arbitraging from Zurich

For example, sell SF100,000 spot @ SF2.1354 gives $46,829–63,
and sell $46,829–63 3 months forward @ SF2.0837 gives SF97,578–91.

The CFC (loss) is SF2,421–09 or *2.42109%** on SF100,000.

The formula now is: $\dfrac{2.0837(F) - 2.1354(S)}{2.1354(S)} \times 100 = -2.42109\%$*

*Reconciliation.
The *spot* (S) rate is used this time as the divisor because the expression is seen as a *direct* one.

Finally, sell SF100,000 spot @ SF3.2746 gives £30,538–08
    and sell £30,538–08 3 months forward @ SF3.2037 gives SF97,834–85.

The CFC (loss) is SF2,165–16 or *2.16516%*‡ on SF100,000.

The formula is: $\dfrac{3.2037(F) - 3.2746(S)}{3.2746(S)} \times 100 = 2.16516\%$‡

‡ Reconciliation.
The *spot* (S) rate is used as the divisor because the expression is seen as a *direct* one.

In all these cases the use of the wrong divisor would give an incorrect reconciliation.

Chapter 10

The Credit Risk and ECGD

In previous chapters we dealt with two of the major risks peculiar to international business. They were:

The Marine risk   (Chapter 5)
The Foreign Exchange risk (Chapter 9).

It is now time to turn our attention to the third risk – the Credit risk. This, of course, is by no means confined to the international sphere of business but because of such factors as the distance from markets, lack of knowledge of overseas events which are likely to impinge on finance and of buyer's credit ratings, and also, increasingly, the upward movement in the length of credit periods, exporters are faced with the possibility that:

(a) They will face delays in receiving payment; or
(b) They will never receive payment.

Now, it is worth mentioning at this stage that in a sense, importers too face a sort of credit risk. True, it doesn't present itself in the form of non-receipt of payment from the exporter! However it can involve:

(a) Delay in receipt of goods;
(b) Shortfall in quantity delivered;
(c) Inferior quality delivered;
(d) Wrong goods delivered;
(e) Non-delivery.

These problems can lead the importer to face financial difficulties in the sense that his ability to on-sell goods is impaired and may cause the loss of customers, or his ability to use the imports in his own production process is impaired. Either way a financial problem is likely which may result in a financial loss.

The importer, however, has certain methods open to him to avoid or, at least limit these problems. They are:

(a) Withholding of payment;

(b) Refusal to accept documents (see chapters on Collections and Letters of Credit);

(c) Inspection of goods in transit;

(d) Use of intermediaries: e.g. a Confirming House;

(e) Use of Bonds (see later in this chapter).

Because of the worldwide decline in the volume of trade, a buyer's market has developed which has led to increasing demands by importers for more competitive pricing, lengthening credits and better delivery performance. As a result they are, perhaps, better placed than ever to limit the problems mentioned above.

The exporter on the other hand, is more pressed than ever; especially when an entire overseas market turns sour due to political events outside his – or his buyer's – control.

Several of the topics covered in previous chapters, have in fact, dealt with methods whereby suppliers can assure themselves that, provided good delivery is made, they will receive payment at least at the end of the agreed credit period, if not before. Readers are advised to re-read the relevant topics which are contained in Chapters 4, 7 and 8.

However, even these, non-recourse, facilities may not cover all eventualities. For example, factoring may not extend to all of an exporter's business, and the sought-after Letter of Credit may not be forthcoming from the importer or his bank.

To overcome these difficulties many countries around the world have established government, or government assisted facilities, to provide cover to their exporters which effectively limit their exposure to losses arising from non-payment.

Later in this chapter a section is devoted to facilities of other countries, but the major part of this chapter is concerned with the facilities available in the UK by the organization called the Export Credits Guarantee Department or ECGD.

ECGD[1]

THE BACKGROUND

ECGD was established in 1919 in order to promote UK exports in the post-war period, but its present range of functions can be said to have begun in

[1]See *ECGD Services Handbook*, 1985.

1931 when it first started to offer whole turnover policies and in 1932 comprehensive policies. ECGD is a separate department of Government, though it is accountable to the same ministers as the Department of Trade. Its headquarters are in the City of London and in Cardiff and it has a regional network of offices throughout the country. It derives its powers from the Export Guarantees and Overseas Investment Act 1978 and although its operations require the consent of the Treasury, in practice the latter has delegated authority to ECGD on matters of everyday business. Only for cases involving new principles or where a very large sum of money is involved will Treasury approval be necessary. An Advisory Council made up of leading bankers and businessmen appointed by the Secretary of State for Trade gives advice on the acceptability of risks for cover which in practice is usually followed. Money is voted annually by Parliament with surpluses being returned to central Government and losses being financed by them. Trading accounts are published annually. ECGD currently covers about one-third of all UK exports.

ECGD has been subject to two official reviews in 1958 and 1972 and was reviewed again in 1983. A committee of enquiry was announced by the Minister of State for Trade and had a very wide remit.[2]

ECGD operates under five sections of the afore-mentioned 1978 Act;

Section 1 – commercial business
Section 2 – national interest business
Section 3 – loans and grants
Section 4 – securities
Section 5 – cost escalation cover (discontinued in 1983).

In this chapter we are concerned principally with ECGD credit insurance cover and also associated bank guarantees, and Sections 1 and 2 are concerned with these and other facilities. Section 1 requires ECGD to conduct its business in such a way as to involve no expense to the taxpayer. Since 1974 it has also to maintain a set ratio of reserve levels to the amount at risk. Policies are to be written and services offered, on terms, and at rates which allow it to meet its costs and accumulate necessary reserves, taking one year with another. In fact, because of the prevailing economic and financial climate in recent times, serious deficits are being incurred in common with similar bodies in other countries. For example, in 1982/83 claims were £584 m and premium income was £346 m.

Section 1 business is by far the most important part of ECGD's work being about 80% of its credit insurance facility. Section 2 business involves the taking of risk not really compatible with a purely commercial approach but is done as a public service in the national interest. For example, certain exports may be given credit insurance cover on terms and at premium rates which do not fully reflect the risks to ECGD but which is regarded as of

[2]See article in the *Financial Times*, 17 August 1983.

Diagram 10.1
ECGD Facilities

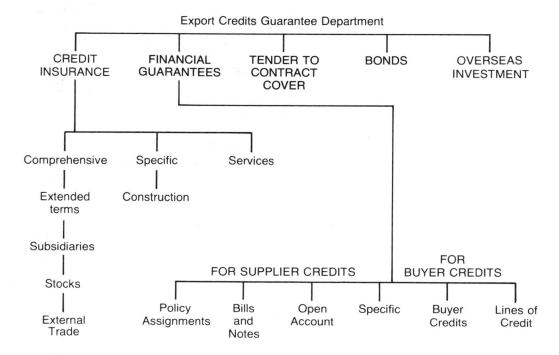

public importance; e.g. selling capital goods on long-term credits to high-risk markets.

The work of ECGD can best be assessed by dividing its activities into three areas:

(a) Credit Insurance;
(b) Financial Guarantees;
(c) Other facilities.

Diagram 10.1 gives an outline summary of these three areas.

CREDIT INSURANCE

This can be defined as "the insurance against non-payment by an overseas buyer due under a properly carried out contract, for a premium (fee) paid by the seller".

As can be seen from Diagram 10.1 credit insurance comprises a variety of areas. Comprehensive cover is the most important, accounting for about 75% of ECGD's business.

Comprehensive Credit Insurance Policy

The term "comprehensive" refers to two aspects of the comprehensive policy:

(a) It is comprehensive in exporter's turnover;

(b) It is comprehensive in cover.

(a) Exporter's Turnover

Exporters who are seeking to cover their export business at the lowest possible cost will need a comprehensive policy, but in order to cover as wide a range of good and bad markets, ECGD insists on covering all, or a wide spread of a particular exporter's turnover. In this way, ECGD is not given only the risky areas to cover leaving the exporter to cover the less risky ones himself. However, by special agreement, certain markets may be excluded.

(b) Cover

It is also comprehensive in cover in that it gives protection for a wide variety of events that could lead to non-payment. These are listed later in this chapter.

This policy is essentially for exports sold on short-term credit where the buyer is required to pay within *six months* from delivery. It must be taken out for a minimum period of twelve months. It is a *continuous* guarantee covering the agreed markets of the exporter and subject to renewal each year. Apart from exporters, merchants, confirming houses and banks may be covered. If needed, cover can run from the date of the contract of sale rather than from the date of delivery, provided the goods are shipped within twelve months from the date of contract. This "pre-credit" risk involves ECGD in extra risk and an additional premium is called for. The exporter must cover all his insured markets in this way or none at all.

Under a comprehensive guarantee, ECGD will not be aware of individual buyers unless a claim is made. However, limits on cover to individual buyers are imposed in principle. For example, a first order of up to £250 by a buyer new to the exporter is covered provided there are no adverse data on the buyer. After that first order, contracts up to a value of £5,000 are covered provided the exporter obtains a satisfactory report on the buyer from a bank or credit information agency. After £5,000, ECGD will require to be notified and its approval sought. The Cardiff offices of ECGD have a computer with nearly 200,000 credit assessments of overseas buyers which can be transmitted to a regional office.

Premiums are paid by the exporter in two ways:

(a) An annual lump sum related to the exporter's turnover;

(b) A monthly payment related to the shipments made that month.

Premium rates have been raised only six times since 1945 but four of these
have been in the period 1979–83. Until the latest increase rates were of the
average order of 32 pence per £100 of covered exports. From 1 July 1983
there were premium increases of up to 15%.

Risks covered
  (i) Buyer's insolvency (defined in the policy), see page 263;
 (ii) Buyer's failure to pay within six months of due date for goods which he
      has accepted;
(iii) Buyer's failure to take up goods which have been despatched to him
      and not the result of the exporter's poor performance;
 (iv) General moratorium on external debt;
  (v) Any other action by the buyer's government which prevents perfor-
      mance of the contract;
 (vi) Political, economic and other measures outside the UK preventing
      payment by the buyer;
(vii) Legal discharge of a debt (but not under the law of Contract) in a
      foreign currency causing a shortfall in payments;
(viii) War and some other events causing an interference with performance
      of the contract;
 (ix) Cancellation or non-renewal of a UK export licence or the restriction
      on exports of UK goods under the "cover from contract of sale" guaran-
      tee.

These nine risks comprise a substantial package of cover for UK exporters
who sell a continuous volume of goods on short-term credit. This is especially so, where the exporter is not a beneficiary under a confirmed Letter of
Credit or has no access to other types of non-recourse export fiance.

The major exceptions that apply are:

 (i) Where the exporter fails to honour his export contract properly;
(ii) Where the exporter has failed to comply with his other conditions of the
     insurance policy.

Under (ii) there is: failure to make premium payments, failure to reveal
adverse credit rating knowledge of buyer when known by exporter, and
failure to comply with the ruling on confidentiality.

The confidentiality rule
ECGD normally insists that its cover of an exporter should not be revealed
to his buyers in order to prevent the latter from entertaining thoughts of
non-payment in the light of the likely indemnification of the exporter by
ECGD.

Risks not covered by the policy
   (i) The marine risk;

  (ii) Failure to obtain authority to import and to make or receive payment;

 (iii) The exchange risk (but see later section on Foreign Currency Contracts Endorsement);

 (iv) Losses arising in the UK (except export licensing);

  (v) Breach of contract by the exporter;

 (vi) Cancellation of the contract by the buyer before the goods are despatched. However certain Public buyers are excluded provided there is no good cause for the cancellation – e.g. exporter's misbehaviour;

(vii) Insolvency or default by the exporter's agent or collecting bank;

(viii) Losses arising from illegal activity in the UK or in the buyer's country.

Buyer and political risks
The risks which *are* covered (nos. i to ix) can be categorized as:

(a) Buyer risks (nos. i, ii, iii);
(b) Political risks (the remaining nos.).

A "buyer" risk is defined as "a risk arising from default due to the action of the buyer". A "political" risk is therefore "one which arises from events beyond the control of the buyer".

Now, the largest number of defaults are in category (b), the "political" risks. This is because of the large number of countries that have been affected by the world recession and who simply do not always have the necessary foreign exchange to meet their importer's liabilities. However, as in most cases, these countries sooner or later are able to replenish their currency reserves, perhaps as part of a package of assistance from the International Monetary Fund (see Chapter 12); "political" risks are often temporary and effectively call for some extra months of credit.

"Buyer" risks, on the other hand, while smaller in proportion, are much more serious as far as ECGD is concerned because they are much less likely to be temporary. This is especially so, when, given a buyer's market, some buyers are encouraged to enter into contracts which are less than viable from their point of view, e.g. they may have difficulty in obtaining the finance to meet their purchases. Unfortunately this category of risk is on the increase and presents a major problem to ECGD. In 1982/83 "political" risk claims were three times as large as "buyer" claims but the former are largely subject to debt rescheduling agreements between ECGD and overseas governments. One way to alleviate the problem is to avoid "cut-throat" competition between export credit organizations around the world, and to that end the Berne Union was established in 1934 (The International Union of Credit and Investment Insurers). ECGD was a founder member. As a result of exchanges between members, and by regular meetings, information about defaulting buyers and claims experience is circulated with a view to establishing sound export credit principles. For example, there are agreements to limit credit periods and to lay down minimum interest rates for longer term credit. (See OECD reference rates later in this chapter.) In spite of this, however, there are lapses of behaviour by some countries and formal protests by aggrieved members of the Berne Union have not been unknown. For example, in 1977 the UK and USA feared that France was prepared to offer the Soviet Union special interest rate terms which allegedly offended against the OECD recommendations.

The "Matching" Principle

ECGD states clearly that where competitors are offering terms beyond these sound principles agreed to, it will be prepared to offer similar terms.

Percentage of Cover for Comprehensive Insurance

There are three grades of cover:

"Buyer" Risks

1. Risks (i) and (ii) – 90% of losses covered.[3]
2. Risks (iii) – exporter must bear a "first loss" of 20% of the full original price and ECGD bears 90% of the balance.

"Political" Risks

3. risks (iv) to (ix) – 90% of losses covered if they arise *before* despatch; 95% of losses covered *after* despatch.

In addition ECGD may be prepared to cover losses resulting from some overseas "Public Buyers" failing to honour the trade contract, providing it was not the result of the exporter's poor performance.

It should be noted that in no circumstances does ECGD offer 100% cover, and in any case, only "losses" are covered, not the value of the goods. For example, if there is an under-payment of receipts, or if no payment at all is received but the goods are resold, only the net loss is covered. In the case of risk (iii) a special provision applies. Suppose the value of the goods is £100,000 and they are re-sold for £80,000. The exporter is required to bear £20,000 loss himself (20% of the full original price), and is then indemnified for 90% of the *balance of the loss*.

As in this case the balance of the loss is zero, there will be no ECGD indemnification! Thus, in the case of risk (iii) the loss due to resale must be more than 20% of the original price if there is going to be any ECGD cover!

---

[3]Note: from 1 July 1983 cover against *private* buyer default reduced to 75%.

This limit of cover for risk no. (iii) (buyer's failure to take up goods) reduces the likelihood of UK exporters despatching goods to uncertain buyers and claiming indemnification from ECGD when they are refused payment.

When Claims Can Be Made

(a) Buyer's insolvency – on proof of insolvency;

(b) Protracted default – on accepted goods, six months after due date of payment;

(c) Failure to take up goods – one month after resale;

(d) Delay in payment transfer – four months after due date, or four months after completion of the transfer formalities, whichever is the later;

(e) For any other cause – four months after the event causing the loss.

Insolvency is defined by ECGD as:

   (i) Buyer declared bankrupt;
  (ii) Buyer has made a valid assignment, etc., in favour of his creditors;
 (iii) A receiver has been appointed;
 (iv) A compulsory winding-up;
  (v) A voluntary winding-up;
 (vi) A Court has sanctioned an arrangment binding on all creditors;
(vii) The substantial equivalents to any of the above.

It is clear from the above, that in no circumstances will ECGD entertain a claim by an exporter as soon as a loss is incurred. In general, some months have to elapse before indemnification can take place, and in the meantime the exporter will have to arrange for temporary finance.

Recovery of Monies from the Buyer

Exporters are not relieved of the responsibilities to try to collect sums owed to them but ECGD can offer advice and help. It will also reimburse the exporter's costs in this regard in the same proportion as it provides credit insurance cover.

Contracts in Foreign Currency

The comprehensive policy guarantee can cover contracts in approved foreign currencies as well as sterling.

Foreign Currency Contracts Endorsement

Although ECGD itself does not offer to cover the foreign exchange risk, an exporter can seek protection from it for exchange losses arising from a forward "close-out" situation, or losses arising from currency borrowing.

For example if a UK exporter has sold forward his expected receipts of $50,000 for £33,000 but due to his buyer's default the money is not received on the due date, the bank will enforce a "close-out" whereby the exporter will (theoretically) buy $50,000 in the then spot market, and deliver them as per his forward contract. Suppose that this incurs the exporter in a cost of £34,000 (sterling having depreciated), there is a "close-out" loss of £1,000.

Provided that the exporter had elected to have a Foreign Currency Contracts Endorsement added to his basic Comprehensive policy, ECGD will indemnify these "close-out" losses so long as they do not exceed 15% of his other legitimate claims on them. The same principle applies to loans of foreign exchange, which on repayment, have to be met by spot purchases of the currency due to buyer's default, resulting in a loss.

ECGD make an additional charge for this facility. However, it is worth noting that any "close-out" or currency borrowing gains by the exporter will go to offset his other losses. In effect, ECGD are prepared to accept the speculative risk of losing or gaining from the non-fulfilment of a forward contract or borrowing contract up to the limit already mentioned.

The Supplemental Extended Terms Guarantee

For those exporters who already hold the Comprehensive guarantee but whose trade warrants the granting of credit terms in excess of six months, e.g. vehicles and engineering goods, the Supplemental Extended Terms Guarantee is available for an additional premium for the same markets as for his underlying policy. Under it, the exporter is permitted to cover contracts where delivery is up to two years and credit is up to five years.

He can also be insured for "close-out" or borrowing losses with a Foreign Currency Contracts Endorsement, which attracts an extra premium.

Selling Goods Through Overseas Subsidiaries or Associates

Where a UK exporting country is selling to one of its overseas-based subsidiaries or associated companies, it may still be able to acquire ECGD cover depending on its control of the overseas organization.

(a) Subsidiaries

ECGD treats sales to a subsidiary and the latter's on-sale of the goods as two legs of a single deal:

Leg 1 – Sale to the subsidiary will be offered cover *only* for "political" risks;
Leg 2 – Onward sale by the subsidiary will be offered normal cover. To qualify for such cover, the UK company must have a *direct controlling interest* in the subsidiary.

(b) Associates

Where the UK firm has no controlling interests in the overseas associate company, ECGD will only be prepared to offer "political" cover for sales to the associate company. In addition, cover for the associate's insolvency may also be purchased.

Overseas Stocks

Apart from the cover already afforded to exporters' *sales* from stocks held overseas, by the Comprehensive policy, cover for stocks held *prior to sale* is also available by way of a Supplementary Stocks Guarantee for losses arising out of such events as war, and stock confiscation, etc. This cover is for stocks held overseas or in transit overseas to replenish stocks. An additional premium is payable.

External Trade Guarantee

Some UK trade consists of goods which are both purchased from and sold to overseas countries. An example would be that of a UK Merchant Company buying goods abroad and selling them abroad. Cover for losses sustained can be purchased with an External Trade Guarantee policy although certain goods which are deemed to be directly competitive with UK exports are not insurable.

Cover is similar to Comprehensive but risks nos. ii, iii and ix are not covered; nor is cover available for losses arising from the imposition of export or import licences.

SPECIFIC GUARANTEES

So far in this chapter we have dealt only with credit insurance cover for UK exports which entail cover for all or an acceptable part of an exporter's turnover. Although this type of credit insurance forms the bulk of ECGD's work, cover is also provided for the one-off, high value, capital goods type of business.

This is available under the Specific Guarantee policy which, as its title suggests, offers cover for a specific contract of sale and involving a credit period of up to five years. ECGD may be prepared to grant cover where the credit period is over five years under its "matching" principle (see earlier in this chapter).

Because ECGD does not benefit from cover across the range of the exporter's business it charges a much higher premium. This can be as high as £5.00% (1985). Cover can be from date of contract or date of shipment.

Foreign Currency Contracts Endorsement cover is available as for the Comprehensive Extended Terms Guarantee.

The range of risks covered is similar to that of the Comprehensive policies except that the top level cover is 90% (against 95% for Comprehensive) and *no cover is given against the failure of private buyers to take up exported goods.*

Note: This last exclusion is in respect of *private* buyers. *Public* buyer default *is* covered. As most of the business written under Specific policies are for sales to the latter this is not a problem for most UK exporters.

Claims are met after similar time periods for Comprehensive cover.

CONSTRUCTION WORKS GUARANTEE

One area which the Specific policy does not cover is for work performed in the buyer's country. Payment is normally made against the presentation of an engineer's certificate or against periodic invoicing of the employer. The latter term (employer) is used in the Construction Works Guarantee in place of "buyer". The guarantee is specific to a particular contract to supply goods and perform services and covers similar risks to those covered in the Specific Guarantee, with 90% cover against loss.

SERVICES POLICIES

Exporters are not the only ones who may suffer losses arising from non-payment from overseas. Any type of service offered to overseas clients, e.g. technical, professional, processing, hiring, supply of know-how, royalty agreements, etc., can be covered for the credit risk by a Services Policy provided the services are performed overseas or are enjoyed overseas by the client.

Services on a Recurring Pattern

When services are offered on a recurring pattern of business, not exceeding a twelve-monthly period, and where credit does not exceed six months, cover is available on similar terms to the Comprehensive policy.

One-off Services

For non-recurring services, cover is available under similar terms to the Specific policy.

Leasing and Hiring

Cover is available for "financial" leasing of UK goods, e.g. contractor's plant, commercial trailers, etc., under the Specific Shipments Hiring Policy. Cover is for sums due to be paid under the leasing agreement for:

  (i) Lessee's insolvency;
 (ii) Lessee's failure to pay within six months of due date;

(iii) Delays of transfer of payment to UK;
(iv) War or other disturbance.

"Operational" leasing can be covered by Comprehensive or Specific types of Service policies. (See Chapter 8 for details of "financial" and "operational" leasing.)

FOREIGN SUB-CONTRACTING

In those cases where a number of sub-contractors have come together to participate jointly in major contracts for the supply of capital goods or services, ECGD may be prepared to offer a UK participant cover against losses arising from failure of the buyer to make payment to the overseas company acting as the main contractor, and also from failure of the main contractor to make payments to the UK participant.

SUMMARY OF ECGD CREDIT INSURANCE FACILITIES

We have now covered in outline the bulk of ECGD's export credit insurance facilities. They may be summarised as:

(a) Comprehensive cover for short-term credit   (goods);
(b) Comprehensive cover for short-term credit   (services);
(c) Comprehensive cover for medium-term credit   (goods);
(d) Specific cover for medium-term credit   (services);
(e) Specific cover for medium-term credit   (goods);
(f) Other cover (subsidiaries, stocks, external trade, construction).

PRIVATE CREDIT INSURANCE

Although ECGD is by far the most important source of export credit insurance cover, there are in the UK some private insurers who are prepared to offer similar facilities. Among them are Credit and Guarantee (Underwriters) Ltd. and Trade Indemnity Company Ltd. In 1981 the latter introduced a "whole export turnover" policy which has similar features to ECGD's Comprehensive policy. For example, credit is limited to six months and cover can be for contracts in foreign currency.

Other private companies include Credit Insurance Association (part of the Hogg Robinson group), and the American Insurance Group. In general, the private sector offers only cover for "buyer" risks although Lloyds of London *can* provide insurance for the "political" risks at a cost!

The *raison d'être* for private sector insurance is that it might be prepared to offer cover for business rejected by ECGD. For example, it might offer cover for selected buyers or selected markets. However, minimum rates are likely to be proportionately higher than for EGCD. Again, some exporters may be willing to take the "political" risks themselves, requiring only to be covered for "buyer" risks. Such cover could be at lower rates than for ECGD. Thus, a UK exporter doing business on a documents against acceptance collection basis with buyers in stable countries, may have no need for the overall cover provided by ECGD's Comprehensive policy.

On the other hand, exporters who are beneficiaries under *unconfirmed*, irrevocable Letters of Credit would need to take up ECGD's policies on the basis that although the Letter of Credit gives them protection from the "buyer" risks, the fact that it is unconfirmed suggests that the UK banks are uncertain about the prospect for currency transmission. (See Chapter 6 on *Collections* and 7 on *Letters of Credit*.)

ECGD FINANCIAL GUARANTEES (FOR SUPPLIER CREDITS)

Under ECGD's credit insurance facilities a UK exporter can cover himself for the possibility of not getting paid. However, by itself, such cover does nothing to provide the exporter with *immediate finance* (shipment finance), but because of the reduction in the risks facing the exporter, banks may be prepared to offer shipment finance either on a with-recourse or without-recourse basis.

POLICY ASSIGNMENTS

Armed with, say, an ECGD Comprehensive policy, an exporter may be able to more easily obtain shipment finance from his bank on a with-recourse basis by way of an overdraft, loan or negotiation of documents.

To that end, the exporter can *assign* his ECGD policy over to the bank by way of security for the finance. In effect, the exporter transfers his rights (if any) under the policy in favour of the bank, either in respect of the whole policy, or for all transactions in specified markets, or for all transactions with a named buyer, or even for individual Bills of Exchange.

In the event of non-payment by the buyer, the exporter claims on ECGD, and any payments received from them are collected on behalf of the bank providing the finance. ECGD will give the bank formal acknowledgement of the arrangement at no extra cost to the exporter.

The major disadvantage of this procedure from the exporter's point of view is that because he may not conform to the conditions under which ECGD offers its cover, he may have no legitimate claim on them in the event of non-payment. As such, the bank itself may have no valid rights, and therefore it will offer its finance on a with-recourse basis. In other words, the bank is relying on the proper performance of the exporter for the security of the policy. Another disadvantage is that policy assignments do not attract pre-ferential rates of interest.

BILLS AND NOTES FINANCIAL GUARANTEE

Where an exporter:

(a) Has an ECGD credit insurance policy;
(b) Is offering credit under two years;
(c) Is a beneficiary under a Promissory Note or Bill of Exchange,

ECGD may be prepared to provide the exporter's bank with an *unconditional guarantee to pay the bank 100%* of any sum six months overdue.

The exporter simply presents the Bills or Notes to his bank on shipment together with the commercial documents, and also a warranty that his ECGD cover is in order.

Because the bank has a 100% guarantee from ECGD which is not subject to the exporter's performance, its risks are virtually zero. *As a result, UK banks have agreed to charge the exporter the preferential interest rate of ⅝% over bank base rate.*

The exporter pays an extra premium for this facility and also signs a recourse agreement with ECGD undertaking to repay them the difference between the sum ECGD pays to the bank and the sum the exporter can claim against ECGD.

For example, if an exporter receives £100,000 by way of a bank facility but, in fact, is only eligible to claim (say) £90,000 under his insurance policy, in the event of a claim ECGD will reimburse the bank for the full £100,000 but re-claim £10,000 from the exporter.

The only exception to the above is where a Bill of Exchange is not accepted by the buyer. In that event the bank retains the right of recourse on the exporter. If the latter fails to reimburse the bank within one month ECGD will meet the bank's claim and then take recourse against the exporter.

OPEN ACCOUNT GUARANTEE

Not all exporters operate on a Bills of Exchange or Promissory Note basis and for these there is the alternative of the ECGD Comprehensive Open Account Guarantee to the exporter's bank on similar terms to the Bills Guarantee. However, exporter's credit to the buyer is limited to six months.

Such a guarantee would be appropriate for exporters who operate on a cash against documents basis or on open account (see Chapter 6). Because there are no supporting financial documents in this case, and payment is made by the buyer direct to the exporter, ECGD is guaranteeing a simple loan from the bank to the exporter. *The guarantee is, therefore, that the exporter will pay the sums borrowed from the bank*, and in order to underline this, the exporter is required to give the bank his own Promissory Note to cover his debt. *Thus, the bank has the right of recourse against the exporter* and if the latter fails to pay, the bank can invoke its guarantee from ECGD, who will pay the bank six months after payment is due. In addition to the premium payment the exporter also has to pay a charge for each Promissory Note handled.

The guarantee to the bank is as for the Bills and Notes Guarantee, namely, for 100% of the bank loan. Once again, the exporter pays interest on the loan at ⅝% above base rate.

Differences between the two guarantees:

Table 10.1

Bill Guarantee	Open Account Guarantee
(a) export credit up to 2 years	export credit up to 6 months
(b) without recourse to the exporter unless buyer refuses to accept Bill of Exchange	with recourse to the exporter
(c) Cost: basic premium	Cost: basic premium plus Promissory Note charge

Note: The preferential rate of ⅝% over base rate is available for *all* UK exports including sales to the EEC.

SPECIFIC GUARANTEES

Where an exporter is selling goods on credit terms of two years or more and where he is covering the credit risk by a Specific insurance policy or an Extended terms guarantee to a Comprehensive insurance policy, he can request ECGD to provide his financing bank with an unconditional guarantee for 100% of any Bill or Note against which payment has not been received three months after due date. These guarantees are available in connection with contracts for capital goods where payment is secured by Bills of Exchange or Promissory Notes. The bank has the same right of recourse against the exporter whose Bills are not accepted by the buyer as in the case of the Comprehensive Bill guarantee. Such bank finance will be *without recourse* to the exporter at a rate of interest fixed in line with the guidelines for officially supported export credit.

INTERNATIONAL CONSENSUS GUIDELINES

Periodically, agreement is reached between members of the organization for Economic Co-operation and Development (OECD) for fixed-rate export finance for credit terms of two years or more. Within the OECD the rate guidelines are supervised under the "International Arrangement on Officially Supported Export Credits". This is an agreement at government level for codes of conduct on such credits with a repayments term of two years or more. It sets ceilings on repayment periods and floors on interest rates.

As at January 1985 the agreement allows for rates and credit periods as shown in Table 10.2.

Table 10.2
Minimum Rates of Interest — January 1985

	Relatively rich markets	Intermediate markets	Relatively poor markets
Minimum interest rates for credits between 2 and 5 years inclusive	12%	10.70%	9.85%
Minimum interest rates for credits over 5 years	12.25%	11.2%	9.85%

Note: These rates do *not* apply to sales to European Economic Community countries. Instead, interest rates for these markets are as set by the commercial banks.

Thus for exports to a developing country, a UK exporter can obtain bank finance under the ECGD Specific Guarantee at a minimum of 9.85% per annum, which he can then pass on to his overseas buyer. These rates are *fixed* for the period of the credit.

Intermediate countries are usually defined as "Eastern European".

Interest Rate Make-up

Because UK banks (along with their counterparts in other OECD countries) are required to offer interest rates at the above guideline rates, it follows that where commercial rates are above these, the banks could be in the invidious position of paying more for their money than they receive! To counter this, UK banks are eligible for ECGD interest equalization for the difference between the above Consensus rates and an agreed commercial rate of return. This has resulted in large subsidy payments by ECGD to UK banks. For example in 1981/82 ECGD paid them £587 m by way of interest subsidy.

Conversely, countries within OECD who have commercial medium-term rates below the Consensus rates had an advantage over those countries whose rates were above. In 1978 ECGD introduced their Foreign Currency Specific Guarantee which permitted UK exporters with contracts on credit terms of two years or more and for a value of over £1 m to opt for financing in US dollars or Deutsche marks. This was beneficial in those circumstances where interest rates for these currencies were below those of the Consensus guidelines. In addition, it alleviated the subsidy payable by ECGD.

In August 1983, OECD approved a new scheme whereby exporters had access to officially-supported loans in seven low interest-rate currencies. Such currencies are defined as those with market interest rates below the Consensus "ceiling" of 12.25% for relatively rich countries.

These rates (which are subject to regular review) are shown in Table 10.3.

These reference rates are market-related and are subject to monthly adjustments. They provide the UK exporter with the ability to offer his

Table 10.3
**OECD Reference Rates for Actual or Potential Low
Interest Rate Currencies Valid from 15 August 1983**

Currency	Rate	Terms
Austrian schilling	9.675% 9.425% 9.55%	2–5 years 5–8 years 8 years plus
Canadian dollar	12.25%	over 2 years
Deutsche mark	9.25% 9.95%	for businesses worth less than SDR40 m over 2 years for businesses worth over SDR40 m over 2 years
Dutch guilder	11.25%	over 2 years
Finnmark	11.65% 11.90%	2–5 years 5 years plus
Japanese yen	8.6%	over 5 years
Swiss franc	6.85% 7.1%	2–8 years, plus 1% fee on undrawn balance 8–10 years, plus 1% fee
US dollar	13.46%	over 2 years
Sterling	13.34%	over 2 years

buyer contracts expressed in these low interest rate currencies as an alternative to the Consensus rates shown in Table 10.2. Like the Consensus rates they are *fixed* for the period of the bank loan but *do not represent an interest rate subsidization* as do the Consensus rates, although, as they are fixed for the period of the loan they could become more or less expensive than fluctuating market rates. However, as with Consensus rates, ECGD interest mark-up is available to the banks. Because the reference rates are not deemed to be "officially supported", i.e. subsidized at the outset, the guarantee to the banks are referred to as "pure cover", that is, cover against non-payment.

Why should a UK exporter want to express his contract in one of these currencies? Well, of course, his buyer might prefer to pay in a currency with which he is familiar e.g. US dollars, or in his own currency, e.g. Swiss francs. Secondly, and in the case of a currency like the Swiss franc, the interest cost to the borrower is lower than for sterling.

On the other hand, both sterling and US dollar interest rates under the Consensus guideline rates (Table 10.2) are lower than their reference rates, so use of these currencies can still be made at costs lower than at market rates.

From the buyer's viewpoint a drawback of paying in a low interest rate currency is that its exchange rate against the domestic currency may appreciate, resulting in higher than anticipated domestic currency costs.

BUYER CREDIT GUARANTEES

So far in this section on ECGD Financial Guarantees we have considered only the *supplier credits*, i.e. guarantees given to banks who provide finance to the *exporter*. In addition, ECGD provides guarantees to banks who are prepared to make loans direct to *overseas buyers* of UK exports. These facilities are known as Buyer Credit Guarantees and are available in two main forms:

(1) Buyer Credit Guarantee

Where a UK exporter is involved in a large contract worth £1 m or more he may prefer to offer his buyer a loan in sterling or an approved currency from a UK bank for a value of up to 85% of the contract value; the balance is payable by the buyer directly to the exporter with a proportion of it provided as a downpayment on the signature of the contract and the remainder on shipment.

ECGD provides a guarantee to the lending bank for 100% of the capital and interest against non-payment by the buyer, and for this the exporter has to pay a premium to ECGD whose value must not be disclosed to the buyer.

On receipt of documents, the buyer draws down the loan to meet payments to the exporter which are made available to the latter by the UK bank making the loan. A Buyer Credit flow-chart is illustrated in Diagram 10.2.

1. Contract of sale
2. Loan arrangement
3. Premium agreement
4. Guarantee agreement
5. Loan facility agreement

As indicated in the above diagram, the loan can be made directly to an overseas buyer or to an overseas bank acting on his behalf.

On completion of the above arrangements, the buyer (who will already have made the cash payment of 10–15% of the contract value to the exporter) can

Diagram 10.2
Buyer Credit Flow-chart

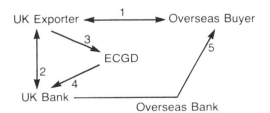

now draw down his loan to meet agreed payments to the exporter which is paid by the UK bank.

In effect, the exporter receives cash on shipment without recourse, except for his breach of the sales contract. Interest rates selected from both the Consensus guideline rates or the references rates are available for Buyer Credits as for the Specific Guarantee. The buyer (as the borrower) accepts full responsibility for repayment as soon as he draws on the loan.

Advantages of a Buyer Credit Guarantee to the Exporter

(a) By arrangement with the buyer, progress payments can be made at intermediate stages of manufacture;

(b) Without recourse finance. Under a Supplier Credit transaction, a non-accepted Bill of Exchange will result in ECGD indemnifying the lending bank and then taking recourse against the exporter, who, if he has a valid credit insurance claim, can receive indemnification, later on, for (say) 90% of his losses. With a Buyer Credit, loans are made directly to the overseas buyer and there is therefore, no recourse against the exporter provided he fulfils his contract properly;

(c) Under a Supplier Credit, the exporter would have to disclose the contingent liability for recourse by ECGD in a note to its accounts. No such disclosure is called for with a Buyer Credit.

One problem with a Buyer Credit is that some buyers may be more familiar with traditional financial arrangements whereby they accept Bills of Exchange drawn by the exporter; also they may not be prepared to accept loans offered by foreign banks for political reasons.

(2) Lines of Credit

An alternative facility is the Line of Credit which enables export contracts with a value as low as £25,000 to be accommodated. The arrangements are similar to Buyer Credits except that the credit is made available to an overseas bank with the usual ECGD guarantee against non-repayment. Overseas importers can utilize such credits available in their own country for the purpose of purchasing UK exports.

Lines of Credit can be of two types:

(a) *Project Credits*. Here the credit is available only for a specific project, and sub-contractors may be able to finance their own import purchases in this way.

(b) *General Purpose Credits*. These are available to intending purchasers of UK exports for a number of different contracts for capital goods. A list of general purpose lines of credit are published by the Department of Trade to inform UK companies of their existence, the recipient country, borrower, arranging bank, and broad eligibility of contracts.

A major advantage of a Line of Credit is that it acts as a "bait", encouraging overseas firms to take advantage of an existing credit line in their own country. All the advantages of a Buyer Credit are available including low, fixed interest rates.

We have now outlined the principal ECGD credit insurance and guarantee facilities, and to conclude this section some of the more important additional facilities now follow. While their aim is not insurance or bank guarantees, nevertheless they have the basic characteristic of assisting UK exporters to sell their goods and services more easily and at less risk.

TENDER TO CONTRACT COVER

Because of the increase in the use of foreign currency invoicing by UK exporters, especially for the sale of capital goods where low, fixed interest rates are available, the problem of fluctuating exchange rates between the time of the tender and the time of the contract award (or rejection) meant that exporters were open to the foreign exchange risk *even if they had covered forward*.

Readers will, perhaps, recall that this problem was overcome in the Comprehensive guarantee and the Specific guarantee by way of the Foreign Currency Contracts Endorsement. The endorsement to the basic credit insurance policy was, however, *subsequent to the contract of sale*.

With large capital goods export contracts, a tender (an offer of sale) is, of course, a *preliminary* to the contract of sale. Months can pass between the tender and a contract award during which time exchange rate changes could drastically alter the *sterling* value of the quoted currency price.

There are, in fact, *two* identifiable but related situations where a problem could arise;

(1) Where a tender is made, forward cover is obtained, but the *tender is rejected*. For example, the tender could carry a price of (say) $50 m. When sold forward for the period of time judged by the exporter to be suitable, realizes a sterling value of £25 m at a forward rate of £1 = $2.

    If, at the time the tender is rejected the spot rate is £1 = $1.50, the exporter will be "closed-out" by having to enter the then spot market to buy $50 m at £1 = $1.50 giving a cost of £33.333 m and a net loss to the exporter of £8.333 m. Here sterling has *depreciated*.

(2) Where a tender is made but no forward cover is obtained and *the contract is won*. Here, the exporter is still seeking £25 m as the value he must receive to make his offer of sale worthwhile, but when the tender is accepted the quote of $50 m realizes *less* than £25 m. Here, sterling has *appreciated*, and a loss is incurred.

Under the Tender to Contract Cover scheme, the exporter gives ECGD an estimated sterling value he wishes to receive under the tender *when he makes it.*

ECGD then provides him with guaranteed forward exchange rates over the period of expected payment. The guarantee is, effectively, that the sterling receipt will be no less than the sterling value of the currency sold forward at the ECGD forward rates. *No forward contract is entered into by the exporter until the contract is won.* On its acceptance, the exporter sells his expected currency receipts forward in the normal way but if the sterling thus realized is less than that guaranteed by ECGD, they will reimburse him up to a value of 25% of the worth of the guaranteed sum. By the same token, any gains made from forward cover are paid over to ECGD. A premium is charged for this service consisting of a flat charge and a sliding rate based on the time between cover and contract award.

COST ESCALATION COVER

Even when UK exporters have covered themselves by taking out both credit insurance and Tender to Contract Cover they still face the possibility of loss resulting from increases in domestic costs during the period of manufacturing large capital goods or the provision of services over time. The Cost Escalation Cover scheme came into operation in early 1975 when UK inflation was running at 16% per annum. In 1975 it was 24.2%; 1976, 16.5%; 1977, 15.9%; 1978, 8.2%; 1979, 12.2%.

Such massive increases in domestic costs could easily wipe out any profit over an extended manufacturing period. ECGD assisted UK manufacturers of export goods with a contract worth at least £5 m and a manufacturing period of at least two years, or UK exporters of services with an extended period of service, e.g. a consultancy service. The scheme did not apply to sales to European Community countries and was subject to annual renewal by Parliament. Only local costs were acceptable for cover and of these only a part was deemed to be eligible for cover. For example, only 75% of UK costs were eligible for cash business and 70% for business on credit terms.

Even then, not all of these proportions of costs were covered; ECGD and the exporter agreed at the outset a threshold up to which increases in eligible costs were borne by the exporter (or his buyer). ECGD compensation then applied to cost increases beyond this threshold up to a maximum amount per annum.

The degree of cover was dependent on the threshold level. Thus, if an exporter chose a low threshold, the degree of cover was lower than if he agreed to a high threshold level. With the deceleration of price and cost increases between 1980–1984 this scheme became much less important. It is no longer available.

GUARANTEES FOR BONDS

A bond (or guarantee) is a written instrument issued to an overseas buyer by an acceptable third party (a bank or insurance company) guaranteeing compliance by an exporter or contractor with his obligations, or that the overseas buyer will be indemnified for a specified amount if the exporter or contractor fails to fulfil his obligations under the contract.

Bonds became much more prevalent in the 1970s when Middle Eastern buyers who were prepared to pay cash or on short-term credit terms, needed to protect themselves from the failure of suppliers to properly honour their contract. In such circumstances, the penalty of the withholding of payment would be unavailable or much reduced.

Because of the misuse of such bonds, the International Chamber of Commerce (ICC) in liaison with other international bodies, has issued the *Uniform Rules for Tender, Performance and Repayment Guarantees*; Publication No. 325 (1978). These rules are shown at the end of this chapter in Appendix 8.

TYPES OF BONDS

(1) Tender Bond

Sometimes called a Bid bond or guarantee. It gives the prospective buyer the assurance that the tenderer will comply with the conditions of the tender should it be accepted by the buyer. By its use, the buyer is aware that all tenders are likely to be genuine. In the event that the tender is accepted and its terms are not honoured by the exporter, the bond issuer is liable to compensate the buyer for the costs involved in re-awarding the contract. These costs will usually be for 2–5% of the tender value. Most tenders which require a Tender bond also call for a Performance Bond in the event that the tender is accepted. Thus, failure to offer a Performance Bond on contract acceptance could be construed as a breaking of the terms of the Tender and could invoke a claim under that bond. Thus, the issuer of a Tender bond may also have to issue a Performance bond for the same contract.

(2) Performance Bond

This is a guarantee to the buyer that the exporter will abide by the terms of the contract; e.g. proper completion. An example of "performance" concerns the case of Edward Owen Engineering, a company contracted to supply greenhouses to the Agricultural Development Council of Libya in 1977. A Performance bond was issued for 10% of the contract value (a typical percentage) but the exporter failed to honour his contract because he found that the Letter of Credit issued in his favour was in a form unacceptable to him. However, in a subsequent judgment by the Appeal Court in London the bond commitment was upheld and the exporter had to meet his liabilities under it.

(3) Advance Payment Bond

Many contracts call for both an advance and progress payments and in these circumstances the buyer is at risk in that good delivery will not be made even though he has parted with (sometimes substantial) sums of money. To protect himself he may call for an Advance Payment bond which guarantees repayment of these monies in that event.

It is important to bear in mind that all of these bonds issued by banks or insurance companies are provided only on the basis that there is full recourse to the exporter in the event that the bond is "called" (a claim is made under the terms of the bond). This is achieved by the issuance of a counter-indemnity taken from the exporter by the issuer.

Conditional and Unconditional (On-Demand) Bonds

All the bonds mentioned above can be of two types:

(a) Conditional

A Conditional bond carries certain stipulations regarding breach of contract; usually that an independent arbitrator has to rule that such a breach has happened. With this type of bond, the buyer has the responsibility to show that default has occurred. Compensation is normally limited to the buyer's own losses or a specified amount whichever is the lower. Banks are not usually prepared to issue such bonds because it involves them in disputes about contract fulfilment and can qualify their reputation for prompt settlement.

(b) Unconditional or On-Demand Bonds

Such bonds carry no terms regarding the validity of a "call"; they can be "called" on demand, i.e. as and when the buyer decides for any or no reason; even if the exporter has honoured his contract to the letter. Compensation is not necessarily limited to the buyer's losses – if any!

Why should an exporter allow himself to be subjected to such an iniquitous liability? Well, buyers may be reluctant to ask for a Conditional bond because of the time-consuming business of showing that default has occurred, and, if they have a good record, may present no problem to the exporter who is confident of being able to meet his contract liabilities. In any case, the order may be for cash payment and a risk element can be written into the quoted price, and without the bond the order may not materialize. However, the dangers of such bonds are illustrated in the previous remarks concerning the unfortunate Edward Owen Engineering company.

THE ROLE OF ECGD

ECGD does not itself issue bonds but provides guarantees to issuers to encourage them to issue bonds which might not otherwise be available.

Performance, Tender and Advance Payment bonds may be covered by an ECGD guarantee to the issuer for 100% of the value of the bond. Under the guarantee ECGD is unconditionally liable to reimburse the bond giver for the full value of the bond "call". In turn, ECGD has recourse against the exporter unless he can show that he is not in default of his contract or, if he is in default, it is because of factors beyond his control and specified in the recourse agreement.

To qualify for ECGD bond support the contract must be:

(a) For £250,000 or more;
(b) On cash or near cash terms;
(c) Insured by ECGD's credit insurance;
(d) For a buyer in the public sector when support is sought for on-demand bonds.

In addition to the above guarantee for *individual* bonds ECGD also offers a *general* facility to insure exporters against unfair "calling" of bonds by incorporating an addendum into the basic credit insurance policy. However, under the Comprehensive policy cover is not available for Tender bonds or for any bonds concerning contracts with private buyers. Naturally a premium is payable by the exporter. Unfair "calling" is defined as a situation where the exporter is shown not to be in default in his performance of the contract, or if there was default, it was due to specified events outside his control.

OVERSEAS INVESTMENT COVER

ECGD also has a facility to cover UK companies making equity investments abroad, or who provide plant or know-how to overseas companies or who make loans overseas with a repayment period of not less than three years. The cover is against:

(a) Expropriation: including nationalization or confiscation, or any other event which causes discrimination against the UK investor;

(b) War;

(c) Restrictions on remittances: including losses due to the inability to remit earnings.

Only new investments are covered and ECGD must be approached before the investment is made. Cover is normally for fifteen years and for 90% of the above losses.

The main aim of this scheme is to encourage the outflow of capital for commercial, profit-making purposes, bearing in mind that the UK is a net *earner* of interest, profits and dividends on its Balance of Payments account. (See Chapter 12.) In addition, some capital outflow can also give rise to cheaper imports of raw materials or component parts, thus adding to UK cost competitiveness, and also to enhanced UK exports resulting perhaps from an overseas investment in plant or machinery or in a distributive establishment for marketing UK products. In the context of ECGD, UK overseas investment carries with it similar implications as for trade credit, namely, allowing the overseas party time to pay.

ECGD FACILITIES VIA AN INTERMEDIARY

We have noted in an earlier chapter that exporters who use intermediaries such as Confirming Houses may be able to obtain the benefits of ECGD indirectly through the intermediaries' own block cover with ECGD. An illustration of such indirect cover is that of Midland Bank Internationals' "Small Exporters Scheme".

"Small Exporters Scheme"

In association with Midland Banks' export house subsidiary, British Overseas Engineering and Credit Company (BOECC) this scheme came into operation in March 1980 for the purpose of giving ECGD credit insurance cover and bank guarantee facilities to those UK exporters with small or intermittent turnover who would find direct cover too expensive or too time-consuming in terms of paper work.

The basic principle of the scheme is that the bank itself takes out block (ECGD) credit insurance cover and then passes this cover on to its customers who are eligible for the scheme. In addition the customer can receive without recourse, fixed interest rate finance.

To qualify, the customer must be an exporter with a turnover up to £250,000 per annum and with no one contract worth more than £15,000. Trade credit must be on a Bills or Notes basis with a maximum of six months from date of shipment. Midland vets the credit-worthiness of the buyer and, of course, everything is subject to the exporter's proper fulfilment of his sales contract.

The scheme operates as follows:

(a) Details of the buyer are provided to the bank for vetting purposes;

(b) On shipment, the Bills or Note together with other documents are presented to the bank and if in order, the exporter's account is credited with 90% of the face value of the financial document less interest and charges;

(c) On the maturity of the Bill or Note, assuming there is no default, the remaining 10% is paid to the exporter;

(d) Interest is charged at 1½% over Midland Bank base rate and is for the period of the credit plus 20 days (to allow for transmission delays);

(e) A charge of 1% (with a minimum of £10) of the value of the Bill or Note is made to cover Midland Bank's premium payments to ECGD and also to cover collection and handling charges;

(f) Sight or unaccepted Term Bills of Exchange are with recourse until they have been paid or accepted. Promissory Notes are with recourse;

(g) Once the finance is without recourse and default by the buyer occurs, the exporter is assured of 90% of his receipts and the bank itself can claim 90–95% of their advance to the exporter from ECGD;

(h) Where currency receipts are expected, sterling finance is available at current forward exchange rates.

Let us look at an illustration of this scheme by way of a hypothetical example:

Example:
A UK exporter draws a 60 day draft Bill for £10,000 on a buyer; Midland Bank base rate is 14% per annum.

On presentation of proper documents he receives		£9,000.00
less interest for 80 days at 15½%	=	305.75
less bank charges at 1%	=	100.00
Net receipts	=	£8,594.25

On final payment by buyer he also receives the balance of 10%		£1,000.00
thus, total receipts if all goes well	=	£9,594.25

Total costs of £405.75 amount to 4.06% of £10,000. No direct premiums to ECGD are payable for this, or any other part of the exporter's turnover.

Suppose, however, that the exporter *had* been covered directly by ECGD. What would his costs have been?

Credit insurance premiums (say) 34p per £100	=	£34.00
Bills and Notes guarantee premium (say) 25p per £100	=	£25.00
Interest at 14⅝% on £10,000	=	£320.55
Total costs	=	£379.55

Although a marginally smaller cost, remember that the exporter will also have to pay premiums for *all* (or a large part) of his export turnover.

Should the overseas buyer not pay on the maturity of the financial instrument then the exporter will lose a further sum of £1,000 under the Small Exporters Scheme. This is similar to the direct cover given by ECGD which is 90% for buyer insolvency (see earlier section in this chapter on Comprehensive cover).

Table 10.4
A Comparison of ECGD Facilities with Factoring, Forfaiting and Letters of Credit

	ECGD credit insurance plus bank guarantees	Forfaiting	Factoring	Letters of Credit
1. degree of cover	90–95% but may be less where buyer refuses goods	100%	100% on "approved" debt	100%
2. interest costs	⅝% over base rates	market rates	market rates	market rates
3. fixed interest rates	for credits of two years or more	yes	no	no
4. subsidised rates	for credits of two years or more	no	no	no
5. recourse on exporter	only if exporter fails to honour his contract or buyer fails to take up goods under a specific policy	no	not on "approved" debt	only with an Unconfirmed Negotiations Credit
6. credit terms	up to six months for Comprehensive cover, otherwise up to five years (or more)	up to about 8 years	not likely to be for more than some months	several months but may be available on a revolving basis
7. foreign exchange risk	only close-out cover and Tender to Contract cover	no	no	yes
8. pre-shipment cover	available at extra cost	only insofar as delivery of the goods is over a period of time after forfaiting	not usual	only by special arrangement
9. claim delays	several months	none	none	none
10. debt recovery	exporter's responsibility	not exporter's responsibility	not exporter's responsibility	exporter's responsibility
11. services	none	none	several	documentation and collection
12. cover for sales to developing countries	may be available at enhanced premium rates	only if bills or notes are "Avalized"	depends on whether the factor "approves" the debt	yes

COMPARING ECGD WITH ALTERNATIVE FACILITIES

Table 10.4 gives a brief outline of the differences or similarities between forfaiting, factoring, Letters of Credit and ECGD.

WORLD-WIDE EXPORT CREDIT FINANCING SYSTEMS

This chapter is concluded by a brief summary of available systems of official support for export credits in member countries of the Organisation for Economic Co-operation and Development (OECD) and is based on their booklet *The Export Credit Financing Systems* published in 1982. This contains summary details for all twenty-two member countries of OECD but here we look at only France, West Germany, Japan and the USA. However, in addition a brief outline of South Korea's facilities are provided as an example of the trend of developing countries' provisions in this field. South Korea is not a member of the OECD.

FRANCE

There are three main bodies who co-operate to provide officially supported export credits. They are:

(1) Banque de France (central bank);

(2) Banque Française du Commerce Extérieur (BFCE) (The French foreign trade bank);

(3) Compagnie Française d'Assurance pour de Commerce Extérieur (COFACE – The French foreign trade insurance company).

COFACE is a joint stock company, part private, part public, and offers credit insurance on similar terms to ECGD. However cover against the Foreign Exchange risk is available for losses over 2.25%. A Cost Escalation scheme and Bond insurance are available.

Preferential financing is offered by the commercial banks in conjunction with the Bank of France and BFCE. COFACE credit cover is a prerequisite for preferential interest rates. However, short-term credits are outside the preferential treatment and are financed by the commercial banks at market rates plus 1%.

Medium-term export credits are rediscounted at preferential rates with the Bank of France after endorsement by BFCE. Credits over seven years are financed directly by BFCE either from Treasury grants or funds raised on the capital markets. Some risks are not covered by COFACE so the Government allows exporters using the COFACE facilities to allocate a sum equal to 10% of the credit granted to a *special tax-free reserve*. This is only possible for medium- to long-term credits.

WEST GERMANY

The Federal Government is responsible for an official credit insurance scheme operated by a consortium authorised to provide facilities in the name of and for the account of the Government. The consortium consists of:

(a) Treuarbeit AG (a public corporation); and
(b) Hermes AG (a private insurance corporation).

Most of the cover given is for single transactions (unlike ECGD) and both buyer and political risks are covered.

Buyer credit guarantees are available for tied loans with German banks providing the finance but unlike the ECGD scheme no 100% guarantees are given to the banks. Instead they must bear at least a 5% margin which is not recoverable from the exporter.

Premium payments are not graduated according to the overseas market but between private and public buyers; the latter incurring the exporter in rates about one-half the value of the former.

Preferential Interest Rates

These are available from a Government-owned body Kfur, and from a Government-supported private company AKA, but in order to be eligible, credit insurance must first be obtained.

Kfur was set up in 1948 to finance domestic reconstruction but since 1955 has provided long-term finance for German exports and is the official agency for the German overseas aid programme. Finance is available mainly for sales to developing countries at 4½% per annum but this low rate is raised by the inclusion of market-raised funds in a ratio of 1 to 3.

Owing to the shortage of official finance, Kfur has had increasing resort to the capital markets, and as a result, only contracts worth up to DM25 m contain the maximum permitted preferential finance.

AKA, a private company, was set up in 1952 as a syndicate of fifty-six commercial banks and is not responsible to any Government body. They have the following facilities:

(1) *Line A*. Loans are made available to the exporter against Promissory Notes which are discounted by AKA.

(2) *Line B*. Mainly provides supplier credits to developing countries with repayment between one and four years. Interest rates are 1½% over the Bundesbank official discount rate.

(3) *Line C*. This is for financing buyer credits at market rates of interest with repayment between two and ten years.

JAPAN

The system in Japan is made up of two main elements:

(1) *The Export Insurance Division (EID) of the Ministry of International Trade and Industry (MITI)*. This Government body is responsible for insuring repayment of export credits.

Cover for a similar facility to ECGD's Comprehensive policy is up to 90% for political risks and up to 60% for buyer risks although certain exports can be covered for up to 80% for buyer risks. For capital goods cover is up to 95%. There is an Export Bill Insurance to cover banks against default of commercial paper accepted by them.

Premium rates are determined by the credit-worthiness of the overseas buyers and markets. No insurance at all is available for "high-risk" markets or for one where default has occurred.

(2) *The Export-Import Bank of Japan (EXIM)*. This Government body, was set up in 1951, and participates with commercial banks in financing medium- and long-term export credits. The interest rate charged is in conformity with the OECD rates (see Tables 10.2 and 10.3) but are a blend of low rate EXIM funds and market-rate commercial bank funds in the ratio of about 65% and 35% respectively. The EXIM part is at a fixed but preferential rate. Buyer credits are only extended to overseas public buyers. Of course, EID cover is a prerequisite for all EXIM finance. Export credits with a repayment term of up to six months are financed entirely by the commercial banks at market rates.

USA

The system in the USA is made up of three major organisations:

(1) *The Export-Import Bank of the United States (EXIMBANK)*. This is an independent Government agency subject to some control by Congress. It operates both credit insurance and bank guarantees in conjunction with the following two organizations:

(2) *Foreign Credit Insurance Association (FCIA)*. This is a group of over fifty private insurance companies.

(3) *Private Export Funding Corporation (PEFCO)*. This is a private corporation owned by fifty-four banks, seven industrial corporations and one investment bank.

The FCIA/EXIMBANK programme offers credit insurance for short- and medium-term business for both buyer and market risks. PEFCO is a major source of capital for medium- and long-term fixed state financing.

FCIA covers buyer risks for its own account up to a certain value per policy; over this it re-insures with EXIMBANK who are also responsible for political risk cover.

EXIMBANK also offers bank guarantees against buyer and political risks for both supplier and buyer credits. Cover is for 100% for political risks and 90% for buyer risks for short- to medium-term credits. For contracts over $5 m, exporters are eligible for direct, long-term, fixed rate loans to the overseas buyer from EXIMBANK.

EXIMBANK also encourages PEFCO to participate in export loans by a process of giving them unconditional guarantees. Interest rates are usually fixed at levels consistent with the cost of raising market funds. There is no automatic officially supported refinancing facility in the USA, nor is there an interest rate support scheme as such.

SOUTH KOREA

South Korea is an example of an advancing, developing country anxious to be able to compete in industrial products, especially capital goods.

The Korean Export-Import Bank (Eximbank) was set up in 1976 and accepted into the Berne Union in 1977. Other developing countries that are members of the Berne Union include Argentina, Hong Kong, India, Israel, Pakistan, Portugal, Singapore and Spain. Mexico and Cyprus are applying for membership.

Eximbank operates as an autonomous agency of the Government and is financed by both public funds and borrowings in the private markets. It is responsible for both an export credit insurance programme and export financing.

Supplier credits are available in domestic currency to Korean exporters of capital goods at a preferential, fixed interest rate with credit terms up to ten years. However, because only up to 80% of the finance is supplied by Eximbank, with the balance coming from the commercial banks, the "blended" interest rate is higher than the preferential rate. Eximbank itself is subsidized by the Government through both interest-free subscriptions and preferential access to credit lines in foreign currency at the Bank of Korea.

Buyer Credits

In order to facilitate an increase in the export of high-value capital goods, Eximbank introduced in 1978 a programme of Buyer Credit facilities in US dollars available in selected banks in overseas developing countries, for re-lending to importers of Korean capital goods. Apart from encouraging the sale of such goods as machinery, plant, ships, vehicles, fertilizers and textile yarns, this scheme is also helping Korean construction companies, especially in the Middle East.

A unique feature of Eximbank is its programme of encouraging Korean imports!

Pre-shipment loans for up to 80% of the contract value of materials purchased abroad are available to Korean importers, provided these materials are necessary for the manufacture of Korean capital goods. These credits are repayable within two years at preferential rates of interest.

WORLD-WIDE EXPORT CREDITS

Some Final Notes

With the increasing numbers of countries entering the field of insuring their exporters against non-payment and also supplying them or their overseas buyers, with fixed rate, preferential credit, it is clear that there is a major division between interest rates for domestic trade and for international trade. An illustration of this can be seen from the fact that it has been estimated that about $7 billion was paid in 1981 to subsidize export credit terms by OECD members. (See IMF survey 13 December 1982.) Another illustration is that while the Consensus guideline rates have remained virtually constant over the past few years, market rates rose substantially.

It is increasingly anomalous that countries are able to obtain preferential terms for their imports by way of facilities granted overseas *and* to return the compliment by also offering preferential terms for the purchase of their exports. In particular, should developing countries be looking for low-cost imports of capital goods for development purposes, or should they be concerned to *provide* low-cost exports to the industrialized countries?

Appendix 8

'Uniform Rules for Contract Guarantees'

International Chamber of Commerce Publication No. 325 (1978)
This code was written with a view to securing uniformity of practice between the parties involved, and endeavours to find a fair balance between their respective interests without losing sight of the commercial purpose of the guarantee. The full text of the 11 Articles is reproduced here.

Scope

Article 1

1 These rules apply to any guarantee, bond, indemnity, surety or similar undertaking, however named or described ("guarantee"), which states that it is subject to the Uniform Rules for Tender, Performance and Repayment Guarantees ("contract guarantees") of the International Chamber of Commerce (Publication No. 325) and are binding upon all parties thereto unless otherwise expressly stated in the guarantee or any amendment thereto.

2 Where any of these rules is contrary to a provision of the law applicable to the guarantee from which the parties cannot derogate that provision prevails.

Definition

Article 2

(a) "tender guarantee" means an undertaking given by a bank, insurance company or other party ("the guarantor") at the request of a tenderer ("the principal") or given on the instructions of a bank, insurance company, or other party so requested by the principal ("the instructing party") to a party inviting tenders ("the beneficiary") whereby the guarantor undertakes – in the event of default by the principal in the obligations resulting from the submission of the tender – to make payment to the beneficiary within the limits of a stated sum of money;

(b) "performance guarantee" means an undertaking given by a bank, insurance company or other party ("the guarantor") at the request of a supplier of goods or services or other contractor ("the principal") or given on the instructions of a bank, insurance company, or other party so requested by the principal ("the instructing party") to a buyer or to an employer ("the beneficiary") whereby the guarantor undertakes – in the event of default by the principal in due performance of the terms of a contract between the principal and the beneficiary ("the contract") – to make payment to the beneficiary within the limits of a stated sum of money or, if the guarantee so provides, at the guarantor's option, to arrange for performance of the contract;

(c) "repayment guarantee" means an undertaking given by a bank, insurance company or other party ("the guarantor") at the request of a supplier of goods or services or other contractor ("the principal") or given on the instructions of a bank, insurance company or other party so requested by the principal ("the instructing party") to a buyer or to an employer ("the beneficiary") whereby the guarantor undertakes – in the event of default by the principal to repay in accordance with the terms and conditions of a contract between the principal and the beneficiary ("the contract") any sum or sums advanced or paid by the beneficiary to the principal and not otherwise repaid – to make payment to the beneficiary within the limits of a stated sum of money.

Liability of the guarantor to the beneficiary

Article 3
1   The guarantor is liable to the beneficiary only in accordance with the terms and conditions specified in the guarantee and these rules and up to an amount not exceeding that stated in the guarantee.
2   The amount of liability stated in the guarantee shall not be reduced by reason of any partial performance of the contract, unless so specified in the guarantee.
3   The guarantor may rely only on those defences which are based on the rules and conditions specified in the guarantee or are allowed under these rules.

Last date for claim

Article 4
If a guarantee does not specify a last day by which a claim must have been received by the guarantor, such last date ("expiry date") is deemed to be:
(a) in the case of a tender guarantee, six months from the date of the guarantee;
(b) in the case of a performance guarantee, six months from the date specified in the contract for delivery or completion or any extension

thereof, or one month after the expiry of any maintenance period (guarantee period) provided for in the contract if such maintenance period is expressly covered by the performance guarantee;

(c) in the case of a repayment guarantee, six months from the date specified in the contract for delivery or completion or any extension thereof.

If the expiry date falls on a non-business day, the expiry date is extended until the first following business day.

Expiry of guarantee

Article 5

1   If no claim has been received by the guarantor on or before the expiry date or if any claim arising under the guarantee has been settled in full satisfaction of all the rights of the beneficiary thereunder, the guarantee ceases to be valid.

2   Notwithstanding the provisions of Article 4, in the case of tender guarantees:

(a) upon acceptance by the beneficiary of the tender and the award of the contract to the principal or, if so provided for in the written contract, or if no contract has been signed and it is so provided for in the tender, the production by the principal of a performance guarantee or, if no such guarantee is required, the signature by the principal of the contract, the tender guarantee issued on his behalf ceases to be valid;

(b) A tender guarantee also ceases to be valid if and when the contract to which it relates is awarded to another tenderer, whether or not that tenderer meets the requirements referred to in paragraph 2 (a) of this Article;

(c) a tender guarantee also ceases to be valid in the event of the beneficiary expressly declaring that he does not intend to place a contract.

Return of guarantee

Article 6

When a guarantee has ceased to be valid in accordance with its own terms and conditions or with these rules, retention of the documents embodying the guarantee does not in itself confer any rights upon the beneficiary, and the document should be returned to the guarantor without delay.

Amendments to contracts and guarantees

Article 7

1   A tender guarantee is valid only in respect of the original tender submitted by the principal and does not apply in the case of any amendment thereto, nor is it valid beyond the expiry date specified in the guarantee or provided for by these rules, unless the guarantor has given notice in writing or by cable or telegram or telex to the beneficiary that the guarantee so applies or that the expiry date has been extended.

2   A performance guarantee or a repayment guarantee may stipulate that
    it shall not be valid in respect of any amendment to the contract, or that
    the guarantor be notified of any such amendment for his approval. Fail-
    ing such a stipulation, the guarantee is valid in respect of the obliga-
    tions of the principal as expressed in the contract and any amendment
    thereto. However, the guarantee shall not be valid in excess of the
    amount or beyond the expiry date specified in the guarantee or provided
    for by these rules, unless the guarantor has given notice in writing or by
    cable or telegram or telex to the beneficiary that the amount has been
    increased to a stated figure or that the expiry date has been extended.
3   Any amendment made by the guarantor in the terms and conditions of
    the guarantee shall be effective in respect of the beneficiary only if
    agreed to by the beneficiary and in respect of the principal or the
    instructing party, as the case may be, only if agreed to by the principal
    or the instructing party, as the case may be.

Submission of claim

Article 8
1   A claim under a guarantee shall be made in writing or by cable or
    telegram or telex to be received by the guarantor not later than on the
    expiry date specified in the guarantee or provided for by these rules.
2   On receipt of a claim the guarantor shall notify the principal or the
    instructing party, as the case may be, without delay, of such claim and of
    any documentation received.
3   A claim shall not be honoured unless:
    (a) it has been made and received as required by paragraph 1 of this
        Article; and
    (b) it is supported by such documentation as is specified in the guaran-
        tee or in these rules;
    (c) such documentation is presented within the period of time after the
        receipt of a claim specified in the guarantee or, failing such a
        specification, as soon as practicable, or, in the case of documentation
        of the beneficiary himself, at the latest within six months from the
        receipt of a claim.
In any event, a claim shall not be honoured if the guarantee has ceased to be
valid in accordance with its own terms or with these rules.

Documentation to support claim

Article 9
If a guarantee does not specify the documentation to be produced in support
a claim or merely specifies only a statement of claim by the beneficiary, the
beneficiary must submit:
(a) in the case of a tender guarantee, his declaration that the principal's
    tender has been accepted and that the principal has then either failed to
    sign the contract or has failed to submit a performance guarantee as
    provided for in the tender, and his declaration of agreement, addressed

to the principal, to have any dispute on any claim by the principal for payment to him by the beneficiary of all or part of the amount paid under the guarantee settled by a judicial or arbitral tribunal as specified in the tender documents or, if not so specified or otherwise agreed upon, by arbitration in accordance with the Rules of the ICC Court of Arbitration or with the UNCITRAL Arbitration Rules, at the option of the principal;

(b) in the case of a performance guarantee or of a repayment guarantee, either a court decision or an arbitral award justifying the claim, or the approval of the principal in writing to the claim and the amount to be paid.

Applicable law

Article 10

If a guarantee does not indicate the law by which it is to be governed, the applicable law is that of the guarantor's place of business. If the guarantor has more than one place of business, the applicable law is that of the branch which issued the guarantee.

Settlement of disputes

Article 11

1   Any dispute arising in connection with the guarantee may be referred to arbitration by agreement between the guarantor and the beneficiary, either in accordance with the Rules of the ICC Court of Arbitration, the UNCITRAL Arbitration Rules or such other rules or arbitration as may be agreed between the guarantor and the beneficiary.

2   If a dispute between the guarantor and the beneficiary which touches upon the rights and obligations of the principal or the instructing party is referred to arbitration, the principal or the instructing party shall have the right to intervene in such arbitral proceedings.

3   If the guarantor and the beneficiary have not agreed to arbitration or to the jurisdiction of any specific court, any dispute between them relating to the guarantee shall be settled exclusively by the competent court of the country of the guarantor's place of business or, if the guarantor has more than one place of business, by the competent court of the country of his main place of business or, at the option of the beneficiary, by the competent court of the country of the branch which issued the guarantee.

The copyright of Uniform Rules for Contract Guarantees, *Publication No. 325 (1978), is held by the International Chamber of Commerce, and copies of the publication are available from the British National Committee of the ICC, Centre Point, 103 New Oxford Street, London WC1A 1QB, and from the Publications Division, ICC Headquarters, 38 Cours Albert 1er – 75008 Paris, or from the ICC's national committees in over 50 countries.*

Chapter 11

Travellers' Finance and Inter-Bank Settlements

In this chapter we are concerned with a number of banking topics:

(1) Providing finance for travellers abroad;
(2) Making an international payment;
(3) Inter-bank settlement (Nostro-Vostro);
(4) The Euro-markets;
(5) London as an international financial centre;
(6) Other bank and non-bank services.

(1) FINANCE FOR TRAVELLERS ABROAD

Anyone going overseas for business or pleasure will want to ensure that they have access to a sufficient supply of finance acceptable in the overseas country. It is convenient to list some of the factors that will help to determine which financial facility is best suited to particular situations. These are:

(A) THE EXCHANGE RISK

It may be possible to use one's own domestic currency in cash form to meet payments overseas. This will be the case where the currency is familiar and not likely to be subject to falls in its value. Even so, acceptance will not be 100% and any depreciation will result in its reduced purchasing power.

(B) SECURITY

Carrying large sums of cash is an obvious security risk and therefore other forms of payment mediums not subject to the same degree of risk is warranted.

(C) ACCEPTABILITY AND COST

Not all currencies and not all forms of payment are acceptable in all parts of an overseas country. Some sellers may insist on a cash payment, or if some other form *is* acceptable, a premium cost may be required.

(D) CONVENIENCE

(i) *Time Convenience*, e.g. finding a bank open for business.

(ii) *Geographic Convenience*, e.g. access to acceptable finance wherever one happens to be.

(E) EXCHANGE CONTROLS

Limits may be imposed as to the quantity of local or foreign currency that may be permitted to leave the country. Very disadvantageous exchange rates may be demanded at exit points.

Bearing these points in mind, let us look at some of the major ways in which finance for travellers abroad may be arranged.

Travellers' Own Currency Notes

As already mentioned it may be possible to use domestic currency in payment abroad; some quantity will always be useful in transit and at ports of departure and arrival. There is no need to make special arrangements but there is a *security* problem in carrying large quantities and there may be an *exchange risk*.

Foreign Currency Notes

Some amount of foreign cash is advisable to meet incidental costs but the same problem of *security* is present and there may be a problem of *exchange control*. Such notes are obviously *convenient* and *acceptable*. Where a traveller is moving between countries a third country currency such as US dollars may be more *convenient* than several changes into different currencies.

Travellers' Own Personal Cheques Backed by a Bank Guarantee Card

Banks in Europe who are part of the Eurocheque encashment scheme will permit holders of Eurocheque Encashment cards to draw personal cheques in sterling with the card acting as a guarantee to the paying bank that the bank issuing the card will honour such drawings up to £50 per encashment.

Features of the scheme include:

(a) No more than two cheques (not exceeding £50 each) to be drawn each day;

(b) No drawings to be made where this will cause the holders' account to exceed the permitted level, although the bank will honour such cheques nonetheless;

(c) Cheques drawn cannot be countermanded by the drawer;

(d) Cheques must be signed in the presence of the bank cashier;

(e) The drawer will be paid the equivalent in local currency less the paying bank's charges.

The scheme allows for convenience and some security. If the card is lost or stolen and it is immediately reported to the issuing bank and confirmed in writing within seven days, the holder's liability for subsequent cheques encashed against the card will cease. There will, of course, be an exchange risk if the local currency is appreciating against the holder's currency. This facility is now being replaced by the Uniform Eurocheques Scheme.

Uniform Eurocheques

A special book of cheques can be provided by banks together with a plastic card to allow the holder to write cheques in any West European currency up to a value of £100 sterling.

The users' domestic bank account will be debited at the exchange rate prevailing at the time of notification in the UK. The plastic card may also be used in some cash dispensing machines. While the cheques themselves are free of charge, there is a fee of £3.50 each year for the card and a 1¼% commission payable on each transaction and bank charges of about 30p per cheque used.

This scheme is superior to that of the Eurocheque Encashment facility in that *any* West European currency can be written and each cheque can be for twice the sterling value. In addition, any number of cheques can be used and there is no need to make a bank visit unless cash is required as the cheques can be used to make any payment desired.

Travellers Cheques

These are available in either domestic or foreign currency including the currency of a third country (e.g. US dollars). They are available in a variety of value denominations. Travellers cheques can be defined as "a bank's promise to pay the holder the sum printed on the cheque provided certain conditions have been observed".

These conditions include:

(a) That they are "first" signed by the purchaser of the cheques in the presence of the bank cashier;

(b) That they are "second" signed by the purchaser of the cheques in the presence of the recipient.

Because such cheques are issued by banks they are much more acceptable than personal cheques (which could "bounce"). They are *convenient* in that they can be carried about; their *cost* is relatively low (banks will charge a commission); *security* is quite good as "second" unsigned cheques which are stolen or lost will be replaced or refunded by the issuing bank if they are notified immediately. Cheques denominated in a currency other than the local one will, of course, be open to the *exchange risk*. Unused cheques are returnable to the issuing bank but if denominated in a foreign currency may involve an exchange loss.

Credit Cards

There are two major credit cards in the UK, Barclaycard and Access. Both are members of international bank card systems. Barclaycard is a member of the VISA system and Access is a member of the Interbank Card Association. They can be used abroad in the same manner as at home, namely by signing the cash voucher to authorize acceptance of the liability of its value by the holder of the card. The denomination will be in the local currency and the holder will be debited in the sterling equivalent on the day that the card company receives notification from the creditor.

In addition, the cards may be used to obtain cash abroad of up to the equivalent of £100 per day in local currency from any bank which is part of the network. A passport is normally required for identification purposes and a charge of 1½% is made.

Credits cards are relatively *secure* as losses, if reported immediately, are replaced by the card company. They are *acceptable* in many hotels and department stores but may be *inconvenient* if cash is required when banks are closed. There is an *exchange risk* where the home currency depreciates against the overseas currency between the time of payment and the time of debit of the card-holder's account. This could be several weeks.

Cheque Encashment by Prior Arrangement (Open Credit)

An "open credit" facility can be arranged whereby the traveller's bank will authorize an overseas bank to honour cheques drawn by the traveller up to a specified value. A specimen of the traveller's signature is sent to the overseas bank for verification purposes. The cheques are drawn in the currency of the traveller who receives the local currency equivalent less charges. Clearly *acceptability* is good and *security* depends on the safe-keeping of the cheque-book. However, *convenience* may be poor in the sense that the traveller is restricted to a particular branch bank and in addition that bank may itself be closed during certain times of the day. There is also an *exchange risk*.

TRAVELLERS' FINANCE AND INTER-BANK SETTLEMENTS

Remittances by Mail, Telegraphic Transfer or by SWIFT

It is possible for the traveller to arrange with his bank to remit specified sums of money periodically to named overseas banks, or alternatively, to remit specified credits coming into his domestic bank account (e.g. salary payments, etc.). Remittances can be in either home or foreign currency. Once again, the paying bank will need a specimen signature of the traveller to compare with his signature for receipt of the funds. Remittances sent by mail (MT) will take longer to arrive but is cheaper; telegraphic transfer (TT) will take only a few hours to be transmitted but is more expensive.

SWIFT (Society for Worldwide Interbank Financial Telecommunications) has been in operation since May 1977 and is a co-operative society created under Belgian law and covers most of Western Europe and North America. It comprises a computer network system between participating banks with two operating centres, in Amsterdam and Brussels, where messages can be stored temporarily before being transmitted to the relevant bank's terminal. Although the cost to the customer will be higher than using MT or TT facilities, the speed of delivery of a message is much greater. This will depend on whether the message is designated "normal" (10 minutes) or "urgent" (one minute). Security is obtained by the use of a password and other inputs of identification. This allows for the exact identification of both the sender and the recipient as well as the type of message being transmitted. Only the specified recipient gains access to the message, although when required the same message can be transmitted to a number of specified recipients.

Advantages of SWIFT

(a) *Speed of Transmission*;

(b) *Improved Security*. Use of this automated electronic system of identification, validation and authentication helps to reduce human errors of judgment (see example at end of this chapter).

(c) *Improved Efficiency*. Use of standardized formats and inbuilt guidance "on screen" reduces the problems of error and misunderstanding; also the reconciliation of statements is made easier. In addition a message can carry a status designation to allow staff to process the most important or urgent messages first. See hypothetical example of a SWIFT message on the next page.

Such remittances whether by MT, TT or SWIFT, offer *security* but may be *inconvenient* if only one bank is authorized to make payment. The *cost* of a TT or SWIFT message will be relatively high. The *exchange risk* will operate as remittances will be at the rate of exchange prevailing on the day when they are made, but due to the speed of SWIFT, funds need not be remitted until the last moment.

A SWIFT Message

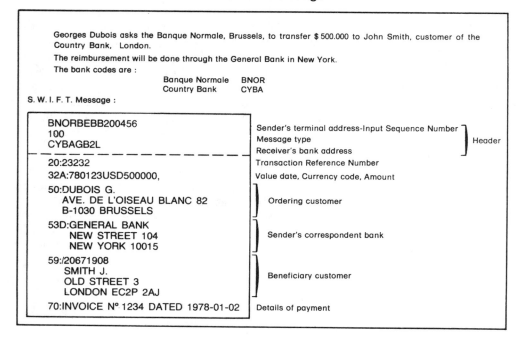

Georges Dubois asks the Banque Normale, Brussels, to transfer $ 500.000 to John Smith, customer of the Country Bank, London.

The reimbursement will be done through the General Bank in New York.

The bank codes are :

Banque Normale	BNOR	
Country Bank	CYBA	

S. W. I. F. T. Message :

BNORBEBB200456	Sender's terminal address-Input Sequence Number ⎤
100	Message type
CYBAGB2L	Receiver's bank address ⎦ Header
20:23232	Transaction Reference Number
32A:780123USD500000,	Value date, Currency code, Amount
50:DUBOIS G. AVE. DE L'OISEAU BLANC 82 B-1030 BRUSSELS	Ordering customer
53D:GENERAL BANK NEW STREET 104 NEW YORK 10015	Sender's correspondent bank
59:/20671908 SMITH J. OLD STREET 3 LONDON EC2P 2AJ	Beneficiary customer
70:INVOICE N° 1234 DATED 1978-01-02	Details of payment

A Non-SWIFT Message

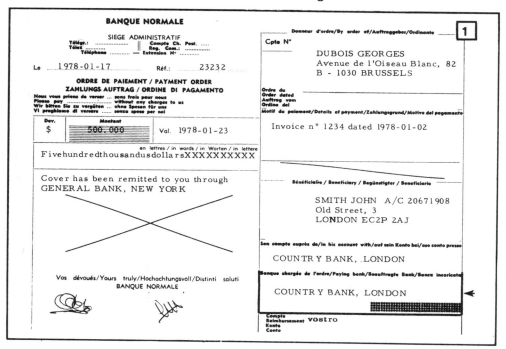

BANQUE NORMALE

SIEGE ADMINISTRATIF

Télégr.: .... Compte Ch. Post. ......
Télex .... Reg. Com.: ....
        Téléphone .... — Extension N° ....

Le 1978-01-17   Réf.:   23232

ORDRE DE PAIEMENT / PAYMENT ORDER
ZAHLUNGS AUFTRAG / ORDINE DI PAGAMENTO

Nous vous prions de verser ... sans frais pour nous
Please pay .... without any charges to us
Wir bitten Sie zu vergüten ... ohne Spesen für uns
Vi preghiamo di versare ...... senza spese per noi

Dev.	Montant	
$	500.000	Vol. 1978-01-23

en lettres / in words / in Worten / in lettere
Five hundred thousand us dollars XXXXXXXXXX

Cover has been remitted to you through
GENERAL BANK, NEW YORK

Vos dévoués/Yours truly/Hochachtungsvoll/Distinti saluti
BANQUE NORMALE

Donneur d'ordre/By order of/Auftraggeber/Ordinante   [1]
Cpte N°

DUBOIS GEORGES
Avenue de l'Oiseau Blanc, 82
B - 1030 BRUSSELS

Ordre du
Order dated
Auftrag vom
Ordine del

Motif du paiement/Details of payment/Zahlungsgrund/Motivo del pagamento

Invoice n° 1234 dated 1978-01-02

Bénéficiaire / Beneficiary / Begünstigter / Beneficiario

SMITH JOHN A/C 20671908
Old Street, 3
LONDON EC2P 2AJ

Son compte auprès de/in his account with/auf sein Konto bei/suo conto presso

COUNTRY BANK, LONDON

Banque chargée de l'ordre/Paying bank/Beauftragte Bank/Banca incaricata

COUNTRY BANK, LONDON   ◄

Compte
Reimbursement vostro
Konto
Conto

Bankers' Draft

Where a company wishes to remit funds overseas for the purpose of financing one of its employees, it is possible for the company to purchase a Bankers' Draft from its own bank for remittance to a specified overseas bank where the employee can obtain cash against it. The drafts can be in any currency and the employee will be paid on his signature of a receipt validated by a specimen signature remitted beforehand. The same factors apply as for an Open Credit except that the Bankers' Draft is substituted for the employee's own personal cheque. This may be necessary when the employee's own bank account is not to be debited. Should the employee be overseas for some time it may be preferable to have an account opened in his name in the overseas country into which his company could remit regular funds.

Travellers' Letter of Credit

Readers should not confuse this type of credit with a Documentary Letter of Credit referred to in Chapter 7. The latter is, of course, used to finance international trade payments while the former allows for travellers abroad to obtain cash. However, there are broad similarities; namely:

(a) They are both issued by a bank in favour of a beneficiary (the exporter, the traveller);

(b) They are payable by a correspondent bank named in the credit.

Although the advent of "plastic" cards and the use of travellers' cheques has greatly reduced the demand for travellers' Letters of Credit, some customers still insist on using this facility. The system operates by the customer making the necessary arrangements with his own bank to issue such a credit to him which he can present to named overseas banks. On such presentation the paying bank will draw a Draft on the issuing bank for the value specified by the traveller (which must be within the total value of the credit). This Draft is signed by the traveller and the signature is verified by reference to the signature on an accompanying document carried by him – a letter of indication – which will have been signed by both the traveller and the issuing bank.

The Draft is then cashed and sent for collection. The traveller will receive the local currency equivalent of the Draft value. The Letter of Credit will be marked with the drawn value and stamped by the paying bank. It will have an expiry date.

If the traveller is likely to be moving around and the Letter of Credit is usable in a number of stated correspondence banks abroad (a circular Letter of Credit), then *convenience* is a major characteristic of the system. However, because of forgeries, some overseas banks may be reluctant to make payment against them even when they have entered into arrangements with the issuing bank. The system allows for *security* in that large amounts of cash need not be carried although the Credit itself could be stolen. In such a case a copy would be required before further cash could be obtained. An *exchange risk* will apply.

The traveller may be called on to pay the full value of the Credit when opened. Alternatively, he may be allowed to pay by debit to his own account, as and when Drafts are received.

Additional Cash Requirements

When existing arrangements prove to be insufficient and additional funds are urgently required, it is possible for travellers to cable their own bank requesting a transfer of funds to a specified bank. An overseas bank may be prepared to offer a cable facility. The funds will normally take one business day to arrive and, of course, the traveller's own account will be debited. The *cost* will be quite high as two cable charges and bank charges are incurred.

(2) MAKING AN INTERNATIONAL PAYMENT

We now turn our attention to the ways in which it is possible for traders to remit payment to an overseas party. There are four methods:

(A) BUYER PAYS BY PRESENTING HIS OWN CHEQUE

This is an uncommon and unsatisfactory method of making payment as:

(i) It may contravene exchange control regulations in the buyer's country;

(ii) It will require the recipient to ask his bank to collect it for him involving charges and delay;

(iii) Payment may be refused when presented.

(B) MAIL TRANSFER (MT)

An importer can request his bank to send an airmail instruction to an overseas correspondent bank to pay the beneficiary or his bank a specified sum of money denominated in either the importer's currency or the beneficiary's currency. The importer's account will be debited (including a currency account if he has one). The transfer will include details of how reimbursement between the banks is to be effected. (See later in this chapter.) As the process will take some time to complete, the beneficiary will have to wait for the funds, and if a large sum is involved, an additional cost will be incurred.

(C) TELEGRAPHIC TRANSFER (TT)

This method employs the transmission of the instruction by cable or telex. It is faster but more expensive than mail transfer; however, if large funds can be moved quickly to the beneficiary, they can earn interest more quickly, and in addition, the importer can delay making the payment until the last possible moment. Instead of the authorized signature of the sender, the authorization is by a test key which is a coded system of numbers enabling the paying bank to verify the instructions.

Banks who participate in the SWIFT system (see previous section) will send a SWIFT message instead of an airmail letter, and an urgent SWIFT message instead of a telegraphic transfer. Of course both they and the recipient banks will need to be participants in the SWIFT system.

(D) BANKERS' DRAFT

This method entails the importer's bank drawing its own draft on an overseas bank, normally on one of its correspondent banks in the beneficiary's country. This draft is then given to the importer to mail to his beneficiary who will be able to present it to the bank upon whom it has been drawn for payment. The importer's account will be debited and if payment has been made in foreign currency, the debit will be either by way of a spot transaction or by applying the draft against an existing forward contract. Alternatively, a currency account could be debited. The drawer bank will advise the drawee bank of the draft and request them to pay against it on presentation.

This system suffers from the delay inherent in the importer himself making a mail remittance and there is also the possibility of the letter being lost in transit.

(3) INTER-BANK SETTLEMENT

We now turn our attention to the methods whereby the banks themselves make settlement with each other as a consequence of their customer's international transactions. To do this all major banks maintain foreign currency accounts with banks abroad which they can instruct to be credited or debited as the case may be. Likewise overseas banks maintain sterling accounts with UK banks which they too can draw on or add to. Special terms are used to refer to these accounts *but readers are advised to remember that these terms are subjective in the sense that they reflect a particular bank's viewpoint.*

For example, the terms used, *nostro* and *vostro*, which are Latin for "our" and "your" respectively are applied in the following ways:

(a) A UK bank's dollar account held in a New York bank will be looked upon by the UK bank as "our *nostro* account with you". But the New York bank will perceive the account as "your *vostro* account with us".

(b) Likewise a sterling account held by an overseas bank with a London bank will be seen by the London bank as "your *vostro* account with us", while the overseas bank will consider it to be "our *nostro* account with you".

To avoid confusion therefore it is wise to label these accounts from the viewpoint of only one of these banks. *For our purposes we shall view the accounts from a UK bank's viewpoint.* When customers wish to remit funds to an overseas recipient (or receive funds from an overseas payer), the banks involved will use their *nostro* or *vostro* accounts to settle the indebtedness arising from their customers' transactions.

In addition, banks use the accounting function of a mirror-image account, called a *record* account which reflects changes happening to the *nostro* and *vostro* accounts. These *record* accounts are held in the banks at home as an accounting device to maintain a running balance of the state of the actual accounts held overseas. When statements are received from the overseas banks, these are used to reconcile with the *record* accounts. Banks are reluctant to hold more cash abroad than is necessary to accommodate their customers' needs, unless they intend to "go long" in a currency (or "go short" for that matter – see Chapter 9) and the use of the *record* account gives some assistance in this respect. It is important however to note that the *record* account is always a mirror image of the real account held overseas. Thus, when the *nostro* account is *credited*, the *record nostro* is *debited*. When the *nostro* account is *debited*, the *record nostro* is *credited*.

Table 11.1 give four hypothetical (and simplified) examples of customers' transactions that are settled by means of crediting or debiting these accounts. For simplicity's sake £1 is the equivalent of US$2 throughout the transactions and no allowance is made for bank charges. The terms *nostro* and *vostro* are as seen as from Bank 'X' in London.

CASE A

A UK customer of Bank 'X' in London wishes to remit £5,000 (in sterling) to a recipient who is a customer of Bank 'Y' in New York. We assume that both banks maintain deposits with each other, namely, Bank 'X' has a dollar *nostro* account with Bank 'Y' and Bank 'Y' has a sterling *vostro* account with Bank 'X'.

The transactions will be as follows:

1. UK customer's account is debited by £5,000;
2. Bank 'X' credits Bank 'Y's *Vostro* account by £5,000;
3. Bank 'Y' will debit its *Record Vostro* account by £5,000;
4. Bank 'Y' will credit its own customer's account by $10,000.

In effect, Bank 'X' in London has simply switched £5,000 worth of sterling liabilities from its own domestic customer to Bank 'Y' (moves 1 and 2).

But Bank 'Y' has received £5,000 (in sterling) for an increase in dollar liabilities of $10,000 to its own domestic customer (move 4). As a result, it is Bank 'Y' who has conducted a foreign exchange transaction by effectively selling dollars to its customer (move 4) and buying sterling from its customer which is deposited in Bank 'X' (move 2). This increase in sterling held

Table 11.1
Nostro/Vostro Accounting

£1 = US$2

CASE	Bank 'X' in London						Bank 'Y' in New York					
	Record Nostro Account		UK Customers' Sterling Account		Bank 'Y's Sterling Vostro Account		Bank 'X's Dollar Nostro Account		US Customer's Dollar Account		Record Vostro Account	
	Debit	Credit	Debit	Credit	Debit	Credit	Debit	Credit	Debit	Credit	Debit	Credit
A			1 5000			2 5000				4 10000	3 5000	
B		2 10000	1 5000				3 10000			4 10000		
C	3 10000			4 5000				2 10000	1 10000			
D				4 5000	3 5000				1 10000			2 5000

"Nostro" = Bank 'X's dollar account held in bank 'Y' (from 'X's viewpoint)
"Vostro" = Bank 'Y's sterling account held in bank 'X' (from 'X's viewpoint)

CASE A. UK customer wishes to remit £5000 to US customer who sells it for spot dollars.
CASE B. UK customer wishes to remit $10000 to US customer from a purchase made with sterling.
CASE C. US customer wishes to remit $10000 to UK customer who sells it for spot sterling.
CASE D. US customer wishes to remit £5000 to UK customer from a purchase made with dollars.

Note: In Cases A and D, Bank 'Y' has exchanged sterling for dollars.
In Cases B and C, Bank 'X' has exchanged sterling for dollars.

at the London bank may not be required and Bank 'Y' may therefore decide to sell it in the market (perhaps to Bank 'X').

Should Bank 'Y' decide to sell its increased sterling asset to Bank 'X' in London, the accounts will be settled as follows (assuming no change in the exchange rate):

Bank 'Y' will debit Bank 'X's dollar *Nostro* account by $10,000;

Bank 'X' will debit Bank 'Y's sterling *Vostro* account by £5,000;

Bank 'X' will also credit its *Record Nostro* account by $10,000;

Bank 'Y' will also credit its *Record Vostro* account by £5,000.

The effect of these entries will be:

(a) To offset exactly Bank 'Y's increased sterling assets and dollar liabilities, thus countering its exposure in sterling;

(b) To reduce Bank 'X's sterling liabilities, but also to reduce its dollar assets – in effect, it has purchased sterling for dollars.

This increase in the supply of sterling will shift the supply curve downwards to the right and cause a depreciation against the dollar (see Diagram 9.1 in Chapter 9).

Such transactions, if multiplied many times over, could have an effect on the exchange rate by moving it to (say) £1 = US$1.99.

CASE B

Here, the customer of the London bank wishes to remit $10,000 to the credit of a US recipient. The transactions are:

1. UK customer's account is debited by £5,000;
2. Bank 'X' credits its *Record Nostro* account by $10,000;
3. Bank 'Y' debits the *Nostro* account by $10,000;
4. Bank 'Y' credits its customer's account by $10,000.

In this case it is the London bank which has decreased its sterling liabilities to its customer (1) but also decreased its dollar assets (3). As in Case A, there could be a resulting foreign exchange deal as Bank 'X' tries to replenish its reduced *Nostro* balances.

CASE C

This time it is the US customer who wishes to remit $10,000 to the UK recipient. The transactions are:

1. US customer's account is debited by $10,000;
2. Bank 'Y' credits Bank 'X's *Nostro* account by $10,000;
3. Bank 'X' debits its *Record Nostro* account by $10,000;
4. Bank 'X' credits its customer's account by £5,000.

In this case Bank 'X' has increased its dollar assets (2) but also increased its sterling liabilities (4). As in case B, it may wish to enter the foreign exchange market, this time to *sell* dollars.

CASE D

Here, the US customer wishes to remit £5,000 to the UK recipient. The transactions are:

1. US customer's account is debited by $10,000;
2. Bank 'Y' credits the *Record Vostro* account by £5,000;
3. Bank 'X' debits Bank 'Y's *Vostro* account by £5,000;
4. UK customer's account is credited by £5,000.

In this case, Bank 'Y' has a reduced liability in dollars (1) but also a reduced asset in sterling (3). It may therefore wish to replenish its sterling in the market.

The four cases represent the basic principle that when banks need to transfer funds for their customers, they do so by a process of debiting or crediting their own accounts held with each other. Whether it is the *Vostro* or *Nostro* accounts which are affected depends on which currency is to be remitted by the customer. *If the UK customer wants to remit sterling then the Vostro account is credited; if dollars, then the Nostro account is debited. If the US customer wishes to remit dollars then the Nostro account is credited; if sterling then the Vostro account is debited.*

When customers wish to remit foreign exchange and they maintain a currency account, it is possible for that account to be debited as an alternative to the debiting of the domestic currency account (B1 and D1). In these cases no foreign currency transaction is effected and banks' currency positions remain unaltered. For example, Bank 'X' will find that its dollar liabilities to its customer falls but so does its dollar assets held in its *Nostro* account. Likewise, Bank 'Y' finds that its sterling liabilities to its customer falls but so does its sterling assets held in the *Vostro* account.

However, the *customers* themselves may not be prepared to allow their currency deposits to fall in this way and they may request their banks to purchase currency on their behalf. In this case there will be the same effects (in principle) on the rates of exchange.

One other possibility is that the remittance or receipt of currency is applied against a forward purchase or sale. In these cases, the same transactions will be carried out but at the agreed forward rates rather than at the current spot rates.

Of course, the actual *transmission* of the instructions to debit or credit depends on the method used. They are:

(a) By Banker's Draft. (See section 2 of this chapter.)

Here, the customer requests the purchase of a Banker's draft in domestic or foreign currency, and his own account is to be debited. If the draft is in *sterling*, the bank will credit the *vostro* account and advise the overseas bank on the credit and ask it to pay against the presentation of the draft by the overseas recipient. As the draft is in sterling it will be drawn on the remitting bank's own head office. The draft is given to the customer who mails it to the recipient who then presents it as above.

If the draft is in the currency of the recipient, then the remitting bank will draw the draft on the overseas bank and ask for the *nostro* account to be debited.

(b) By Mail or Telegraphic Transfer (See section 2 of this chapter.)

Here the instructions are sent directly from the remitting to the paying bank, but the accounts are debited or credited as in (a).

We also need to consider the situation where a *third* currency is involved. For example, where a UK customer needs to make a dollar payment in favour of a French recipient and vice versa. Let us assume that the recipient requires payment in his own currency. Table 11.2 illustrates the necessary transactions.

Table 11.2
Payment in a Third Currency

	London Bank			New York Bank				Paris Bank			
	Customers £ Account		Record $ NOSTRO		London Bank's $ NOSTRO		French Bank's $ NOSTRO		Record $ NOSTRO		Customer's FF Account	
	D	C	D	C	D	C	D	C	D	C	D	C
CASE A	5000			10000	10000			10000	10000			50000
CASE B		5000	10000			10000	10000			10000	50000	

We assume that £1 = $2 = FF10.

CASE A

The London bank asks its New York correspondent to make payment of $10,000 to a French recipient who (we assume) does not maintain an account at that bank. To effect this payment the New York bank debits the London bank's *Nostro* account and credits their French correspondent's *Nostro* account. At the same time they ask their French correspondent to pay the French franc equivalent to the French recipient.

The French bank debits the *Record Nostro* account, and the London bank credits its *Record Nostro* account and debits its customer's account.

The London bank has a reduced sterling liability of £5,000 and a reduced dollar asset of $10,000. It may need eventually, to replenish its depleted dollar balances by buying dollars in the market.

The New York bank has merely transferred $10,000 from the UK bank's *Nostro* to the French bank's *Nostro*.

The French bank has increased dollar assets of $10,000 matched by increased French franc liabilities of FF50,000. It may eventually need to deplete its swollen dollar deposits by selling dollars to the market.

CASE B

Here we assume the opposite transaction; namely where the French customer wishes to transfer $10,000 to a UK recipient. The transactions are the reverse of Case A.

The Result Is

The London bank has increased dollar assets and increased sterling liabilities. The New York bank has merely transferred $10,000 from French bank's *Nostro* to the London bank's *Nostro*. The French bank has reduced dollar assets matched by reduced French franc liabilities.

The above two sets of cases have assumed either:

(a) Two banks, each in a different country but each holding an account with each other (Table 11.1).

(b) Two banks, each in a different country but neither of them holding an account with each other. However, they do both have accounts with the *same* third correspondent bank in a third country (Table 11.2).

In addition to these two common situations there could also be a set of cases where two banks, each in a different country, neither of them holding an account with each other or with any one third bank, but both holding accounts with other correspondent banks in each others' country. In these cases the flow of remittances between the two principal banks would involve either the instructions to their respective correspondents overseas to debit the principal bank's *Nostro* accounts and to credit the other principal bank's accounts, or to credit the account of the correspondent bank in the same country and asking them to credit the other principal bank's own account. The method adopted will depend on whether the domestic currency of the remitter or the remittee is being transmitted.

(4) THE EURO-MARKETS

From time to time we have made reference to the possibility of traders and investors borrowing foreign exchange as an alternative to borrowing domestic money (see Chapters 8 and 9). This is done in the so-called Euro-dollar market; "so-called" because the market is neither solely in Europe nor solely in dollars, although a large proportion is, in fact in dollars traded in London and other European centres.

A Euro-dollar can be defined as a dollar deposit held in a bank outside the US. Likewise Euro-sterling consists of sterling held in banks outside the UK.

In addition, these "off-shore" deposits are on-lent to borrowers at interest rates influenced, but not totally determined by rates in the US or other home countries. These "off-shore" dollar deposits have emerged for a number of reasons, including:

(a) Regulation Q in the US put restrictions on the interest US banks could pay on certain deposits;

(b) Restrictions in the UK in the late 1950s on the use of sterling to finance non-UK trade encouraged the use of dollars for this purpose;

(c) The transfer of dollars from US to non-US banks (e.g. by Eastern European countries; multi-national corporations).

As a result of these and other factors, there developed a growth of dollar balances held at banks outside the US. These balances could be lent and borrowed free of US restrictions (or indeed any other country's restrictions).

For a variety of reasons, London became (and still is) the capital of the Euro-dollar market. Factors include:

(a) Geographic position;
(b) Language;
(c) Absence of regulation;
(d) Expertise of "The City".

To illustrate how a Euro-dollar comes into existence we can trace a series of hypothetical transactions. These are shown in Table 11.3.

We assume that a US bank (Bank 'A') carries dollar accounts for a resident oil company, an OPEC customer, the Federal Reserve, a London bank (Bank 'B') and the Exchange Equalization Account.

While some of these dollar balances are non-US resident owned they are not yet Euro-dollars according to the definition given earlier.

Let us assume that the US oil company pays for its purchase of oil from the OPEC customer of the bank. There is therefore both a debit and a credit put through the ledgers in Bank 'A'; namely, transactions 1 and 2.

Now let us also assume that the OPEC depositor decides to transfer his funds to a London bank, perhaps for reasons of interest rates or the appeal of the diffusion of large deposits amongst several nations' banks. These are shown as items 3 and 4.

Table 11.3

The Creation, Use and Destruction of a Euro-dollar Deposit

Bank 'A' in New York

Account	$D	$C
US oil company's account	1	
OPEC's account	3	2
Federal Reserve Board's account		16
Bank 'B's account (NOSTRO)	13	5
EEA's account	15	11

Bank 'B' in London

Account	$D	$C	£D	£C
UK exporter's account	9	8		
OPEC's account	7	4		
Record NOSTRO account	6	14		
UK exporter's account				10

Bank of England's EEA's £ account

Account	£D	£C
	12	

Note: (a) All transactions are assumed to be for identical values or equivalents.
(b) Exchange rates are assumed to be unchanging.
(c) Bank charges are ignored.

Item 4 *is* the Euro-dollar deposit. However, as the London bank has had the deposit transferred to its account in New York we must also show its *Nostro* account as credited (item 5). It will, of course, *debit* its *Record Nostro* (item 6).

In effect, the New York bank has merely transferred its dollar liabilities from an OPEC customer to the London bank. *There has been no change in its overall liabilities.*

However, Bank 'B' is now in a position to on-lend this deposit to borrowers anywhere in the world. By the process of on-lending, the account with the New York bank is merely transferred to the credit of new holders each time the money is on-lent. Note that the owner of these funds – OPEC – has an asset with a *London* bank. It is that London bank which has a matching asset with a US bank, but this is of no interest at all to the OPEC customer, who will look to the London bank for the withdrawal of his funds!

Let us now suppose that the OPEC depositor purchases UK goods and pays for them by a transfer of dollars. (Items 7 and 8.) It is now the UK exporter who owns the dollar deposit in London. Nothing has happened to the owner-ship of the account in New York!

However, let us also assume that the UK exporter wishes to hold sterling; he therefore sells his dollar deposit for a sterling deposit. Item 9 indicates the debiting of his dollar account, and item 10 indicates the crediting of his sterling account.

Now, if the Exchange Equalization Fund (EEA) is used to buy these dollars, then its dollar account will be credited in the New York bank (item 11) and its sterling deposits will fall (item 12). Both these operations represent activities in the foreign exchange market as distinct from the others which are Euro-currency activities.

As the EEA is holding the dollars directly with a US bank and not via a London bank as was the case with the UK exporter and the OPEC holder, the New York bank will debit the London bank's *Nostro* account and the *Record Nostro* will be debited (items 13 and 14). See Chapter 12 for details of the EEA.

The Euro-dollar deposit has now been destroyed. Although dollars owned by a non-US resident remain (the property of the EEA) it is no longer placed on deposit outside the US banking sector.

Finally, it is assumed that the EEA buys Federal Reserve Treasury Bills and items 15 and 16 are entered. The dollar deposit is now to the credit of a US resident (the Federal Reserve) and is entirely within the US monetary system.

What have been the effects of these transactions?

(1) Trade in oil and UK exports have been financed;

(2) US oil company has reduced dollar deposits but an increase in oil stocks;

(3) The UK exporter has an increase in his sterling balances;

(4) Bank 'A's net liabilities have remained unchanged with four debits and four credits cancelling each other out;

(5) Bank 'B's dollar and sterling liabilities are likewise unaltered;

(6) The EEA has reduced its sterling assets but increased its dollar assets (US Treasury Bills);

(7) The Federal Reserve Board has an increase in dollar deposits matched by an increase in Treasury Bill liabilities.

Now, this is a highly simplified account of what may happen and not all these events must automatically take place. Nevertheless, it does serve to illustrate how a Euro-dollar (or any other) deposit can be formed, used by its recipients, and eventually eliminated.

In practice the Euro-markets are largely wholesale in character with banks on-lending large sums for fixed periods of time, with either fixed or floating rates of interest. Loans can be for up to a few months in the shorter end of the market and for up to several years in the medium end. Roll-over loans can also be arranged whereby banks on-lend to customers with interest rates adjusted over agreed time periods. The quoted rates will be a given mark-up over LIBOR (the London Inter-Bank Offered Rate), which is the rate at which the lending bank is able to attract a deposit of the currency from another source. Apart from adjusting the rate of interest, a roll-over loan can also allow for currency switches and in addition permit a change (usually a reduction) in the value of the outstanding loan. Long-term loans can also be arranged through a Syndicated Euro-loan facility which is organized by a consortium of banks.

Traders who seek to raise finance may well consider the borrowing of a Euro-currency as an alternative to borrowing the domestic currency, and also as an alternative to forward cover (see Chapter 9). Factors which have to be considered are:

(a) Cost of Forward Cover;
(b) Rates of interest;
(c) Currency to be paid or received;
(d) Likely changes in exchange rates;
(e) The degree to which the transactor is prepared to accept risk.

Euro-Bonds

In addition to the Euro-currency markets there are also the *Euro-Bond* markets with bonds sold on up to twenty-five years maturity denominated in a currency other than the currency of issue where the sale is effected; e.g. a dollar bond sold in Germany and elsewhere. They are underwritten by an *international* syndicate of banks.

Foreign Bonds

A *Foreign Bond*, on the other hand, is denominated in the currency of the country where it is sold, but by a non-resident borrower; e.g. a US company floating a DM bond in Germany and underwritten by a syndicate of banks from one country.

Bond Issuers

Bond issuers (borrowers) are governments, international institutions like the World Bank, multinational companies and banks, etc. Bonds are issued in all the major currencies and can range in value from $10 m to $500 m per total issue, although investors can purchase individuals bonds for as little as £5,000.

Types of Bond

There are various types of bonds, e.g.:

(a) *Fixed Rate Bonds*. These pay a fixed interest rate annually based on a 360 day year.

(b) *Floating Rate Notes*. Interest is paid twice per year usually, but adjusted periodically to a specified margin over a given reference rate (e.g. LIBOR).

(c) *Drop-lock Bonds*. Here the interest rate floats but should it fall to a specified level the bond converts to a fixed rate for the rest of its life.

(d) *Bonds with Warrants*. These give the investor the right to purchase shares in the issuing company at a price fixed at the date of the bond issue.

(e) *Convertible Bonds*. Here the investor has the option to convert the bond into the shares of the issuing company at a price fixed at the time of issue of the bond.

(f) *Sinking Fund Bond*. The issuer guarantees to buy back his bond at pre-determined times, either from the market or from individual holders.

(g) *Purchase Fund Bonds*. Here the issuer is only called on to buy back the bonds if they fall to a market price below the one at the time of issue.

(h) *Call Bonds*. Here the issuer has the right to make repurchases of his bond at any time but only at a premium price.

Benefits to Borrowers

(i) Various capital markets around the world can be tapped to yield various currencies at maturities up to twenty-five years and at competitive rates of interest;

(ii) Some types of bonds (e.g. Call Bonds) give the borrower the opportunity to buy back the issue and float another bond when interest rate considerations make this an attractive possibility;

(iii) Bonds are issued in the "name" of the borrower and no underlying security is called for;

(iv) Use of a syndicate of banks through which the bonds are issued assures the borrower of the best terms available.

Benefits to Investors

(i) The prestigious names of the borrowers and syndicates together with a very low default rate gives the investor a low risk security;

(ii) Investors have a wide choice of currency to select from including bonds issued in Special Drawing Rights (SDRs) and European Currency Units (ECUs) (see Chapter 12);

(iii) A wide range of bond maturities and rates of interest are available;

(iv) Interest is paid gross of tax;

(v) There is a vigorous secondary market allowing for speedy liquidation;

(vi) Bonds are issued as bearer certificates for ease of sale. However, there are two international agencies – EUROCLEAR and CEDAL, who are prepared to both hold bonds for safe keeping on behalf of investors and also to arrange for them to be cleared.

(5) LONDON AS AN INTERNATIONAL FINANCIAL CENTRE

Reference has already been made to London as the capital of the Euro-markets, perhaps responsible for one-third of all world transactions in Euro-currency business. But London has other claims to financial importance, some of which have been referred to in earlier chapters, e.g. Confirming Houses and Export Houses. Of course, London is the site of the world's major insurance centre, Lloyds of London; the commodities markets etc., but here we are concerned with London as an international *banking* centre. Some facets of this include:

(a) *Advances in Sterling and Euro-currencies.* Short- and medium-term to businesses, local authorities, banks and financial institutions and to the world's money markets.

(b) *Deposits in Sterling and Foreign Currencies, Including the Certificate of Deposit (CD).* This is a bearer document stating that a deposit of a certain amount has been placed with a particular bank for a given period and at a particular rate of interest. The CD is a negotiable asset and can be resold in a secondary market. Sterling CDs were first issued in October 1968 along the lines of the dollar CDs introduced into London by the First National City Bank of New York in 1966. CDs are issued in multiples of £10,000 with a minimum of £50,000 and from three months to five years maturity. The advantage to a holder of a CD is that ownership can be transferred by handing the certificate to the new owner without incurring the costs that would normally be associated with cashing the deposit before maturity. Thus CDs give both an interest rate related to maturity and liquidity.

(c) *The Inter-Bank Market*. This provides a mechanism whereby banks can take and place sterling deposits between banks in London. The main lenders are merchant banks, overseas and foreign banks in London, savings banks and the clearing banks and their subsidiaries. In addition a number of non-banks, such as pension funds, companies, insurance companies, etc., also place funds in the market.

(d) *Growth of Foreign Banks*. In 1960 there were 77 such banks in London but by 1981 there were 379, with US and Japanese banks predominating. They compete with the UK banks for inward and outward business of their countries of origin and also in the taking and placing of foreign currencies from or to UK and overseas residents.

(e) *Consortium Banks*. There are about 29 such groups in London and they are defined as banks owned by other (usually foreign) banks, with no one owning bank having more than a 50% direct shareholding. Their growth has been due to the increase in the large borrowings of multi-national corporations whose requirements would be difficult to meet by a single bank.

(f) *Banking Clubs*. These are co-operative groupings of European banks formed to offer reciprocal lending arrangements including syndicated lending. There are three clubs involving UK banks, namely:

Associated Banks of Europe Corporation (ABECOR);
European Banks International Company (EBIC);
The Inter-Alpha Group.

(g) *The Merchant Banks*. Amongst other facilities, they offer documentary collections, Letters of Credit, Acceptance Credits, foreign exchange, advances in sterling and Euro-currencies, deposits in sterling and Euro-currencies, Euro-bond issues, international underwriting of Bond issues and dealing in the Bond secondary markets, private placements of unquoted securities with large institutional investors overseas, international corporate finance, project finance, export finance and ECGD credits, gold and commodity dealings, factoring and leasing.

(6) OTHER BANK SERVICES

Finally in this chapter we consider some of the non-financial services offered by UK banks to customers dealing in international transactions. They include:

General economic reports on overseas markets;
Information about overseas exchange control regulations;
Status reports on prospective buyers overseas;
Names of overseas agents;
Information on documentation;
Trade restrictions overseas;
Introductions to banks abroad, etc.

Information is also available from:

Commercial and Trade Departments of foreign embassies in the UK;
Commercial and Trade Sections of British High Commissions and embassies overseas;
Chambers of Commerce;
Business Reference libraries;
Trade Associations;
Confederation of British Industry (CBI);
The British Importer's Confederation;
United Kingdom Trade Agency for Developing Countries (UKTA);
HM Customs and Excise.

Publications include:

British Business, weekly, published by the Department of Trade and Industry;
Export Times published by Export Times Publishing;
Export Direction published by Thompson Magazines;
Croner's Reference Book for Exporters published by Croner Publications Ltd., also their *Reference Book for Importers*;
Handy Shipping Guide published by Wilkinson Bros. Ltd.;
Lloyds Loading List published by Lloyds of London Press Ltd.;
Importers' Check List published by British Importers' Confederation.

Finally, no list would be complete without a mention of the British Overseas Trade Board (BOTB).

British Overseas Trade Board

The BOTB provides information, advice and help to UK exporters by amassing and disseminating information on overseas markets. It was set up in 1972. It offers:

(a) *Advice on individual markets*;

(b) *An Export Marketing Research Scheme.* This is designed to help UK companies do market research abroad. It offers a free advisory service and grants may be available towards the cost of market research including up to 33⅓% towards the cost of commissioning consultants, the employment of professional management to re-organize an export department, and the setting up of a new market research department. Total cumulative financial help is limited to £20,000 per firm;

(c) *An Overseas Status Report Service.* This gives information about the interests and capabilities of overseas companies including the scope of its activities, and if it is to act as an agency, its ability to cover the area it claims to operate, etc. This service is *not* a credit rating facility which may be available from banks or a commercial enquiry agency.

(d) *Market Entry Guarantee Scheme.* This scheme is to help the smaller exporter to enter new overseas markets. Certain overhead costs of market entry may be financially assisted by the BOTB. These include, overseas office accommodation, staff costs, travel expenses, sales promotion, overseas warehousing, commercial and legal costs (e.g. patents, trade marks, licences, etc.). One half of these costs may be funded by the BOTB, which makes a flat-rate charge of 3% of its funding, and also takes a levy on sales receipts. The minimum funding for any one venture is £20,000, the maximum is £150,000.

(e) *Overseas Trade Fairs.* This is to encourage UK companies who participate in such fairs with the BOTB providing space and shell stands at special rates. Travel costs may also be assisted. BOTB can also give help in publicizing such fair participation.

(f) *Overseas Seminars and Symposia.* Where such meetings can be reasonably expected to lead to an increase in UK exports. BOTB may be able to contribute towards the cost of hall hire, public address systems, projectors, translation, printing, local publicity, graphics, and in some cases travel support.

(g) *Market Advisory Service.* This service gives a prospective exporter information about the prospects for selling particular goods and how best to exploit the opportunities, including local representation abroad. Details about local demand, competition, the attractiveness or otherwise of the proposed export product, etc., are also available under this scheme.

(h) *Outward Missions.* This scheme is to encourage UK exporters to visit overseas markets and contributions towards the costs of such visits are available from BOTB.

(i) *Inward Mission.* Under this facility, companies which wish to bring to the UK foreign businessmen, journalists, etc., who may be able to influence UK exports, can be granted financial assistance for travel costs, interpretation costs, etc.

Projects and Export Policy Division

Apart from the above facilities, the Projects and Export Policy Division (PEP) of the Department of Trade, which operates under the guidance of BOTB, offer an *Overseas Projects Fund*. This is to help UK exporters in their pursuit of major overseas projects with financial assistance toward pre-contractual expenses and feasibility and consultancy studies. Projects with a potential UK content of £50 m or more will be considered.

PEP also operate a *World Aid Section* which gives UK exporters information about opportunities for the provision of goods and services under the aid programmes run by the international lending agencies such as the World Bank Group (International Bank for Reconstruction and Development, International Development Association, and the International Finance Corporation), the Inter-American Development Bank and the European Development Fund. The World Aid section collects and monitors project information from these bodies.

Publicity Unit

Finally, the BOTB has a Publicity Unit which advises exporters on the free publicity services obtainable from the Central Office of Information (COI) and the BBC External Services. Access to foreign journalists based in London is also possible. There is also a Statistics and Market Intelligence Library at the Department of Trade in London which offers trade data and general background information on many overseas countries. The reading room contains a large collection of directories.

Chapter 12

The Monetary and Financial Background

In this chapter we stand back from the details of the day-to-day activities of traders, investors and banks and look at the monetary and financial environment in which these activities take place. In particular we shall be touching on the following:

(a) How *countries* finance their external debt;
(b) How countries obtain long-term development finance;
(c) The fixing of exchange rates by international agreement;
(d) The major factors that have led to changes in (c);
(e) The UK balance of payments and its significance as an indicator of external debt.

To do this the chapter is divided into the following sections:

(A) The International Monetary Fund;
(B) Major changes in the system;
(C) The World Bank group;
(D) The European Monetary System;
(E) The UK Balance of Payments.

(A) THE INTERNATIONAL MONETARY FUND (IMF)

This was set up in 1946, with its headquarters in Washington, USA with an original membership of 44, now 147 member states (September 1984). The aim of the IMF was to:

(a) Avoid exchange rate competition between member states whereby each tried to achieve an export price advantage over competitors by pushing the rate for their currencies down – but to no lasting effect as other countries did the same;

(b) Remove exchange controls on at least the movement of money to finance trade with a view to an expansion of trade;

(c) Establish a system which allowed for a degree of exchange rate flexibility so that balance of payments imbalances could be righted through an acceptable level of depreciation.

To achieve these ends each member was given a quota determined by its population size, gross domestic product, its trade volumes and its level of international reserves. The quota itself determined:

(a) The members' voting rights; each member having 250 basic votes plus one vote for each $100,000 of quota;

(b) The degree to which a member could obtain financial assistance from the IMF;

(c) The degree to which a member was required to supply its own currency to the IMF;

(d) The distribution of Special Drawing Rights.

Quotas were expressed in US dollars of the weight and fineness in effect on 1 July 1944, namely $35 equal to one Troy ounce of gold. Although gold was given the role of determining the value of the US dollar, was used in part to make up members' subscriptions to the IMF, and was still a major reserve unit, it was no longer used as in a Gold Standard to rigidly fix exchange rates without alteration, nor was it used to help determine domestic money supplies. Its principal function then, was to give the US dollar a basic value, and indeed like all other members, the US had to support its rate of exchange, in its case by supporting the world's gold markets to ensure that gold never moved beyond 1% either side of its $35 parity. This gave a flexibility of $34.65–$35.35 but in practice the movement upwards was restricted to $35.20. The US authorities achieved this by selling to, or buying gold from the free markets. However, the US obligation to exchange gold for US dollars at the parity rate only extended to overseas monetary authorities. By this process, the dollar reserves of other countries were effectively "backed" by the US promise of supplying gold in exchange on demand. Thus holding dollars was as good as holding gold; better in fact, because dollar assets yielded a return, while gold had a cost in terms of storage and security.

Other members established parity for their currencies against the US dollar. For example, the UK set the pound sterling at $4.03 with the same degree of 1% flexibility, and was prepared to support sterling in the foreign exchange markets by the same process of buying and selling. To achieve this, the Exchange Equalization Fund (EEA) which had been established in July 1932 was used by the Bank of England on behalf of the Treasury to maintain the gold and dollar reserves of the UK and to use them to buy sterling when its exchange rate fell towards $3.99 and sell sterling when it rose towards $4.06.

The result of this system could be said to be a gold-dollar exchange system. That is currencies could be exchanged for dollars at an almost fixed rate of exchange, and dollars themselves could be exchanged for gold at any equally fixed price.

SUBSCRIPTIONS

Members subscribed to the IMF a sum equal to their quota, made up of 25% gold and 75% in their own currency. The latter is held by the IMF in the form of non-interest bearing, non-marketable notes except for a small amount of cash deposit at members' Central Banks. The IMF exchanges the notes for the currency when it is needed to supply other members with finance. However, only the subscriptions of the members whose currencies were convertible could be used by the IMF to finance other members, and in practice for a number of years it was primarily the US dollar which fulfilled this function. In effect, the IMF was an organization which received dollars from the US subscription and made them available to other members who had Balance of Payments problems.

PURCHASES AND REPURCHASES

The IMF doesn't use the terms "lending" and "repaying" to describe its operations but rather the terms "purchasing" and "repurchasing". The reason is simply because the IMF *sells* members' currencies to members in need, in return for the equivalent receipt by the IMF of the buying members' currency. For example, if the UK needed US dollars, it could obtain them in certain circumstances from the IMF by buying them for sterling at the parity rate of exchange. In effect the IMF acts like a *foreign exchange market* except that:

(a) Purchases are conditional;

(b) Access is by member governments only;

(c) Puchases need to be "repurchased" within a certain period of time;

(d) Transactions are not likely to affect the private markets in the same way as a private transaction.

However, purchases (or drawings) were limited according to the following rule:

"The IMF will not hold a member's currency in excess of 200% of that member's quota".

Thus, with a quota of (say) $1,000 m a member has to subscribe $250 m in gold and $750 m in its own currency. Each time it makes a drawing (purchase) from the IMF, it has to give the IMF the equivalent in its own money. It can go on doing this until the IMF has that member's currency equal to twice that member's quota.

For example, as each annual drawing right was limited to a value equal to 25% of its quota, a member with a quota of $1,000 m could draw up to $250 m worth of foreign exchange each year (or a cumulative amount if no drawings had been made in any one or more years). As the member had already subscribed its own currency to a value of 75% of its quota ($750 m worth), there remained a drawing right value of 125% of its quota, i.e.

1st year drawing	$250 m (gold (now reserve) tranche)
2nd year drawing	$250 m (1st credit tranche)
3rd year drawing	$250 m (2nd credit tranche)
4th year drawing	$250 m (3rd credit tranche)
5th year drawing	$250 m (4th credit tranche)
total drawing	= $1250 m = 125% of quotas
Add subscription	= $ 750 m in domestic currency
Total IMF holding	= $2000 m in members' own currency = 200% of quota.

The first drawing was called a "gold tranche drawing" as it represented the value of the gold subscription. Now it is called the "reserve tranche drawing". This drawing right is automatic and unconditional – members can call upon it as a right. Subsequent drawings are called "credit tranche drawings" to emphasize that with them, members are receiving foreign currency in excess of their own gold (or reserve) subscriptions. These drawings are not automatically obtainable and they carry IMF conditions. These become increasingly severe with drawings in the upper credit tranche levels.

Members may be able to obtain currency in this way if they are in Balance of Payments need. However, interest is payable to the IMF which is mostly passed on to the country whose currency the IMF is selling. Currently (1983) the IMF levies charges on credit tranche drawings by way of a service charge of 0.5% plus an annual charge of 6.6%.

Members are designated debtors or creditors depending on the IMF holdings of their currencies. Thus, members whose currencies the IMF is holding above the original 75% of quota level are designated "debtors", while members whose currencies the IMF is holding below the original 75% of quota level are designated "creditors".

A purchase of currency has to be eventually offset by a repurchase, usually within three to five years. A repurchase consists of the debtor member returning foreign exchange to the IMF in return for its own currency. However, the denomination of the currency or currencies of repurchases is for the IMF to determine. This is so, because if it were left to the decision of the repurchasing member, the IMF could be left holding other members' currency in excess of 75% of their quotas as a direct result of the repurchase by another member. This would be tantamount to one member getting another member into debt with the IMF by the process of a repurchase, and this offends against a cardinal IMF principle which is that *any one member's debt status can only be as a result of that member's own purchases.*

CONDITIONALITY

It has already been pointed out that credit tranche drawings are subject to IMF conditionality. This usually takes the form of an agreed economic policy programme aimed at achieving a viable Balance of Payments position over an appropriate period of time. This programme could include, public sector financing, interest rates, domestic money supply and the exchange rate. The IMF may make definite proposals to a prospective borrowing member to depreciate its currency as a condition of the drawing by that member. If successful, the programme will (hopefully) eventually enable the member to make an IMF repurchase and so terminate its debtor position. If, prior to a drawing, a member has imposed exchange controls designed to limit the outflow of foreign exchange, for example, a moratorium on payments under Letters of Credit, the IMF will usually require the lifting of such controls as one condition of the drawing.

(B) MAJOR CHANGES IN THE SYSTEM

The benefits of the IMF system (called the Bretton Woods system because it was at Bretton Woods, in New Hampshire, USA in July 1944, that the Articles of Agreement were drafted and signed by forty-four nations) can be said to have been:

(a) Fixed but adjustable exchange rates;
(b) Fewer competitive depreciations;
(c) Finance for debtor members;
(d) The encouragement of debtor members to take remedial action;
(e) A reduction in restrictions on current account transactions.

However, there were a number of difficulties which eventually led to dramatic changes in the system. They were:

(1) The inability of the IMF to put pressure on *creditor* members to take steps to reduce their Balance of Payments surpluses;

(2) The eventual decline in the acceptability of the US dollar at the fixed parity to gold;

(3) The growth of large speculative funds in the Euro-markets.

(4) UK devalued sterling from $2.80 to $2.40 in November 1967. This diverted attention to the problem of the US dollar.

Continued gold purchases in the London free gold market pushed the price of gold beyond its IMF parity ceiling of $35.20. On 15 March 1968 the UK authorities closed the market temporarily. It re-opened two weeks later under the two-tier gold system. This permitted the *private* price for gold to be unrestricted and therefore unsupported by Central Banks. This meant that they no longer had to supply gold to the market out of their reserves. This was especially important for the US who was primarily responsible for fixing the dollar price of gold, and whose gold reserves were falling rapidly.

However, gold transacted *between* Central Banks was still to be at the parity price of $35 per fine ounce of gold. Of course the system could only work if the Central Banks desisted from selling gold to the private market at more attractive prices than they could obtain in the official market. Some such sales were, in fact made, but little gold changed hands via the official market.

The US dollar was clearly over-valued against a number of currencies including the Deutsche mark and the Japanese yen. However, neither Germany nor Japan wished to revalue their currencies. Instead pressure was put on the US to devalue the dollar. This could only be achieved by changing the dollar's parity to gold and apart from the US being unwilling to do this, it would have meant that the system's major currency would no longer have an immutable value in terms of gold – no longer "as good as gold". This, it was believed, would undermine the entire system. The US was unhappy about taking such a step for other reasons as well. They were:

(i) An increase in the official dollar price of gold would have benefited the gold producing areas like South Africa and the Soviet Union;

(ii) Most developing countries held little gold so they would reap little benefit;

(iii) Some major industrial countries like Japan, who held large dollar reserves would effectively incur a loss in the gold value of their reserves, while others, notably France who had been following a policy of exchanging officially held dollars for US gold, would receive a boost to the value of their gold reserves.

Pressure on the US dollar mounted and on 15 August 1971 President Nixon announced that the US authorities would no longer honour its IMF obligation to sell gold to other Central Banks in return for dollars. In effect, the US dollar became inconvertible into official gold and the parity rate of $35 became meaningless.

On 18 December 1971 international agreement was reached by the Smithsonian Agreement of the Group of Ten countries (the major industrial countries. This included a devaluation of the US dollar to $38 per ounce of gold and a revaluation of several currencies against the dollar, notably the Deutsche mark by 13.58% and the Japanese yen by 16.58%. However, as the gold value of the pound sterling remained unchanged the new rate was £1 = $2.60; the only time that sterling was revalued against the dollar in post-war history. In addition parity margins were widened from 1% to 2¼%.

Renewed speculation against sterling resulted in the pound sterling being floated on 23 June 1972. This policy was in accordance with the then UK authority's philosophy of ending the "stop-go" economic pattern that had become so discredited. The idea was to allow the pound to fall to whatever level the market deemed necessary and to concentrate on reviving the domestic economy. Whether or not this policy would have been successful is debatable, but in any case the oil price rise of October 1973 soon acted to depress the economies of all oil importing countries.

Attention once again reverted to the US dollar and renewed speculation led to a second dollar devaluation, this time to $42.22 per ounce of gold on 12 February 1973.

On 19 March 1973 the European Economic Community's "snake" which had started on 24 April 1972 (the agreement to limit fluctuations between their participating country's currencies to a 2¼% margin) was no longer subject to the "tunnel" (the limit of 4½% to changes of the "snake" currency's movements against the US dollar). In effect, the value of the dollar was no longer going to be maintained by European Central Bank intervention. This was therefore tantamount to a general float of all major currencies, with the exception of the currencies within the "snake" itself. (See the "European Monetary System" later in this chapter.)

The net results of all these changes can be said to have been:

(i) A termination of the fixed but adjustable system of exchange rate determination;

(ii) Wildly fluctuating rates; e.g. the all-important US dollar/German mark rate has moved from $1 = DM2.36 in 1976, to $1 = DM1.73 in 1979, to $1 = DM2.54 in 1983 and over DM3.07 in September 1984. These rates represent a dollar depreciation of about 27% followed by an appreciation of about 73%!

(iii) The end of the US dollar's "immutable" relationship with gold;

(iv) An almost complete cessation of industrial countries' drawings from the IMF. For example, in 1971 they had made collective drawings totalling SDR1362 m. This fell to SDR322 m by 1973, and, if we exclude the UK drawings, there have been virtually none by these countries ever since. In effect the IMF has become an organization funding the developing nations' Balance of Payments deficits and this has led to changes discussed further on in this chapter.

(v) A phasing out of gold as a monetary asset and a measure of currency value. For example, on 1 July 1974 the value of the Special Drawing Right (SDR) was no longer determined by its gold "content", i.e. ⅟₃₅ of an ounce of gold = one SDR, but by a "weighted basket" measurement (see later in this chapter). IMF began auctioning one-third of its gold subscriptions on 2 June 1976.

Now, throughout the changes that took place in the world's monetary system 1968–1974, the IMF was essentially an onlooker. Its most important members took unilateral or collective measures outside its auspices and by the mid-1970s its Articles of Agreement were looking sadly ineffectual.

The first major amendment of IMF Articles came on 1 January 1970 when the first allocations of SDRs were made, and on 1 April 1978 the second Amendment to IMF Articles became effective.

THE SECOND AMENDMENT TO IMF ARTICLES

On 1 April 1978 IMF Articles were amended as follows:

(a) Termination of the requirement that members maintain fixed parity rates. Members to be permitted to determine their own currency arrangements, with the qualification that the IMF was to operate "surveillance" over such arrangements by a process of consultation, with a view to preventing competitive depreciations.

(b) The fiction of an official price for gold was discontinued. Members were not permitted to link their currencies to gold. Gold subscriptions gave way to "Reserve" subscriptions.

(c) Restrictions on the use of SDRs were relaxed.

(d) The IMF substituted the concept of "a freely usable currency" for "a convertible currency" reflecting the need for it to use additional currencies for drawing right purposes.

Even before the Second Amendment, the IMF had taken steps to meet its members' needs by the introduction of a number of facilities. These are:

(1) January 1962, the General Arrangement to Borrow

This empowered the IMF to increase its resources by borrowing from ten of its industrial members plus Switzerland (a non-member). These arrangements have been extended several times and the most recent renewal ends in October 1985. Currently (1983), about SDR6.8 billion is available. Large drawings were made by such members as the UK (in 1964) and the US (in 1978). (See also "Future Changes" later in this chapter.)

(2) February 1963, Compensatory Financing Facility

Members who experience short falls in export earnings, especially for primary products, that are temporary and largely beyond the members' control may obtain additional drawings of up to 100% of their quota. Repurchases must be made within three to five years. To date SDR11.6 b has been drawn.

(3) June 1969, Buffer Stock Facility

This is to assist those members who are helping to fund approved international buffer stocks designed to stabilize prices of primary goods. Repurchases must be within three to five years and up to an additional 50% of quota can be obtained. To date SDR0.48 b has been drawn.

(4) September 1974, Extended Facility

Because of the oil price shock in October 1973 and the subsequent imbalances to many members' Balance of Payments, the IMF introduced this facility which allows for drawings of up to 140% of quota in addition to compensatory financing, buffer stock financing, the oil facility and the first credit tranche. Repurchases are required within four to ten years. So far some SDR4.04 b has been drawn.

(5) June 1974 and April 1975, Oil Facilities

These temporary facilities were offered to members to counter the Balance of Payments effects of the oil price rise of October 1973. Repurchases are required within seven years and SDR6.9 b was drawn. The facility is now fully drawn.

(6) June 1975, Oil Subsidy Account

This facility reduced the cost to members who drew on the IMF Oil Facilities by subsidizing the interest charges they thus incurred. Subsidies were made to twenty-five members totalling SDR186.8 m. Final payments were made in August 1983.

(7) May 1976, IMF Trust Fund

This IMF Trust Fund was financed from the sale of one-sixth of IMF gold holdings held, during the period 1976–1980. Some 25 million ounces of gold was sold in 45 auctions raising US$5.7 b. From January 1977 to March 1981 loans on concessional terms were made from the Trust Fund to members with low per capita incomes and a Balance of Payments problem. Repayments are required within ten years. The Trust Fund was terminated in March 1981. In addition to loans, the IMF also distributed part of the profits from the gold sales to developing members on the basis of their share in total IMF quotas on 31 August 1975. Distributions were completed in 1980.

(8) February 1979, Supplementary Financing Facility

This facility is offered to those members who, having already exhausted drawings under the Extended Facility, are seen as in need of additional assistance. They can draw up to an additional 140% of quota which is financed out of IMF borrowing. Repurchases must be within seven years. SDR6.5b has been drawn. The facility has now been replaced by the Enlarged Access Policy (see (10)).

(9) March 1981, IMF/Saudi Arabian borrowing agreement

In line with its policy of increasing its resources through borrowing, the IMF concluded an agreement with the Saudi Arabian Monetary Agency (SAMA) to borrow up to SDR8b over two years with the possibility of further amounts in the third year.

(10) May 1981, Enlarged Access Policy

As a result of the full commitment of the Supplementary Financing Facility (SFF), and also as a result of the new IMF borrowing arrangements, the Enlarged Access Policy was introduced on the same terms as the SFF except that drawings could be up to 150% of quota annually or 450% over a three-year period.

FUTURE CHANGES

(1) Increase in Quotas

Several increases in quotas have been made over the years and another increase (the eighth) is proposed for 1984, which is expected to bring total quotas to SDR90b (from SDR61b). 25% of the increase is to be paid for in Special Drawing Rights or in other members' currencies prescribed by the IMF. Increases are subject to the members' own approval.

(2) Enlargement of the General Arrangements to Borrow (GAB)

A proposal to increase from SDR6.4b to SDR17b the size of IMF possible borrowings was agreed to in principle in February 1983. Participating members are: Belgium, Canada, Germany, France, Italy, Japan, Netherlands, Sweden, UK, US and Switzerland. It is expected to be effective in 1984.

(3) IMF borrowings from non-GAB lenders

In addition to the enlargement of the GAB, it was also agreed in principle to permit IMF borrowings from non-GAB members and, by implication, the possibility of IMF borrowings from the private capital markets of member countries.

To conclude this section there follows some data on the IMF and its activities as at 29 February 1984.

Table 12.1
Quotas

Total quotas SDR88,998.5 million, of which:

USA	17,918.3 m
UK	6,194.0 m
Germany	5,403.7 m
France	4,482.8 m
Japan	4,223.3 m
Saudi Arabia	3,202.4 m
Canada	2,941.0 m
Italy	2,909.1 m
China	2,390.9 m
India	2,207.7 m

= SDR51,873.2 m or 58.3% of the total

Table 12.2
Total Purchases to Date of the Top Eleven Drawers Cumulative Since 1947 in Order of their Total Drawings

Total purchases to date = SDR77,652.9 million, of which

		As % of current quota
UK	12,517.6	202
India	5,830.5	264
USA	5,827.1	33
Yugoslavia	3,809.6	621
Italy	3,171.0	109
Brazil	3,479.7	238
Argentina	2,721.7	245
Turkey	2,505.2	584
France	2,465.9	55
Pakistan	2,149.3	393
South Africa	1,882.3	206

Table 12.3
Holdings of Members' Currencies as a Percentage of their Quotas

(a) *IMF holdings above 350%**		(b) *IMF holdings below 40%*	
Ivory Coast	456.2%	Singapore	25.8%
Uganda	452.9	Trinidad and Tobago	29.2
Sudan	445.9	Paraguay	33.4
Turkey	434.3	Malta	36.2
Mauritius	417.5	Libya	36.6
Yugoslavia	416.6	Saudi Arabia	37.4
Dominica	386.8		
Morocco	386.6		
South Korea	384.7		
Liberia	375.4		
Kenya	364.5		
Zambia	357.9		

(c) *IMF holdings of some major members*

USA	46.3%
UK	67.1
France	71.2
Japan	67.8
Canada	81.3
China	93.0
India	254.6
Italy	66.8

*Enlarged Access Policy.

Table 12.4
**Currencies Used in Purchases to Date as a
Percentage of Total Purchases to Date**

US dollars	31.6%
SDRs	16.2
Deutsche marks	11.7
Saudi riyals	7.8
Yen	5.9
Guilders	3.2
Italian lire	2.7
Belgian francs	2.6
Sterling	2.7
Canadian dollars	2.6
Others	13.0

SPECIAL DRAWING RIGHTS (SDRs)

We now need to consider SDRs in more detail. In the previous section of this chapter we noted that throughout the 1960s and beyond the US dollar became subject to speculative pressures on the world's foreign exchange markets. This was due principally to the large Balance of Payments problems of the USA and the increasing imbalance between holdings of dollars abroad and US gold reserves. Any correction seemed to imply an improvement in the US Balance of Payments to reduce overseas dollar balances. However, it was believed such an adjustment could, by reducing international reserve levels, have a deflationary impact on world trade. To avoid this happening the IMF was empowered to issue a new unit to be called the Special Drawing Right unit.

This new unit was first allocated to participating members of the IMF on 1 January 1970, and in subsequent years as follows:

1970–72   SDR   9.3 billion
1979–81   SDR 12.1 billion
Total to date SDR 21.4 billion

To accommodate the new unit the IMF has set up a Special Drawing Right Department (separate from the General Department which deals with "ordinary drawing rights" already described in the previous section).

The SDR allocations are made from the SDR Department on the basis of existing quotas. For example the USA has received 21.3% and the UK 8.9% of the total SDR allocations.

Allocations are made without any reciprocal subscription to the IMF and have the status of official reserve assets alongside gold and currencies. In the beginning the value of an SDR was set at $\frac{1}{35}$ of an ounce of gold giving them an equal value to the US dollar. When the dollar was devalued in 1971 and 1973 the SDR retained its gold value. This changed the dollar/SDR rate from

   SDR1 = US\$1 (1970)
to SDR1 = US\$1.08571 (1971)
to SDR1 = US\$1.20635 (1973)

Subsequent events have further altered the dollar/SDR rate as we shall see
later in this section.

Allocations are made when the IMF deems it necessary to bring international reserve levels up to what it regards as adequate to meet the trade and
payments needs of its members. It has the power to cancel existing allocations but has never done so. SDRs are not allocated to any party other than
participating members of the IMF although the IMF permits fourteen "other
holders" of SDRs, other than IMF members. These include the Bank for
International Settlements and the World Bank.

Use of SDRs

The basic purpose of the SDR allocation was to permit members with Balance of Payments difficulties to draw on their SDR holdings to settle their
debt just as they might draw on their dollar reserves. However SDRs are *not
directly* usable to settle debt. For example, they cannot be sold to the private
foreign exchange markets for currency, nor can they be sold to importers to
use to pay for imports. SDRs are essentially *public sector assets* and transferable only between participating members and "other holders".

SDRs Can Be Used in Three Main Ways

(1) By Bilateral Agreement

Two IMF members may agree to exchange SDRs for currency. For example,
the Philippines may well sell SDRs to Singapore for US dollars which can be
used by the Philippines to settle their international debt either by selling the
dollars directly to their importers to by selling them for other currency in the
private market and using the proceeds to sell to their importers.

(2) By IMF Designation

A member with a Balance of Payments need can request the IMF to desig-
nate another member whose Balance of Payments and reserves are strong,
to purchase its SDRs for currency. However, no member may be required to
hold a total of SDRs beyond a level of three times its own allocations.

(3) By Payment to the IMF in a Repurchase

The IMF may agree to accept SDRs from a member making a repayment
(repurchase) of its drawings from the General Department. In this way the
General Department has built up holdings of SDRs which it can use in the
ordinary way by meeting members' purchasing requirements from the General Department. One advantage of this is that SDRs used in repurchases do

not affect other currency holdings of the IMF which might be above the 75% position levels.

Limitation on Use of SDRs

(a) Clearly, use is limited by total holdings, which in turn, depend on allocations plus purchases.

(b) Users of SDRs are liable to an interest rate charge where their holdings fall below their allocations. Holdings above allocations attract interest. All interest is payable in SDRs and is calculated by reference to the weighted average yields or rates on short-term market instruments in the USA, Germany, the UK, France and Japan. It is calculated weekly and at 29 February 1984 was 8.67% per annum for interest payers and 7.307% per annum for interest receivers.

SDR users therefore, need to retain a minimum level of SDRs to service their interest payments or, if these are insufficient, must *purchase* SDRs through a bilateral arrangement or by an ordinary drawing from the IMF's General Department.

Other uses of SDRs

(a) Participants can arrange to buy or sell SDRs for *forward* delivery;

(b) They can also arrange SDR loans and make repayment in SDRs;

(c) SDRs can be used as security for a loan;

(d) SDRs can be used in donations.

Since 1970 and up to July 1982 SDRs have been used as in Table 12.5.

Table 12.5
Use of SDRs

By designation	25.7%
By agreement	21.6%
By repurchase	17.2%
By subscriptions	16.2%
By interest payments	15.7%
Other	3.5%

In addition some 16.2% of all drawings from the IMF's General Department have been in SDRs.

How SDRs are valued

Earlier in this section we saw that the SDR was originally linked to gold at the same ratio as the US dollar, namely SDR1 = $\frac{1}{35}$ of an ounce of gold.

However, because of the policy of removing gold as a numeraire it was decided to abandon the SDR/gold link as from 1 July 1974. Beginning on that date the SDR was valued on a weighted basket basis using sixteen currencies. Values are calculated daily using noon middle market London rates. Calculations are shown in Table 12.6.

Column A shows these market rates against the US dollar as at 28 June 1974.

Column B shows the rates expressed in terms of one SDR where because of two US dollar devaluations one SDR had a value of US$1.20635. Thus if US$1 = DM2.52, then DM2.52 × 1.20635 = DM3.04 = SDR1.

Column C contains the percentage weights ascribed to each currency by the IMF. They represent the use of each currency in trade, payments and reserve holdings.

Column D is found by finding the weight percentages of each value in column C. Thus, 33% of $1.20635 = $0.40 and 12.5% of DM3.04 = DM0.38, etc. The total of column D represents the total value for one SDR, however to add the contents of this column we need to convert them to a common denominator.

Column E shows the conversions into US dollars using market rates, e.g. if US$1 = £0.41 then £0.045 = $\frac{1}{0.41} \times 0.045 = \$0.109756$ etc., etc. Of course, the total of column E is $1.20635. By this process, it was possible to calculate the currency value per SDR each day.

Table 12.6
SDR Value Calculations – Original Weightings

	A Market rates per US$1 as at 28.6.74	B Calculated per SDR1, where SDR1 = US$1.20635 due to 2 US$ devaluations	C % weights	D "Basket" components of SDR1	E Expressed in $ values (other expressions possible)
USA	$1	$1.20635	33	$0.40	$0.40
Germany	DM2.52	DM3.04	12.5	DM0.38	$0.151
UK	£0.41	£0.495	9	£0.045	$0.109
France	FF4.8636	FF5.8672	7.5	FF0.44	$0.091
Japan	Y287	Y346.2	7.5	Y26	$0.091
Canada	C$0.9809	C$1.1838	6	C$0.071	$0.072
Italy	L649.4	L783.4	6	L47	$0.072
Netherlands	DG2.579	DG3.111	4.5	DG0.14	$0.054
Belgium	BF37.9	BF45.7	3.5	BF1.6	$0.042
Sweden	SK4.31	SK5.2	2.5	SK0.13	$0.030
Australia	A$0.66312	A$0.8	1.5	A$0.012	$0.018
Spain	SP6.079	SP7.333	1.5	SP0.11	$0.018
Norway	NK5.4711	NK6.6	1.5	NK0.099	$0.018
Denmark	DK60.79	DK73.33	1.5	DK1.1	$0.018
Austria	Sch18.238	Sch22	1	Sch0.22	$0.012
South Africa	R0.67973	R0.82	1	R0.0082	$0.012
Totals			100%	= SDR1	= $1.20635

Table 12.7
New SDR Weightings Effective 1 July 1978

	Weights	"Basket" component
US dollar	33%	$0.40
D mark	12.5	DM0.32
Sterling	7.5	£0.050
F Franc	7.5	FF0.42
Yen	7.5	Y21
Canadian dollar	5.0	C$0.070
LIT	5.0	LIT52
Guilder	5.0	DG0.14
B Franc	4.0	BF1.6
SA riyal	3.0	SAR0.13
S Krone	2.0	SK0.11
Iran rial	2.0	IR1.7
Australian dollar	1.5	A$0.017
S peseta	1.5	SP1.5
N Krone	1.5	NK0.10
Austrian schilling	1.5	AS0.28
	100%	SDR1

It was decided to replace the Danish krone and South African rand by the Saudi Arabian riyal and the Iranian rial with effect from 1 July 1978. Also, from that date new weightings were ascribed to the sixteen currencies, as shown in Table 12.7.

The effect of these new weightings was to reduce sterling, the Canadian dollar, Italian lire, and Swedish krona, as components of the SDR basket and increase Dutch guilders and Belgian francs as components, apart from replacing the South African rand and Danish krone by Saudi Arabian riyals and Iranian rials. Changes of this nature are considered every five years to adjust the "basket" to changed circumstances.

Change in the SDR "Basket" Effective 1 January 1981

In order to enhance the SDR both as a reserve asset and a unit of account further changes in its valuation were made with effect from 1 January 1981. The sixteen component currencies were reduced to five which have the weights shown in Table 12.8.

Table 12.8
New SDR "Basket"

	Weights		"Basket" component
US dollar	42%		$0.54
D mark	19%		DM0.46
Yen	13%		Y34
F Franc	13%		FF0.74
Sterling	13%		£0.071
	100%	=	SDR1

As in the previous tables, any one currency's SDR value can be found by converting the "basket" components total into the required currency at market rates. For example, if the total of the "basket" column equals $1.28571 at market rates and the dollar value of the Deutsche mark is DM1.883046, then the SDR value of the Deutsche mark is 1.28571 × 1.883046 = DM2.421051.

These new weightings reflect the importance of the currencies in trade and payments based on the value of exports of goods and services and the use of these currencies as reserve assets over the period 1975–1979. A new weighting structure is expected to be effective from 1 January 1986.

Because the SDR is an amalgam of five currencies its value tends to be more stable than any one of its component currencies (see Chapter 9). This enhances its use not only as a reserve asset but also as a unit of account (a measure of value). In addition, the reduction to five components simplifies the weekly IMF calculations for SDR interest rates.

SDRs in the Private Sector

Although private commercial banks have not been designated by the IMF as "other holders" of SDRs there is nothing to stop them offering services to their customers in which the SDR is used as a unit of account. As a result of the above-mentioned simplifications in the valuation of SDRs, this has now become a more practical proposition. For example, one of the first banks to offer both sight and term deposits was Banque Keyser Ullman en Suisse SA in the mid-1970s. Sight SDR deposits were usable as an ordinary current account with no interest payable but a minimum of SDR30,000 deposit was required, payable, of course in a national currency. Likewise, the SDR deposit was convertible into national currency on demand. Term deposits were for three or six months but other durations were possible for sums in excess of SDR250,000.

In January 1981 Natwest Bank started to offer deposit accounts, CDs, and syndicated credits denominated in SDRs. At the same time a London market for SDR denominated CDs was formed by the following banks:

Barclays Bank Group
Chemical Bank International Group
Citibank
Hong Kong and Shanghai Banking Corporation
Midland Bank Limited
International Westminster Bank Limited
Standard Chartered Bank Limited.

Minimum CDs of SDR1 million was offered with maturities up to twelve months. They are issued against, and repaid in US dollars and other currencies.

In fact, any private party can hold SDR denominated claims but there is no IMF liability to exchange SDRs for currency. That is the responsibility of the issuer of the claim (a bank).

The stimulants to the private market have been:

(a) High interest rates for the US dollar;
(b) Exchange rate volatility;
(c) A simplified "basket" of five currencies permit banks to hedge their liabilities by either holding spot currencies or buying forward.

Apart from deposits and CDs, Euro-Bonds denominated in SDRs have also been issued.

Of course, the SDR is not the only composite unit available. There is nothing to stop a bank offering a tailor-made composite but this would have the disadvantage of transferring the claim by first "decomposing" it into its constituent parts, thus incurring transactions costs. Other composite units include:

(a) Barclays Bank "B" Unit;
(b) The European Currency Unit (ECU) (see later in this chapter).

For uses of SDR denominated trade contracts, see section in Chapter 9 dealing with ways of reducing the exchange risk.

No chapter on the international monetary system as first established at Bretton Woods in 1946 would be complete without a reference to the sister organization of the IMF, namely the World Bank Group.

(C) THE WORLD BANK GROUP

Where the IMF was given the function of assisting members with Balance of Payments problems, the World Bank Group was established to provide long-term investment capital for development purposes. The Group has three organizations of which the International Bank for Reconstruction and Development (IBRD) is the largest.

IBRD

The organization receives subscriptions from much the same membership as the IMF. However, these are only partly paid (10%) with the balance being on call should the IBRD require financial assistance. No such call has been made to date. It does not rely on these subscriptions for its investments but rather uses them as security for selling its own Bonds on members' capital markets. Because of this security it has been able to raise medium to long-term money at lower rates of interest than would otherwise have prevailed. For the first five years of its life lending was devoted to European reconstruction, but since the early 1950s it has been mostly concerned with the development of its poorer members. Its brief is to lend only to those members, or agencies of members who would not be able to attract private capital on reasonable terms.

Basic principles of lending include:

(a) To invest in those programmes designed to promote economic development;

(b) To lend only the foreign exchange costs;

(c) To provide multilateral finance, i.e. use of funds in any member country offering best tenders;

(d) Projects must be technically and financially feasible;

(e) Members must be able to service the debt.

The bank's capital is to be increased to US$72 b and its liquid assets as at June 1982 amounted to US$8 b. Annual net profits are running at US$600 m and the bank boasts that it has not suffered a single loss since its inception. Total lending to June 1982 has been about US$71 b of which about US$13 b has been repaid or sold to other parties leaving US$58 b of committed loans. However of this US$29 b remains undisbursed, to be drawn down over the next six to seven years.

The bank does not participate in debt rescheduling or change the terms of a loan. Its loans are largely for project purposes, although this is now being relaxed.

The outstanding debt of the bank at 30 June 1982 was about US$34 b. It is in sixteen different currencies with an average life of seven years all at fixed interest rates. 30% of it is held by central banks or governments who hold IBRD paper as part of their foreign exchange reserves. The balance comes from the private financial markets with US$6–7 b held in the USA, and similar amounts in Switzerland, Germany and Japan. Current interest costs are about 8.2% per annum. Interest charges are currently 11.6% per annum on average.

Changes in Borrowing Practices in 1983

It is proposed to borrow about US$9 b in fiscal 1983, some of which will be by way of short-term, variable-rate instruments for the first time. It is expected that with falling rates, the cost to the bank will be reduced. As a consequence, the rate for lending will be determined every six months during the life of the loan.

INTERNATIONAL DEVELOPMENT ASSOCIATION (IDA)

In order to meet the development needs of the poorest member countries the World Bank decided to establish IDA in 1960 as a "soft loan" window of the bank.

Finance for IDA comes mainly from special member subscriptions, which because of the terms of IDA credits are almost the sole source of finance. As a result subscriptions have to be "replenished" every few years to permit IDA's ongoing work.

Credits are allocated only to those members whose GNP per capita is at the lower end of the range. For example, India has taken a significant proportion of credits; also, Pakistan, Kenya and Ethiopia. Credits have been granted for such purposes as transportation, agriculture, electric power and education. By easing the terms of repayment the bank has been able to pay more attention to the social rather than the economic returns of any given project. More recently, credits have been advanced for urbanization, water-supply and population control projects.

Credits are made available up to fifty years at a nominal charge of ¾% per annum, with a grace period of ten years before repayments become due. From 5 January 1982 a new charge of a half per cent on undisbursed balances is being made.

Because of the Balance of Payments problems of many subscribing members, including the USA, subscription "replenishments" have become increasingly difficult. Several countries that have been recipients of IDA credits have now "graduated" and are now only accessible to IBRD loans. They include, Chile, Turkey, Jordan, Ivory Coast and Colombia.

Total IDA credits to 1982 have been US$29.4 b (worth US$40 b in 1982 dollars).

INTERNATIONAL FINANCE CORPORATION (IFC)

The third and last member of the World Bank Group is the IFC which was established in 1956 as an affiliate organization with US$78 m in capital subscribed by its members.

IFC is a complementary body to the other two organizations in that its brief is to provide investment capital for manufacturing and commercial enterprises as opposed to investments in so-called "infra-structure" projects. Although its investments are small by comparison, they totalled US$4.1 b to 1981, its importance extends beyond these figures insofar as it encourages outside capital to participate in its ventures. These are by way of taking up both equity and fixed interest claims. Thus, four and a half times as much outside capital has been encouraged to invest in members' private sector. Sectors such as energy resources, foodstuffs, especially improved processing and storage, and tourist facilities have been recipients of IFC and associated capital.

The main aim of IFC is not so much to obtain a return on capital, although modest returns have been made, but to pioneer entrepreneurial investments and skills in the higher-income developing countries to improve their industrial and commercial output, especially in the export industries and organizations. Unlike its sister bodies, IFC provides venture capital and is thus open to entrepreneurial loss-making.

In addition to providing capital it offers technical and managerial help which manifests itself in it taking up board positions. However, when an enterprise is deemed to have "got off the ground", the IFC tends to sell its holdings for re-investment elsewhere. Like its sister institutions, it operates on an International Competitive Bidding (ICB) basis, where funds are spent on procuring goods anywhere in World Bank member countries.

CO-FINANCING

The World Bank Group has entered into co-financing arrangements both with commercial banks and export credit organizations like ECGD. These fall into three broad categories:

(1) Joint Financing

Here the IBRD acts as a supervisor of both procurements and disbursements subject only to the veto of the partner who funds an agreed percentage of the finance, e.g. with ECGD participation (up to 1971).

(2) Parallel Financing

Here each participant administers its own part of the project but with general consultation. This has become more common as the IBRD requirement for ICB (see above) did not meet the aims of a partner such as ECGD who looked to finance the procurement of its own exporter's goods (see Chapter 10).

(3) Unorganized Parallel Financing

Here the project is divided into separate sections with each partner taking responsibility for a part. Usually the IBRD takes the civil works contract with ECGD getting the capital equipment contract. The borrower has to negotiate separate agreemeents with both bodies although the IBRD still appraises and supervises the entire project. In all Parallel Financing the IBRD will call for a "cross-default" clause to protect the entire project. This clause allows the IBRD to stop disbursements of funds if the borrower defaults on any part of his liabilities.

Co-financing with Commercial Banks

Because commercial banks tend to lend on shorter terms than the IBRD the scope for such Co-financing tends to be limited to such self-liquidating projects as public utilities and transportation. The IBRD acts as a disbursement channel and recipient for service payments and, again, insists on a "cross-default" clause.

(D) THE "SNAKE" AND THE EUROPEAN MONETARY SYSTEM

Reference in this chapter has already been made to the European Community "snake" which came into operation on 24 April 1972. It comprised the German mark, French franc, Italian lire and Belgian and Luxembourg franc and limited movements in rates between each of these currencies by a maximum of 2¼%. However, movements of rates against outside currencies (e.g. the US dollar) could be up to 4½%.

A diagrammatic illustration of this arrangement known as the "snake in the tunnel" is shown in Diagram 12.1.

In Diagram 12.1 the mark and French franc are shown as moving together within the 4½% limit against non-participating currencies. This is a hypothetical representation only. Central bank intervention in the foreign exchange markets by both the strong and the weak currency countries were required to maintain these relationships. For example, if the Deutsche mark moved towards its ceiling against the US dollar and this caused the mark/ franc rate to move beyond their 2¼% limit, then the Bundesbank and the Banque de France would have to sell marks and buy francs.

In May 1972 the UK and others joined the system but the UK and Eire left in June 1972. There were in fact no less than six attempts to join and seven attempts at leaving the system by seven countries. For example, France joined in April 1972 but left in January 1974; joined again in July 1975 but left in March 1976.

On 19 March 1973 the "snake" left the "tunnel"; i.e. the upper and lower limits of the movement against the US dollar were lifted and a general float against the US dollar ensued, leaving the "snake" limits intact. However, because of the fluctuation stresses in the foreign exchange markets, by the end of 1978 the "snake" comprised only Germany, Denmark, Norway and the Benelux countries.

To give some idea of these fluctuations, the mark had appreciated by some 68% against the US dollar and Italian lire had depreciated by some 31% against the US dollar in the period 1972 and 1978. In order to bring the "snake" currencies within their cross-limits, several currency realignments were effected.

Diagram 12.1
The "snake" in the tunnel

Table 12.9
ECU "Basket" – 1 March 1979[2]

	% weight	Currency amount
German mark	33.02	DM0.82800
French franc	19.89	FF1.15000
UK sterling	13.25	£0.08850
Dutch guilder	10.56	DG0.28600
Italian lire	9.58	LIT109.00000
Belgian franc	9.23	BF3.66000
Danish krone	3.10	DK0.21700
Irish pound	1.11	£I0.00759
Luxembourg franc	0.35	LF0.14000
	100.00 =	ECU1

One of the obvious problems causing these realignments, and thus exchange rate fluctuations, was the differences between participating countries' economic and financial policies. If greater stability was to be obtained then a process of "convergence" of such policies was required. The new European Monetary System (EMS) which replaced the "snake" incorporated convergence rules within its structure.

THE EUROPEAN MONETARY SYSTEM (EMS)

At the heart of the EMS system is the European Currency Unit (ECU) which is a "basket" of fixed amounts of the nine participating currencies determined by "weights" resulting from these countries' GNP and world trade. The EMS started on 13 March 1979 with the ECU "weights" and resulting currency amounts shown in Table 12.9.

Thus one ECU is the combined value of all the nine currency amounts and to find the ECU rate for any one currency the same procedure is followed as for the SDR calculation (see earlier in this chapter, Table 12.6), namely, by converting each currency component into a common denominator currency at market rates of exchange.

In order to measure effective exchange rate changes for the EMS currencies *central rates* were agreed on 24 September 1979 and from these rates, *cross-parities* can be calculated which are required to be maintained within a 2¼% margin.

Several realignments of the central rates have had to be made in order to accommodate economic and financial differences within the EMS countries. Table 12.10 give the original central rates and those obtaining as from 22 May 1983 and 22 July 1985.

These central rate changes allow members of the EMS to more easily maintain their rate margins.

[2]New "basket" composition effective 17 September 1984.
DM 32.0% (DM 0.719); FF 19% (FF 1.31); £15.0% (£0.0878); DG 10.1% (DG 0.256); LIT 10.2% (LIT 140); BF 8.2% (BF 3.71); DK 2.7% (DK 0.291); I £1.2% (I £0.00871); LF 0.3% (LF 0.14); Greek Drachma 1.3% (GD 1.15).

Table 12.10
ECU Central Rates

	From 24.9.79	From 22.5.83	From 22.7.85
One ECU = DM2.48557		2.24184	2.23840
= FF5.8552		6.87456	6.86402
= DG2.74748		2.52595	2.52208
= LIT1,159.42		1403.49	1520.60
= BF & LF39.8456		44.9008	44.8320
= DK7.36594		8.14104	8.128570
= £I0.649822		0.72569	0.724578

Cross-rates are found by relating pairs of central rates, e.g.:

$$ECU1 = DM2.24184 \quad \text{and} \quad FF6.87456$$

Therefore $\quad DM1 \quad = \dfrac{6.87456}{2.24184} = FF3.06648$

Each participating Central Bank is required to intervene to keep the daily market rate for its own currency against all other EMS currencies within 2¼% of its cross-parity. The three currencies which are exceptions to this rule are the UK and Greece, whose currencies are included in the ECU "basket" but do not participate in the EMS limits, and Italy, whose currency is allowed to move by up to 6% against its cross-parities.

To calculate the 2¼% (or 6%) margin limits, factors of 1.0227531 and 0.9777531 are used against the cross-parities. These factors are reciprocals of each other and differ by twice the 2¼% margin.

Thus, if the DM/FF central cross-parity is DM1 = FF3.06648 (see above) then the limits are 3.06648 multiplied by the two factors, giving FF3.13625–FF2.99826. The German mark is required to be maintained within this band.

THE DIVERGENCE INDICATORS

In addition to limits imposed on cross-parity charges, there is also a limit set by changes of any participating currency against the ECU itself. This limit is called a "divergence indicator".

The formula for calculating the "divergence indicator" is $0.75 \times 2.25\%$ (or 6%) $\times$ (100 − ECU basket weight).

Thus, for the German mark we have:

$0.016875 \times (100 - 0.828) = 1.6735275\%$.

When the daily exchange rate for the Deutsche mark moves to the 1.6735275% limit either way against its ECU rate (See Table 12.10), there is a "presumption" that the authorities concerned will take steps to correct the situation. There is, however, no *obligation* for it to take such steps but consultation between Central Banks will ensue to discuss the changes, presumably a greater convergence in domestic policies.

The concept of a "divergence indicator" is not just to give an early warning of currency rate changes that could call for rectification, but more importantly to indicate whether any one currency is appreciating or depreciating against the rest as a whole (as embodied in the ECU), which may be happening even though no other currency is *necessarily* moving outside its 2¼% margin. *In such circumstances, the onus of adjustment falls on the currency moving outside its "divergence" limits.*

EMS FINANCIAL PROVISIONS

The European Monetary Co-operation Fund (EMCF) which was created in April 1973 and served as a clearing agency for "snake" operations, was empowered to receive monetary reserves from all the member states of the European Community and to issue ECUs against such assets. 20% of members' gold and gross US dollar reserves have been exchanged for ECUs in the form of revolving three month "swaps". Although the UK does not participate in the currency limitations, she is a holder of ECUs. ECUs can be used by Central Banks to purchase their own currencies which are held in excess by other Central Banks, who have intervened in the market to support its own currency. Thus, if the Bundesbank had purchased French francs in order to keep the mark within its central cross-parity limits, some could be exchanged for French ECUs. This has the effect of protecting the value of the reserves of such members.

CREDIT FACILITIES

To assist members whose reserves are insufficient to meet intervention requirements, a number of credit arrangements are available:

(1) *Very Short-term.* Unconditional finance is available up to a forty-five day limit. (Not available to the UK.)

(2) *Short-term.* Three months unconditional finance. The UK is permitted restricted drawings.

(3) *Medium-term.* Two to five year finance subject to the Council of Ministers' conditions.

THE UK AND THE EMS

Although the UK participates in the credit arrangements of the EMS and sterling is a component of the ECU "basket", she does not participate in the 2¼% margin limits (Greece is also a non-participant.)

Such participation was seen by the UK as likely to require considerable intervention by the Bank of England in the foreign exchange markets, also a requirement to converge UK domestic financial and economic policies with those of other EMS countries. This was not believed to be in the UK's best interests.

However, a report by a House of Lords committee in September 1983 suggested that circumstances had so changed that UK membership should now be considered, and as a member, the UK would be able to more effectively influence any move towards a restructuring of the currency system. They pointed out that:

(a) The EMS was flexible;
(b) Oil price movements were less volatile;
(c) UK inflation had come into line with other EMS countries.

(E) THE UK BALANCE OF PAYMENTS (BOP)

To conclude this chapter we look at the concept of the "Balance of Payments" and, in particular, that of the UK.

DEFINITION

"A record of transactions between the residents of the reporting country and non-residents."

The purpose of the BOP account is to quantify the value of all assets and liabilities exchanges between residents and non-residents in order to determine whether there is a situation calling for a policy change, e.g. an exchange rate change.

A UK resident is defined as a person living permanently in the UK and corporate bodies located in the UK, but not their overseas branches and subsidiaries. Persons who enter or leave the UK for one year or more are regarded as having changed their residence status for BOP purposes. The only exception to this concerns public employees working abroad as agents of the UK authorities (e.g. embassy and military personnel) who are always UK residents.

The BOP account is maintained on a double-entry basis, with any one transaction recorded as both a credit (+) and a debit (−). However, unlike traditional double-entry, the two entries originate from different sources. For example, an export is, of course, shown in the trade section as a credit, but the offsetting entry will be shown in the section relevant to the way in which the export is being financed: e.g. if under a trade credit arrangement, then the (−) sign will appear against "Export Credit", but if the export goes as part of a grant to a developing country, the offsetting entry will appear under "Transfers".

Basically, there are two sources of information:

(a) From the transactors themselves;
(b) From the banks who provide data on money transactions.

It is unlikely that these two sources will provide exactly the same values due to (i) inaccuracy, (ii) omissions, (iii) time lags. The basic principle followed is that the banking data is correct, and any shortfall in the transactor's data is deemed to be due to the above factors. To balance the account therefore, a special entry is made, called the "Balancing Item".

SIGN CONVENTIONS

A (+) sign indicates a *decrease in UK assets*, e.g. a sale of exports, a financial instrument, or property/real capital; or an *increase in UK liabilities*, e.g. borrowing from non-residents. Both changes result in an *inward flow of finance*.

A (−) sign indicates an *increase in UK assets*, e.g. a purchase of imports, financial instruments, or property/real capital; or a *decrease in UK liabilities*, e.g. repayment of outstanding loans from non-residents.

BREAKDOWN OF THE BOP ACCOUNT

There are three distinct sections:

(1) The Current Account

This comprises:

(a) Visibles (goods) = the Trade Balance;
(b) Invisibles (services) = the Services Balance.

Services Include: transport, financial services such as banking and insurance, general government such as military and diplomatic expenditure, transfers (defined as official, i.e. grants to overseas countries, and private, i.e. gifts by individuals, etc.), and interest, profits and dividends, both official and private sector.

(2) Investment and Other Capital Transactions

These include:

(a) Investments in companies, property and financial instruments (long-term);

(b) inter-government loans;

(c) Trade credit;

(d) Currency borrowing and lending;

(e) The "sterling balances", i.e. sterling reserves owned by overseas governments, and overseas private sector sterling holdings;

(f) Sterling lending to non-residents;

(g) Other non-UK bank borrowing or lending;

(h) SDR allocations (shown as (+) entries).

(3) Official Financing

This section includes all transactions entered into by the UK authorities in their reactions to the transactions in the rest of the BOP account. They include:

(a) Transactions with overseas authorities, e.g. with the IMF, and borrowings from other Central Banks;

(b) Foreign currency borrowing by the UK, i.e. Euro-dollar facilities (repaid in 1980 and 1981);

(c) Foreign currency borrowing by UK public bodies under the Exchange Cover Scheme;

(d) Changes in the Official Reserves (including SDRs and ECUs). Note, a receipt of SDRs is shown as a (+) in section (2) and is shown as a (−) in this section.

Table 12.11 is a summary of the UK BOP account for 1981.

Analysis of Table 12.11

Exports comfortably exceeded imports in both years although oil exports played (and continue to play) a dominant role in this surplus. Services con-

Table 12.11
UK Balance of Payments. £ million

	1981	1982
Exports (fob)	£50,977 m	£55,546 m
Imports (fob)	£47,969 m	£53,427 m
Visible balance	+ £ 3,008 m	+ £ 2,119 m
Services (net)	+ £ 4,249 m	+ £ 3,844 m
Interest, profits and dividends (net)	+ £ 1,257 m	+ £ 1,577 m
Transfers (net)	− £ 1,967 m	− £ 2,112 m
Invisible balance	+ £ 3,539 m	+ £ 3,309 m
Current account balance	+ £ 6,547 m	+ £ 5,428 m
Capital		
Long-term capital (net)	− £ 7,309 m	− £ 7,309 m
Inter-government (net)	− £ 336 m	− £ 337 m
Trade credit (net)	− £ 847 m	− £ 1,389 m
Currency borrowing (net)	+ £ 1,462 m	+ £ 4,173 m
Sterling balances (net)	+ £ 2,756 m	+ £ 4,572 m
Sterling lending (net)	− £ 2,954 m	− £ 3,243 m
Other (net)	− £ 366 m	+ £ 682 m
SDRs	+ £ 158 m	—
Capital flows balance	− £ 7,436 m	− £ 2,851 m
Official financing		
Transactions with overseas authorities	− £ 145 m	− £ 163 m
Currency borrowing	− £ 1,587 m	+ £ 26 m
Reserves	+ £ 2,419 m	+ £ 1,421 m
Official financing balance	+ £ 687 m	+ £ 1,284 m
Balancing Item	+ £ 202 m	− £ 3,861 m

tinue to show surpluses emphasising the role of "City" services and the net return to the UK of interest, profits and dividends resulting from capital investment placed abroad. Transfers comprise the grant element in overseas aid and overseas subscriptions, etc.

The huge net outflows of long-term capital will hopefully accrue further returns to the BOP in future years in interest, profits and dividends. Inter-government loans include UK lending to developing countries which are tied to the purchase of UK exports, as well as subscriptions to the World Bank Group and other bodies.

Trade credit indicates that the UK is a net credit provider and assists in the sales of our exports. Currency borrowing represents the activities of the London Euro-banks, and the changes in the sterling balances represent increases in overseas holdings of sterling financial assets. Sterling lending includes advances and overdrafts to overseas residents by UK banks and sterling Bills of Exchange discounted, other than for UK export credit.

What conclusions can we draw from these figures?

Current Account. A large trade surplus was accrued, although much of this can be ascribed to oil exports. In addition a large invisible surplus obtained, offset somewhat by transfer outflows. The net Current Account balance was in large surplus.

Capital Account. Very large net long-term outflows (in both Direct and Port-folio Investments) were added to by net Trade Credit and sterling lending outflows. To offset these outflows partially, there were net inflows of currency borrowing and an increase in the sterling balances. Net Capital outflows were in excess of the balance on Current Account in 1981 but much less in 1982.

These Capital flows should be read as the borrowing and lending by UK residents with non-UK residents. Effectively, the UK as a whole borrowed short-term and lent long-term. This is a viable position so long as (a) sterling is not subject to speculative attack and (b) long-term assets yield a higher return than short-term liabilities.

Official Financing. These items represent the activities of the UK authorities in their financial dealings overseas. Thus, transactions with overseas authorities are short-term loans/repayments made with other governments and overseas bodies and also the UK's position in the IMF.

Currency borrowing represents Euro-dollar borrowing/repayments by the UK authorities, public corporations, and local authorities.

The Reserves represents changes in the level of the UK's gold, dollars, other currencies, SDRs and ECUs.

Official financing should be seen as measures taken to finance the surpluses or deficits elsewhere in the Balance of Payments. In effect, the Reserves were drawn down but debt was also repaid.

The Balancing Item consists of all errors and omissions due to incomplete records and timing and valuation differences. They are also believed to be other short-term capital flows not shown elsewhere.

Summary. Large surplus on Current Account more than offset by large net outflow of long-term capital, but countered by inflows of short-term capital; a net repayment of official debt together with a fall in the Reserves.

Verdict? The UK more than paid its way for the year and substantially added to its stock of overseas assets. However, the rise in short-term liabilities could prove a problem if sterling were to be subject to a speculative attack. Although the Balance of Payments is a record of *past* transactions, it is taken by both the private financial market and by the IMF as an indicator of the financial viability of a country. For example data which is taken as poor could lead to a large-scale sale of the currency, forcing the authorities to take emergency action. The IMF may also make it a condition of its facilities that an unacceptable Balance of Payments must be corrected by appropriate steps, i.e. government spending, interest rates, taxation, etc.

FINAL NOTE

In a sense we have come full circle. Starting with the activities of traders, hedgers, arbitrageurs, speculators, investors and their use of bank and non-bank services, we have seen that – given the international obligation that have been entered into – there will be implications for the country as a whole. This in turn can lead to policy decisions which result in changes in the parameters in which the private sector operates.

FURTHER READING

IMF

Macbean, A. I. and Snowden, P. N. 1981. *International Institutions in Trade and Finance*. George Allen and Unwin.

SDRs

IMF Survey (supplement), May 1981. Barclays International booklet. 1982. *Currency deposits; SDRs and ECUs.*
IMF Survey, 12 January 1981, *Federal Reserve Bank Quarterly Review*, Winter 1981–82 (for comment on private use).

World Bank Group

MacBean and Snowden (above).
World Bank Annual Reports.
IFC Annual Reports.

For IDA

Finance and Development. December 1982. IMF, Washington.

EMS

"The Long Road to EMS". *Euromoney*, January 1979.
IMF Survey (Supplement on EMS) 19 March 1979.
"Review of EMS". *IMF Survey*, 27 June 1983.

UK Balance of Payments

Central Statistical Office. *UK Balance of Payments*, annually in October.

For the theory of Balance of Payments presentation, see *Bank of England Quarterly Bulletin*, December 1964 and article by P. V. Allin in *Statistical News*, February 1977.

Index